ECOLOGIES
AGENTS
TERRAINS

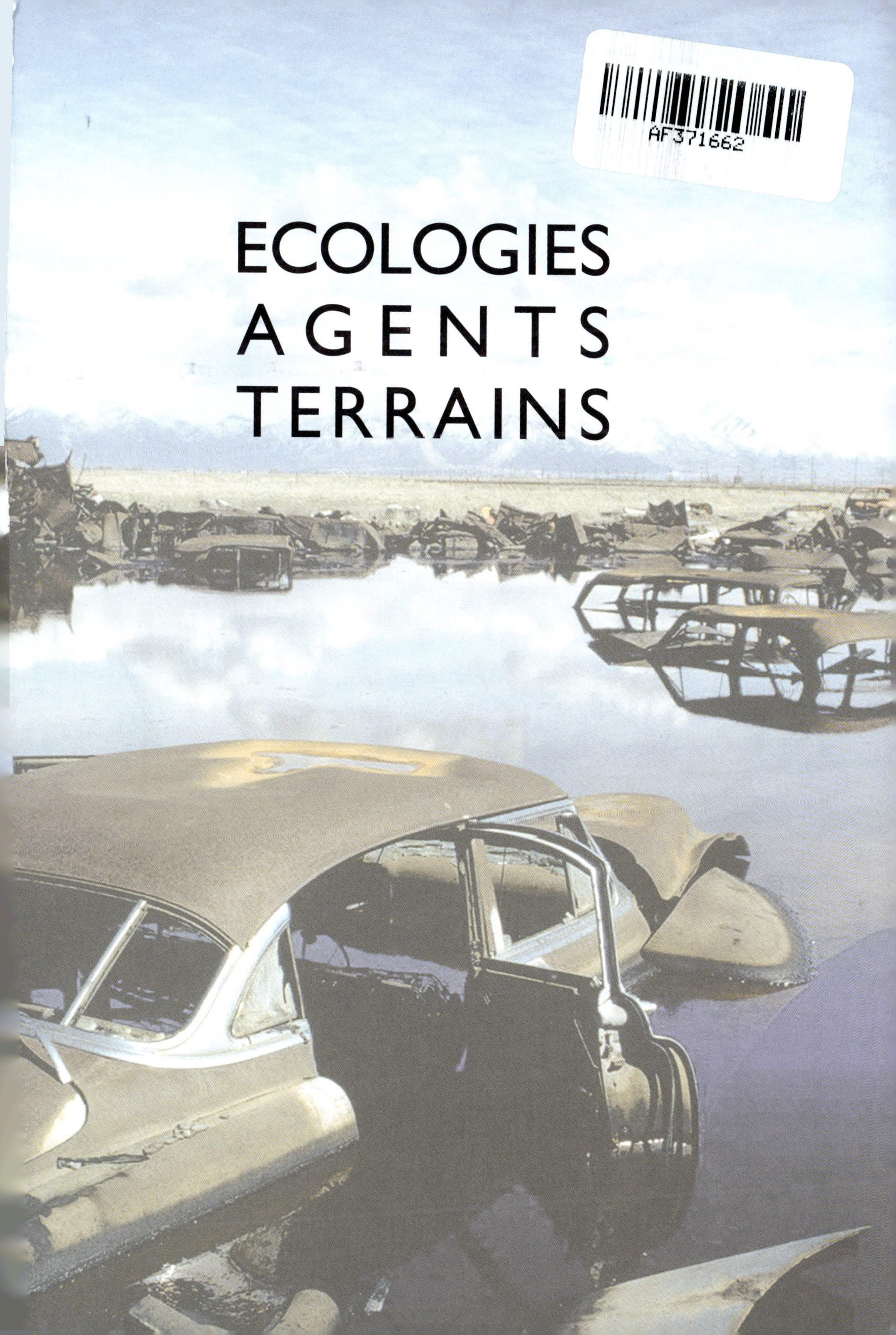

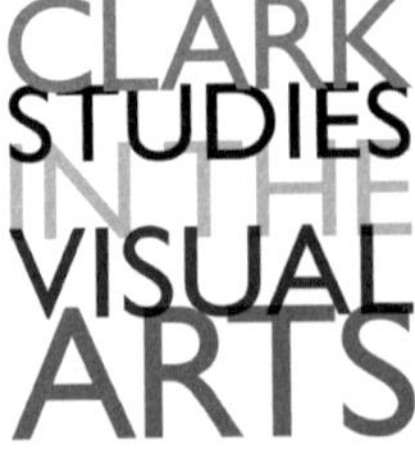

CLARK
STUDIES
IN THE
VISUAL
ARTS

ECOLOGIES
AGENTS
TERRAINS

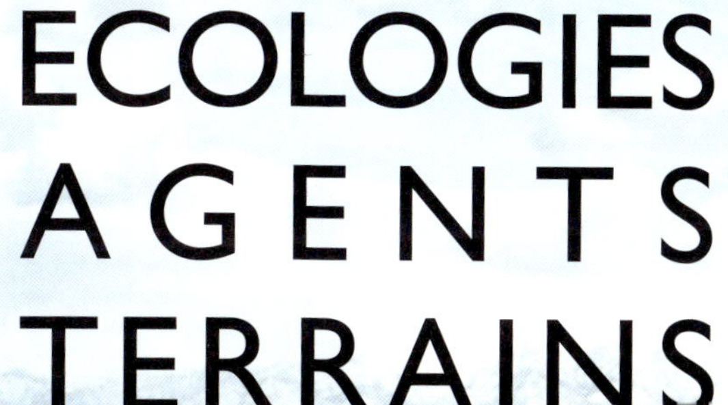

Edited by Christopher P. Heuer and Rebecca Zorach

Clark Art Institute
Williamstown, Massachusetts

Distributed by Yale University Press, New Haven and London

This publication was conceived by the Research and Academic Program at the Clark Art Institute. A related conference, titled "Ecologies, Agents, Terrains," was held May 4–6, 2017, at the Clark. For information on programs and publications at the Clark, visit www.clarkart.edu.

Produced by the Publications Department of the Clark Art Institute, 225 South Street, Williamstown, Massachusetts 01267

Anne Roecklein, *Managing Editor*
Kevin Bicknell, *Assistant Editor and Rights Coordinator*
Ashton Fancy, *Publications Assistant*
Samantha Page, *Publications Assistant*
Anne-Solène Bayan, *Publications Intern*

Copyedited by Sharon Herson
Designed by David Edge
Layout by Carol S. Cates
Proofread by Kara Pickman, Pickman Editorial
Printed by Die Keure, Bruges, Belgium
Distributed by Yale University Press, New Haven and London
www.yalebooks.com/art

Printed and bound in Belgium
10 9 8 7 6 5 4 3 2 1

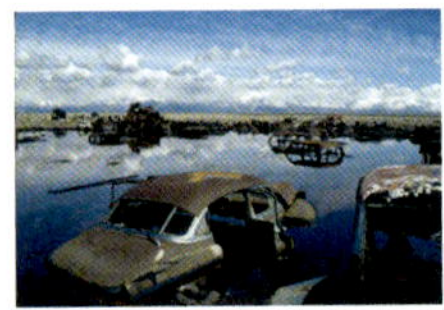

Title page and divider illustration: Bruce McAllister (American, b. 1946), "Abandoned automobiles and other debris clutter an acid water- and oil-filled five-acre pond; it was cleaned up under EPA supervision to prevent possible contamination of [the] Great Salt Lake and a wildlife refuge nearby," April 1974, from DOCUMERICA: The Environmental Protection Agency's Program to Photographically Document Subjects of Environmental Concern, 1972–77

Library of Congress Cataloging-in-Publication Data

Names: Heuer, Christopher P., editor. | Zorach, Rebecca, 1969– editor. |
    Sterling and Francine Clark Art Institute, issuing body.
Title: Ecologies, agents, terrains / edited by Christopher P. Heuer and
    Rebecca Zorach.
Description: Williamstown, Massachusetts : Clark Art Institute, 2018. |
    Series: Clark studies in the visual arts | A related conference, titled
    "Ecologies, Agents, Terrains," was held May 4–6, 2017 at the Clark. |
    Includes bibliographical references.
Identifiers: LCCN 2018002689 | ISBN 9781935998327 (publisher: clark art institute)
    | ISBN 9780300233162 (distributor: yale university press)
Subjects: LCSH: Ecology in art.
Classification: LCC N8217.E28 E29 2018 | DDC 704.9/43—dc23 LC record available at
    https://lccn.loc.gov/2018002689

Contents

Terrains

Introduction

Christopher P. Heuer and Rebecca Zorach

> In the realm of social ecology, Donald Trump and his ilk—another form
> of algae—are permitted to proliferate unchecked.
>
> —Felix Guattari, "The Three Ecologies" (1989)

In November 1971, the brand-new Environmental Protection Agency announced a massive photographic project, DOCUMERICA. For the next seven years, the EPA would send photographers around the country to photograph the environment—broadly understood—of the United States. Photographers imagined "environment" not only as natural, but also as social and architectural. One of Bruce McAllister's photographs for the project served as the cover image for the program of the conference on which this volume is based (fig. 1). The photo captures a

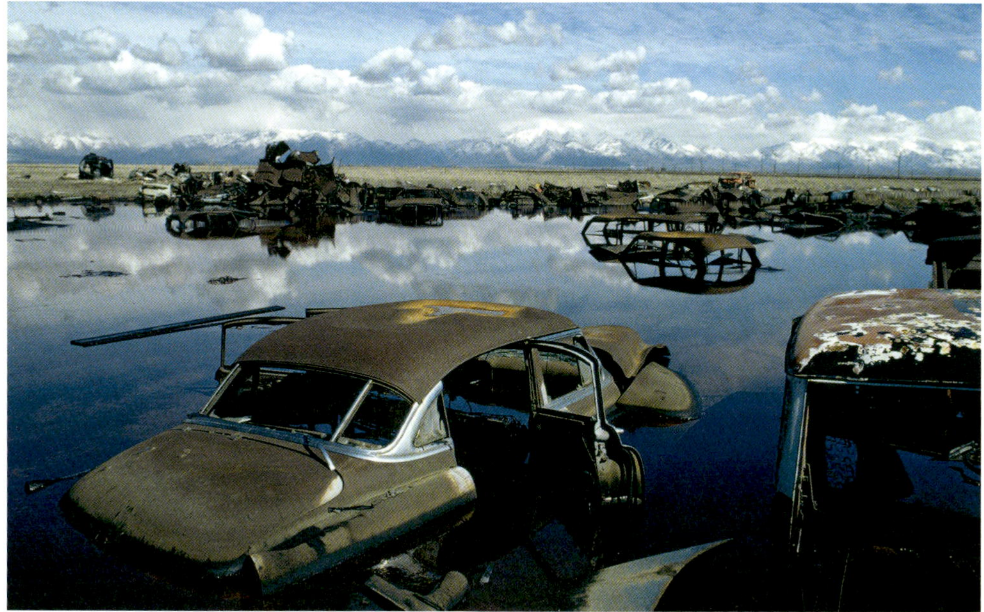

Fig. 1. Bruce McAllister (American, b. 1946), "Abandoned automobiles and other debris clutter an acid water- and oil-filled five-acre pond; it was cleaned up under EPA supervision to prevent possible contamination of [the] Great Salt Lake and a wildlife refuge nearby," April 1974, from DOCUMERICA: The Environmental Protection Agency's Program to Photographically Document Subjects of Environmental Concern, 1972–77

"site-specific sculpture" of a different ilk but somehow related to Robert Smithson's iconic *Spiral Jetty* (1970); its caption reads:

> Abandoned automobiles and other debris clutter an acid water- and oil-filled five-acre pond; it was cleaned up under EPA supervision to prevent possible contamination of [the] Great Salt Lake and a wildlife refuge nearby. (Photo by Bruce McAllister, near Ogden, Utah, April 1974)

Another image, from closer to the present: Terry Evans's *Petcoke Piles with Sprinklers at KCBX Site on Calumet River* (2014; fig. 2), from the Museum of Contemporary Photography's exhibition *Petcoke: Tracing Dirty Energy*. This is the Calumet region, southeast Chicago in particular, where residents have been on the receiving end of toxic waste for decades. Here, BP and Koch Industries plants refining tar sands petroleum left huge piles of powdery petcoke upwind of hundreds of thousands of residents. Residents organized to fight back. They had to call the EPA and city and state officials to account to do their jobs, eventually forcing changes and winning a settlement.

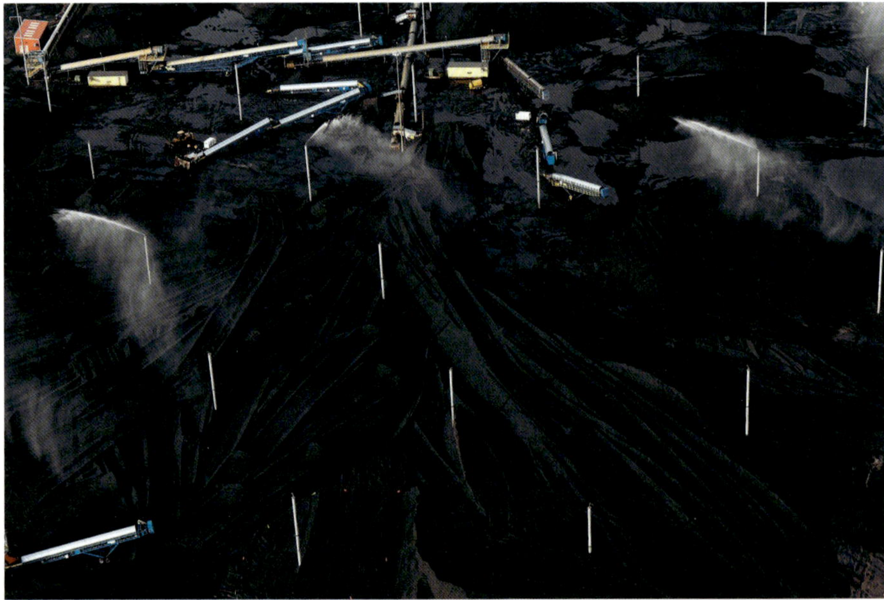

Fig. 2. Terry Evans (American, b. 1944), *Petcoke Piles with Sprinklers at KCBX Site on Calumet River*, 2014. Photograph. Museum of Contemporary Photography, Columbia College Chicago

The environmental activism we thought we understood was accustomed to fighting the EPA to hold it to account, to force it to honor its own laws and standards rather than caving in to the industrial polluters that likewise lobby it, and with much more money, from the other side. But now we live in even stranger times. The week before our conference at the Clark, the EPA took down its climate change website, saying that it was "updating language to reflect the approach of new leadership." On June 1, 2017, as first drafts of these collected papers were due, the United States signaled its decision to pull out of the Paris Climate Accord—already widely understood as a half measure. On August 15, as revised drafts of the essays began to arrive, President Trump signed an executive order revoking a 2015 order by then-President Obama to "create a new flood risk reduction standard for federally funded projects."[1] Four major hurricanes battered the United States and the Caribbean in the month that followed. When we initially planned this conference, we didn't think we'd find ourselves facing the dismantling or gutting of even the *moderate* protections the EPA provided, considering the withdrawal of the world's biggest economy from the Paris deal, or imagining that this malevolent fraud of a president would be so shamelessly kleptocratic that some people would actually be *relieved* when he acts like a "normal" American leader and drops bombs on other countries. Or that Attorney General Jeff Sessions—too much of a racist to be a judge in 1986—would be obtaining a conviction carrying a year in prison against activist Desiree Fairooz *for laughing at Jeff Sessions.*

If something as notoriously ineffectual as the arts and humanities can draw attention to the natural and social ecologies that surround us, if they might effect shifts in consciousness that make social change, it would seem this project would take on new urgency now.[2] And yet we feel a profound mismatch between the academic timescale and the scale of shifting political and societal winds. One of us has in her home two pieces of furniture—a bench and a cabinet—made from shipping crates salvaged from the MCA Chicago's 2006 exhibition *Massive Change* and lightly altered for another exhibition project by the artist collective Material Exchange. If Material Exchange had not taken them, the MCA would have just thrown them out, and these large wooden objects—like most art shipping crates—would have gone to a landfill. *Massive Change* was just one of a series of art exhibitions that seek to address issues of environmental "change"—the destructive effects of human actions—but without (as far as we can tell) fundamentally altering business as usual in the institutions of the art world, or the academy.[3]

What is it possible actually to expect of art, art criticism, or art and architectural history, in terms of making real change, producing real resistance?

We came to this project, too, with an interest in eco-criticism and what is being called "new materialism"—the work of Jane Bennett and others—and the sense that art history, with its long history of thinking seriously about materiality and the agency of objects, had something to contribute to this emerging field.[4] At the same time, we had some skepticism about the direction it was taking and the questions it occluded. Feminist scholars have created a robust discussion around the relationship of gender oppression to the suppression of "nature," though the ideological weight laden on the term "nature" also produces justified skepticism.[5] The frequent omission of race from discussions of environmentalism was noted nearly fifty years ago by Nathan Hare in his 1970 piece "Black Ecology" in *Black Scholar*.[6] Such concerns also emerge from responses to the journal *October*'s recent questionnaire on new materialism. As part of our early organizing meetings, we read both the *October* issue and a short response that was accidentally (we are told) left out of that issue, Huey Copeland's "Tending-toward-Blackness," which critiques new materialism as a retrenchment that leaves aside uncomfortable questions about human hierarchies. Copeland points out that "in the name of universal values and transcendent theoretical schemas," new materialist discourses risk abetting white supremacy, as when the editors of one anthology sweep aside, in a single facile gesture, "fashionable constructivist approaches and identity politics."[7] In response to the *October* questionnaire, Mel Y. Chen makes a similar point: "To what extent then are new materialisms serving as structural condescensions, themselves new technologies engaged in acts of forgetting, in which lived differences such as race, class, sex and ability no longer serve as necessary considerations because fictions of scale mark them as irrelevant?"[8] Alongside these critiques of new materialism we revisited the "old" materialism of Marxism, thinking with Jason Moore about capitalism's creation of hierarchies of "human" action on exploited "nature" (in which many humans are ideologically crammed into the "nature" side of the divide).[9] Visual art and art history bring in questions not only of beauty, but also of the artifact, the shelter, human action in its usefulness *or uselessness*. They also suggest the possibility of changing consciousness as a way of creating change. We also read Brett Bloom's *Petro-Subjectivity*, which confronts us with the ways in which fossil fuel dependency powerfully shapes our consciousness, and suggests the capacity of art to intervene therein.[10] Along these lines, Félix Guattari's classic essay "The Three Ecologies" pointed us to questions of social ecology and the ecology of consciousness as well as to the "natural environment"—in addition to its prescient description of the current occupant of the White House as invasive species that serves as our epigraph.[11]

Originally, we organized the presentations that lie behind these collected essays into pairs of concepts, devised on the basis of presentation abstracts: Aesthetics, Conflicts, Nations, Matter, Energy, and Flow. These themes were intended to spark dialogue among papers but not to restrict their implications or confine their complexities. Each of them remains in play in this book. But new connections emerged, both in the conference and as final versions of the essays developed. There were other intersecting tensions at stake: history and the present; the relationship of race and social justice to environmental activism (which come together, but all too infrequently—and all the more pressingly—in environmental justice movements); the urban and the rural; and the relationship—conflict?—between the aesthetic and symbolic properties of "environmental" artworks (not just beauty or wonder, but abstraction, dissonance, critique) and their potential for instrumental action or symbolic communication. A few new questions we did not anticipate in the initial framing can be cited here: the temporality of artworks as well as that of history; the palpable sense of crisis. In circumstances like these, can we have business as usual anymore? (In similar circumstances, artists have decided to stop making art or to make art differently, scholars have shifted focus, some have found the urgency to be even more productive, others have been exiled, silenced, murdered.) And if not, what should we do? In our final organization, we have used the three framing concepts of the conference and book title to organize scholarly essays (including contribtions by both editors) into groups of four, with each section followed by an intervention that works in a different medium or genre. These contributions are each labeled with a descriptive term that indicates its deviation from a standard academic essay, though they are also analytical. As we explain more fully below, "Ecologies" speaks to interrelationships among concepts, physical objects, and life forms; "Agents" focuses on particular makers and doers, whether human or nonhuman; and "Terrains" emphasizes the sites and spaces, physical or conceptual, within which these inquiries play out. Most of the essays could fit in all three categories, and our primary goal remains the same: to create conversations among them that are generative rather than limiting.

"Ecologies" addresses the physical and social ecologies of artworks and of art history, artworks as ecologies, and questions of interaction—between artworks and their environment, among physical entities, artworks, and individuals. We understand ecology through Félix Guattari's "Three Ecologies," that is, the physical ecology of "the natural environment"; the social ecology of human interactions; and the ecology of individual consciousness. The texts in this initial section address questions of interaction in terms of chemistry, biology, and society, and the metaphoric ecologies of our disciplinary divides. James Nisbet's "The Ecological Site" resists the seductions of a phenomenological approach to site-specific sculpture. Nisbet revises modernist art historical understandings of such works as Richard Serra's *Shift* (1970–72) by considering the many ecologies in which it is situated. Sonya S. Lee, in "An Eco–Art History of Weathered Stone Sculptures from Southwest China," addresses the ecology of weathered stone in medieval Buddhist sculpture. Lee also analyzes the disciplinary ecology that segregates art historical investigations from the results of conservators' physical examination of the works, and finds new insights in bringing these approaches together.

Like Lee's essay, Vittoria Di Palma's addresses the question of disciplinary ecologies. In "Character and the Climatic Imaginary," Di Palma discusses the association of architectural aesthetics, climate, and health in seventeenth- and eighteenth-century European and colonial contexts. By placing her text in this section, we highlight the question of relationships, rather than the more obvious and literal focus on "terrain," which would allow it to fit equally well into our final section. Closing this section, Jessica L. Horton's essay, "'All Our Relations' as an Eco–Art Historical Challenge: Lessons from Standing Bear's Muslin," considers the question of relationality through Indigenous making and practices that respond to the "violent dislocations that are . . . a strong connection to the past." She studies this question in relation to Standing Bear's depiction of the Battle of Little Bighorn painted in watercolor on a six-foot square of muslin. Her piece introduces the crucial issue of Indigenous people's relationship to ecology, land, and politics, one that was on all our minds as we prepared this conference during the Standing Rock Sioux tribe's heroic struggle to preserve their land rights in the face of the construction of the Dakota Access Pipeline, a struggle that intersects with Horton's essay at several junctures.

The artist project documentation that follows is the work of the international collaborative Ghana ThinkTank (GTT), whose small-scale interventions constellated our days of gathering, helping to create a genuine "ecology of activism" throughout the meeting. Members curated events considering, as they put it, "Third World solutions to First World problems" in very concrete ways. How to reshape the language used by the left to talk about environmental precarity, avoiding loaded terms like *global warming, green,* or even *crisis*? Is such a project even feasible? GTT offered a sequence of collaborative workshop-performances in which participants had opportunities both to reflect on these questions and to propose real-world solutions, some of which are addressed in GTT's essay, cowritten with Sonnet Coggins and Terence Washington, "Talking About the Man in the Moon, Combating Climate Change with Art."

As we put together an initial statement describing this conference, we wrote that "art history may seem to have come late to the eco-critical turn, but it is perhaps because it was—in some sense—already there." Part of what this statement refers to is the centrality of the term "nature" to the history of art history. In Western aesthetics, "Nature" with a capital *N* and "Art" with a capital *A* have a long history of intertwining, intimate collaboration, and antagonism. Looking to the three terms of our title—Ecologies, Agents, Terrains—Art in this sense associates itself with Agency (not only because they both start with *A*): it's what humans do to shape their world, to set themselves over against it, to make new things out of it, consciously and intentionally. The essays under the heading "Agents" put agency into question, thinking about the agency of the nonhuman, of nature, of artworks, but also of individual artists and human actors. Robert Felfe's "Premodern Geosphere: Nature's Workshop, Treasure House, and Deep Time" addresses the agency of Nature as artist and architect through a series of key interwoven moments from the intellectual history of early modern Europe, particularly in the realm of the natural sciences. What kind of alternatives might early modern reflections on the agency of Nature "herself" provide us in the present? Dylan Miner's "*Gichi-mookomaanan miinawaa Gichi-maazhigaa-aabkook // From Big Knives to Big Pipelines*" is, as he puts it, "about images and stories as living beings." Speaking from an Indigenous position, in a way that is both scholarly and autobiographical, Miner considers raw materials, tools, images, art history, and the stories that they gather around themselves. Rebecca Zorach's "'Welcome to My Volcano': New Materialism, Art History, and Their Others" addresses the privileging of nonhuman agency in new materialism in relation to questions of human agency. In particular, what happens to humans who have historically been denied the status of human when nonhumans are granted, at least in theory, new forms of reciprocity? Does such an approach restrict the capacity for action of those who desperately need tools for political struggle? From this perspective, she examines artworks by Rebecca Belmore and a collaborative film by artists

Jérôme Havre, Cauleen Smith, and Camille Turner as generative allegories of agency, whether through individual struggle or collective survival. Chelsea Mikael Frazier's "Thinking Red, Wounds, and Fungi in Wangechi Mutu's Eco-Art" considers related questions. She draws on a body of theoretical and creative work she characterizes as *black-fem* (theory and practice) to establish a critique of mainstream environmental discourse that can serve as the backdrop to a multilayered account of Mutu's work, considering the ecological implications of the color red, the depiction of wounds, and fungal forms. Implicitly, she presents an expansive view of the artist's agency through Mutu's capacity to help make sense of "our damaged present." Sarah Kanouse's performance, "My Electric Genealogy," appears here in a necessarily partial collection of texts and images, as "Notes on a Performance-in-Progress." Kanouse braids together personal and environmental histories of postwar Southern California, in essence to *enact* the dialectic between private and public spheres of ecological anxiety. She eschews the brutely psycho-biographical, however, to offer a gorgeous situating of herself—and by extension, us—in the networks of communication, capital, and resources that the art world leaves mostly unexamined. It is impossible not to be implicated, although some are more implicated than others.

Essays in "Terrains" address physical place, understood in terms of regions, areas, and land, but also the background or context within which the operations we are looking at take shape. They engage directly with the "terrain" of art and architectural history, but also with land and place understood in physical terms, and, especially, the shifting, slippery terrain of solid and liquid forms of water, of earth congealed, rearranged, and atomized. Terrain, therefore, does not land us on solid ground. Verity Platt's essay, "Ecology, Ethics, and Aesthetics in Pliny the Elder's *Natural History*," considers the ancient world as a terrain on which ideas about Western art and aesthetics play out, but also the idea of *natura* as a ground and origin for thinking and making art—as well as a physical location where questions of imperial power and its interventions into the environment unfolded, with Pliny himself directly implicated therein. Jeffrey Jerome Cohen and Julian Yates's "Ark Thinking" considers the physical and conceptual foundations of architecture as imperfect barrier to ecological crisis through the telling and retelling of the story of Noah's Ark. The piece experiments with the *form* of the essay itself, setting us, appropriately enough, adrift in a sea of reference and images that they—two by two—resist placing in some diachronic order of form. Instead, what we glimpse is the model for withstanding, and describing, what they wonderfully call "announced catastrophe," a phenomenon as current in our Holocene as in Genesis. Meanwhile, both Maggie M. Cao's "The Entropic History of Ice" and Christopher P. Heuer's "A Post-Critical Arctic?" point north. Cao weaves a vivid social history of nineteenth-century America's addiction to refrigeration, and to the unexpected colonial and epistemological complexities that ice harvesting—a need before electricity—wrought. Art has an unexpected role to play in this story. The icescapes of Frederic Church (which, as Cao shows, bewildered contemporary critics in their emptiness) engaged racial anxieties about "whiteness" in the wake of the Civil War, at the same time as ice was emerging as an elite commodity in places like the Caribbean. There, as Cao puts it, "ice, art, and race were inextricably bound together by practices of perception as well as technologies of globalization." Heuer, meanwhile, interrogates some recent "activist" art practices that invoke the Far North as both a literal site (indeed, a terrain) and a condition. Deliberately polemical, Heuer traces a pattern of practices wherein Church's sublimity lives on, practices that, in our neoliberal image-world, have unexpected consequences for the idea of environmental "dialogue." Can art today still maintain a stentorian I/thou relationship to its object of critique (in this case, a melting Arctic?), a standpoint of blunt elegy or action?

The Center for Land Use Interpretation (CLUI), a Culver City–based institute, closes this volume with a final nonstandard intervention, a photo essay titled "Peripheral and Central Places in the USA." CLUI defamilarizes this equation to compelling and, as Heuer argues, hopeful ends. CLUI's photo essay turns the idea of the cartographic archive on its head. Offering a reading of American landscape that dispenses with both the tragic *and* the scenic, but fusing both, the Center's images refuse to disassociate the natural from the human. As CLUI director Matthew Coolidge puts it: "Humans are a part of nature and nature shouldn't be something considered exclusive of humans." With this, perhaps, we are spurred to rethink the notion of terrains as binaries of humans and environment—lopsided or harmonious. Paradoxically, perhaps, it is archival practices like CLUI's and Kanouse's—dispensing with self-righteously "environmental" rhetoric in favor of more incongruous modes of inquiry—that might prove to be our moment's most ecologically sensitive practices of all.

It is no secret that the usefulness of a term like "nature" dissolves in the confrontation between its ideological uses (divisions between the natural and the unnatural) and the distinct possibility that *everything* that happens is, in fact, natural. Is it natural to make art, or to do politics, or to decimate other life forms?

Was it *natural* when, in the confirmation hearings for the US Attorney General, Desiree Fairooz laughed at the statement that Senator Jeff Sessions's record of "treating all Americans equally under the law" was "clear and well-documented"? Natural because involuntary, a biological reflex: laughter caused by an objectively, verifiably, *laughable* statement. But if it were an intentional laugh, an exercise of agency, a laugh designed to disrupt, would it not also be natural? Consider these lines from the opening of Elizabeth Bishop's "One Art": "The art of losing isn't hard to master; / so many things seem filled with the intent / to be lost that their loss is no disaster." But if things, of whatever *nature*, are "filled with the intent to be lost," it doesn't mean we have to let them go without a fight. Can we still have business as usual? What would it look like not to? Can we harness laughter? Can we shape forms of collectivity that acknowledge nonhuman beings but engage human agency? As people who operate, most of us, inside institutions, can we ask our institutions to operate differently, can we ask ourselves to operate differently in those institutions, can we extricate ourselves from their inertia? Even a little bit? A little bit more than we thought we could? Would it be recognizable if we did?

1. US Federal Government, Executive Order 13690 of January 30, 2015.

2. We do not here attempt anything like a comprehensive state of the field, but note that we are also inspired by the recent work of T. J. Demos, for example his *Decolonizing Nature: Contemporary Art and the Politics of Ecology* (Berlin: Sternberg Press, 2016); Yates McKee, such as his "On Climate Refugees: Biopolitics, Aesthetics, and Critical Climate Change," *Qui Parle* 19, no. 2 (2011), 309–25; and Alan C. Braddock and Renée Ater's special issue of "Art and the Anthropocene," *American Art* 28, no. 3 (2014), among other recent writings.

3. Mark C. Taylor's neo-theological *Sensing Place* show from 2016, for example, and its accompanying catalogue, *Recovering Place: Reflections on Stone Hill* (New York: Columbia University Press, 2016.) A selection of other recent exhibition catalogues, in chronological order, might include Sue Spaid with Amy Lipton, eds., *Ecovention: Current Art to Transform Ecologies* (Cincinnati: Contemporary Arts Center, 2002); Stephanie Smith, ed., *Beyond Green: Toward a Sustainable Art* (Chicago: Smart Museum of Art, University of Chicago; New York: Independent Curators International, 2005); Serene Huleileh, ed., *Still Life: Art, Ecology, and the Politics of Change* (Sharjah, United Arab Emirates: Sharjah Biennial, 2007); Jennifer Allora et al., *Greenwashing: Environment, Perils, Promises, and Perplexities* (Turin: Fondazione Sandretto Re Rebaudengo, 2008); Francesco Manacorda and Ariella Yedgar, eds., *Radical Nature: Art and Architecture for a Changing Planet, 1969–2009* (London:

Koenig Books, 2009); Anik Fournier et al., eds., *Undercurrents: Experimental Ecosystems in Recent Art* (New York: Whitney Museum of American Art, 2010); and Ine Gevers, ed., *Yes Naturally: How Art Saves the World*, trans. Pierre Bouvier and Jacqueline Schoonheim (Amsterdam: Niet Normaal Foundation Rotterdam, 2013).

4. Jane Bennett, *Vibrant Matter: A Political Ecology of Things* (Durham: Duke University Press, 2010). This approach also draws on the work of Bruno Latour, for instance in his *Reassembling the Social: An Introduction to Actor-Network-Theory* (New York: Oxford University Press, 2005). Artists have long highlighted the complex relationships humans have to materiality. See, for example, A. Laurie Palmer, *In the Aura of a Hole: Exploring Sites of Material Extraction* (London: Black Dog Publishing, 2014), a poetic history of the extraction of minerals that tries to account for the entanglements of these materials in beauty, meaning, memory, danger, damage, and social life.

5. See "Feminism & Ecology: Earthkeeping / Earthshaking," *Heresies: A Feminist Publication on Art and Politics* 13 (1981). The problematizing of "nature" is not restricted to feminist approaches; see, for instance, Timothy Morton, *Ecology without Nature: Rethinking Environmental Aesthetics* (Cambridge: Harvard University Press, 2007).

6. Nathan Hare, "Black Ecology," *Black Scholar* (April 1970): 2–8, http://www.tandfonline.com/doi/abs/10.1080/00064246.1970.11728700 (accessed November 7, 2017).

7. Diana Coole and Samantha Frost, eds., *New Materialisms: Ontology, Agency, and Politics* (Durham: Duke University Press, 2010), 19; cited in Huey Copeland, "Tending-toward-Blackness," *October* 156 (Spring 2016): 141–44, 142; Emily Apter et al., "A Questionnaire on Materialisms," *October* 155 (Winter 2016): 3–110.

8. Mel Y. Chen, "Questions of Matter and Materialism," *October* 155 (Winter 2016): 22.

9. Jason W. Moore, *Capitalism in the Web of Life: Ecology and the Accumulation of Capital* (London: Verso, 2015).

10. Brett Bloom, *Petro-Subjectivity: De-Industrializing Our Sense of Self* (Fort Wayne, Ind.: Breakdown Break Down Press, 2015).

11. Félix Guattari, "The Three Ecologies," *new formations* 8 (Summer 1989): 131–47 (trans. Chris Turner).

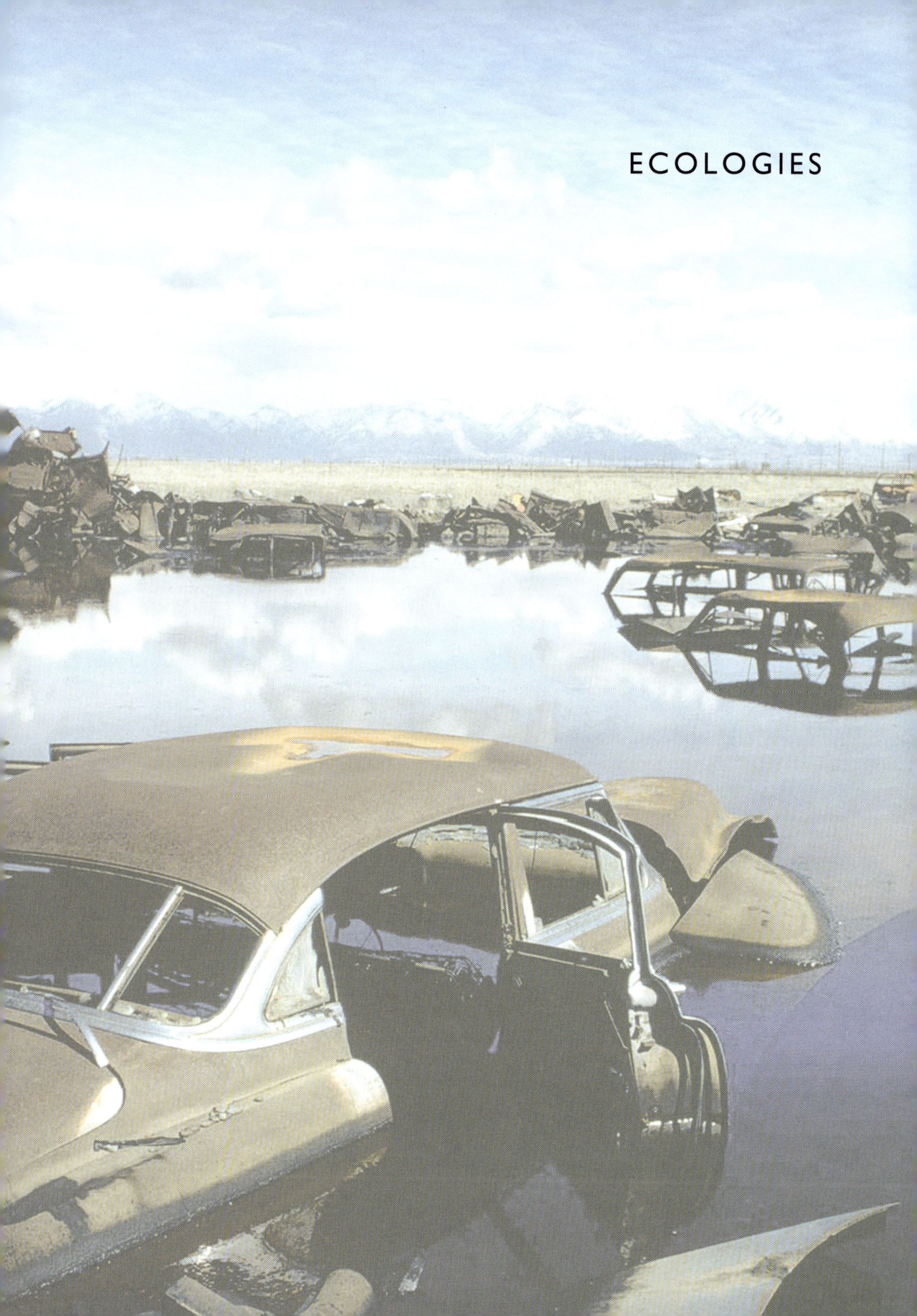
ECOLOGIES

The Ecological Site

James Nisbet

Richard Serra's site-specific sculpture *Shift* (1970–72), like many outdoor sculptures and artworks of the postwar land art movement, is known to spectators primarily through its photographs. Despite being located on farmland in King City, Ontario, just north of the major international metropolis of Toronto, it receives less foot traffic than the more celebrated and appreciably more remote earthworks of the American West by Serra's contemporaries Walter De Maria, Michael Heizer, Nancy Holt, and Robert Smithson. In art historical publications—including both monographs on Serra and more general literature on land art—*Shift*

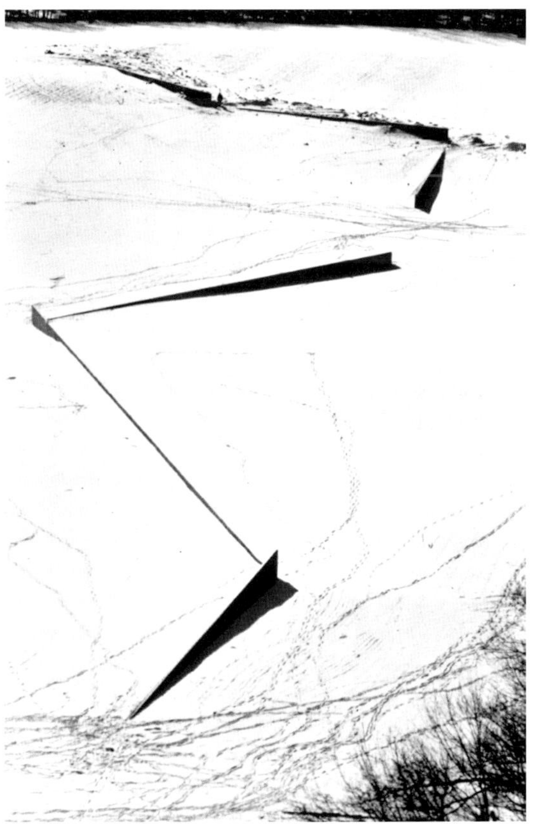

Fig. 1. Gianfranco Gorgoni (Italian, b. 1941), photograph of Richard Serra's *Shift*, 1970–72. © Gianfranco Gorgoni

is unfailingly represented by a series of photographs taken at the time of the work's completion by Gianfranco Gorgoni, the go-to documentarian of the American land artists.[1] These images depict *Shift* in winter, some with snow covering the ground, some with exposed dirt around the six low-lying concrete walls that compose Serra's sculpture, but each characterized by a tendency to eschew all but the most meager traces of life in the frame.

Looking more closely at one of these photographs (fig. 1), which by dint of its pervasive presence in Serra's literature has become the most iconic and in turn representative shot of *Shift*, we see the work from a slight elevation. Viewed from such a vantage, one might expect a complete and comprehensible view of the work, but instead, Gorgoni's print makes it difficult to immediately grasp the essential details of Serra's piece. Looking in places more like an abstract drawing than a documentary photograph, this image presents *Shift*'s six discrete walls in a stark landscape blanketed by snow and marked intermittently by the meandering tracks of a few ambulatory viewers, one of whom stands in a bulbous winter coat at the terminus of these tracks, appearing as much like an ink blot on the page as a person in the world. Proceeding forward from the back of the frame, heavily exposed shadows cast by *Shift*'s walls cut through the landscape, melding concrete and shaded snow into a sequence of thin, black wedges that do not lay upon the surface of the land so much as puncture and disrupt its planar continuity. Unless provided the bare traces of orientation afforded by details such as the tree branches that appear scratched into the lower right corner of the photograph or hints of daylight breaking through the stand of trees across its upper edge, this composition might read as entirely unmoored from a living environment, let alone an agricultural field nestled in ecologically diverse forestland. In this and additional views by Gorgoni that are similarly bleak and intensely formal, *Shift* appears as if enclosed in a time capsule, abstracted from the ongoing processes of the place in which it was made and still exists.

In contrast to the especially halted quality of this and its other documentary images by Gorgoni, however, *Shift* was created out of a prolonged exercise of moving through and inhabiting the land shared between Serra and the artist Joan Jonas. As Serra explains this process:

> In the summer of 1970, Joan and I spent five days walking the place. We discovered that two people walking the distance of the field opposite one another, attempting to keep each other in view despite the curvature of the land, would mutually determine a topological definition of the space. The boundaries of the work became the maximum distance two people could occupy and still keep each other in view. The horizon of the work was established by the possibilities of maintaining this mutual viewpoint. . . . What I wanted was a dialectic between one's perception of the place in totality and one's relation to the field as walked. The result is a way of measuring oneself against the indeterminacy of the land.[2]

This intertwined relationship among movement, visibility, and topography would inform *Shift*'s final composition: six slabs of poured concrete, eight inches wide, each guided in direction and length by the contours of the site, which Serra

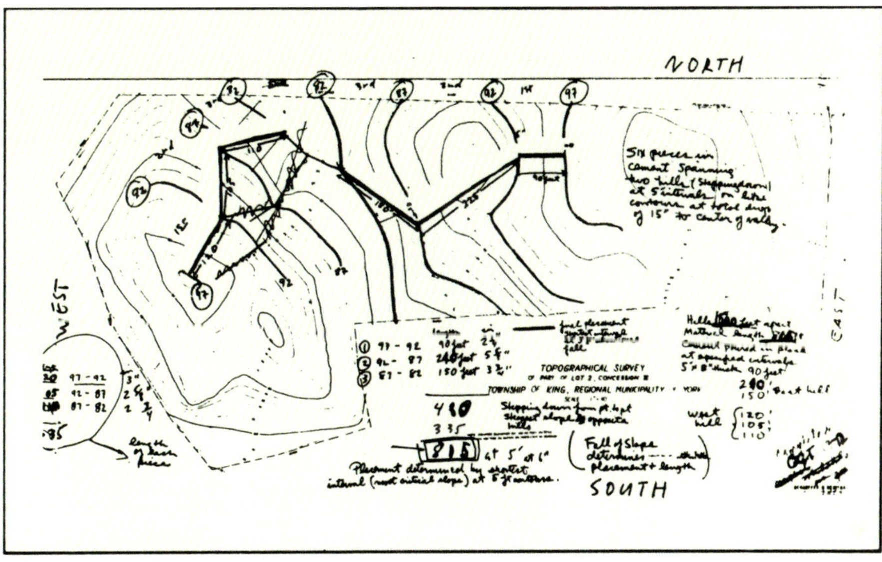

Fig. 2. Richard Serra (American, b. 1938), preparatory drawing for *Shift*, 1970–72. © 2017 Richard Serra/Artists Rights Society (ARS), New York

had resurveyed in the planning stages at a grade of one-foot contour intervals (fig. 2).[3] Beginning at the two extreme points of distance set out by his and Jonas's movement through the field, Serra erected walls in the direction of the most significant drop in elevation in the land, extending each wall until this vertical drop reached a height of five feet, subsequent walls being set out through the same process. Varying in length and direction, the three walls on each side of the field zig and zag toward the three walls on the other, meeting in an open space in the center. For Serra,

> the space between the two sets of walls—across an open plane of approximately 120 feet—implies a center to the work. This center would coincide with both the measured center of the field and a gravitational or topological center of the land mass. However, this is not the center of the work. The work does not concern itself with centering in that way. The expanse of the work allows one to perceive and locate a multiplicity of centers.[4]

This interpretation of *Shift*'s multiple and moving "centers" is provocative, whether we understand those centers to be actual, physical locations or more figurative notions of establishing stability and orientation. Understood in either sense, such active *shifting* internal to Serra's work strongly resists the inert quality of its photographic presence within his published oeuvre.[5] We might contrast Gorgoni's photographs of *Shift*, for instance, with the way that the work has been depicted in more recent newspaper articles and online publications, whose photographic illustrations not only tend to be in color rather than in black and white, but also show *Shift* in its present condition, covered in varying degrees of plant growth in a field still farmed annually for a rotating crop of corn, wheat, and soy.

These stark differences between the representation of *Shift* and its actual existence—between a static environment and a mutable one—highlight the potential contribution of this work to discussions of ecological perspectives and methods in art history. To be clear, this is not because *Shift* is located outdoors, as any work of art, whether placed outside or inside a museum or gallery, exists within an ecosystem. Nor is this because *Shift* has experienced a divide between its photographic documentation and its reality on the ground, as this disparity is true of many earthworks. *Shift* is instead especially valuable as an object for thinking about the intersection of ecology and art history because of its manifestly extreme conditions. These imbalances comprise both *Shift*'s extremes in appearance between image and site, and also, as we will see, alterations to its environment. Such polarities bring to light a series of changing ecological relationships pertaining to *Shift* that might otherwise be difficult to discern and especially to directly experience in artworks with less volatile histories of representation and setting.

At present, the prevailing concept for addressing issues of location in the history of late modern art is "site specificity." This term dates from the first wave of land art—encompassing *Shift* alongside its more recognized contemporaries south of the border—and describes an artwork that is made for one particular place and can exist only in that place. Site specificity was first popularly disseminated by a distinction Smithson drew in his own practice between a "site" as the place in which he made artwork and a "non-site" as the portable objects, photographs, texts, and so forth that could be displayed anyplace.[6] Importantly, while it is now commonplace to refer to outdoor projects of Smithson, Serra, and others as "site-specific," this is not the term that Serra used at the time he finished *Shift* in the early 1970s, primarily describing the location of his outdoor sculpture with the terms "land" and "place."[7] Serra himself didn't begin to deploy the language of site specificity in public statements until approximately 1980, which is important to recall, because the traction of site specificity as a key term within art history took particular hold during that very decade on account of a controversy surrounding one of Serra's own projects. *Tilted Arc* was installed in lower Manhattan in 1981 using public funds, and soon began receiving complaints from a small number of federal white-collar workers employed in the area, leading to a public hearing to discuss relocating the sculpture. Despite Serra's own testimony that moving the sculptural element of *Tilted Arc* was tantamount to negating its site specificity and therefore the work as a whole, this sculptural element was removed from its site in 1989, effectively destroying the artwork.[8] In addition to its notoriety in the art world at the time, this episode has subsequently proven crucial to the discourse of site specificity for its congealing effects. In the 1980s, to be on the "right" side of the emerging culture wars—that is, the side of personal freedom and artistic expression, and against that of politically right-wing, Reaganite, and increasingly evangelical conservatism—meant siding with Serra and his account of *Tilted Arc*. While critical for the political climate of the day, the carryover of this position into the twenty-first century has all but barred any dents or inroads into thinking through the broader implications of site specificity's original formulation.

This ingrained understanding of site specificity has deeply limited the reception of *Shift*, and with it, more robustly ecological ways of interpreting the relationship between artworks and their environments of display. By the term "ecology," I refer both to a branch of the natural sciences that investigates the ways in which living species interrelate within particular environments and to a more general approach to understanding the interconnections affecting the experience of such environments. As distinct from an "environment," which derives etymologically from the root verb "environ," and implies a spatial approach to defining place, ecology is delimited by relationships rather than physical boundaries. Such an approach to ecology, however, is also exceedingly broad in scope and difficult to concretize, let alone to visualize. The essay that follows will therefore work through a series of historical and ongoing ecological relationships affecting *Shift* as means to convey the complications posed by addressing site as an ecological notion.

It is necessary, therefore, to begin with a more exacting examination of site specificity as a concept and interpretative framework, addressing a revisionist version of the term that emerged in the 1990s, which, I will argue, well described a new body of contemporary artwork to appear at that time but did not adequately problematize the fundamental tenets of the site specificity fashioned in the preceding decades. A good part of the limitations to this latter concept lie in its adopting a version of phenomenology riven by claims, on the one hand, for the importance of spectators' temporal awareness in moving through a site, and, on the other, a version of subjectivity that strips temporality almost entirely from that site itself. In actuality, this framework produces a deeply atemporal relationship between an artwork and its site. What is more, its unsound assumptions have been perpetuated, whether explicitly or implicitly, through subsequent iterations of site specificity. Thus, rather than adding on to this existing genealogy, my intervention seeks to return to the initial formulation of site specificity to root out and work through its contradictions, in order to articulate an approach to the ecology of site that categorically decenters the enduring notion that only physical and cognitive acts of human agency truly shape the form and meaning of artworks.

Moving from the discourse of site specificity to a series of recent events affecting the material conditions and environment of *Shift*, I will next address both the urban development of King City and the seasonal cycles of growth in *Shift*'s agricultural field. In so doing, I will also identify and examine a different version of atemporality to emerge in current discussions of vibrant materiality in the humanities. These concerns of time and duration are especially important to understanding *Shift*, not only because the work's site has changed substantially during its forty-five-year lifespan, but also on account of ongoing questions regarding how to ethically and responsibly conserve site-specific artworks. For while the sense of ecology in this argument is primarily engaged with questions of knowledge rather than those of more activist environmentalisms that seek to directly advocate for the care of ecosystems, the continued life of outdoor artworks can no more be divorced from the former approach than from the latter. To accept the necessity of ecological change over time as an integral condition of site specificity means that ideas about art conservation must also internalize principles of ecology, including the fundamental reorganizations that take place in ecosystems over time. The implications for an ecological understanding of conservation are as profound as those for site specificity, suggesting a dramatically revised approach to such fundamental criteria of conservation as authorship and the primacy of original materials.

Thus, rather than simply articulating a third wave of site specificity, this argument will attempt to lay out the necessity of incorporating ecological perspectives into art historical interpretations of site and environment, balancing these against the imperative of humanistic expression to resist simply importing theories and models from the sciences. As situated at the very intersection of this tension, *Shift* at once exceeds the discipline's existing environmental frameworks of interpretation and offers instructive insights for forging more thoroughly entangled approaches to the ecology of site.

By the conclusion of the *Titled Arc* ordeal in 1989, site specificity had been cemented in its descriptive meaning for critics and historians alike, and, in the process, had become the presumptive way to experience location-based artworks of the preceding two decades. In the wake of *Tilted Arc*, however, the approach of artists themselves to site specificity took a new turn. Artists including Renée Green, Christian Philipp Müller, and Mark Dion, for instance, retained environmental specificity in their respective practices while also referring to social constructions and histories of environmental knowledge and experience. In a 1995 essay titled "The Functional Site," James Meyer described this second wave of site specificity as an "operation occurring between sites, a mapping of institutional and textual filiations."[9] Miwon Kwon would soon provide the most definitive account of these emergent practices in her 2002 book *One Place after Another*, casting their relation to place as "a discursively determined site that is delineated as a field of knowledge, intellectual exchange, or cultural debate."[10] While both arguments opened new horizons for thinking about site-specific art, they have also had the effect of reinforcing an assumption that the outdoor sculpture created by Serra and others should remain bound within the terms of first-wave site specificity.[11]

The site-specific art of those preceding decades of the 1960s and 1970s was initially addressed by both critics and artists through a paradigm of direct, perceptual experience at the site of the work, which was a reading deeply influenced by the art-critical reception of Maurice Merleau-Ponty's philosophy of phenomenology. To critique Meyer and Kwon for not challenging this position is not to suggest that phenomenology did not deeply impact the reception of land art's site-specific earthworks, but instead to draw a distinction between the range of interpretations that might describe first-generation site-specific sculpture and the entrenchment of the phenomenological take. To do so, we must first pause upon the considerable influence of Rosalind E. Krauss, whose impact on postwar scholarship began with criticism written in the 1960s and continued with her first long-form scholarly publications the following decade. Krauss's essay "Allusion and Illusion in Donald Judd," published in *Artforum* in May 1966, for instance, offered the first significant incorporation of Merleau-Ponty's phenomenology for postwar sculpture.[12] The English translation of Merleau-Ponty's *The Phenomenology of Perception* had appeared in 1962 (initially published in French in 1945), at approximately the same time that a number of American sculptors, including Judd, led a minimalist turn in sculpture that focused on the object-quality of simple geometric forms. Bodily perception occupies the main argument of *The Phenomenology of Perception*, emphasizing the primacy of the living, breathing human body in any experience and understanding of the larger world around it by way of the perceptual fields this body traverses. Such perceptual fields, Merleau-Ponty argues, are only ever partial views of an object that unfolds in time. "The world is not what I think," he maintains, "but what I live through."[13] For Krauss, this philosophy provided a compelling means to address the unfolding quality of the minimalist object in space, which, despite its use of rational, prismatic shapes, exceeded understandings of either space or time as knowable in advance of the spectator's direct encounter.

This is not to say that Merleau-Ponty's ideas themselves directly influenced the reception of postwar sculpture, so much as the cast they assumed in the art criticism of Krauss and others. Alex Potts, for instance, has written compellingly about the aspects of Merleau-Ponty's philosophy that fall beyond this art historical reception, including the latter's political position on Marxist historical materiality.[14] Indeed, an entire study could be written on the comparison between Merleau-Ponty's arguments in their original form and the vast permutations that his arguments have undergone in postwar aesthetics.[15] Within this larger field of discourse, it has been Krauss's particular version of Merleau-Ponty that has been most influential to the field of contemporary art history for addressing postwar sculpture and site-specific art. As such, I am less concerned with teasing out these distinctions between Krauss's adaptation and Merleau-Ponty's original argument than with thinking through the implications of the former for how art historians understand site specificity. That is, it is less "phenomenology" at stake here than the consequences of Krauss's forceful version of it—especially concerning time-based spectatorship and abstraction—on the discipline.

To begin with temporality, it is instructive to return to Krauss's *Passages in Modern Sculpture*, which, upon its publication in 1977, did much to both solidify and canonize a phenomenological view of site-specific sculpture shaped by the influence of minimalism. In the concluding pages of this text, she turns to the recent completion of *Shift*, alongside that of *Double Negative* (1969–70) and *Spiral Jetty*, writing:

> Contemporary sculpture is indeed obsessed with the idea of passage.
> We find it in . . . Serra's *Shift*, in Smithson's *Jetty*. And with these images

of passage, the transformation of sculpture—from a static, idealized
medium to a temporal and material one—that had begun with Rodin
is fully achieved. In every case the image of passage serves to place
both viewer and artist before the work, and the world, in an attitude of
primary humility in order to encounter the deep reciprocity between
himself and it.[16]

In describing the encounter between a spectator and these outdoor artworks,
Krauss emphasizes a particular notion of duration and physical movement—en-
capsulated by her term "passage"—that renders temporality as something that
unfolds for the spectator in relation to the work of art as encountered in the
particular place it was made and continues to reside. Despite Krauss's choice of
language, however, the "reciprocity" in this relationship is uneven, as "passage" is
something activated overwhelmingly by the human spectator rather than a relationship that coexists between the spectator and the admittedly slower and more
gradual movement transpiring in and around the work. Such division foregrounds
an impasse in Krauss's argument that the ensuing reception of site specificity has
not addressed: the difference between the temporality of real-time perception on
the part of a human subject viewing an artwork and the atemporality of privileging the static form of that work at one given moment—usually, the moment it
was completed. This is to say that Krauss's influential version of phenomenology
does not present an actual reciprocity between subject and object with respect to
temporality but rather a split between the subject as bound to experiential time
and the object as free of any duration excepting that brought to bear by the human agency of the spectator.

All the images Krauss calls upon in *Passages in Modern Sculpture* to illustrate her claims, not only about *Shift*, but also about *Double Negative* and *Spiral
Jetty*, were shot by Gorgoni; all feature one or two isolated figures encountering
these works in the manner dramatized by her argument. These figures tend to
be shown as silhouettes—whether standing at the cusp of and upon the ramp of
Double Negative, at the point of intersection between the long arm wrapping out
of *Spiral Jetty*'s coil and the shoreline of the Great Salt Lake, or upon the snow-
covered ground at *Shift* (figs. 3 and 4). Taken together, these images contribute to
the anthropocentric notion of time characteristic of Krauss's phenomenology, depicting the environments of these site-specific artworks in the most reductive possible fashion. But more than a merely anthropocentric point of view, this brand of
phenomenology also tends to pare down subjectivity to the motor faculties of the

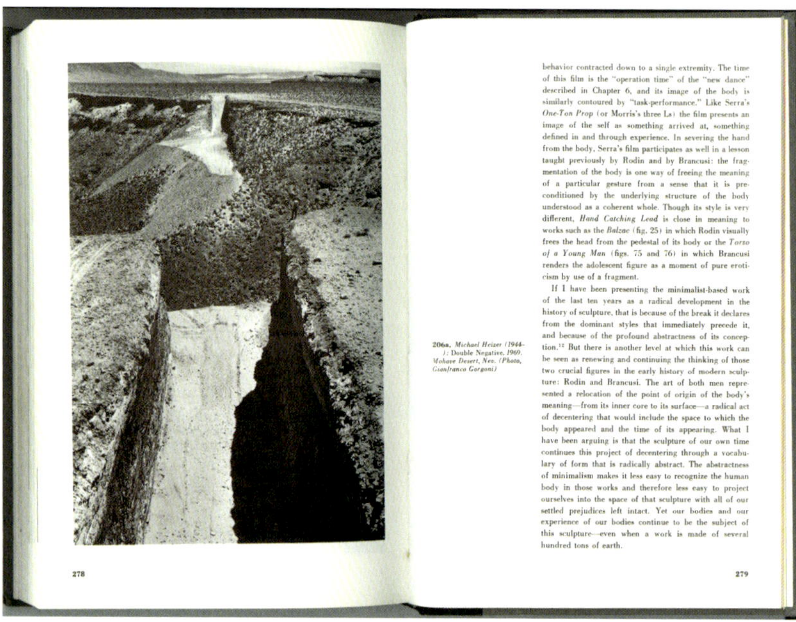

Fig. 3. Gianfranco Gorgoni, photograph of Michael Heizer's *Double Negative*, 1969, published in Rosalind E. Krauss, *Passages in Modern Sculpture* (1977). © Gianfranco Gorgoni

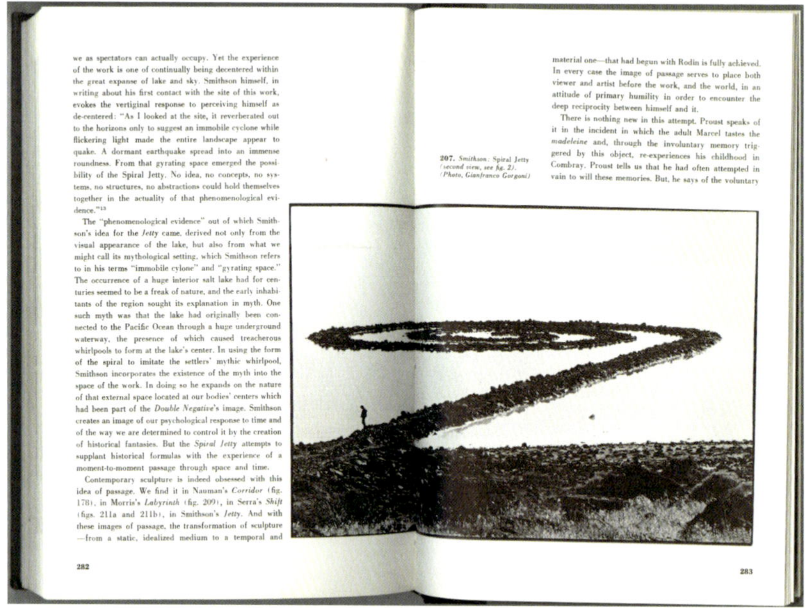

Fig. 4. Gianfranco Gorgoni, photograph of Robert Smithson's *Spiral Jetty*, 1970, published in Rosalind E. Krauss, *Passages in Modern Sculpture* (1977). © Gianfranco Gorgoni

human sensorium, seeing and moving through the site overcoming any personal histories or feelings that individuals might bring to the experience of that place.

Crucially, this impulse to emphasize subjectivity, while at the same time radically reducing and generalizing it, further intersects with an equally distinct version of abstraction at play in Krauss's phenomenological aesthetics. In a 1983 essay on Serra, written for a French audience, Krauss again focused on *Shift*, casting it, notably, as a witting or unwitting instantiation of Merleau-Ponty's ideas. In a quite remarkable, extended description, she moves from the movement of Serra and Jonas upon the field of *Shift*, into the internalization of phenomenology by minimalist sculpture, into, finally, a claim about Serra's abstraction as part of a "primordial, preobjective world."[17] Though there are many ways to understand abstraction that might contribute to environmental knowledge and experience, as modeled through Gorgoni's photographs and Krauss's understanding of site specificity, abstraction is tantamount to the closed shape of sculptural form. Moreover, this narrow sense of abstraction generates, in Krauss's account, "aesthetic operations . . . that produce what could be called the abstract subject."[18] This abstraction of subjectivity is different from the modern quantification of perception in nineteenth-century psycho-physics and gestalt psychology that has been examined by scholars such as Jonathan Crary.[19] Rather than casting the human faculties of perception in strictly mechanical terms, Krauss's notion "abstracts"—in the active, transitive sense—perceptual experience as being, paradoxically, individual and temporal, on the one hand, while universal and unchanging, on the other.

To further unfold this point, we might consider Krauss's next major treatment of *Shift*, in a catalogue essay for Serra's first MoMA retrospective in 1986. Here, she writes:

> Moving over the grounds of the work, one experiences the walls as elements in constant transformation: first as line, then as barrier, only to become line once more. From the vantage of high ground, the upper edges of the walls are the vectors along which one sights as one stands above them looking down, and they thereby establish one's connection to the distance. Whereas from the vantage of one's "descent" they broaden and thicken to become an enclosure that binds one within the earth. Felt as barrier rather than as perspective, they then heighten the experience of the physical place of one's body. Without

> depicting anything specific, the walls' oscillation between the linear and
> the physical articulates both a situation and a lived perspective. And it
> does this in the most abstract way possible: by the rotation in and out
> of depth of a plane.[20]

Though an evocative portrayal of *Shift*'s formal properties in the language of conventional sculpture in the round, this account nonetheless reiterates her position on site specificity, and by implication, its legacy. The "constant transformation" Krauss describes is one bounded entirely by formal properties, such as line and plane, and is equally contingent upon the particular interests of the spectator who traverses *Shift*'s site. "The physical place of one's body," likewise, becomes a similarly formal proposition, free of land rights, political constraints, weather, or any other mode of being situated that might arise in the encounter between a body and a site. The "lived perspective" that emerges from this perceptual awareness is thus perspectival in the most geometric, abstract, and "abstracted" sense, confirming the force of a phenomenological framework that relies upon a restrictive construction of temporality experienced by a subject narrowly construed as a mobile, perceptual faculty who traverses an object-field that fluctuates only in accordance with the agency of that subject. While this account may jibe well with the presentation of *Shift* in Gorgoni's photographs of the early 1970s—which illustrate each of Krauss's subsequent discussions of *Shift* following *Passages in Modern Sculpture*—it is far less apposite to the seasonal cycles affecting the condition and appearance of the work throughout the agricultural year, and, moreover, the considerable changes that have reshaped King City during the past four decades.

The environment surrounding and containing *Shift* has indeed changed substantially since 1972, primarily because the sculpture and its parcel of land are owned by the Toronto-based development company Hickory Hill Investments, having been purchased from Serra's original patron, Roger Davidson, when he sold his farmland in 1974.[21] The presence of *Shift* in Davidson's sale of land was then entirely ignored by Hickory Hill for thirty years, until 2004, when members of King Township's city council moved to register the artwork as a provincial heritage site. During approximately the same period of time, Hickory Hill began to build both condominiums and single-family homes on its real estate holdings in King City, altering the demographics and organization of the town from a small rural, agricultural community to a growing exurb connected by commuter rail to

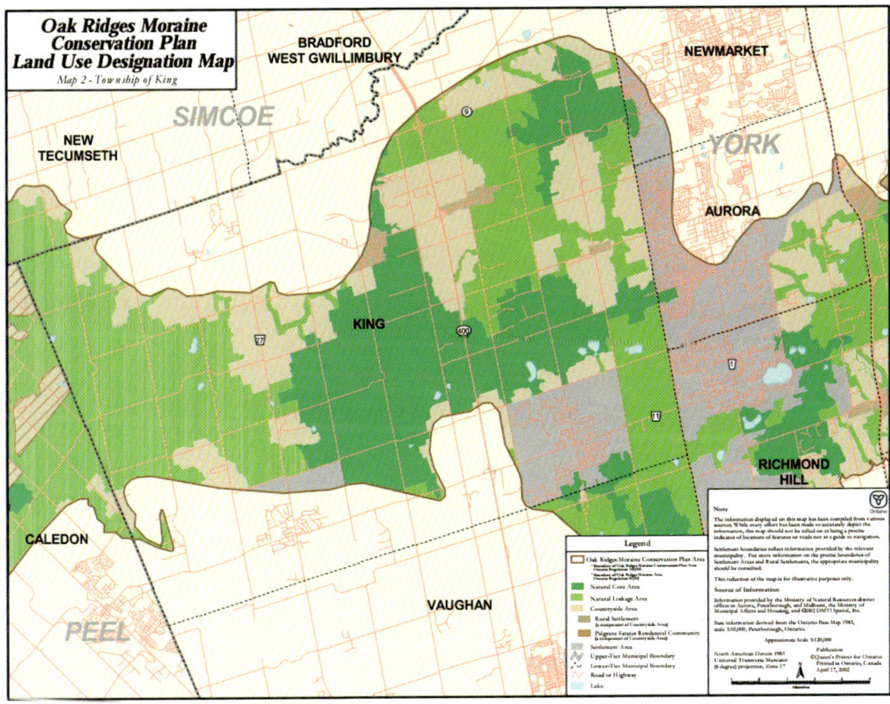

Fig. 5. Township of King, section of the Oak Ridges Moraine Area Land Use Designation Map, 2002. Ontario Ministry of Housing

Toronto. While rapid alterations to King City generated uncertainty about the future of *Shift*, Hickory Hill staunchly resisted attempts to legally protect Serra's sculpture and site, claiming any such designation "inappropriate and unnecessary" for "a private piece of art on private property" already protected ecologically by the Oak Ridges Moraine Conservation Act, which had been passed in 2001 to control growth within the Moraine north of Toronto and protect its "ecological and hydrological integrity."[22]

The Oak Ridges Moraine Conservation Act does include King City, but collapsing its approach to ecological preservation with that of artistic preservation is not so straightforward. The Oak Ridges Moraine Conservation Plan, established in 2002 to enact the goals of the act, divides the Moraine's 733 square miles into four zones: Natural Core Areas, Natural Linkage Areas, Countryside Areas, and Settlement Areas. *Shift* lies within a Natural Core Area (fig. 5), which, of the four designations, carries the most restrictions for new construction, but does not prohibit human development altogether, permitting building projects for agriculture, infrastructure, personal businesses, and recreation.[23] From this list, it is clear that the plan bars Hickory Hill from turning *Shift* into a high-end courtyard for mid-rise condominiums, but it does not prevent other arrangements that could significantly alter the sculptural work and its site. This potential threat to *Shift*'s future under the plan is further compounded by the fact that it lies right on the border of a Settlement Area, the zone allocated for the greatest density of real estate construction and human traffic.

In all, the specious sleight-of-hand in Hickory Hill's claim regarding the artistic protection provided by the Oak Ridges Moraine Conservation Plan bears striking similarity to the sophistry applied to *Tilted Arc*'s site specificity by federal administrators. While, in the former case, Hickory Hill turned the 2002 conservation plan into an erroneous and misleadingly elastic interpretation of "conservation," in the latter, Dwight Ink, the acting administrator for the General Services Administration in Washington, DC, which commissioned and owned *Tilted Arc*, skewed the meaning of site specificity to suggest that any site provided for *Tilted Arc* would become its "specific" site and therefore satisfy Serra's stipulations for his work.[24] Unlike the case of *Tilted Arc*, however, in February 2013 Hickory Hill lost its argument and the approximately ten acres of land encompassing *Shift* were conferred "cultural heritage value" under the Ontario Heritage Act, a designation that specifically protects *Shift* as an artwork.[25] While an important victory for the longevity and integrity of the work, this decision does not end questions pertaining to *Shift*'s preservation, as King City's suburbanization is but one variable among many in the work's ecological site specificity.

What does it mean to address *Shift*'s site specificity as ecological? At a basic level, the interrelationships affecting it encompass not only the field where the sculpture is located, but also the ever-expanding circuits of influence beyond this acreage that include the local politics of real estate development and more widespread influences, such as the impact of climate change on the experience of Serra's work. As compared to someone standing in this field in 1972, the spectator who visits *Shift* today encounters a place whose plants, animal life, and bug populations have been affected by a range of human and nonhuman actions. I have already noted some of the material changes that have taken place at this site, including the rotating agricultural crops and plant growth at the base of the sculpture. Yet, to truly recognize *Shift*'s site as a living environment, we need to further acknowledge its longer history.

Such a consideration begins with the strips of forest along the edges of the field that frame the spectator's view of the work. Until the nineteenth century, the land upon which King City is located was a "tall prairie-and-oak savanna with mixed softwoods," inhabited and managed by the Indigenous Mississauga people.[26] This land was then irrevocably altered when seized by British colonists and allotted for farming, displacing the native inhabitants and significantly reducing the complexity of local ecosystems. This is to say that prior to Serra and Jonas's arrival in 1970, a geometric partitioning and reshaping of the land had already transpired. That Serra and Jonas could see across the apparently open expanse of this farmland to grasp its topology was less a condition of neutrality or absence—an empty ground preceding sculptural form—than a remainder of the violence done to both human and nonhuman ecologies at that site. The patches of forest surrounding *Shift* today only further underscore this discrepancy between forested and nonforested land in southern Ontario, indicating that the openness and visibility of the latter is always already colonial and appropriative.

The strips of forest surrounding the field were also undergoing a transformation at the time of *Shift*'s completion. Until the late 1950s, this forest had been grazed by cattle owned by local farmers, who cut it back regularly for easy mobility. But upon the sale of this land to Davidson, the field in which *Shift* is located began to be rented for farming to contractors who only tilled specific plots and didn't reside on the land or maintain it. Davidson also discontinued the husbandry of cattle on his farm, effectively ending the practice of cutting back the forest. Today Hickory Hill continues to rent the field and not to touch its surrounding forest, meaning that since the 1950s, this forest has grown increasingly mature and more complex.

Within the field itself, alterations to all manner of species have been affected during the recent past both by macro-level events occurring at the scale of the planet and those at a more micro level by local actions undertaken by Hickory Hill. Bird populations that would have been present overhead or nesting in the forest at *Shift* in early spring or late fall of the early 1970s have been altered by changing weather and temperature patterns.[27] Residents of King City who have lived near *Shift* for its entire lifespan confirm such changing patterns. The birds that residents used to see regularly, but have now disappeared, or all but so, are extensive and include bobolinks, bluebirds, tanagers, thrushes, catbirds, king birds, killdeers, flickers, swallows, starlings, redheaded woodpeckers, hairy woodpeckers, chickadees, nuthatches, rose-breasted grosbeaks, and warblers.[28] Geologists, atmospheric scientists, and farmers bring more observations into the conversation. Such serial accounts of living and nonliving connectivity have in fact become commonplace in the environmental humanities in recent years, giving rise to what philosopher Ian Bogost calls the "Latour litany," in reference to the lists of interconnected living and nonliving actants that appear in accounts of ecomateriality inspired by Bruno Latour's Actor-Network Theory (ANT).[29]

As Latour himself explains, ANT can be a misleading name, in that it doesn't provide a theory of either actors or networks, as such, but instead offers a method of addressing the associations among the immense range of things that shape social formations. "Even though most social scientists would prefer to call 'social' a homogenous thing," he explains, "it's perfectly acceptable to designate by the same word a trail of *associations* between heterogeneous elements."[30] Emphasizing the instability and movement created by the associations that form among such "heterogeneous elements" as birds, weeds, single-family homes, and airborne particles, the radical openness of ANT to social behavior and experience may help account for the impact of actants upon *Shift* as local as a city council and as global as ocean tides. But in addressing this all-encompassing aspect of his method, Latour clarifies that "big does not mean 'really' big or 'overall,' or 'overarching,' but connected, blind, local, mediated, related. This is already an important contribution of ANT since it means that when one explores the structures of the social, one is not led away from the local sites . . . but *closer* to them."[31]

In keeping with the distinction drawn above between Merleau-Ponty's phenomenology and its art historical reception, it is actually not Latour's ANT itself that has most impacted approaches to ecological description and analysis in the humanities so much as its reception through newer theories of materiality. In the most impactful of these, Jane Bennett's *Vibrant Matter: A Political Ecology of Things* (2010), the author describes a pile of debris in a Baltimore storm drain as a kind of Latour litany that very nearly gets at the kind of ecological awareness through which I would like to characterize *Shift*.[32] In the chapter that follows from this description, Bennett goes on to articulate a "thing-power" and "vital materiality" that persist not only in garbage scattered in a gutter, but also in examples drawn from literature, legal history, and philosophy. First introduced by asking "modern, secular, well-educated humans" to suspend their tendency to conceive "human agency . . . as the ultimate source" of all agency in the world, Bennett's argument expands to further case studies addressing topics including electrical blackouts, food consumption, stem cells, and hurricanes in order to argue for a notion of "vibrant matter" that is vitalist at the same time as being inherently political. In doing so, Bennett attends to the agential force of nonliving things as always embroiled in the balance of institutionalized practices of power. In this way, her account most closely approaches what I am attempting to say about *Shift*, as compared to other accounts of what has been dubbed "new materialism" or "object-oriented ontology" that too easily dispose with socially rooted forms of ideological and institutionalized power in favor of giving voice to a multivocal life of things that inhabit a plane of existence unhinged from pasts of bias and repression, as the editors also discuss in their introduction through the responses of Mel Y. Chen and Huey Copeland to a recent survey about materialist impulses in contemporary scholarship.[33]

Such critiques point us to one of the fundamental limitations generated by Bennett's approach: her version of Latour's active materiality and distributive agency ultimately leaves aside the ideological implications of duration. Bennett's own canon of historical thinkers is rich and scattered across the long history of European philosophy, as, in her words, she "pursues a materialism in the tradition of Democritus-Epicurus-Spinoza-Diderot-Deleuze."[34] But instead of laying out a historical trajectory of thinking about materiality, these thinkers operate in Bennett's argument in the present tense of description. That is, while hers and similar approaches to vibrant materiality have been effective in expanding the scope of the objects and agents that scholars address, these accounts also tend to produce synchronic systems that, while different from the anthropomorphic variety of atemporality in Krauss's phenomenological aesthetics, produce a similar upshot in limiting the life of objects to a universalizing presentism.

The ecological perspective of materiality, however, need not be presentist. On this point, it is crucial to bear in mind that ecology was not always grasped by way of ecosystems, and these ecosystems, in turn, were not always thought to be subject to the effects of time. To briefly summarize, while ecology itself is a field of modern science dating back approximately a century and a half, the notion of an ecosystem was created considerably later.[35] First coined in 1935, "ecosystems" initially designated interconnections defined primarily by the agency of animal organisms, particularly through the model of the food chain.[36] But following the conclusion of the Second World War and the rise of cybernetics, ecosystems were reordered around more robust systems theories derived from new computing technologies, which produced the influential paradigm of the "steady-state" ecosystem, characterized, like informational code, by a consistent order that is both predictable and unchanging.[37] Steady-state ecology was the dominant explanatory model and means to imagine global connectivity through-out the long 1960s, when a public consciousness about environmentalism arose through such signal events as Rachel Carson's publication of *Silent Spring* in 1962 and the first Earth Day demonstrations in 1970, only to be challenged the fol-lowing decade when ideas drawn from chaos theory began to encroach upon the conceptualization of ecosystems. Based on longer-term studies, scientists in the 1970s, at just about the time that *Shift* was completed, realized that ecosystems do not have a natural and timeless steady state, but instead consist of a balance of relationships that can be fundamentally altered over time by the influx of both immediately disruptive and more incrementally unruly factors.[38] This revised understanding of ecosystems, in turn, has impacted the concept of succession in ecology, which also dates from the early twentieth century, and had also assumed that communities of species do not fundamentally change over time.[39] Following the decline of steady-state ecology, succession was likewise revised to recognize that, over time, some species decline in prevalence and influence, others increase, and others still disappear or colonize in ways that alter the balance of a particular ecosystem. This can take place as a "primary succession," wherein an ecosystem forms in a previously barren region, or a "secondary succession," in which a new organization of ecological relations replaces a previous one. Based on its roots in theories of chaos, this revised notion of succession also acknowledges that such alterations are typically unpredictable, and, therefore, not the work of a rational, or, at least, singular agency.

The idea of succession is also provocative for thinking about the ecology of site as durational rather than atemporal in either of the phenomenological or materialist modes that I have outlined. From this notion of the ecosystem as being open to revision over time, we might consider, for instance, whether *Shift* has undergone changes so fundamental as to constitute a succession of its relationship to site. That is, to consider whether the effects to *Shift* have been so extensive as to recast its site specificity as a different kind of work, one less at-tuned to experiencing topological shape and more to grasping the complexities of change within living environments. The implications of understanding *Shift* in these terms would be considerable, particularly with respect to ongoing complexi-ties of its conservation.

We might consider, for instance, what it is like to see *Shift* during the late summer and early fall in a year when its field is planted with corn (fig. 6). Within these

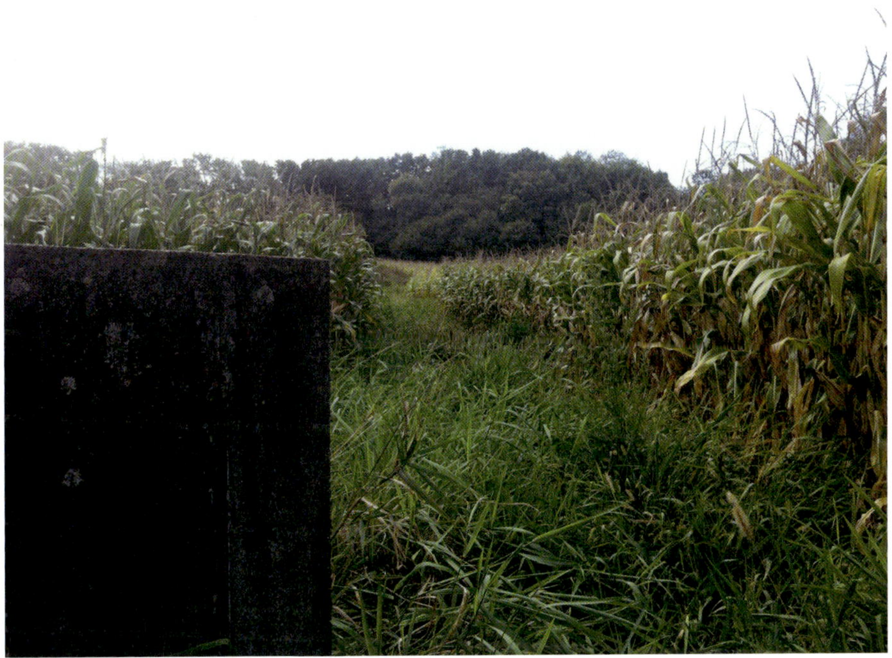

Fig. 6. Richard Serra, *Shift* (detail), 1970–72. Concrete, six sections: 60'' × 90' × 8''; 60'' × 240' × 8''; 60'' × 150' × 8''; 60'' × 120' × 8''; 60'' × 110 × 8''; 60'' × 105' × 8''. Photographed 2017

conditions, its sculptural walls have to be sought out through blind exploration amidst the tall stalks growing across the site. Then, even when the walls have been located, restricted visibility necessitates that no more than one or two walls are visible at any one time. Rather than markers rising up from the flat topography of the land, in such conditions these walls instead become pathways sunken beneath the tops of the stalks, creating a route of travel through an allover array of vegetation.

Even when planted with low-lying soybean plants, as it was in summer 2017, *Shift* can be significantly affected by local weather. Spring 2017 was in fact particularly rainy in southern Ontario, giving rise to an especially dense cluster of wild plants around *Shift* that summer that almost entirely covered its walls, leaving them visible only in small patches (fig. 7). In this state, the shape of the land was visible, while the shape of the sculpture itself had become something left mostly to the spectator's imagination. This is to say that the relationship between sculptural object and its environmental contingencies was still vital to experiencing the site—as is essential to the foundational ideas of site specificity—but not in terms of the formal lines and planes of the sculpture Serra originally installed

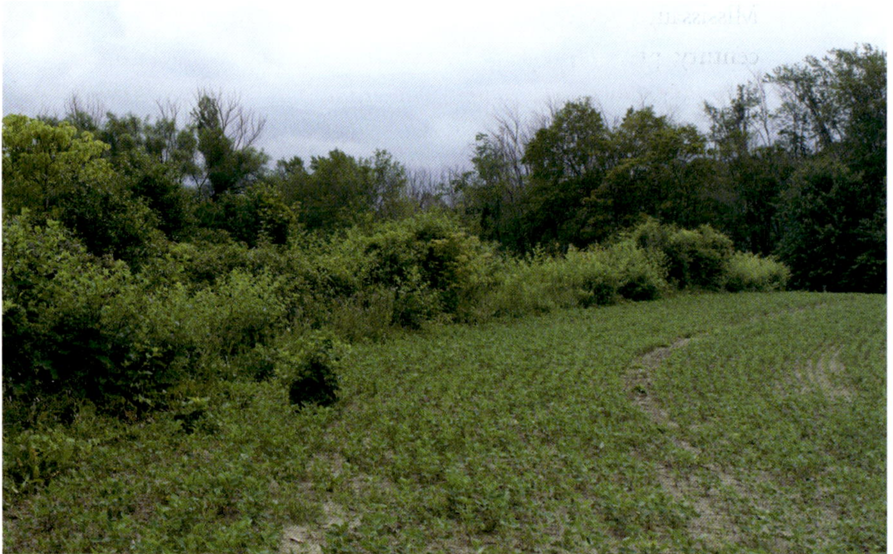

Fig. 7. Richard Serra, *Shift* (detail), 1970–72. Concrete, six sections: 60" × 90' × 8"; 60" × 240' × 8"; 60" × 150' × 8"; 60" × 120' × 8"; 60" × 110' × 8"; 60" × 105' × 8". Photographed 2017

on this site in the early 1970s. Instead of being a visible shape, the sculptural presence of *Shift* had taken on a new role as barrier to the farmer's plow.

Cultivated fields tend to be monocultural habitats, being seeded only with a single crop. The presence of *Shift* in the center of such a field, however, prevents uniformly even harvesting, plowing, and seeding, giving rise to the colonization of many different kinds of plants, including those both native to the region, such as goldenrods and asters, and non-native, such as burdock and many of the grasses. As such, *Shift* still relies on contingency as a sculptural presence, but this is a contingency of rain and ecological diversification that differs quite dramatically from the typical conditions of an agricultural field.

Shift's present state has also been directly affected by its recent public exposure, encompassing not only heritage committee meetings but also an unsuccessful attempt by the Art Gallery of Ontario to acquire the work and increase public access.[40] This increased attention has in turn prompted Hickory Hill to further "protect" *Shift* by installing a chain-link fence to keep the public away from the work. For while *Shift* has always existed on private property, spectators had previously never been barred from entering the site. Now, to experience *Shift* in person, visitors to the site must willfully cross "No Trespassing" signs and scale a fence. This is the same "private property" that had been taken from the

Mississauga two centuries earlier, but which had been, for much of the twentieth century, private property by law, but in practice a field open to the public. To encroach today on such land is a far more self-conscious and brazen act of intrusion, once again recasting the universalism of phenomenological subjectivity as not only (and still) colonial, but also, in a different valence, resistant to terrestrial privatization.

Taken together, these and other changes brought about by factors ranging from Hickory Hill's activities to local weather patterns suggest that a transformation has in fact occurred in the relation of *Shift* to its site approaching a secondary ecological succession. One of the challenges in theorizing these changes holistically, however, lies in the fact that they have not simply affected the site's ecosystem as such, but, instead fluctuations to this ecosystem have affected how the site operates as a work of art. As a point of contrast, consider Alan Sonfist's *Time Landscape* that he installed in 1978 at the northeast corner of La Guardia Place and West Houston Street in New York City. Covering an area 25 x 40 feet, it originally comprised three planting zones, each consisting of different stages of maturity of the forest that once covered Manhattan Island, ranging from grasses to saplings to developed trees. Today, the work remains in place, but nearly forty years of growth have obscured the once-precise borders among its three zones. While *Shift* began as a sculptural object within a specific site and only over time developed an increasingly blurred distinction between object and site, this lack of separation has always characterized *Time Landscape*. Unlike *Shift*, the increasing maturity of the small forest growing at *Time Landscape* and its ecological succession over time is an element of the work anticipated from the beginning. From Serra's various notes and statements, there is no evidence to suggest he planned for *Shift* to do this as well. As such, the more unpredicted alterations transpiring in the relations between the sculpture element of *Shift* and the ecology of its site present challenging questions about the work's conservation. While *Shift* has been protected from demolition or a similarly disastrous fate by the Ontario Heritage Act, this ruling does not answer the question of how *Shift* might be best cared for in the near and distant future. This is because conserving Serra's work, from the perspective of art conservation, is no longer a straightforward proposition of attempting to maintain *Shift* in its original condition, if we understand that condition to be what is pictured in Gorgoni's photographs or described by Krauss. To cut away all of the growth around the work, cease the cultivation of the field, and perhaps even cut back the woods surrounding it would be to create a new work approximating the appearance of *Shift* in 1972, rather than to restore it as such. That work has been succeeded by a new ecological reality.

Related issues of art conservation have been addressed in disparate ways with Walter De Maria's *Lightning Field* and Robert Smithson's *Spiral Jetty* (see fig. 4), which are both maintained by the Dia Art Foundation. The latter was gifted to the foundation in 1999 at a time when the work was submerged underwater, a condition that lasted from soon after its completion in the early 1970s until 2002. After *Spiral Jetty* resurfaced, encrusted in a cap of white salt, former Dia conservator Francesca Esmay began a project of documenting the work aerially to track a number of factors, including water level, the drift of *Spiral Jetty's* circular coil, and buildup of silt deposits against it. While Dia continues to document these processes, it has yet to take any actions to conserve the coil itself. In an interview, Esmay describes such deliberations as follows:

> For conservators, when we consider intervention and treatment on a work of art, we often think about preserving "original materials" and strive to align any intervention with the "artist's intent." In the case of *Spiral Jetty*, both of these issues are not straightforward since the original materials of the object arguably began changing the very instant the artwork was completed. Therefore, citing an original condition to use as a benchmark for a restoration is very challenging, if not impossible.[41]

Notably, in deciding not to touch the rocks and dirt that comprise the sculptural form of *Spiral Jetty*, Dia has instead focused its attention on the view shed around the work, attempting to preserve the appearance of approaching and standing before Smithson's earthwork that spectators would have encountered in 1970. In doing so, Dia has opposed local proposals involving oil extraction, but as recently as 2015, stated that it would not act to raise the water level along the lake's north shore surrounding the *Spiral Jetty*, despite a sustained drought that had effectively marooned Smithson's work.[42]

Dia has also resolved to conserve *The Lightning Field*'s view shed by acquiring a land easement south of the work from local ranchers to prevent that land from being developed or commercialized.[43] Unlike its treatment of *Spiral Jetty*, however, Dia has also subjected the sculptural element of De Maria's *Lightning Field* to more direct conservation, replacing selected poles over time that had been damaged by the local climate and undertaking a more significant and systemic effort to reinforce the entire structure of the *The Lightning Field*'s four hundred poles in 2012.[44] Considering Esmay's stated criteria of "original materials" and "artist's intent," the difference between Dia's approach to conserving *Spiral Jetty* and *The Lightning Field*, respectively, appears to arise more from the latter criterion than from the former. Although Smithson died in a plane crash in 1973 and therefore couldn't participate in Dia's decisions, he wrote extensively during his lifetime about his own work and famously valorized the concept of material entropy, which for him denoted the gradual breakdown of recognizable form over time.[45] Further, from statements by Smithson such as "nature does not proceed in a straight line, it is rather a sprawling development," Dia and others have inferred that the artist would not choose to resist any effects to *Spiral Jetty* wrought by the vicissitudes of erosion, coastal drift, and drought over time.[46] De Maria, to the contrary, expressed no such conceptions of entropy about his sculpture and, still being alive and active in his practice at the time of *The Lightning Field*'s conservation, served as ultimate arbiter of its proper care.

Between these two limit cases, we might return to *Shift* with Esmay's criteria of "original materials" and "artistic intent" to further consider the complications involved in its artistic conservation. Under the concept of ecological succession, I have already discussed how the materials involved in the experience of *Shift* have expanded and mutated in a number of unexpected ways since Serra's installation of the work. What is more, these alterations in the material composition of *Shift* as both sculpture and site have been influenced by many currents of agency, suggesting that the singular agency of Serra as the creator and judge of *Shift*'s proper state has dissipated into more of a distributed network. Serra didn't plant or plan the weeds around *Shift*, but they are now a constituent part of the work. He had nothing to do with the crop rotation of its field, but this rotation deeply impacts the appearance and meaning of the piece throughout the calendar year. This does not mean that Serra's opinion about the ongoing conservation of *Shift* should not carry weight, or that the guidelines of the Ontario Heritage Act, or even the input of Hickory Hill, can or should unilaterally make conservation decisions. As *Shift*'s authorship has become dispersed among these various entities, so too has its future come to increasingly depend upon the interrelated interests of these often-competing parties.

While this dispersed condition of *Shift* is markedly different from its original formation as a site-specific sculpture by a single artist on the land of a single, private patron, this new condition of the work also points to the insufficiencies of succession as a scientific concept for considering the duration of site-specific art. This is because succession assumes a new balance achieved within an ecosystem that entirely supplants previous states of that same ecosystem. While *Shift* may well have achieved such a succession on its site itself, spectators of the work cannot overlook the impact of Gorgoni's photographic representations of the work with which I began. Rather than being simply historical or outmoded documents, these photographs, and in fact, all of the images of *Shift* in circulation that depict its site across the near half-century of its existence, compose a record of the work as precisely the kind of durational object that resists the diminished subjectivity of art critical phenomenology or the synchronic time splices characteristic of new materialism. Against the presentism of living relationships within biological ecosystems themselves, those of artistic ecosystems carry the memory of past states of the work, which may no longer be directly accessible, but do not disappear in the same abrupt manner as in biological ecosystems. While in one sense, *Shift* is not the site-specific work that it once was and has experienced something akin to a succession, in another, those past states of the work still inform our understanding of it in the present. Such a view of site specificity gives rise to a richer palimpsest of the ever-changing conditions at *Shift*'s site, layered in dialogue with the photographic and descriptive fragments of it that we have from the late twentieth century. This suggests that rather than being simply documents of the work in and of itself, the photographs of *Shift* are an ever-growing and increasingly nuanced invocation of the work's previous conditions. What *Shift* is in the present moment is not depicted in such photographs, but they are nonetheless integral to understanding the totality of the work. For this totality cannot be encompassed in one set of ecological relations alone, but only in the unfolding of such relations over time.

To visualize the kind of ecological site specificity that I have attempted to articulate for *Shift*, I'd like to conclude by proposing a virtual diagram, by which I mean one that is best imagined rather than pictured on the page. My speculative assertion is that the work of art, understood ecologically, necessarily exists in a dynamic condition between any single extremity that might falsely identify or overly determine it. Thus, rather than a static diagram with points to be pictured, the ecological site exists in a state of perpetual motion, within a blurry field of interpenetrating scales and bandwidths, never settling on any single state. The present essay has articulated two important spectra along which such relations move. With respect

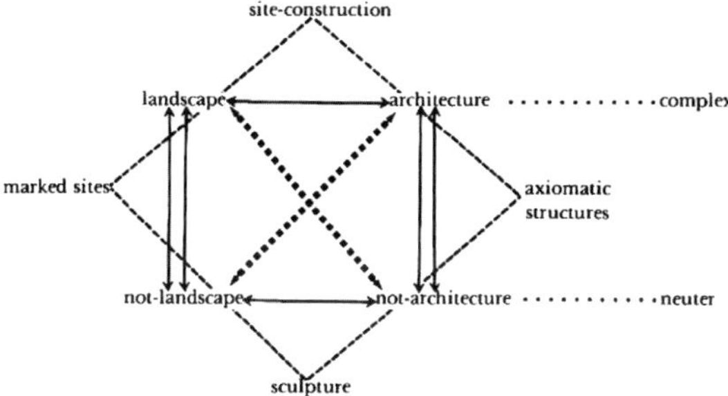

Fig. 8. Rosalind E. Krauss (American, b. 1941), diagram in "Sculpture in the Expanded Field," *October* 8 (Spring 1979)

to human agency and non-agency as one such spectrum, some new materialisms and object-oriented ontologies exist at a far point of non-agency that elides human rights and institutionally entrenched forms of bias altogether, whereas at the other end, positions too endowed in human agency, such as Krauss's phenomenology, lock the artwork into the anthropocentric fallacy that the materiality of art ultimately exists within and for human subjectivity. A similar spectrum exists for the continuity of ecosystems: if all is stability, we find ourselves in the worldview of late 1960s systems ecology, akin to a computer programmed for predictable outcomes in both the short and the long runs of time. If all is chaos or lack of stability, we inhabit the purview of the apocalyptic futurist who can see nothing outside of complete ecological collapse, or, in other terms, someone who doesn't see the possibility of succession, only the deterioration of what once was. In the space between these untenable extremes, the ecological artwork exists as subject to chaotic and sometimes dramatic change, sustains cultural meaning over time, and resists the possibility that only intentional or especially human agency will govern its presence in the world.

This kind of duration means that the ecological artwork's in-between condition is not fixed in place upon its completion, but continues to move over the course of time, within dynamic fields of engagement established one upon the other, again, and again. While past positions of such fields may disappear in the direct environment of the work itself, these are the states captured and recalled in the kind of images and descriptions considered throughout this essay. Thus, rather than simply rejecting the iconic images of *Shift*, I maintain that their difference from the present state of the work does not so much discredit these images as documentation of the work so much as set its current appearance in an accumulation of relationships that have grown increasingly knotted over the past four decades. *Shift*'s site specificity is not a single or a steady state. It exists instead as a movement or montage between the appearance of the work at the moment of encounter and the available archive of its appearances across time. In turn, this shuttling between the ever-changing ecological state of artworks and their photographic record produces a specifically art historical notion of ecological succession, related to but distinct from its scientific counterpart.

One cannot invoke a diagram of environmental art, whether virtual or otherwise, without calling to mind another notorious diagram, that which appears in Rosalind E. Krauss's seminal 1979 essay "Sculpture in the Expanded Field" (fig. 8).[47] This diagram, which she adopted from a structuralist Klein group, marks out a series of new positions in the conception of sculpture that arise from its combination with and/or exclusion of considerations of landscape and architecture. In Krauss's reading, for instance, earthworks such as *Spiral Jetty* and *Double Negative* exist as "marked sites" rather than as pure sculpture because they are part of a kind of "landscape" while also being distinguishable as an artwork that, as such, is therefore "not landscape." Without delving too deeply into this argument, which has experienced numerous afterlives and permutations in contemporary scholarship and criticism, I will instead close by noting the fundamentally different outlook on the relationship of artwork and site offered by the kinds of diagrams before us.[48] Where Krauss's Klein group places works into categories premeditated by discourse, the virtual field I invoke insists instead on the impossibility of fixed positions in the existence and duration of artworks.

Written shortly after the publication of *Passages in Modern Sculpture*, "Sculpture in the Expanded Field" sought to further Krauss's argument that modernism's purist conceptions of medium—focusing on sculpture, but including painting as well—had run their course, giving rise to what she called a postmodern condition. According to Krauss, "within the situation of postmodernism, practice is not defined in relation to a given medium—sculpture—but rather in relation to the logical operations on a set of cultural terms, for which any medium—photography, books, lines on walls, mirrors, or sculpture itself—might be used."[49] While undoubtedly "expanding" the criteria of modernist art beyond the its narrow interpretation of media, especially that of Krauss's early mentor Clement Greenberg, the postmodern field to emerge from this argument and its renowned diagram still relies on a kind of apriority, not of singular artistic media like painting and sculpture, but of cultural production as the working out of already extant terms and ideas. While ostensibly rejecting Greenbergian modernism, the expansion described by Krauss's postmodernism still operates in the imaginary of that kind of modernism. Instead of using what Greenberg once described as "the characteristic methods of a discipline to criticize the discipline itself" to elicit the specificity of each medium, her postmodernism defined a broader, but nevertheless equally self-critical and inert space of cultural interpretation.[50] As loath as I may be to raise the tired specter of Greenberg once more—particularly in the concluding lines of this argument—it is necessary to do so to emphasize that the continued influence of site specificity as a key term in contemporary art history still carries forward the basic premise that environmental art remains fixed upon human agency and environmental stability, even through its revisions by Meyer and Kwon, wherein anything outside the artist or embodied spectator either isn't included in the photographs or is left outside the written accounts. This universe of interpretation has no place for the vastly different versions of *Shift* that have arisen since its initial completion. What I'm proposing, then, is less a further expansion of the same kind of field than a categorical reorientation. The very basis of the terms and distinctions to arise in the first and second waves of site specificity constitute but one vector among a host of others in the consideration of site specific sculpture, or, for that matter, environmentally situated art understood more broadly.

It may seem a rather straightforward proposition to suggest that artworks, and especially environmental artworks, change over time, but closer consideration of this proposition for *Shift* has revealed far more complex considerations. With respect to site specificity, it is clear that sites are not fixed to the prevailing conditions present at either the moment an artist finishes working or the condition depicted in a site's initial documentation. But, in allowing for a more variable, interrelational, and, thereby, ecological conception of how such sites are affected by myriad forms of agency over time, my own earlier suggestion—that changes at that site occur through all-encompassing, ecological successions—must be balanced against the traces of documentation that artworks accrue over their lifespan. For paintings or freestanding sculpture maintained in private collections or museums, these traces tend to be relatively invariable. But for outdoor artworks, the dramatic transformations of a site that can take place over relatively short periods of time give rise to a more dialectical understanding of how the present condition of the artwork corresponds to its previous states. Such a dialectic is but one perspective toward new frameworks that finally shed the lingering vestiges of modernism's human-centered world, and begin to allow more ecological outlooks on the physical, environmental, and worldly lives of artworks.

Thanks to the organizers and all of the participants at the "Ecologies, Agents, Terrains" seminar and conference at the Clark. Their insightful comments and conversation helped to shape this argument in a number of meaningful ways, especially so, the editorial advice of Rebecca Zorach and Samantha Page. Thanks also to Simone Estrin, Elma Feindell, Michael Crossley, Mark Cheetham, and Elizabeth Hutchinson.

1. On the prevalence of Gorgoni's photographs of *Shift*, see Richard Serra and Clara Weyergraf, *Richard Serra: Interviews, Etc. 1970–1980*, exh. cat. (New York: Hudson River Museum, 1980); Rosalind E. Krauss, *Richard Serra/Sculpture*, exh. cat., ed. Laura Rosenstock (New York: Museum of Modern Art, 1986); Hal Foster and Gordon Hughes, eds., *Richard Serra (October Files)* (Cambridge: MIT Press, 2000); Kynaston McShine, *Richard Serra Sculpture: Forty Years*, exh. cat. (New York: Museum of Modern Art, 2007); and Philipp Kaiser and Miwon Kwon, *Ends of the Earth: Land Art to 1974*, exh. cat. (Los Angeles and Munich: Museum of Contemporary Art and Haus der Kunst, 2012). As will be discussed below, Gorgoni was also the primary photographer of Heizer's *Double Negative* and Smithson's *Spiral Jetty*. He did not shoot *The Lightning Field*, however. John Cliett was hired by the Dia Art Foundation to photograph *The Lightning Field* upon its initial completion, on the condition that he give up the copyright to his own images. On issues pertaining to these latter photographs, see my discussion in James Nisbet, "A Brief Moment in the History of Photoenergy: Walter De Maria's *Lightning Field*," in *Ecologies, Environments, and Energy Systems in Art of the 1960s and 1970s* (Cambridge: MIT Press, 2014).

2. Richard Serra, "Shift," in *Writings, Interviews* (Chicago: University of Chicago Press, 1994), 11.

3. Ibid., 12.

4. Ibid., 13.

5. While it is true that any still photograph reduces the temporal quality of sculpture in the round, the argument here is that Gorgoni's photographs of *Shift* do so in an exceptionally reductive manner. On photography of sculpture in general, Serra has commented: "If you reduce sculpture to the flat plane of the photograph, you're passing on only a residue of your concerns [by] denying the temporal experience of the work. . . . With most sculpture, the experience of the work is inseparable from the place in which the work resides." Richard Serra and Douglas Crimp, "Richard Serra's Urban Sculpture," in Serra and Weyergraf, *Richard Serra: Interviews, Etc. 1970–1980*, 170.

6. See Robert Smithson, "The Spiral Jetty," in Gyorgy Kepes, *Arts of the Environment* (New York: George Braziller, 1972).

7. Serra, "Shift," 11–13.

8. See Clara Weyergraf-Serra and Martha Buskirk, eds., *The Destruction of* Tilted Arc: *Documents* (Cambridge: MIT Press, 1991).

9. James Meyer, "The Functional Site," in *Space, Site, Intervention: Situating Installation Art*, ed.

Erika Suderburg (Minneapolis: University of Minnesota Press, 2000), 25.

10. Miwon Kwon, *One Place after Another: Site-Specific Art and Locational Identity* (Cambridge: MIT Press, 2002), 26.

11. Kwon's text, for instance, opens with an oft-cited "Genealogy of Site Specificity" that lays out three moments in the development of the concept: the late-1960s primacy of place in outdoor earthworks, a critique of art world institutions developed predominantly in the 1970s, and the advent of more discursively framed projects in the 1980s and 1990s. She clarifies further that although her "three paradigms of site specificity . . . are presented somewhat chronologically, [they] are not stages in a neat trajectory of historical development. Rather, they are competing definitions, overlapping with one another and operating simultaneously in various cultural practices today." Ibid, 30. While I would note that Kwon rightly acknowledges the imbrication of her three categories, the mainstay of artworks she analyzes that exemplify the overlap and integration of her three categories are those created in the 1980s and 1990s, thereby privileging the synthesis realized by that more contemporary work as opposed to that of the preceding decades.

12. Rosalind E. Krauss, "Allusion and Illusion in Donald Judd," *Artforum* 4, no. 9 (May 1966): 24–26.

13. Maurice Merleau-Ponty, *Phenomenology of Perception*, trans. Colin Smith (London: Routledge, 1962), xvi–xvii.

14. Alex Potts, "The Phenomenological Turn," in *The Sculptural Imagination: Figurative, Modernist, Minimalist* (New Haven: Yale University Press, 2001), esp. 207–13.

15. See, for instance, Stephen Melville, "Phenomenology and the Limits of Hermeneutics," in *The Subjects of Art History: Historical Objects in Contemporary Perspectives*, ed. Mark A. Cheetham, Michael Ann Holly, and Keith Moxey (Cambridge: Cambridge University Press, 1998).

16. Rosalind E. Krauss, *Passages in Modern Sculpture* (New York: Viking Press, 1977), 282–83.

17. See Rosalind E. Krauss, "Richard Serra, a Translation," in *The Originality of the Avant-Garde and Other Modernist Myths* (Cambridge: MIT Press, 1985), 267.

18. Ibid., 262.

19. Jonathan Crary, *Techniques of the Observer: On Vision and Modernity in the Nineteenth Century* (Cambridge: MIT Press, 1990).

20. Rosalind E. Krauss, "Richard Serra Sculpture," in *Richard Serra/Sculpture*, 31–32.

21. The property itself is currently managed by Great Gulf, a real estate company hired by Hickory Hill, but which is not, as has been erroneously reported in some recent articles, a subsidiary of Hickory Hill. Kathleen Schofield, Executive Vice President of Land Development, Great Gulf, correspondence with the author, July 26, 2017.

22. Oak Ridges Moraine Conservation Act, 2001, S.O. 2001, c. 31, https://www.ontario.ca/laws/

statute/01031 (accessed August 24, 2017).

23. See Oak Ridges Land Use Designations, http://www.moraineforlife.org/living/legislation.php (accessed August 24, 2017).

24. Weyergraf-Serra and Buskirk, *The Destruction of* Tilted Arc, 11.

25. James Adams, "Richard Serra's Installation *Shift* Set to Become a Site of 'Cultural Heritage Value,'" *Globe and Mail*, February 26, 2013.

26. L. Anders Sandberg, Gerda R. Wekerle, and Liette Gilbert, *The Oak Ridges Moraine Battles: Development, Sprawl, and Nature Conservation in the Toronto Region* (Toronto: University of Toronto Press, 2013), 36.

27. See, for instance, Peter P. Marra et al., "The Influence of Climate on the Timing and Rate of Spring Bird Migration," *Oecologia* 142, no. 2 (January 2005): 307–15.

28. Elma Feindell, conversation with the author, July 13, 2017.

29. Ian Bogost, *Alien Phenomenology, Or, What It's Like to Be a Thing* (Minneapolis: University of Minnesota Press, 2012), 38.

30. Bruno Latour, *Reassembling the Social: An Introduction to Actor-Network-Theory* (Oxford: Oxford University Press, 2005), 5.

31. Bruno Latour, "On Recalling ANT," in *Actor Network Theory and After*, ed. John Law and John Hassard (Oxford: Blackwell, 1999), 18.

32. Jane Bennett, *Vibrant Matter: A Political Ecology of Things* (Durham: Duke University Press, 2010), 4.

33. Mel Y. Chen, response to "A Questionnaire on Materialisms," *October* 155 (Winter 2016): 21–22; and Huey Copeland, "Tending-toward-Blackness," *October* 156 (Spring 2016): 141–44. It is notable that Bennett also articulates a less anthropocentric reading of Merleau-Ponty than that received by modernist art history (*Vibrant Matter*, 29–30), which she draws from Diana Coole, "Rethinking Agency: A Phenomenological Approach to Embodiment and Agentic Capacities," *Political Studies* 53, no. 1 (2005): 124–42; and Diana Coole, "The Inertia of Matter and the Generativity of Flesh," in *New Materialisms: Ontology, Agency, and Politics*, ed. Diana Coole and Samantha Frost (Durham: Duke University Press, 2010), 92–115.

34. Bennett, *Vibrant Matter*, xiii.

35. The term "ecology" is attributed to the German naturalist Ernst Haeckel, whose original formulation *Ökologie* in the nineteenth century was created by combining the Greek roots *oikos*, meaning "household," and *logos*, "knowledge." *Generelle Morphologie der Organismen*, 1866.

36. For the food chain model, see Charles Elton, *Animal Ecology* (New York: Macmillan, 1927); for the first cited use of the term "ecosystem," see A. G. Transley, "The Use and Abuse of Vegetational Concepts and Terms," *Ecology* 16, no. 3 (July 1935): 284–307.

37. For an influential distillation of the steady-state model of ecology at the height of its influence,

see Eugene P. Odum, "The Strategy of Ecosystem Development," *Science* 164, no. 3877 (April 18, 1969): 262–70.

38. For an excellent account of this transition within the intellectual history of ecology, see Daniel Botkin, *Discordant Harmonies: A New Ecology for the Twenty-First Century* (Oxford: Oxford University Press, 1990).

39. See Frederic E. Clements, *Plant Succession: An Analysis of the Development of Vegetation* (Washington, DC: Carnegie Institute, 1916).

40. James Adams, "AGO Agrees to Talks for Serra Sculpture," *Globe and Mail*, September 23, 2010; and James Adams, "Fight Waged over Richard Serra Sculpture in Field North of Toronto," *Globe and Mail*, August 13, 2012.

41. Richard McCoy, "Extending the Conservation Framework: A Site-Specific Conservation Discussion with Francesca Esmay," *art21* (July 21, 2009), http://magazine.art21.org/2009/07/21/extending-the-conservation-framework-a-site-specific-conservation-discussion-with-francesca-esmay/#.WZ9ouXeGORs (accessed November 8, 2017).

42. See Kirk Johnson, "Plans to Mix Oil Drilling and Art Clash in Utah," *New York Times*, March 27, 2008; Anny Shaw, "'No Intervention' Needed to Protect *Spiral Jetty* from Drought," *Art Newspaper*, September 25, 2015), https://web.archive.org/web/20170828155817/http://theartnewspaper.com/news/conservation/no intervention-needed-to-protect-spiral-jetty-from-drought (accessed November 27, 2017).

43. See Jeffrey Kastner, "Entropy and the New Monument," *Artforum* 46, no. 8 (April 2006): 167–70.

44. Carol Vogel, "Campaign Aims to Restore Weather-Abused 'Lightning Field,'" *New York Times*, June 7, 2012.

45. This point about Smithson's commitment to entropy is raised in a number of articles that support Dia's decision not to physically conserve the sculptural coil of *Spiral Jetty*. See, for instance, Ben Eastham, "We Can't 'Save' Smithson's *Spiral Jetty*, and it Would be Wrong to Try," *Apollo* (October 8, 2015), https://www.apollo-magazine.com/we-cant-save-smithsons-spiral-jetty-and-it-would-be-wrong-to-try (accessed November 8, 2017).

46. Robert Smithson, "Cultural Confinement," in *Robert Smithson: The Collected Writings*, ed. Jack Flam (Berkeley: University of California Press, 1996), 155.

47. Rosalind E. Krauss, "Sculpture in the Expanded Field," *October* 8 (Spring 1970): 30–44.

48. On the various afterlives of Krauss's expanded field essay and its iconic diagram, see Spyros Papapetros and Julian Rose, eds., *Retracing the Expanded Field: Encounters between Art and Architecture* (Cambridge: MIT Press, 2014).

49. Krauss, "Sculpture in the Expanded Field," 42.

50. Clement Greenberg, "Modernist Painting," *Arts Yearbook* 4 (1961): 103.

An Eco–Art History of Weathered Stone Sculptures from Southwest China

Sonya S. Lee

Introduction

It is tantalizing to look at weathered stone sculptures. When trying to make sense of objects like these, we face a host of challenges that are well illustrated in an example from southwest China (fig. 1). This is a high-relief sculpture carved on the back wall of a small niche (no. 253) that belongs to a series of pictorial niches occupying much of a major cliff face at a Buddhist devotional site named Beishan in Dazu, Chongqing (fig. 2). It shows a bald-headed monk in a long, flowing robe and with a halo behind his head, standing on a pedestal side by side with another figure of equal size, both surrounded by ten groups of smaller figures distributed on the side walls. The statue remains in good enough shape for us to decipher its iconographic identity and appreciate its aesthetic appeal. At the same time, the

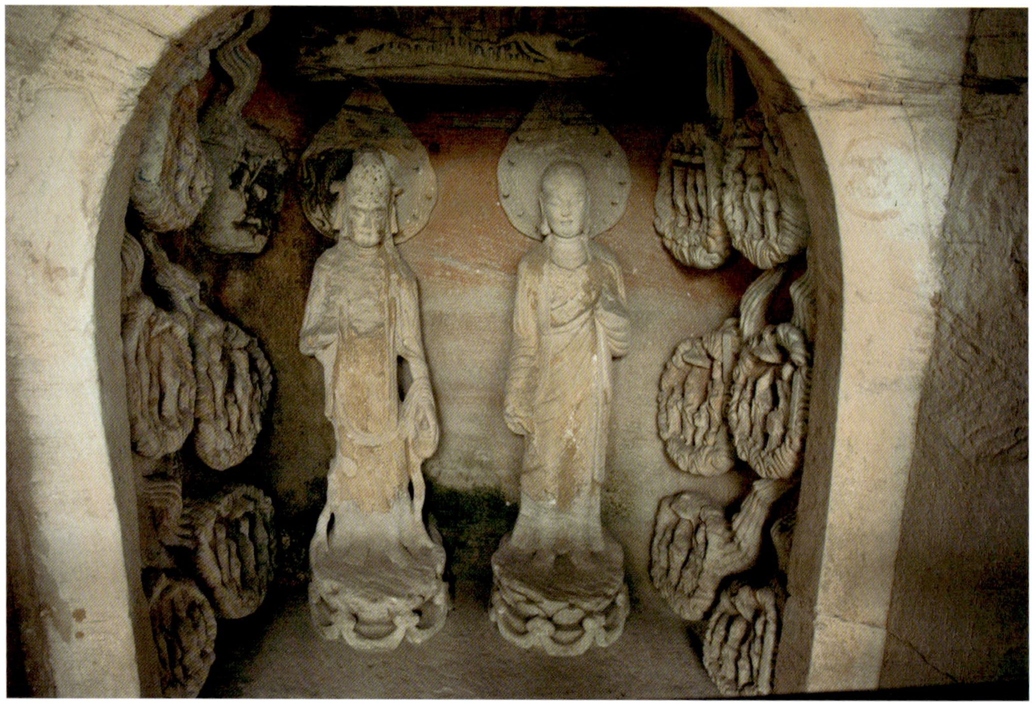

Fig. 1. Avalokiteshvara, Kshitigarbha, and Ten Kings of Hell, 10th century. Niche 253, Beishan, Dazu, Chongqing. Sandstone, 61 3/4 × 48 × 33 7/8 in. (157 × 122 × 86 cm.)

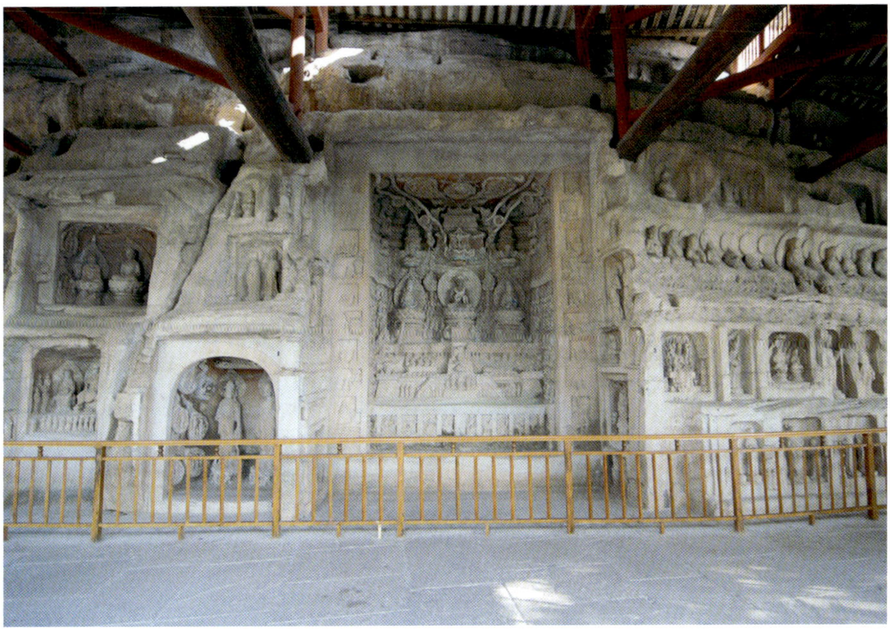

Fig. 2. Overview of Niches 222–255, 10th century. Beishan, Dazu, Chongqing. Sandstone

many signs of deterioration in its physical form do evoke a sense of loss, prompting us to wonder how glorious the figure might have once appeared when first completed and how much it has been diminished under the relentlessness of the elements and the passage of time.

This brief description of what a viewer's first encounter with a weathered stone sculpture might be like is helpful to introduce two distinct modes of looking that are pertinent to the study of these works. The first, which is favored by historians of Chinese religious art, is primarily concerned with gleaning information from the sculpture as part of a broader attempt at interpreting the past through material culture. Accordingly, the kind of information useful for this purpose concerns the work's iconography, function, style, and placement within the larger setting, as well as the cultural meanings attached to it by its patrons, makers, and viewers. In this particular case, the sculpture with which we began the essay can be identified as Kshitigarbha Bodhisattva, a Buddhist savior deity who specializes in rescuing sentient beings from hell and whose identity is chiefly denoted by an appearance as a young monk wearing earrings and necklaces.[1] The pairing of this motif at Beishan with Avalokiteshvara, another savior bodhisattva in Chinese Buddhism, was popular among lay devotees on account of their miraculous power

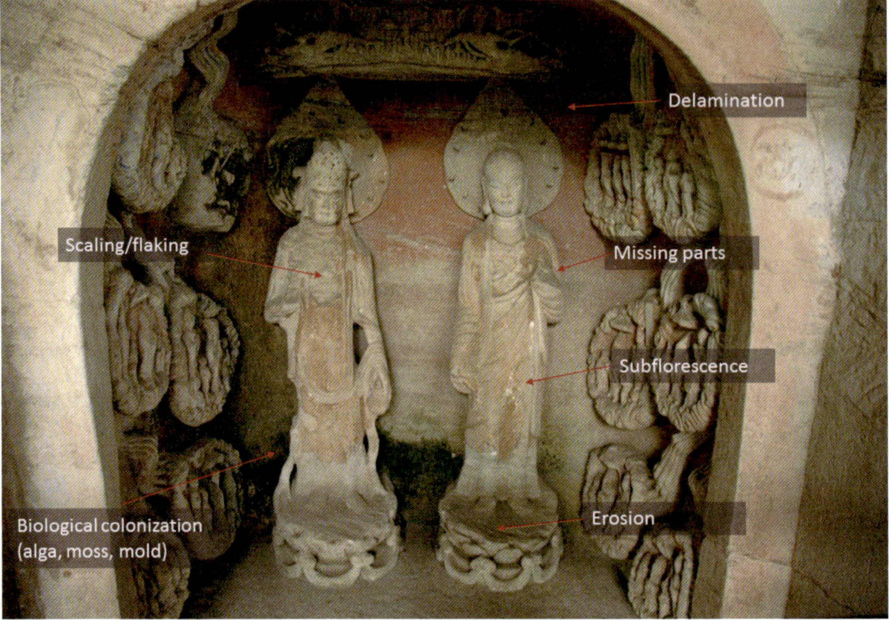

Fig. 3. Different kinds of deterioration found in Niche 253, 10th century. Beishan, Dazu, Chongqing

to save humans from worldly troubles. It was further enhanced by the addition of Ten Kings of Hell to the same assemblage, indicating the rapid dissemination of the concept of purgatory throughout the tenth century that would dramatically transform the Chinese imagining of the passage from death to rebirth from that time onward.[2] The second mode of looking, by contrast, is associated with stone conservators, who tend to concentrate on the work's physical condition and those factors that have contributed to its deterioration over time. For our example at Beishan, a trained professional would readily identify many of the damages therein as indicated in figure 3, including delamination, scaling / flaking, subflorescence, erosion, biological colonization, and missing parts.[3]

The two modes of looking described above are deeply ingrained in their respective disciplines, namely, art history and heritage conservation. This is not a surprise, considering that there is plenty of information for each group to mine when dealing with a relatively well-preserved work like the Kshitigarbha Bodhisattva. But the need to reconsider the value of the approach that each group espouses becomes all the more apparent when we turn to examples that defy expectations. At Beishan there are many statues whose appearance has been reduced to illegibility due to severe weathering, as illustrated in Niches 181 and 183, both located

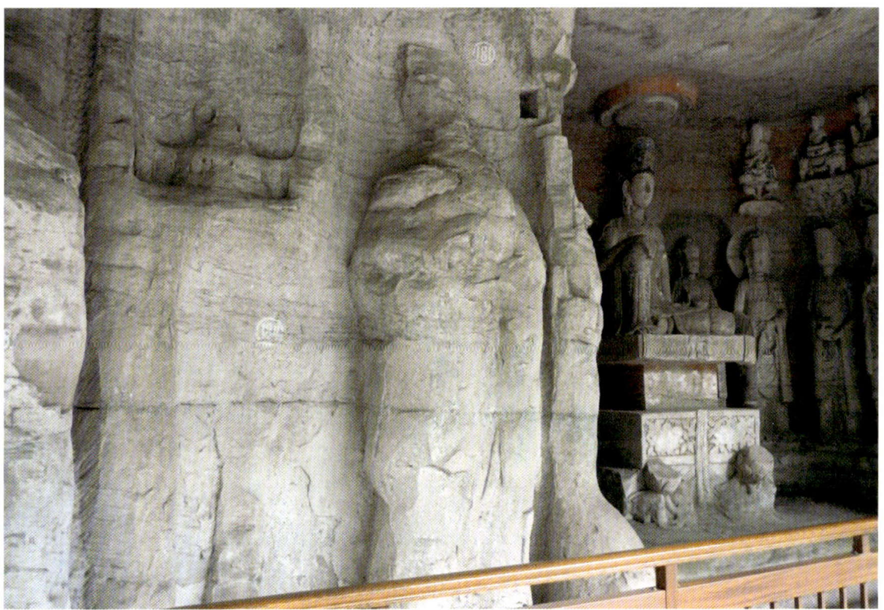

Fig. 4. Niches 180, 181, and 183, 10th century. Beishan, Dazu, Chongqing. Sandstone, height of statue in Niche 181: 122 in. (310 cm.)

on the left exterior wall immediately outside the large-scale Niche 180 (fig. 4). While the set of life-size statues inside the latter are frequently featured in publications on the famed cave complex, the worn-out relief carvings just outside the niche are categorically ignored.[4] The contrast in treatment underscores the pervasive practice in art history to focus on better-preserved works in order to carry out historical interpretations about the making of Buddhist images in China as understood through their iconography, style, and patronage. The lack of interest in weathered stone sculptures, more fundamentally, is rooted in a tendency to cast the object of research as something arrested in a particular point in time and space, a projected repository of historical meanings from which one can retrieve through analysis and then interpret as a form of social history.[5] Within this scheme of things, weathered stone sculptures do not quite fit into the paradigm, because their original appearance, the entry point into the interpretative process, has already been compromised.

Rather than ignoring weathered stone sculptures as before, this essay recognizes at the outset their value as a significant resource on the complex relationship between art and the environment. To tap further into the topic's potential, it is thus necessary to adopt a different approach that would enable us to better understand what these objects can tell us about the ecological context of which they are a part, as well as the mindset and practice that their human caretakers have brought to their maintenance in response to the changing environment. To this end, this essay proposes an eco–art history of weathered stone sculptures, a methodology that aims to reconcile two radically different concepts of time that define the subject, namely, geological time, as represented by the material of stone and its setting, and historic time, as marked by the creation of the relief sculpture and its continued presence at the site. The intertwining of these two temporalities in many ways determines how we make sense of the damages we see in the work. Possible interpretations may range from accepting the perceived deterioration as part of the natural process of transformation to which a rock is subject throughout its lifespan on this planet, to construing it as a form of violence inflicted by natural or human forces that diminishes the work's original appearance either at a given moment or continually over time. Regardless, because the effects of geological and historic times on material objects require different tools to assess and methods to interpret, it is all the more important to bring art history and heritage conservation into dialogue with each other. Central to such a cross-disciplinary inquiry is the reconceptualization of the subject of research as a work that is constantly changing rather than as one frozen in time and space. By making the passage of time a focus in my analysis, I emphasize the importance of considering those factors that contributed to the changes in the sculpture's material state through time, as well as the subsequent interventions made to restore the object's function and thereby extend its lifespan. Conservation science proves to be useful for providing critical information on which art historians can base further studies of these aspects. At the same time, applying the art historical lens to the treatment of weathered stone sculptures can help historicize conservation practices in modern times, thereby affording us the long view needed to understand today's techniques and methods in relation to those of the past. An eco–art history of weathered stone sculpture, in short, demands one to look at the stones the way a stone conservator would but to think like an art historian in explicating the data at hand.

In what follows, I plan to demonstrate more concretely what an eco–art history of weathered stone sculptures might entail and how it could help illuminate the way people in a specific cultural and ecological context have responded to nature through the creation and preservation of material objects. Accordingly,

I will concentrate on one case study, namely, the Buddhist cave temple Beishan located in the Dazu District of Chongqing. After a brief introduction to the site and its setting, I will discuss different types of deterioration commonly found there. Since my goal here is historical rather than scientific, the ensuing analysis is not about proposing any treatment method or advancing our knowledge of stone deterioration. Rather, it is about understanding weathered stone sculptures in relation to the kinds of ecological conditions at work in their setting and the interventions made both in the past and in the present to preserve these works in such a context. In the case of the Dazu materials, I am particularly interested in explaining the remarkable transformation in cave design that occurred between the ninth and tenth centuries and the twelfth and thirteenth. I believe the change was made possible by significant advances in the technology of cave building, as builders and carvers became more daring in their attempts at creating monumental sculptures on mountain cliff faces.

Stone Deterioration at Beishan

Dazu District is one of the major centers of Buddhist material culture in China. There are over fifty thousand extant pictorial images distributed across more than forty cave complexes. Beishan, literally meaning "the North Mountain," is one of the most important sites in the area due to its close proximity to the county seat and the existence of the earliest images made in the area, which date to the late ninth century.[6] Pictorial images at Beishan are mostly relief carvings on cliff surfaces, organized into discrete compositions that fill up the interior of shallow rectangular niches. There are also a number of large excavated spaces that extend deeply into the rock, with life-size statues set up inside in stagelike assemblages. The majority of the niches, 252 in total, are located near the top of the hill, which is about 1,800 feet above sea level, spanning several large cliff faces along the same plane. All the pictorial niches are now sheltered under a series of wooden-framed structures erected by the local management unit (fig. 5). Their well-kept appearance, along with the sophisticated monitoring equipment nearby, is a clear indicator of the site's current status as an UNESCO World Heritage Site and a top-priority protected heritage property in China. The structures' very existence also points to the greater ecological setting of which Beishan is a part. It is, in a nutshell, a humid subtropical monsoon climate, with an average annual rainfall in Dazu close to 48 inches (1,218 mm) in 2016 and the yearly relative humidity at 85

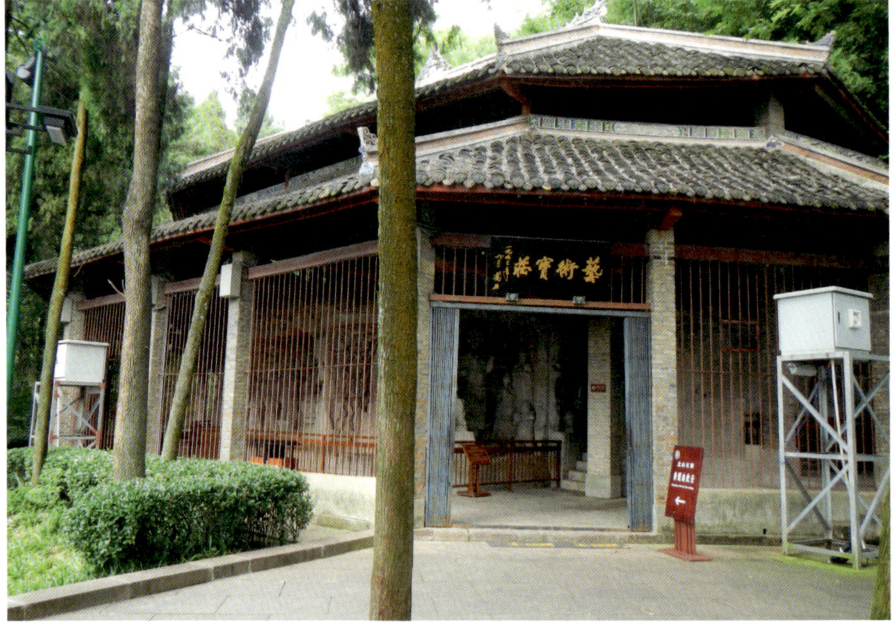

Fig. 5. Wooden-framed shelter at Beishan, Dazu, Chongqing, built in 1952–53; metal bars installed in 1995

percent.[7] The abundance of water in the form of rainfall and humidity is key to understanding the kinds of stone deterioration evident at Beishan.

As noted earlier, various types of deterioration can be identified inside the Kshitigarbha niche at Beishan, including delamination, scaling/flaking, subflorescence, erosion, biological colonization, and missing parts. As it turns out, all these damages are common throughout the entire site as well. What is worth pointing out is that they are caused either directly or indirectly by the presence of water and salt in the stones. Biological colonization offers a helpful starting point for the discussion, as it is a reliable indicator of high water content in the stone. The appearance of algae, moss, and mold on stone surfaces reveals a situation where the substrate remains moistened for long periods of time.[8] Upon a closer look, this problem is in fact pervasive in the area around the Kshitigarbha niche, with the moisture appearing to concentrate near the bottom of the cliff face (fig. 6). In other sections where many deeply excavated spaces are located side by side, however, moisture is found considerably farther inside the rock formation. In the case of Niche 177, one can see water flowing out from the back wall on a day with high humidity (fig. 7). Perhaps the most troublesome spot at Beishan is located near Niche 197, where water constantly streams out from the top even on a dry day;

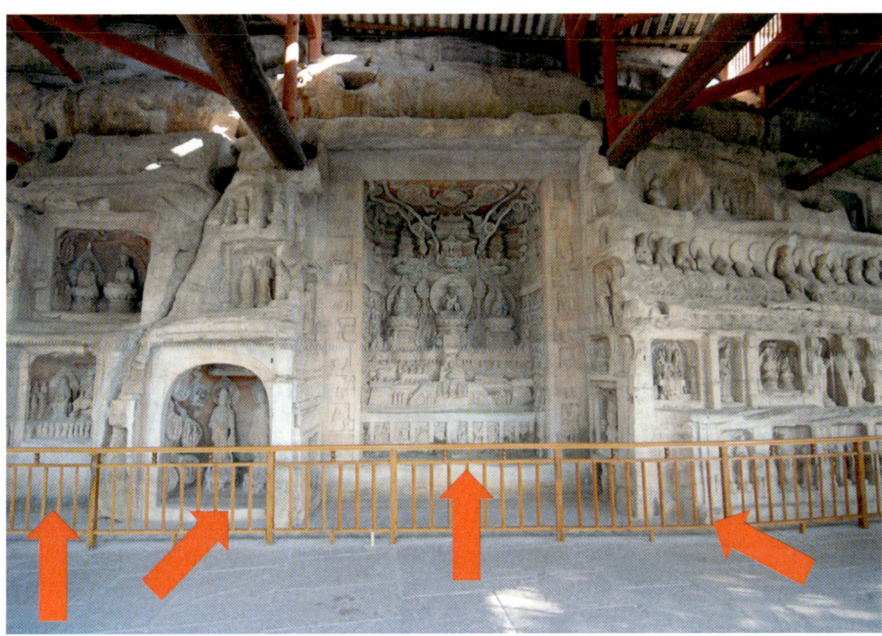

Fig. 6. Instances of biological colonization, indicated by red arrows, in the vicinity of Niches 222–255. Beishan, Dazu, Chongqing, August 2016

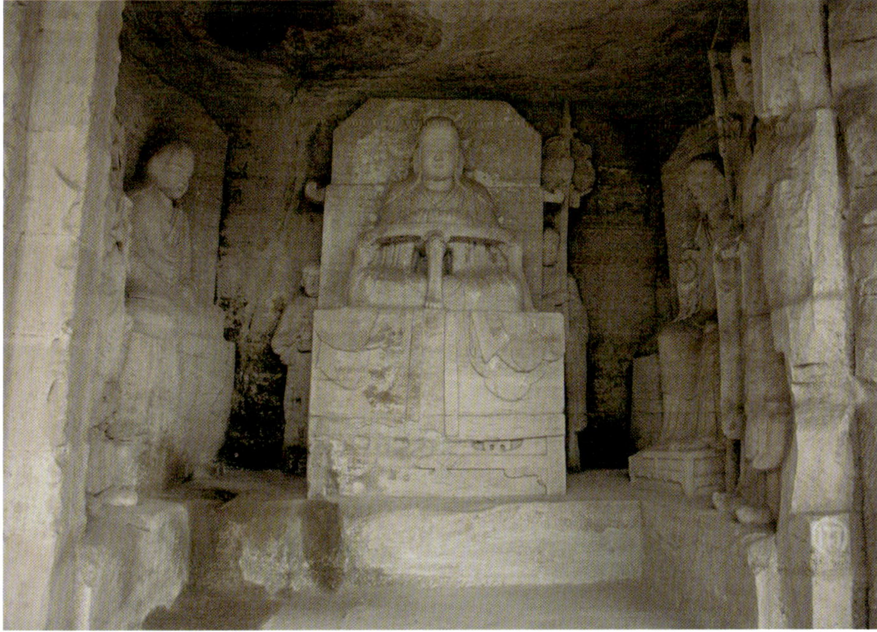

Fig. 7. Water seeping out from the interior of Niche 177 on a dry day with some humidity. Beishan, Dazu, Chongqing, July 2012

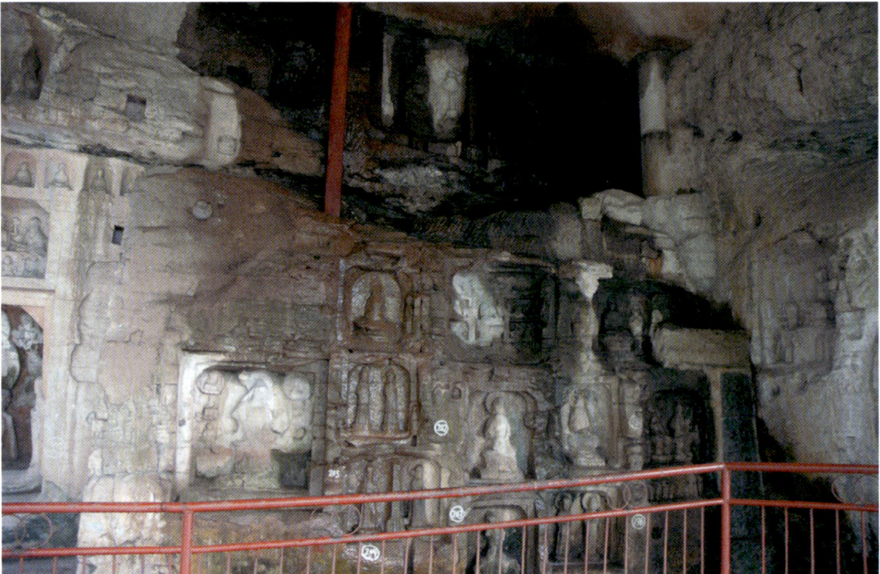

Fig. 8. Water drenching from a spot above Niche 197 on a rainy day. Beishan, Dazu, Chongqing, November 2015

the entire wall surface would be drenched when it rains (fig. 8). The considerable amount of moisture present at the Beishan hilltop is due to rainfall and the general humid condition of the area as expected. A lesser known but equally important reason lies in the use of over two acres of land at the hilltop as a rice field by the local residents in the early 1950s, which likely contributed to an increase in the underground water reserve in the mountain over the years.[9]

For the untrained eye, it might seem alarming to see water constantly gushing over valuable cultural artifacts like the stone reliefs at Beishan. But this is actually a common phenomenon in the formation of sandstone or sedimentary rocks in general. More to the point regarding stone deterioration is the fact that the weathering characteristics of stones are influenced by their chemical properties, physical structure, and geological origin. In the case of biological colonization, the stone's mineral composition and cement type, as well as porosity and permeability, play as key a role as environmental factors such as water availability.[10] It is thus critical to turn to the type of stone found at Beishan. The most common throughout Dazu, including this site, is a kind of sandstone rich in feldspar and quartz and cemented by clay and calcite.[11] It has relatively high porosity but a fairly stable structure due to its mineral composition. Although minerals such as feldspars and clay are weathering-prone, the sandstone can still remain durable so long as the mineral structure stays intact and the water can get in and out without hindrances. The growth of microorganisms on the stone surface, however, can lead to changes in moisture circulation patterns and temperature response. This means that the biological growths could form a sheet of biofilm on the surface that might slow or block the evaporation of water out of the stone.[12] Another fact to keep in mind is that sandstones have large pores that make them more sensitive to salt crystallization than stones with lower porosity.[13] If there is salt present in the water, this would make the stone already affected with biodeterioration even more vulnerable to salt crystallization, thus leading to scaling and flaking of the surface. One additional negative effect of biodeterioration is that it could also accelerate the accumulation of atmospheric pollutants, which might result in the formation of black crusts that can lead to severe decay as well.[14]

With today's advances in science and technology, we now know about the properties of stones as well as the reasons and processes of their deterioration more than ever before. But the artisans in Dazu must have had some knowledge of the phenomenon, too. They would not have been able to explain the weathering factors and processes in the same scientific terms we have today, but they did know enough about the property of sandstones to come up with designs that could minimize their decay and implement measures to prolong their lifespan in a very humid environment. After all, the practice of carving monumental sculptures on cliff faces has been in Dazu since the ninth century and is still a living heritage today. The tradition's longevity underscores an enduring fascination with creating cultural monuments in the middle of nature as much as a continual pursuit of knowledge and technology needed to materialize this fascination.

Wooden-Framed Shelters at Cave Temples

Among the simplest yet most effective interventions taken to preserve the stone carvings at Beishan are the wooden-framed shelters erected around the cliff faces. These shelters were recently renovated by the Dazu Rock Carvings Academy, the official management unit in charge of all the heritage sites in the district (figs. 2 and 5). They maintain more or less the same design that has been used over the years, namely, a semi-freestanding post-and-beam structure in wood that shapes around the cliff's carved section in front, with some of the roof beams attached directly to the cliff on one side for structural support and a screen of metal bars on the other side forming the front of the structure.[15] There are two such structures at Beishan, each covering the two main sections of the site. An earlier version of these shelters was introduced at Beishan in 1952, shortly after the management unit was established by the local government. It was part of a larger conservation project the staff undertook at the time, which included the creation of a drainage system around the site, the stabilization of the pathway in front of the niches, and the confiscation of the hilltop rice field mentioned earlier.[16]

The idea of erecting a shelter around a cultural monument may seem rudimentary, but it is no doubt the most straightforward way of protecting the work from direct exposure to rain, while promoting adequate air circulation throughout the site. Another benefit of the structure is to provide shade for the stones so they are not exposed directly to sunlight. This in turn would help reduce fluctuation in temperature of the stone surface in the freeze–thaw cycle. It is a well-established fact that any dramatic fluctuation in temperature can cause serious cracking and splitting, which would in turn undermine the stability of the stone. Besides providing protection for the monument from the elements, the shelter also affects considerably how the site is visited and interpreted, from controlling access to the monument to shaping the visitor experience and mediating the relationship between the site and the surrounding landscape through its design. In short, the practical benefits of using a shelter are as many as the symbolic ones.

With all the practical, aesthetic, and interpretive functions they bring, it is not a surprise that protective shelters are commonly utilized around the world to preserve exposed archaeological ruins in situ.[17] What is significant about the specimens in China lies in how integral they were to the original design and intended purpose of Buddhist cave temples in premodern China. Rather than a self-conscious intervention prompted by modern conservation concerns and values, wooden shelters were often planned to be part of cave temples from their inception or added not long after completion in order to prolong the existing system of practice and meaning for future generations. Yungang Caves in Shanxi province, a site first established by the emperors of the Northern Wei dynasty (386–535) in the second half of the fifth century, offer an outstanding example to illustrate this point. According to the sixth-century geographical text *Shuijing zhu* by Li Daoyuan (d. 527), some of the caves are reported to have had wooden-frame structures resembling actual freestanding temple buildings as early as a few decades following their completion.[18] Although the record has provided little detail on the appearance of the shelters, the practice of maintaining wooden structures in front of the cliff face did continue in subsequent times. Yungang underwent a major revival during the Liao dynasty (907–1125), when elaborate structures

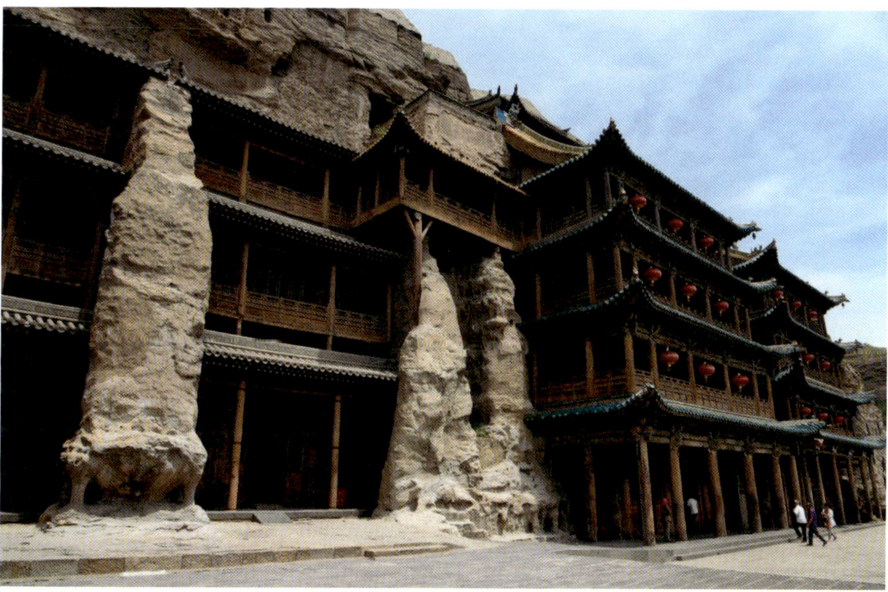

Fig. 9. A view of the exterior of Caves 5 and 6, Yungang Caves, Shanxi; structures rebuilt in the 17th century. Sandstone

were built as antechambers attached to the exterior of many existing cave units. As Su Bai has argued, this combination of excavated spaces inside the mountain and wooden structures in front constituted what has been referred to as the "Ten Temples of Yungang," now corresponding to Caves 1 to 20.[19] The copious strut holes lining the outer frames of cave entrances and the unearthing of wooden elements and roof tiles dating to the eleventh century from the ground in front of Caves 5 to 20 provide compelling material evidence for the Liao date. The impressive scale of some of the front structures was apparently maintained in succeeding dynasties, as can be seen in a recent photograph showing the massive, multistoried structures outside Caves 5 and 6 to the right, which were rebuilt in the mid-seventeenth century (fig. 9).[20] Clearly, these shelters were meant to be permanent attachments to the cave units, providing additional interior space for worshippers and their monastic guardians to carry out certain devotional activities therein. Of particular significance was the act of touring the multistoried structure, which would allow the visitors to see the colossal images inside the caves in close range and from different angles (fig. 10).

Although established on a far smaller scale and in a different part of China centuries later, Beishan nonetheless followed the practice of erecting wooden shelters in front of cave temples as exemplified by Yungang. As indicated by the strut

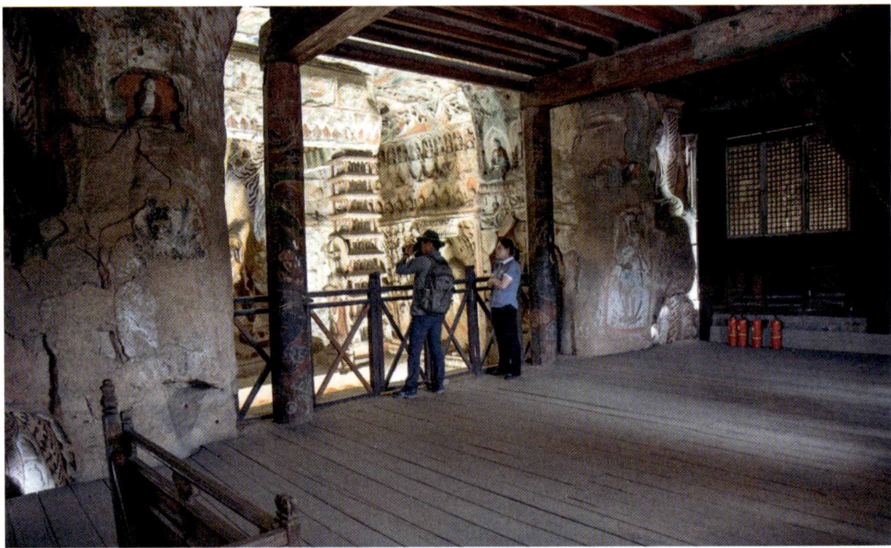

Fig. 10. Viewing images in Cave 6 from a platform inside the shelter, Yungang Caves, Shanxi, June 2017. Sandstone

holes around the outer frames of numerous niches such as Nos. 116 and 117 (fig. 11), there were once modest structures built in front of individual or small groups of pictorial niches throughout the site. While it is difficult to determine their date without any in situ inscriptions or archaeological finds nearby, we can reasonably assume that they were built long before the twenty-first century. Because the majority of the carvings at the Dazu site are positioned on the cliff face rather than set deep inside excavated hollows, the shelters appear to serve more of a protective function of shielding the stone carvings from rain and sunlight than a symbolic one in providing a communal or ritual space for the visiting devotees, as in the case of Caves 5 and 6 at Yungang. What also distinguishes Beishan from its predecessor is the more sporadic history of patronage it had in later times. One negative effect that resulted from having fewer patrons to sponsor restoration over time was the shelters' vulnerability to decay. Because they were built of wood, these structures would have perished long ago unless they were under regular maintenance. I would argue that the perceived impermanence of these wooden shelters was likely a source of motivation for cave builders in Dazu to experiment with a rather different way of protecting the stone carvings, which arguably resulted in the creation of a new style in monumental sculpture that would become the artistic trademark of Dazu rock carvings from the twelfth century onward. A closer look at Baodingshan and other sites in its vicinity helps us further explore this point.

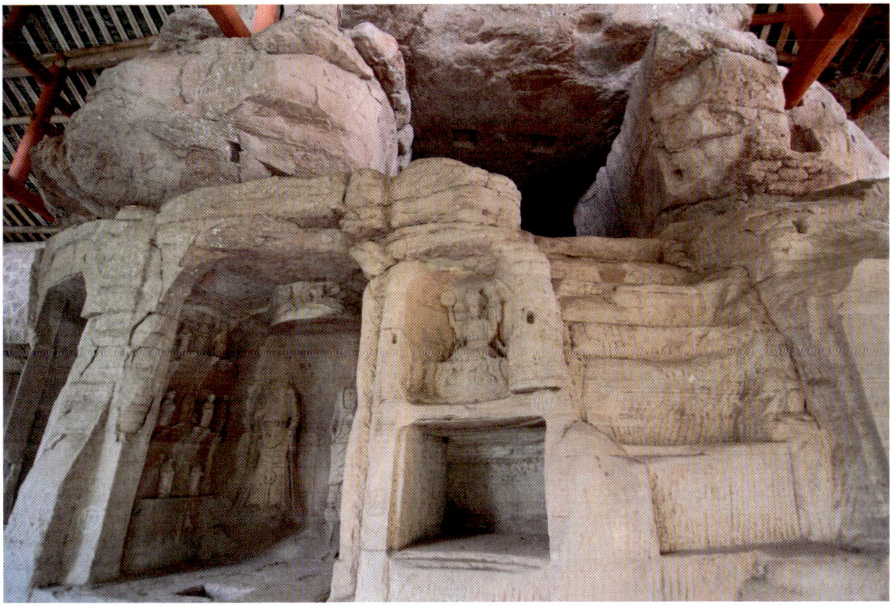

Fig. 11. Overview of Niches 116 and 117, 10th century. Beishan, Dazu, Chongqing. Sandstone, Niche 117: 73 5/8 × 44 7/8 × 39 in. (187 × 114 × 99 cm.)

The Monumental Style Reconsidered

Baodingshan, literally meaning the "Summit of Treasures," is no doubt the best-known example of Dazu's monumental style. Founded by a local preacher named Zhao Zhifeng sometime in the late twelfth or early thirteenth century, the site comprises thirty-one sets of large-scale relief carvings distributed along the cliff faces of a U-shaped gully. Their style marks a radical change from that of Beishan in terms of scale, compositional format, and figuration, as well as carving technique. It has been pointed out by a number of scholars in the past that the new style was key to realizing the intended function of Baodingshan as a teaching ground for Zhao Zhifeng's followers. Angela Howard is perhaps the most explicit in explaining how different aspects of this monumental style helped shape the viewer's response to and understanding of the site's rich pictorial contents, arguing that "representation was squarely placed at the service of religion."[21] While I agree with her insights into the religious purpose of the style, I think it is equally important to consider the development from a technological perspective. In fact, a close observation of the carvings reveals that the monumental style was also practical in preserving the carvings, as it was in tune with the unique ecological setting of the site. To take the Three Worthies of Huayan section as an example, the entire cliff

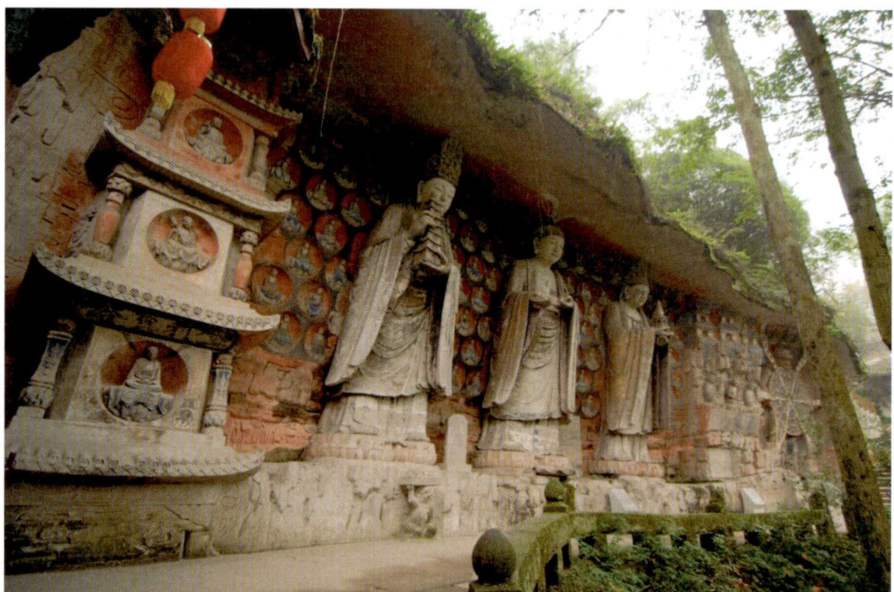

Fig. 12. Overview of the section featuring the Three Worthies of Huayan, 12th–13th centuries. Baodingshan, Dazu, Chongqing. Sandstone, 322 $^7/_8$ × 570 $^7/_8$ in. (820 × 1450 cm.)

surface is carved at a sloping angle, with the mass of the stone concentrating near the top rather than at the bottom, so that the figures appear to be leaning out of the stone toward the viewer (fig. 12). Another notable feature of the new format is the creation of a massive awning that protrudes out of the cliff over the entire composition from the top. Both features work seamlessly together to compensate for the lack of a front wall to shield the carvings from rainwater, as can be seen in the photograph taken on a rainy day, which shows how the entire cliff face remained dry while the ground in front was moist.

As the original awning for the Three Worthies of Huayan at Baodingshan has for the most part stayed in shape and performed its intended function through-out the centuries, it is difficult to imagine what damage the carvings might have suffered in its absence.[22] But at a smaller site nearby named Guangdashan, we do have such an example, which is helpful for considering the shift from the tradition of building shelters to one without. Located at an outcrop a kilometer southwest of Baodingshan, Guangdashan consists solely of a single niche in which there are three half-bust figures representing the theme of the Three Worthies of Huayan (fig. 13). Both the central Buddha and the bodhisattva on the right remain rela-tively intact despite significant discoloration, but the bodhisattva to the left was so badly damaged that the entire body has been reduced to the mere silhouette of its stone core. A comparison of two photographs taken at Guangdashan about thirty years apart, one in the 1980s and the other in 2014, reveals some major changes that took place at the site during this short period of time (fig. 14). For one, a band of looters made an attempt at hacking away the head of the left bodhisattva on the evening of January 3, 1997. As the management unit later discovered, much of the figure was in fact the product of a restoration made sometime in the seventeenth or eighteenth century, and the clay portion of the bodhisattva crumbled into pieces during the attempted looting.[23] The earlier episode of deterioration was apparently caused by a large dent in the awning directly above, which in turn exposed the figure more directly to rain and sunlight. For another, the discoloration on all three figures, as evident in the more recent photograph, was the result of a number of factors, including soot from incense burning, soiling, and acid rain. Regardless of which caves are responsible and to what degree, it is truly stunning to see how much color loss occurred in just three decades.

The recent changes at Guangdashan evidently represent the kinds of damages that are more than the usual effects resulting from the natural processes of decay that have been discussed with examples from Beishan. What we are dealing with instead is symptomatic of some of the most pressing problems in preserving cultural monuments from ancient times in the modern world. Indeed, rapid economic development, industrialization, and urbanization have

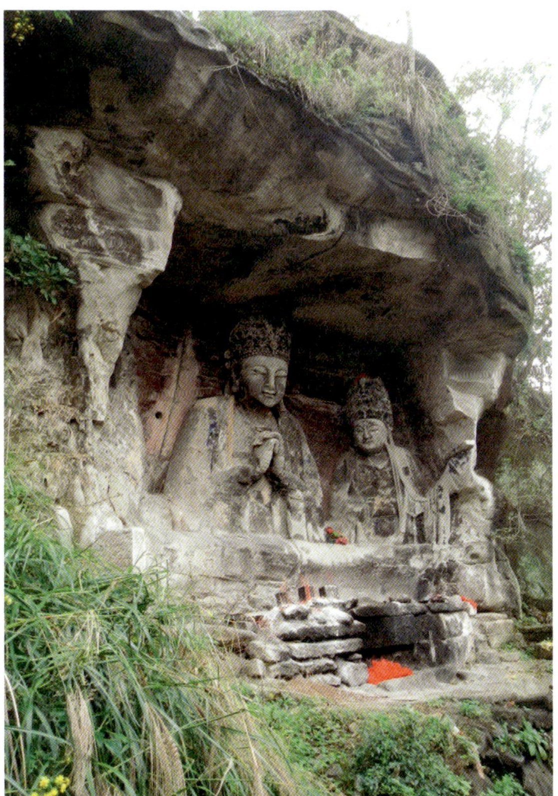

Fig. 13. The Three Worthies of Huayan, 12th–13th centuries. Guangdashan, Dazu, Chongqing. Sandstone, 181 1/8 × 267 3/4 × 110 1/4 in. (460 × 680 × 280 cm.)

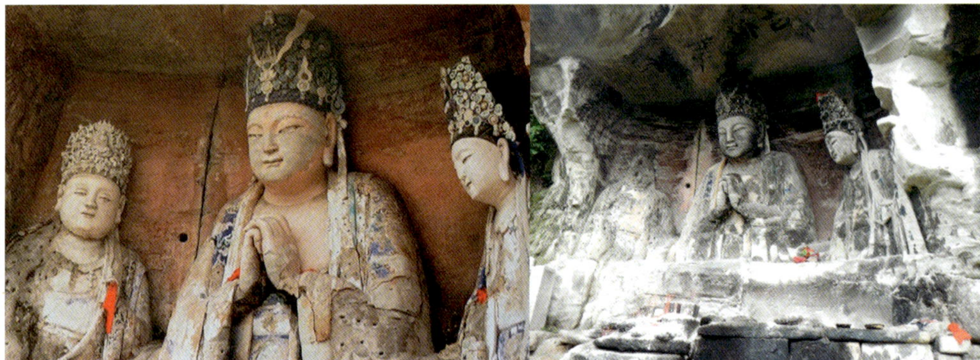

Fig. 14. Changes in the condition of the carvings at Guangdashan. *Left*: photograph taken by Angela Howard, 1980s. *Right*: photograph by author, 2014

given rise to acid rain, a popular term referring to acidic pollution in the atmosphere caused by the release of sulfur oxides, nitrate oxides, and carbon dioxide into the air through the burning of coal.[24] Although the evidence at hand is far from conclusive, the carvings at Guangdashan do fit the classic descriptions of the direct effects of acid rain on stones: the remainder of the bodhisattva figure on the left is in an exposed position where it is regularly washed by rain due to the dent in the awning. As a result, the acidic content in the rainwater likely contributed to the rapid mineral dissolution and surface recession in this statue. The central and right figures, however, are in a more sheltered position, so they are less prone to drastic decay, but the reaction products probably have accumulated on the stone surface, resulting in the formation of what appear to be black crusts.[25] Either way, the acid rain problem in Dazu is clearly serious, and there is no simple solution in sight because the source of the pollution is far away from the site and hence beyond the control of the local management unit, or even the district government. As for the looting of antiquities, this has been a serious problem in China since the second half of the nineteenth century when Buddhist sculptures became desirable collectibles in the Western art market.[26] Significantly, Dazu had not been greatly affected until the mid-1990s, not long after the local management unit began to publicize the carvings in a bid to secure the nomination for the World Heritage Site inscription.[27] Although security was beefed up at all major sites in the region in recent years, thefts have continued to occur on a regular basis.[28]

To return to my initial point about the role of technology in the formation of an artistic style, the two examples of the Three Worthies of Huayan theme respectively at Baodingshan and Guangdashan have demonstrated the need to gauge it in relation to other factors, whether religious, political, or economic. Although we do not yet have enough information about the techniques and processes utilized by cave builders in Dazu, it is at least clear from our examples that the results share effects similar to those of wooden front shelters in protecting the carvings from direct exposure to rainwater. What is more, there is the added benefit of freeing the entire cliff face from any obstruction inevitably caused by the presence of wooden-frame structures or scaffoldings, which in turn allows the sculptors to create relief sculptures of impressive scale or complex compositions across large areas without losing the overall visual unity. As Howard has reminded us, all these are essential features of the monumental style in Dazu rock carvings. An eco–art history of these stone sculptures can further our understanding of the subject by considering their creation in relation to the local ecological conditions as well as the various methods of dealing with such conditions that cave builders in the region had attempted over the years through image-making, repair, and restoration. The connections to emerge from the inquiry would help shed new light on key developments in the history of Dazu caves while also broadening the scope of scholarship, which so far has concentrated overwhelmingly on the style and iconography of the carvings, as well as their religious and social meanings at the moment of creation.

Conclusion

This essay has examined a range of damages that occurred on stone sculptures at cave temples in Dazu. By adopting the conservator's way of looking and the art historian's method of analysis, I have shown that weathered stone sculptures are an enormously rich source of information on the ecological context of which they are a part, as well as on the interventions taken in response to this particular environment to ensure the durability of the works. As it turns out, the many types of stone deterioration evident at a site like Beishan are interrelated, as we cannot understand one without accounting for the other, be it biological colonization, flaking/scaling, or subflorescence. Likewise, the remedies introduced to address the problems reveal an understanding of the root causes that manifested under diverse guises. In the case of the wooden shelter, the concept was simple but effective in fulfilling the structure's intended function of shielding the carvings from direct sunlight and rain. But as we have seen at Guangdashan, the recent damages rendered by looters and air pollutants are far more devastating and difficult to resolve than normal processes of decay to which all stones in the open are subject.

While the eco–art history of weathered stone sculptures hitherto presented does not offer any immediate remedy to all these problems, I do believe that it represents a viable way for art historians to join the larger efforts to integrate sustainability perspectives into the preservation of cultural monuments. This can be done most fruitfully through collaboration with conservators in designing and carrying out studies that could yield significant new data for addressing fundamental questions about art and the environment on which the formulation of new strategies for sustainability are to be based.

As my discussion on the formation of the monumental style in the later history of Dazu caves has demonstrated, technical studies on carving methods and techniques would be key to explicating one of the most significant changes in cave design of southwest China by linking it to preservation methods of an earlier era. In a region where cave builders were constantly in search of innovative ways to create new works as well as repair and preserve old ones, it thus becomes imperative for researchers to account for both kinds of activities when analyzing the results at the sites. In so doing, we would be on firmer ground to consider how humans managed to prolong the lifespan of cultural monuments built into the very fabric of nature. As for the question why people chose nature to be the venue and at times the medium for creative endeavors of all sorts, eco–art history provides an alternative way to consider the issue of agency in the creation of this type of religious art and architecture. In previous studies, the extent to which technology had enabled the realization of religious ideas in material form, or conversely, how religion acted as an impetus behind technological innovation, has been a major point of debate. Now that we have expanded our critical looking to include the awesome effects of nature on the artistic material through time, the question of who is truly responsible becomes all the more difficult to answer.

As Randall Curren and Ellen Metzger have argued, "sustainability is not a science but an art of social coordination."[29] Their insight might sound self-evident, but it is undeniable that there is much to be gained when different groups of stakeholders work together to preserve cultural heritage in a time when the world's biocapacity is diminishing and conflicts over resources are on the rise. Conservators and art historians can do their part by collaborating through research, education, and public outreach. Undertaking a project such as a study of weathered stone sculptures might seem insignificant in a world full of big problems. It is nevertheless a necessary step forward.

1. Zhiru Shi, *The Making of a Savior Bodhisattva: Dizang in Medieval China* (Honolulu: University of Hawaii Press, 2007), 124–26.

2. Ibid., 125–30, 150–52.

3. The terms used here are based on Véronique Vergès-Balmin, ed., *Illustrated Glossary on Stone Deterioration Patterns = Glossaire illustré sur les formes d'altération de la pierre*, English-French ed., Monuments & Sites 15 (Paris: ICOMOS [International Council on Monuments and Sites] and ISCS [International Scientific Committee on Stone], 2008).

4. See, for example, *Zhongguo shiku diaosu quanji* (A treasury of Chinese cave temple sculpture), vol. 7: *Dazu*, ed. Li Yisheng (Chongqing: Chongqing chubanshe, 1999), pl. 20; and Wenhe Hu, *Anyue Dazu fo diao* (Buddhist carvings in Anyue and Dazu) (Taipei: Yishujia chubanshe, 1999), pl. 20.

5. Keith Moxey offers an insightful discussion of this approach in relation to issues of presence in art history in his *Visual Time: The Image in History* (Durham and London: Duke University Press, 2013), 53–71.

6. According to the Wei Junjing stele (text by Hu Mi; dated 895), the site was founded by Wei Junjing, governor of Changzhou, who built a military garrison at the same location at the end of the Tang dynasty. As the highest ranked official in the area, Wei likely took possession of the land and carried out the construction. For a transcription of the stele text, see "Dazu shike yishu bowuguan," *Dazu shike mingwenlu* (Collection of inscriptions from Dazu stone carvings) (Chongqing: Chongqing chubanshe, 1999), 37–43.

7. The data is based on a report provided by the Dazu District government at http://www.cqdz.gov. cn/Subsite/glxzf_02/Text_Show.asp?ClassID=1020000&id=327383 (accessed May 26, 2017).

8. Vergès-Balmin, *Illustrated Glossary on Stone Deterioration Patterns*, 66–67.

9. Deng Zhijin, "Dazu shike weixiu gongcheng sishi nian huigu" (Reflections on forty years of restoration work in Dazu rock carvings), in *Dazu shike yanjiu wenji* 2 (Collected essays on rock carvings of Dazu 2), ed. Dazu shike yishu bowuguan (Chongqing: Chongqing chubanshe, 1997), 572.

10. T. Warscheid and J. Braams, "Biodeterioration of Stone: A Review," *International Biodeterioration & Biodegradation* 46, no. 4 (2000): 345.

11. Li Hongsong, *Shizhi wenwu yanshi cailiao liehua tezheng ji pingjia fangfa* (A study on the features of stone deterioration in stone monuments and their assessment methods) (Beijing: Wenwu chubanshe, 2014), 15.

12. Warscheid and Braams, "Biodeterioration of Stone," 344.

13. Siegfried Siegesmund and Rolf Snethlage, eds., *Stone in Architecture: Properties, Durability*, 4th ed. (Berlin: Springer, 2011), 113.

14. Warscheid and Braams, "Biodeterioration of Stone," 344.

15. The roof structure existed long before the metal bars were installed in 1995 to enhance security. See

Chen Mingguang, ed., *Dazu shike dang'an (ziliao)* (Records of the Dazu rock carvings) (Chongqing: Chongqing chubanshe, 2012), 201.

16. Additional ditches were added a few years later in 1956, so that the drainage system was extended to over 230 meters long. There was another round of improvement made at Beishan in 1990, during which time the shelter and the drainage system throughout the site were upgraded. See Deng, "Dazu shike weixiu gongcheng sishi nian huigu," 569–84.

17. For a discussion on the early history of protective shelters as a method of conservation, see Nicholas Stanley Price and Jukka Jokilehto, "The Decision to Shelter Archaeological Sites: Three Case-Studies from Sicily," *Conservation and Management of Archaeological Sites* 5, nos. 1–2 (2001): 19–34. For their application today, see Neville Agnew, "Methodology, Conservation Criteria and Performance Evaluation for Archaeological Site Shelters," ibid., 91–105.

18. *Shuijing zhu, juan* 13 (the "Leishui" chapter). Pertinent passage cited in Chen You and Sun Hua, "Zhongguo shikusi baohuxing jianzhu de sheji yu shiqian" (Designs of protective structures for Chinese cave temples and their realization), *Sichuan wenwu* 2 (2015): 79.

19. Su Bai, *Zhongguo shikusi yanjiu* (Studies on cave temples and monasteries in China) (Beijing: Wenwu chubanshe, 1996), 56–58, 94–99.

20. Shinka Taketaro and Nakagawa Tadayori, *Rock-Carvings from the Yun-kang Caves*, with photographs by Yamamoto Akira and Kishi Masakatsu (Tokyo: Bunkyudo; Peking: Yamamoto Photographic Studio, 1921), pl. 94.

21. Angela Howard, *Summit of Treasures: Buddhist Cave Art of Dazu, China* (Trumbull, Conn.: Weatherhill, 2001), 160.

22. While the awnings above various sections at Baodingshan were repaired or reinforced in the 1950s, the Liu Benzun section was not part of the project. See Deng, "Dazu shike weixiu gongcheng sishi nian huigu," 576–77.

23. The information was provided to me by Guo Xiangyi, who was the director of the Dazu Rock Carvings Art Museum at the time. The looting was recorded in Chen, *Dazu shike dang'an (ziliao)*, 208.

24. For a concise discussion on the subject and the related literature, see Eric Doehne and Clifford A. Price, *Stone Conservation: An Overview of Current Research*, 2nd ed. (Los Angeles: Getty Conservation Institute, 2010), 10–15.

25. Ibid., 11.

26. See J. Keith Wilson and Daisy Yiyou Wang, "The Early-Twentieth-Century 'Discovery' of the Xiangtangshan Caves," in *Echoes of the Past: The Buddhist Cave Temples of Xiangtangshan*, ed. Katherine R. Tsiang (Chicago: Smart Museum of Art, the University of Chicago; and Washington DC: Arthur M. Sackler Gallery, 2011), 105–29; and Daisy Yiyou Wang, "Charles Lang Freer and the

Collecting of Chinese Buddhist Art in Early-Twentieth-Century America," *Journal of the History of Collections* 28, no. 3 (2016), 401–16.

27. The head of a Buddha figure inside the Multi-Treasure Pagoda at Beishan was stolen on June 5, 1995, marking the first theft in Dazu since the founding of the People's Republic of China. Dazu police arrested the perpetrators and recovered the head a few weeks later. See Chen, *Dazu shike dang'an (ziliao)*, 199–200, 203–4.

28. A Buddha head from Niche 169 was stolen from Beishan; the head of Avalokiteshvara from Shizhuanshan in April 2008. Both incidents are respectively reported in Chen, *Dazu shike dang'an (ziliao)*, 225 and 236.

29. Randall Curren and Ellen Metzger, *Living Well Now and in the Future: Why Sustainability Matters* (Cambridge: MIT Press, 2017), 181.

Character and the Climatic Imaginary

Vittoria Di Palma

In recent years, "ecology" has emerged as a central concept of contemporary thought, expanding beyond its traditional domain of the natural sciences to assume a prominent place in discussions regarding art and design. Yet the question of how a scientific, purportedly objective, data-driven ecological approach might engage with subjective aesthetic concerns is very much unresolved. At times, the two approaches are even cast as being diametrically opposed. Contributing to this problem is the assumption that ecology is a young, or at least youngish, discipline. The term "ecology" was coined by Ernst Haeckel in his *Generelle Morphologie der Organismen* of 1866. It is the branch of biology that deals with the relationships between living organisms and their environment, with "environment" defined as "the complex of physical, chemical, and biotic factors (such as climate, soil, and living things) that act upon an organism or an ecological community and ultimately determine its form and survival."[1] But although the term "ecology" may have been coined in the nineteenth century, the concept of "environment" has ancient roots. In this essay, I would like to argue that although ecology as a field of study is, strictly speaking, a modern invention, many of its fundamental principles have significant continuities with earlier forms of environmental knowledge. Furthermore, by examining the development of some of these earlier environmental ideas, it may be possible to find a way to bridge some of the distance that now often appears to separate ecology and aesthetics.

Environment

In Western thought, the notion of "environment" can be traced back to Hippocrates (460 BCE–370 BCE), and in particular to his treatise *Airs, Waters, Places.* Hippocrates was a physician (the Hippocratic oath recited by all newly minted doctors upon graduation is derived from his writings), and his concern in *Airs, Waters, Places* was to establish causal relationships between bodies and climates. *Airs, Waters, Places* has survived in a fragmentary form, consisting of two principal parts: a first section that analyzes the effect of climate on the health of individuals, and a second section (more important to my analysis here), which seeks to establish causal correlations between climate and national character.

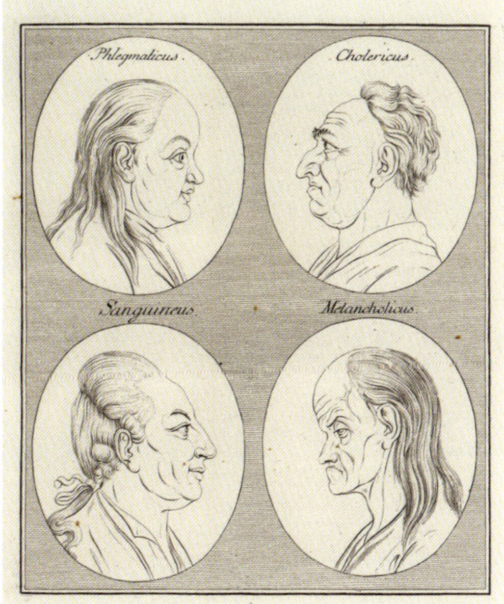

Fig. 1. Illustration of four humors in Johann Kaspar Lavater, *Physiognomische Fragmente zur Beförderung der Menschenkenntnis und Menschenliebe* (Leipzig, 1775–78). Clark Art Institute Library, Williamstown, Massachusetts

Hippocrates's theories were dependent on an understanding of the human body as governed by the humors. Human temperaments were determined by the presence of certain substances—blood, phlegm, black bile, and yellow bile—in the body. The preponderance of any one of these bodily fluids would result in the person having a particular dominant temperament. Thus, people with a lot of blood had a sanguine temperament and tended to be optimistic and social. Those with a great deal of yellow bile were choleric, short-tempered, and fast. Melancholics, who tended to be analytical, wise, and quiet, were dominated by black bile, while phlegmatics, who were relaxed and peaceful, were found instead to have large amounts of water (fig. 1). The theory of the humors had a long afterlife, remaining fundamental to how the body was understood to operate well into the eighteenth century. It also became a subject for the fine arts. In 1672, Charles Le Brun developed a grand sculptural program, the *Grande Commande* for the Parterre d'Eau at Versailles. It was to include twenty-four statues in the form of personifications of the classic quaternities: in addition to the four humors (Choleric, Sanguine, Melancholic, Phlegmatic; fig. 2), it was also to include: the four parts of day (Morning, Noon, Evening, Night); the four seasons (Spring, Summer, Fall, Winter); the four parts of the world (Europe, Africa, Asia, America); the four elements (Air, Fire, Water, Earth); and the four forms of poetry (Lyric, Epic, Pastoral, Satirical), plus four groups representing the four abductions (Persephone by Pluto, Cybele by Saturn, Orethya by Boreas, Coronis by Neptune). But the doctrine of the humors was not the only aspect of Hippocratic theory that was to have a long and significant afterlife. Equally influential were Hippocrates's ideas about interactions between bodies and climates.

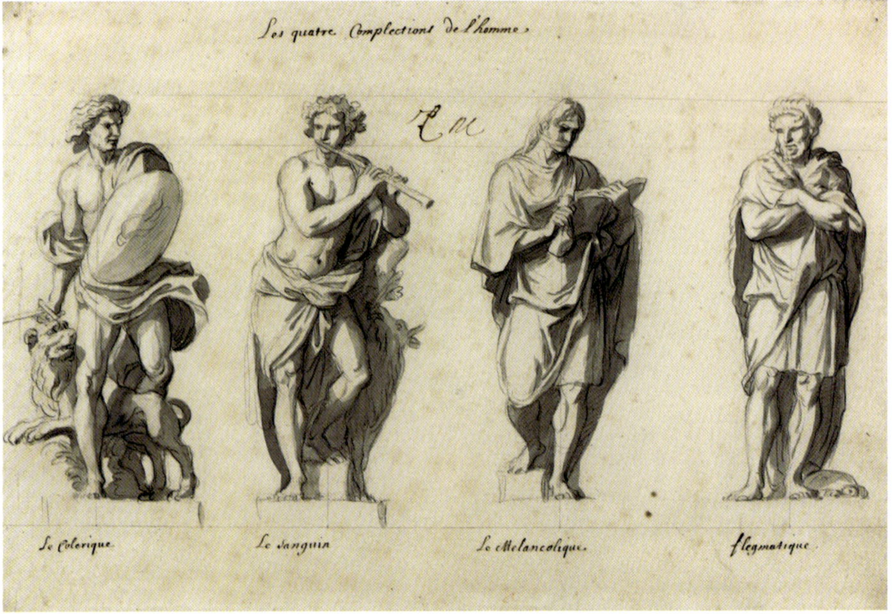

Fig. 2. Charles Le Brun (French, 1619–1690), *Les quatre complections de l'homme, Grande Commande*, 17th century. Ink drawing, 12 ³/₄ × 19 ¹/₈ in. (32.4 × 48.6 cm). Musée national des châteaux de Versailles et de Trianon, Versailles (inv. MV7907)

In the first part of *Airs, Waters, Places*, Hippocrates was concerned with establishing principles that would help doctors with their diagnoses if they found themselves in the position of being called to practice in an unfamiliar town. The task of identifying a disease correctly could be helped greatly, he argued, by knowing the characteristics of the locality, in particular the qualities of its air (or climate) and its water. Hippocrates's ideas about the beneficial or ill effects of different surroundings were repeated by Vitruvius in Book I of *De architectura*, and by that means found their way into many Renaissance city-planning treatises and ideal city plans.[2]

The second part of *Airs, Waters, Places* expands on these ideas regarding the effects of climate on individuals by examining the influence of climate on groups of people or, in other words, on the relationship between climate and national temperament. Focusing on the differences between European and Asian peoples, Hippocrates argues that the mild climate of Asia encourages both vegetation and human beings to grow to great beauty and size.[3] Because seasons are relatively uniform, the inhabitants of Asia are subject to "no mental shocks nor violent physical change, which are more likely to steel the temper and impart to it a fierce passion than is a monotonous sameness."[4] This makes them more gentle, less warlike, and prone to despotic government. Northern Europeans, on the other hand, are wild, unsociable, and full of spirit. The "frequent shocks to the mind" imparted by the constantly varying climate eradicates all traces of tameness and gentleness, which results in their being both independent and brave.[5]

Hippocrates developed these specific observations into broader generalizations about the correlations between peoples and the type of landscapes they inhabited. Mountain dwellers have large physiques, and are wild and fierce. Valley dwellers tend to be "broad, fleshy, and dark haired" and are more bilious than phlegmatic. Inhabitants of low marshy places have protruding bellies and large spleens, while those who live in a high land that is level, windy, and watered will be tall but rather tame of character. Finally, people who dwell on thin, dry, bare soil, in areas with great contrasts in climate from season to season, will have fair hair, hard physiques, and be stubborn and independent. *Airs, Waters, Places* posited the environment, understood as a combination of landscape and climate, as the great determinant of both individual and societal character.

These ideas about character and climate were also repeated by Vitruvius in abbreviated form, this time in Book IV of *De architectura* in the chapter entitled "Climate and Houses," and by this means likewise found their way into Renaissance treatises on architecture.[6] We can thus say that by the Renaissance, many of Hippocrates's ideas regarding climatic influence on sites and populations had become common tropes in architectural treatises. It was in the seventeenth century, however, that Hippocratic ideas were taken up once more and given renewed consideration by doctors. They combined revived interest in exploring the role played by the environment on human health with emerging notions of environments themselves as more changeable than fixed. This confluence of concerns led to the beginnings of a systematic approach to weather observation, and, in a related development, to the emergence of a comprehensive theory regarding the relationship between climate and artistic expression.

From Environment to Weather

In England, the institution most centrally involved with promoting the practice of observing and recording the weather was the Royal Society. Soon after the Society's establishment in 1660, founding Fellow Robert Hooke published "A Method for Making a History of the Weather." Hooke's article consisted of a questionnaire that directed attention to particular phenomena; promoted the use of instruments like barometers, hygrometers, and wind gauges (fig. 3); attempted to standardize the nomenclature of atmospheric conditions; and provided directions for creating a table that would present a month's worth of weather in such a way that it could be comprehended by the eye in a single glance (fig. 4).[7] Royal Society Fellows were inspired by Hooke's recommendations, and their observations were shared both orally, in presentations to the Society at its monthly meetings, and in print, through publication in the Royal Society's periodical, *Philosophical Transactions*. Thanks to these efforts, the practice of keeping a weather journal became increasingly popular, and thermometers, barometers, and hygrometers became fashionable household accessories.[8]

It is striking to note that many of the individuals who took up and remained most committed to the practice of weather observation were not only Fellows of the Royal Society, but also doctors. In question six of his article, Robert Hooke had asked: "What Effects are produc'd upon other bodies [by the weather]: As what Aches and Distempers in the bodies of men: what Diseases are most rife, as Colds, Fevours, Agues, &c. What putrefactions or other changes are produc'd in other bodies; As the sweating of Marble, the burning blew of a Candle, the blasting of Trees and Corn; the unusual sprouting, growth or decay of any Plants or Vegetables: the putrefaction of bodies not usual; the plenty or scarcity of Insects; of several Fruits, Grains, Flowers, Roots, Cattel, Fishes, Birds, any thing notable of that kind?"[9] In this passage, we can discern an underlying belief that weather is correlated with disease. Furthermore, the effects of the weather are not confined to people: Hooke's question presumes that the weather also affects roots, grains, flowers, and fruit; insects, birds, fish,

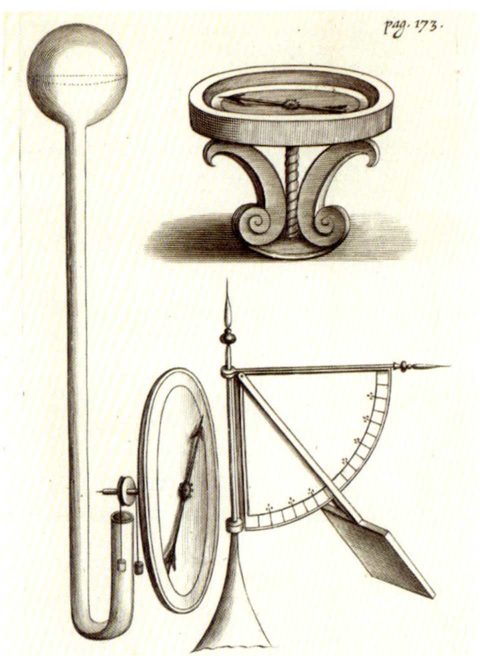

Fig. 3. Robert Hooke (British, 1635–1703), "A Method for making a History of the Weather," in Thomas Sprat, *The history of the Royal-Society of London, for the improving of natural knowledge* (London, 1667). The Henry E. Huntington Library and Art Gallery, San Marino, California (RB 600851)

and cattle. These correspondences indicate that Hippocratic notions about the role of the environment on health were part of Hooke's set of assumptions when approaching the topic of the weather.

Observing the weather became important to the Royal Society's larger project not only on account of the knowledge that would be amassed regarding climatic conditions, but also because of the light it would shed on the effects those climatic conditions had on living organisms. Furthermore, and even more importantly, by reorienting the focus from stable environmental conditions to the mutable weather, attention shifted from describing fixity to chronicling change. And once doctors and scientists and the interested public at large began to think about those environmental changes they were unavoidably subject to due to the variable weather, it became possible also to think about engineering change by becoming the architects of their own environments.[10]

The physician John Arbuthnot (1667–1735; FRS 1704) was one Royal Society Fellow who was interested in both climate and health. In 1733, he published *An Essay Concerning the Effects of Air on Human Bodies* to address a topic that he felt had been conspicuously neglected by his fellow physicians. Two years earlier, Arbuthnot had published a book on food and drink, *An Essay Concerning the Nature of Aliments, and the Choice of them, According to the different Constitutions of Human Bodies*; in it, he had promised to write additional treatises on the other so-called "non-naturals": air, rest, and motion. However, Arbuthnot died in 1735, and the essay on air was ultimately the only one of these other subjects to find its way into print.

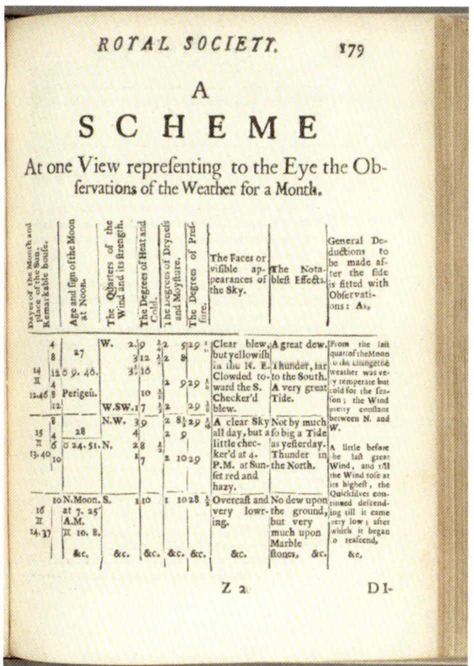

ROYAL SOCIETY.   179

A
SCHEME
At one View representing to the Eye the Observations of the Weather for a Month.

Dayes of the Month and place of the Sun. Remarkable houses.	Age and sign of the Moon at Noon.	The Quarters of the Wind and its strength.	The Degrees of Heat and Cold.	The Degrees of Dryness and Moysture.	The Degrees of Pressure.	The Faces or visible appearances of the Sky.	The Notablest Effects.	General Deductions to be made after the side is fitted with Observations: As,
4 8 14 Ⅱ 4 12.46 12	27 12 ☌ ♓ 46. Perigeū.	W. W.SW.	2.9 3.12 3.16 10 7	½2 ½2 ½2 ½2	5 29 ½ 8 2 9 29 ½ 2 29 ½	Clear blew, but yellowish in the N. E. Clowded toward the S. Checker'd blew.	A great dew. Thunder, far to the South. A very great Tide.	From the last quarter of the Moon to the changeᵗʰᵉ weather was very temperate but cold for the season; the Wind pretty constant between N. and W.
15 4 Ⅱ 6 13.40	28 ☿ 24. 51. N.	N.W. 3.9 4 28 Ⅱ 7	2 8½ 29 ½ 2 9 2 1029	A clear Sky all day, but a little checker'd at 4. P.M. at Sunset red and hazy.	Not by much so big a Tide as yesterday. Thunder in the North.	A little before the last great Wind, and till the Wind rose at its highest, the Quicksilver continued descending till it came very low; after which it began to reascend,
16 Ⅱ 14. 37	10 N. Moon. S. at 7. 25' A.M. Ⅱ 10. 8.	1.10	1 1028 ½	Overcast and very lowring.	No dew upon the ground, but very much upon Marble stones, &c.	&c,
&c.	&c.	&c.	&c. &c. &c.			&c.		

Z 2   DI-

According to Arbuthnot, the topic of air had been conspicuously neglected by physicians. Although "Philosophers, Mathematicians, Chymists, and the Professors of Agriculture and Gardening" had "attended to the Effects of Air on the Subjects of their several Arts," doctors had not given great consideration to the question. Self-consciously following in the footsteps of Hippocrates, whom Arbuthnot calls the great "first Founder of our Art," he resolved to take the first steps to remedy this lacuna, and urged his fellow physicians to observe their local climatic conditions on a regular basis and to record their observations in journals. Arbuthnot hoped that if this practice were to become widespread, it might "perhaps reduce the Physiology of the Air to a Science."[11]

To Arbuthnot it seemed "preposterous that there should be so many minute Inquiries about the Qualities of every Drug which we take but seldom, and none into the Effects of a Substance that we take inwardly every Moment."[12] The reason for this, Arbuthnot guessed, was because air was "one of those Ingesta, or things taken inwardly, which neither can be forborn nor measured in Doses."[13] Invisible and largely insensible, air was a challenging subject of study. Arbuthnot's solution to these difficulties is signaled by his choice of title: *An Essay Concerning the Effects of Air on Human Bodies.* Arbuthnot shifted the focus of study from the air itself, to its effects.

Arbuthnot defines air as "that thin Fluid which surrounds the Earth in which we move and breathe." Although invisible, air is a component of all fluids and solids, of every entity, whether animal, vegetable, or mineral. Bodies are full of air, but the air is also full of bodies: soil, water, plants, and animals perspire, emitting particles in the form of "steams," or "effluvia," which get mixed up with the air. Through respiration, and a more generalized permeability, every animal, every plant, every stone, becomes filled both with air and with effluvia emanating from its immediate environment. The intermixing of bodies and air makes organisms and their environments inseparable. This symbiotic relationship, however, is more beneficial in some places than in others. Because environments differ, the contents and quality of the air changes from place to place. City air is dirty, full of steams emanating from its human and animal inhabitants, and stagnant due to crowded streets and buildings. The high ranges surrounding mountain valleys prevent air from circulating and cause noxious effluvia to linger. The air of riverbanks is humid, hot, and consequently extremely unhealthy. Swamps, however, are the worst of all: their moist and foggy air, their dead and rotting vegetation, and their slimy amphibious creatures emit particularly noxious effluvia. All of these environments are to be avoided if possible, especially if one is selecting a site for a dwelling place. Furthermore, since air exists as a continuous fluid, and because its motion accelerates processes of mixture, sites can affect one another even if they are located at some distance: the air of a seemingly ideal site with well-drained ground can be adversely affected if it is located near a swamp. Air thus is both locally inflected and part of a larger extended system that has no regard for property lines or other culturally determined boundaries.

These ideas were to have a significant impact on the process of colonization. Some decades later, the physician James Lind (best known for having found the cure for scurvy) extended Arbuthnot's ideas in *An Essay on Diseases Incidental to Europeans in Hot Climates: with the method of preventing their fatal consequences,* which examined the relationship between the diseases contracted by Europeans in North America, Africa, the Middle East, India, and the Caribbean and the air of the countries in which these diseases flourished.[14] By any account the book was wildly successful: it went through six editions over the next forty years, was translated into German (going through two editions), and in 1811 an American edition was published in Philadelphia from the sixth London edition. The book is testimony to a significant environmental anxiety that was a fundamental component of colonial encounters. Contributing to and heightening this anxiety was the fact that the source of these often-fatal diseases was the air, which by being invisible was difficult to evaluate and monitor, and by being necessary for respiration could not be prevented from interacting with and indeed entering the body. But the significance of Arbuthnot's ideas extended well beyond the medical sphere. In fact, Arbuthnot's strategy of examining the air through its effects had an important parallel in art and architectural theory.

Character

The concept of character, which centered on the question of how a work of art or architecture could communicate to its viewers, was the subject of sustained theoretical interest during the seventeenth and eighteenth centuries, particularly in France.[15] Its beginnings are to be found in Charles Le Brun's *Conférence sur l'expression* of 1668, which attempted to establish a system for conveying the character or emotional state of a figure in a painting (fig. 5). Basing his ideas on Descartes's *Traité des passions* of 1649 and *Traité de l'homme* of 1664, Le Brun devised a system for depicting fleeting emotions through various dispositions of facial features, in particular the angle and cast of the eyebrows (fig. 6). The goal, for

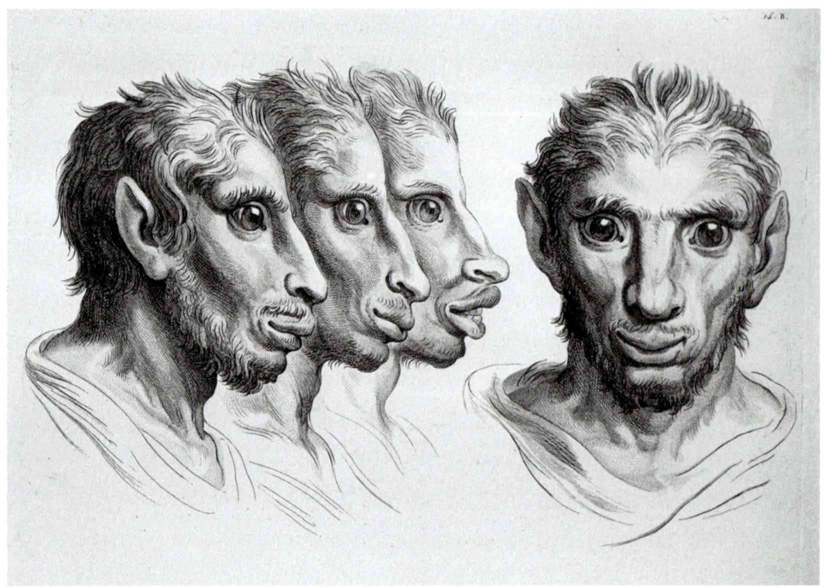

Fig. 5. Charles Le Brun, "Study of a man's head in relation to that of a donkey." Pen and ink, 8 $^3/_4$ × 12 $^7/_8$ in. (22.2 × 32.6 cm). Musée du Louvre, Paris (28053recto)

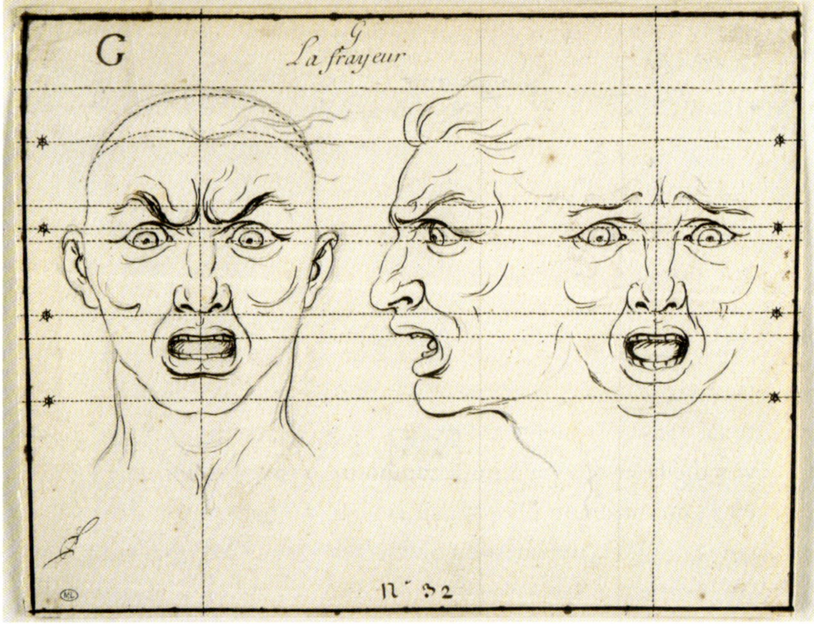

Fig. 6. Charles Le Brun, "La Frayeur. Expressions of the passions of the soul: Fright." Pen and black ink, black chalk, on white paper, 7 $^5/_8$ × 10 $^1/_8$ in. (19.5 × 25.6 cm). Musée du Louvre, Paris (28296, fol. 40; GM6496)

Le Brun, was to develop a way to communicate the emotions of the painting's figures powerfully and directly to its spectators; it was a formula, in other words, for the artistic creation of effect.

But it was Le Brun's younger contemporary and fellow academician Roger de Piles who extended these explorations beyond the depiction of the character or mood of an individual figure to the expression and communication of the character or general mood of a scene. The central question for de Piles was: how can a scene as a whole have an emotional effect on its spectators? In his treatise of 1708, *Cours de peinture par principes*, de Piles aimed to determine the grounds by which high art could be differentiated from technically accomplished craft, and thus to establish the definition of "true painting."[16] Along with extended discussions of painterly techniques like line, color, shading, and composition, the book included a long section on landscape painting. Works by the great masters of landscape, Nicolas Poussin and Claude Lorrain in particular, were associated with different moods, or modes. Poussin, whose cerebral landscapes and noble themes evoked the geometrical perfection of a vanished Classical world, was the exemplar of the heroic mode. Claude, whose landscapes are characterized by limpid skies, clear light, harmonious forms, and soft colors, excelled at the pastoral mode. Each of these two modes was associated with a particular effect: whereas Poussin elevated the mind through the contemplation of glorious thoughts and actions, Claude soothed the spectator with placid visions of a Classical Arcadia.[17] The principal means of communicating effect was through what de Piles termed the *tout-ensemble*. The *tout-ensemble* (translated as "the whole together") was an aspect of composition according to which all the parts of a painting were so mutually interdependent that none would dominate any other.[18] A successful *tout-ensemble* ensured that a painting, rather than being perceived by the eye as a collection of disparate objects, was instead seen all at once (compare the scattered spheres in the fourth register of figure 7, which have no effect, to the bunch of grapes in the third register, which produces a strong effect). In other words, the *tout-ensemble* was the facet of a painting's composition that guaranteed a unified and powerful effect on the emotions of its spectators.

When the question of effect was extended from painting to architecture, the central question was reformulated as: how can a building elicit a particular mood and communicate its purpose to visitors and users? The theoretical vehicle of this question was the concept of character. In its early formulations, architectural character was understood to involve the transmission of a building's status,

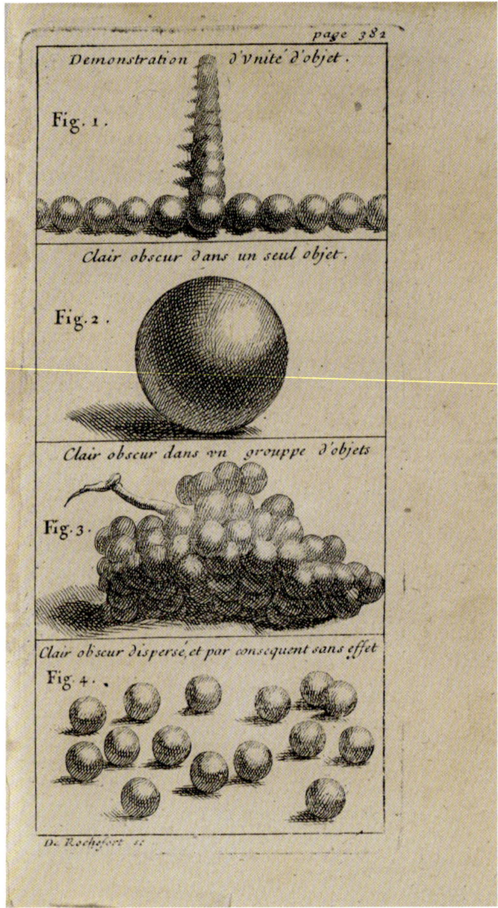

Fig. 7. Roger de Piles (French, 1635–1709), illustration of the *clair-obscur* and the *tout-ensemble*, in *Cours de peinture par principes* (Paris, 1708). Rare Books and Manuscript Library, Columbia University, New York

conferred on a public edifice by its purpose (high in the case of a church; low in the case of a slaughterhouse), and on a private residence by the occupation and social standing of its owner. The status and purpose of a building were made evident, in a basic sense, by means of its size, materials, workmanship, and ornamental details. Over the course of the eighteenth century, however, due to the concurrent development of aesthetics as a discipline—which shifted discussions about the principles of beauty to debates over the nature of taste, thereby displacing the site of inquiry from the object to the subject—the definition of architectural character changed too, and began to have less to do with decoding decoration and more with formulating how and by what means a building could make an impact on its spectators.

In his *Livre d'architecture* of 1745, Germain Boffrand associated particular building types with different moods. "Architecture," he writes, "although its object may seem to be no more than the use of material, is capable of a number of genres that bring its component parts to life, so to speak, through the different characters that it conveys to us."[19] By using the Classical orders and their ornaments as a poet deploys different genres of poetry, the architect can make a salon convey a feeling of gaiety, or a mausoleum one of sadness. "Buildings must proclaim their purpose to the beholder," Boffrand wrote; "if they fail to do so, they offend against expression and are not what they ought to be."[20] In a similar vein, Jacques-

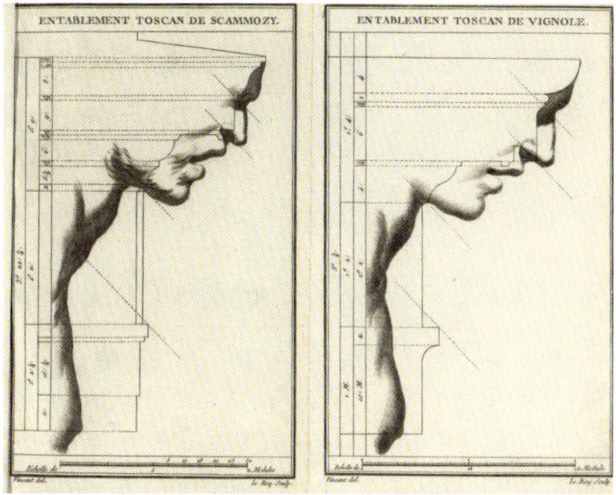

Fig 8 Jacques François Blondel (French, 1705–1774), "Entablement Toscan de Scammozy; Entablement Toscan de Vignole," in *Cours d'architecture, ou Traité de la décoration, distribution & construction des bâtiments* (Paris, 1771–77). ETH-Bibliothek Zürich, Alte und Seltene Drucke

François Blondel declared in the chapter on *caractère* in his 1771 *Cours d'architecture* that "a building must, at first glance, announce itself for what it is." This communication of purpose was to be achieved through the deployment of architectural character, whose variants included "pastoral," "naive," "frivolous," "terrible," "mysterious," "dissembling," and "vague." A temple should be grand; a palace, magnificent. Defensive buildings must be solid; buildings of pleasure, light; monuments, sumptuous; private houses of rich individuals, beautiful. Architecture was to be a language so universal that every individual, native or foreign, would be able to understand it at first sight, and a building endowed with character should have the power to "sweep the spectator off of his feet, move him to tears, and, so to speak, lift up his soul to a state of contemplative admiration" (fig. 8).[21]

It was in the 1780s, however, that the concept of architectural character was fully developed according to a sensationalist construction of knowledge. Both Nicolas Le Camus de Mézières and Étienne-Louis Boullée believed that by studying landscape and, in particular, the interaction between the objects of nature and the human body, it would be possible to understand, and subsequently mimic, the mechanisms by which particular sensations were produced. Sensation was understood to be the wellspring of emotion; thus, the orchestration of sensations became the basis for creating architectural effect. Boullée defines character as "the effect of the object which makes some kind of impression on us."[22] For Boullée, the sight of a lush valley cradling the mirrored surface of a lake illustrates the formal means by which pleasing emotions might be generated, while "the tragic appearance of thick woods and gloomy forests" instructs the architect how to induce the opposite feelings of melancholy and dread. In order to give a building character, the architect must "make judicial use of every means of producing no other sensations than those related to the subject." This careful curation of sensations would ensure that buildings elicited a mood appropriate to their function: a church successfully endowed with character would inspire a feeling of veneration; a theater, pleasure; a palace of justice, respect and fear; a cenotaph, solemnity and gloom.[23] By synthesizing the lessons of landscape, architects could create buildings that would be perceived in a single instant as unified objects, producers of sensations so closely affiliated that the mental processes of reason and judgment could be dispensed with. Character thus became identified as the most effective mechanism for generating powerful, automatic effects.

Climate, Character, Effect

In England, the first architectural theorist to articulate a notion of character was Robert Morris (1703–1754). Very little is known about his life or activities, but he did publish three books of architectural theory in a span of eight years: *Lectures on Architecture* (1734); *An Essay Upon Harmony, as it relates chiefly to Situation and Building* (1739); and *The Art of Architecture: A Poem in Imitation of Horace's Art of Poetry* (1742). In *The Art of Architecture*, published three years before Boffrand's treatise on the same subject, Morris applied Horace's principles of rhetorical expression to architectural form, writing:

> But choice of Place must be the Builder's Care,
> For various *Climates*, various *Modes* prepare.
>
> . . .
>
> All these the Architect must study well;
> From the proud *Palace* to the humble *Cell*.
> The barren *Mountain*, and the rural *Shade*;
> The mingled gay Profusion, Nature made,
> To fit and tally, Art requires his Skill,
> From the *moist Meadow*; to the *brown-brow'd Hill*,
> The silent *shady Grove*, or *silver Rill*.
> To give a Grandeur to the *Opening Lawn*;
> And pleasing Softness, to the *solemn Dawn*;
> To join the *vivid*, with the *vernal* Bloom;
> Where scarce a Sun Beam wanders thro' the Gloom.[24]

But even earlier, in *An Essay upon Harmony*, Morris drew upon de Piles's notion of the *tout-ensemble* to talk about the relationship between buildings and their settings. In *An Essay upon Harmony* of 1739, Morris explained that harmony exists both in the viewer, as a kind of sense, or taste, and in objects, as a set of formal qualities. The taste or sense of harmony is instinctive, implanted in all human beings at birth by nature. Although responses will vary according to the qualities of the object (different shapes, different textures, and different colors produce different sensations, which affect our passions and give rise to a range of emotional reactions), all human beings respond in the same predetermined way. Thus, by disposing the notes of a melody, the words of a sentence, the colors of a painting, the outlines of a building, or the plantings of a landscape garden, the artist can produce a variety of moods in his or her viewers: "we are vivid, gay, joyous, or more calm and sedate, according to the Variety of Objects, or similar with the Gloom, or Solitude, of the Spot."[25]

Yet the harmony that Morris championed was more than an architectural reinterpretation of painterly concepts. Morris also relied upon Arbuthnot's understanding of air when he discussed a related term, which he called "situation." Although Morris noted that "Convenience should be the first care of the builder," when choosing a site for a house (with convenience defined as being located relatively near to a town and having water, wood, pasture, and fertile soil in plentiful supply), "the placing of the Building on a Spot, where Health is most likely to be enjoyed, is particularly to be observed." This entailed being as far as possible from swamps and mountain valleys. Swamps are afflicted with "dead and stagnant Waters, which impregnate the grossest and most unwholesome Air," while "Vallies enclosed by Hills or Mountains" are infected by "the Rains which settle [and] send forth contagious Vapours." An ideal site, instead, would be located on rising ground near a running stream: there the "Air is . . . free and in perpetual Motion, and the Earth . . . purg'd from Damps and Vapours."[26] Situations were integrated in a physical sense by virtue of the pervasive qualities of their air, but they could also be integrated in an aesthetic sense, if they achieved a state of "ocular harmony." Ocular harmony is produced when all the elements of a scene, or environment, work together, from the overall view of the building in its setting, to the outline and massing of the building as a whole, to the most minute ornamental details. When a building harmonizes with its situation, all the elements of the environment produce similar sensations, resulting in a unified effect. And it is in this notion of a unified environment, one that produces a set of sensations that reinforce one another to produce a powerful effect, that we can discern the essence of the concept of architectural character.

Morris combines the notion of character as inherited from the Hippocratic tradition and its associated notions of the effects of the air on bodies and societies with an artistic notion of character as related to the ability of a work of art to produce an emotional response. The common term in both of these notions of character was "effect." Just as the properties of air could best be studied through their effects on human bodies, so character was a design method that depended on a nonverbal, sensation-based system of effect in order to have an impact on the emotions of its viewers.

By making the focus of inquiry not the object, but its effects, de Piles and Morris are key figures in a larger transition that moves the focus of inquiry from beauty to taste, from object to beholder, from production to reception—central, defining characteristics of what in 1735 Alexander Baumgarten named "aesthetics." Yet, as we have seen, these ideas were not isolated from developments occurring in the study of environments and climates.[27] Morris's incorporation of Arbuthnot's ideas about air and the requisite environmental qualities of a good site suggests that Morris's concept of "situation" assumed a complex atmospheric environment in which all components—air, water, soil, stone, trees, plants, insects, birds, animals, humans, and their cultural productions like buildings—were embedded in a thick medium of continuously intermixing particles. In a very literal way, the objects and elements of a given site or situation were fundamentally *of that place*, at the same time that they also formed part of a mobile, changing, fluid continuum. In other words, what begins to emerge at this moment in the first decades of the eighteenth century is a concept of air as an active agent, an agent capable of dissolving boundaries between object and environment, and perhaps even capable of undermining the very notion of an object itself.

1. *Oxford English Dictionary* online (accessed April 29, 2017).

2. See Vitruvius, *On Architecture*, trans. Richard Schofield, intro. Robert Tavernor (New York: Penguin Books, 2009), 20–33. For Renaissance treatises that incorporate discussions of these ideas, see Leon Battista Alberti, *On the Art of Building in Ten Books*, trans. Joseph Rykwert, Neil Leach, and Robert Tavernor (Cambridge: MIT Press, 1992); Andrea Palladio, *The Four Books of Architecture*, trans. Robert Tavernor and Richard Schofield (Cambridge: MIT Press, 1997); and Sebastiano Serlio, *On Architecture*, trans., with intro. and commentary by Vaughan Hart and Peter Hicks, 2 vols. (New Haven: Yale University Press, v. 1, 1996; v. 2, 2001).

3. "Some physiques resemble wooded, well-watered mountains, others light, dry land, others marshy meadows, others a plain of bare, parched earth." Hippocrates, *Airs, Waters, Places*, trans. W. H. S. Jones (Cambridge: Harvard University Press, 1923), I.109.

4. Ibid., I.115.

5. Ibid., I.133.

6. See Vitruvius, *On Architecture*, 166–82 and note 2 above.

7. Robert Hooke, "A Method for Making a History of the Weather," in Thomas Sprat, *The History of the Royal Society of London for the Improving of Natural Knowledge* (London, 1667), 173–79.

8. Jan Golinski, *British Weather and the Climate of Enlightenment* (Chicago: University of Chicago Press, 2007).

9. Hooke, "A Method for Making a History of the Weather," 174–75.

10. See, for example, Fellow of the Royal Society John Evelyn's *Fumifugium: or The Inconveniencie of the Aer and Smoak of London Dissipated. Together with some Remedies humbly proposed by J. E. Esq.* (London: W. Godbid for Gabriel Bedel and Thomas Collins, 1661).

11. John Arbuthnot, *An Essay Concerning the Effects of Air on Human Bodies* (London, 1733), x.

12. Ibid., vii.

13. Ibid., vi.

14. James Lind, *An Essay on Diseases Incidental to Europeans in Hot Climates: with the method of preventing their fatal consequences* (London, 1768).

15. The principal eighteenth-century treatments of character are: Germain Boffrand, *Book of Architecture*, ed. and intro. Caroline van Eck, trans. David Britt (Aldershot: Ashgate, 2002); Jacques-François Blondel, *Cours d'architecture* (Paris, 1771), I; Nicolas Le Camus de Mézières, *The Genius of Architecture: Or, the Analogy of that Art with our Sensations*, trans. David Britt, intro. Robin Middleton (Santa Monica: Getty Publications, 1992); Etienne-Louis Boullée, "Architecture, Essai sur l'art," in Helen Rosenau, *Boullée and Visionary Architecture* (London: Academy, 1976); A.-C. Quatremère de Quincy, "Caractère," in *Encyclopédie Méthodique: Architecture* (Paris, 1788): 1:477–518. See also Vittoria Di Palma, "Architecture, Environment and Emotion: Quatremère de Quincy and the Concept of Character," *AA Files* 47 (September 2002): 45–56; Sylvia Lavin, *Quatremère de Quincy and the Invention of a Modern Language of Architecture* (Cambridge: MIT Press, 1992): 137–47; Louis A. Ruprecht, *Classics at the Dawn of a Museum Era: The Life and Times of Antoine Chrysôstome Quatremère de Quincy* (London: Palgrave MacMillan, 2014); Werner Szambien, *Symétrie, Goût, Caractère: Théorie et terminologie de l'architecture à l'âge classique, 1550–1800* (Paris, Picard: 1986); Anthony Vidler, "From the Hut to the Temple: Quatremère de Quincy and the Idea of Type," in *The Writing of the Walls: Architectural Theory in the Late Enlightenment* (Princeton: Princeton Architectural Press, 1987): 147–64.

16. Roger de Piles, *Cours de peinture par principes* (Paris: 1708), trans. as *The Principles of Painting*

(London: for J. Osborn, at the Golden Ball, in Pater-Noster Row, 1743).

17. Ibid., 200–59.

18. Ibid., 104–14.

19. Boffrand, "Principles of architecture derived from Horace's *Art of Poetry*," *Book of Architecture*, 8.

20. Ibid.

21. Blondel, *Cours d'architecture*, 1:378–434.

22. Boullée, "Architecture, Essai sur l'art," 89.

23. Ibid., 82–113.

24. Robert Morris, *The Art of Architecture: A Poem in Imitation of Horace's Art of Poetry* (London, 1742), 19–20.

25. Robert Morris, *An Essay upon Harmony, as it Relates Chiefly to Situation and Building* (London, 1739), 18–20.

26. Ibid., iii–iv.

27. There is also an intriguing parallel between de Piles's discussion of a unified visual impact and his use of a table to grade the great painters and Robert Hooke's weather table that represents to the eye "At one View . . . the Observations of the Weather for a Month." Foucault identified the table as an index of the eighteenth century's classifying spirit, but this parallel suggests another perspective instead—that of information being seen and comprehended as a unified totality, or integrated system, rather than as a collection of discrete and isolated elements.

"All Our Relations" as an Eco–Art Historical Challenge: Lessons from Standing Bear's Muslin

Jessica L. Horton

A Common World?

In 2012, the Sydney Biennale featured a Lakota phrase as its title. "All our relations" is a translation of *Mitákuye Oyás'iŋ*, a humble prayer that addresses humans, animals, plants, rivers, mountains, and other beings as common kin in a framework of reciprocity (fig. 1).[1] The artistic co-directors, Plains Cree artist and curator Gerald McMaster of the Siksika First Nation and Dutch curator Catherine de Zegher, strove to transform the banal biennial format into a model of planetary interconnectedness. Theirs was a vision consonant with the broader ecological turn that has occasioned this volume. The curators took their cue from philosopher and anthropologist Bruno Latour's declaration, "critique is past."[2] They observed cultural producers around the world "moving on" from a century defined by "separation, negativity, and disruption as strategies of change." Rather, "inclusionary practices of generative thinking, such as collaboration, conversation, and compassion" were urgently needed to compose a common world.[3]

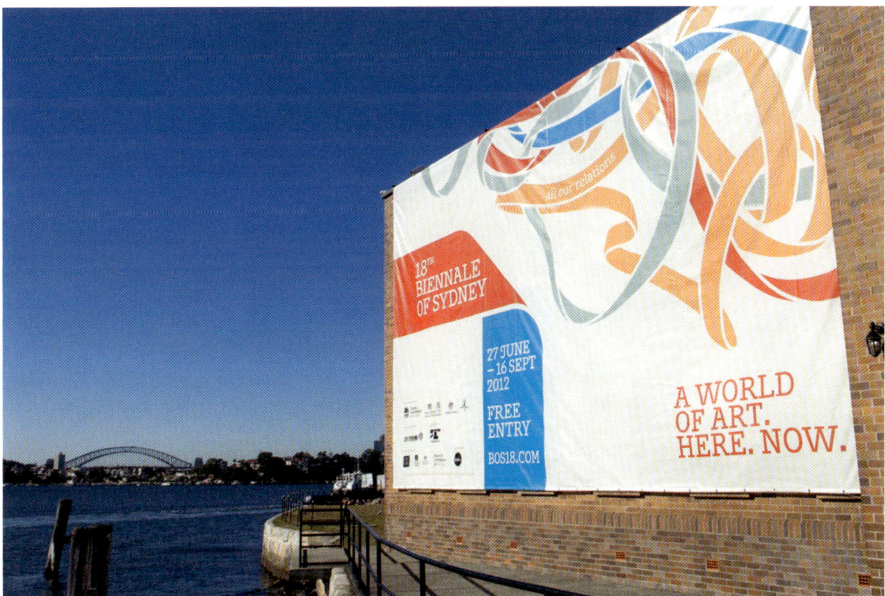

Fig. 1. Exhibition signage on Cockatoo Island for the 18th Biennale of Sydney, 2012

The exhibition incorporated an unprecedented number of Indigenous artists from the Americas and Australia alongside sympathetic global peers. Paintings of ancestral dreamings by Dorothy Napangardi (Walpiri) hung next to model log cabins of *Frontier Land* (2011) by Alan Michelson (Mohawk) (fig. 2). The Arizona-based collective Postcommodity cut open the floor of the Art Gallery of New South Wales to expose raw earth (fig. 3) and filled the gallery with songs performed by Aboriginal residents of Sydney.[4] Yet the phrase, "all our relations," printed in English on celebratory streamers, floated curiously free from the particular history it had survived: one of US treaty-breaking and state-sponsored violence against people and land, ongoing struggles for decolonization and cultural renewal

against all odds. In contrast to the popular pronouncements of frontier closure that opened the previous century, the Oceti Sakowin people, the seven bands of Lakota, Dakota, and Nakota people who form the Great Sioux Nation, continue to pray in a colonial present.

In the fall of 2016, another Lakota phrase moved and mobilized. *Mni Wiconi* expresses respect for the vital connection between human bodies and the liquid veins of *Unci Maka*, Grandmother Earth.[5] Widely translated as "water is life," the words traveled far from Standing Rock in North Dakota, where Oceti Sakowin members and allies first set up a peaceful camp to stop the construction of the Dakota Access Pipeline (DAPL) across sacred sites and waterways—nota-

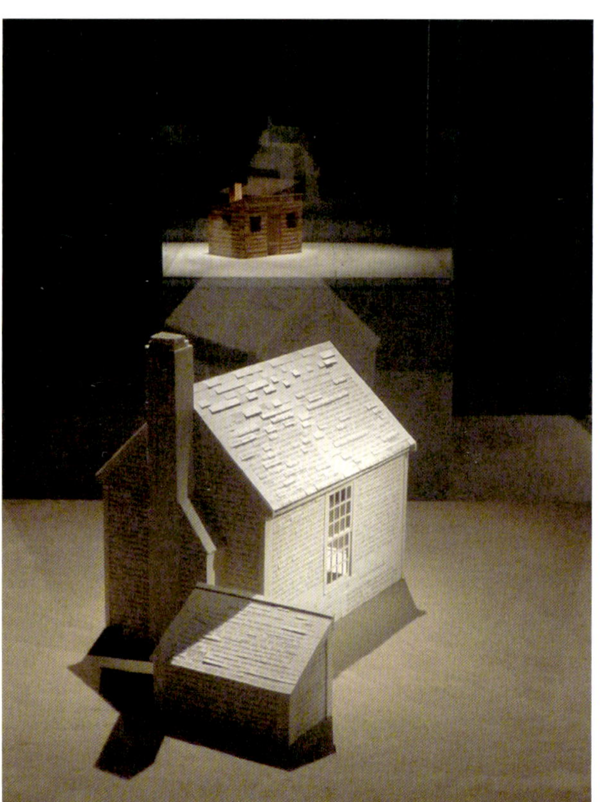

Fig. 2. Alan Michelson, *Prophetstown* (installation view), 2011. Foreground: *Henry David Thoreau Cabin*. Handmade paper, archival ink, and archival board, 10 ³/₄ × 7 ³/₄ × 10 ³/₄ in. (27.3 × 19.7 × 27.3 cm). Background: *Attack*. Handmade paper, black paper, archival board, and acrylic paint, 9 ¹/₂ × 7 ¹/₂ × 8 in. (24.1 × 19.1 × 20.3 cm). Art Gallery of New South Wales, 18th Biennale of Sydney, 2012

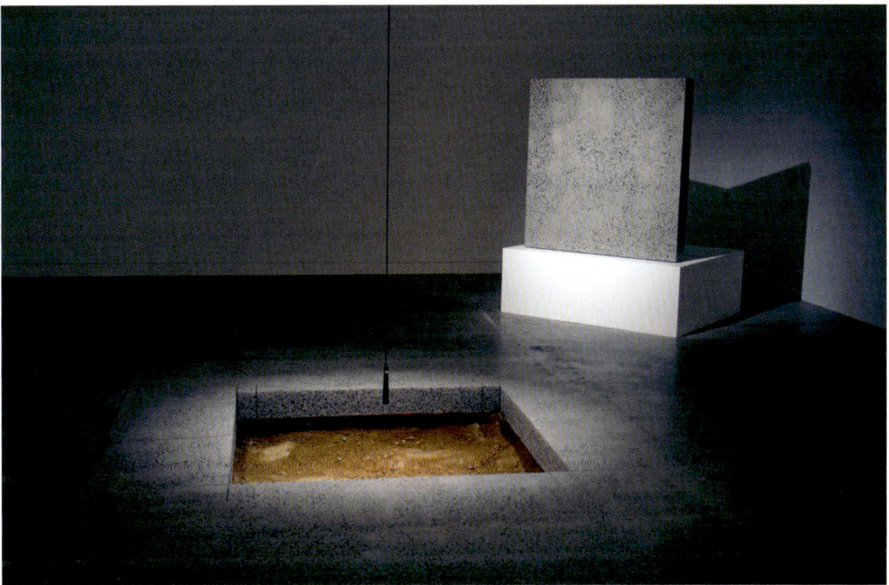

Fig. 3. Postcommodity, *Do You Remember When?* (installation view), 2012. Site-specific intervention and mixed media installation (cut concrete, exposed earth, light, sound). Art Gallery of New South Wales, 18th Biennale of Sydney, 2012

bly, the Missouri River—the previous spring. The broad mobilization popularly known as NoDAPL built upon decades of Indigenous and environmental justice activism, including Idle No More, "a peaceful revolution to honour Indigenous sovereignty and to protect the land & water" begun by First Nations women and allies in Canada in 2012.[6] Crowds from San Francisco to Tokyo embraced a concise cosmopolitical alternative to the devastating logic of resource extraction driving not only a pipeline invasion, but also the neoliberal lockdown of the planet.[7] Close to my home in Philadelphia, more than sixty members of the Jewish community wove "water is life" into the Hebrew verses of "The Waters of Babylon" during a peaceful sit-in at banks funding the pipeline (fig. 4). They continued to sing while nine were arrested in the lobby of a local branch of Wells Fargo.[8]

Without question the translation of an Indigenous prayer into ecological revelation for all has inspired impressive acts of solidarity worldwide. I write from the position of white settler ally, art historian, and being made of water, who has been galvanized, like so many others, by NoDAPL's proliferating words and images. Yet the two cases that I have briefly outlined raise questions about "all our" responsibility to history. How might the ecological webs we spin incorpo-

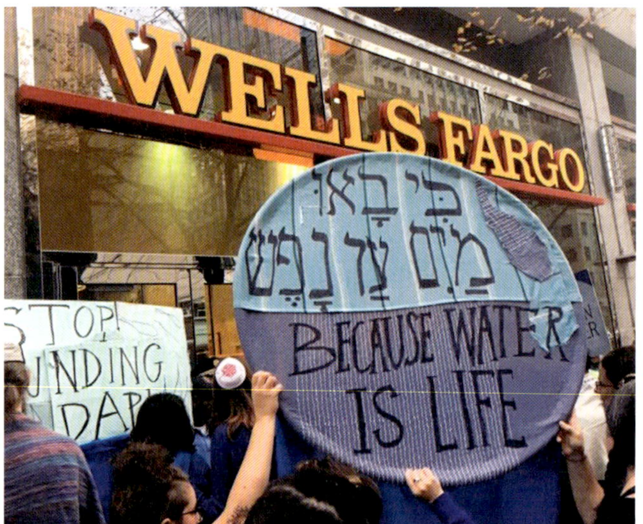

Fig. 4. Protesters from the Jewish community in Philadelphia conduct a sit-in at a Wells Fargo Bank.

rate, rather than obfuscate, violent dislocations that are, in fact, a strong connection to the past? What kind of "eco–art history" might we compose to confront, critique, and cross traumatic divisions engendered by settler colonialism, a process out of which our discipline was forged and with which it remains entangled? Such questions bind ethical activism to a scholarly praxis attentive to Indigenous and environmental justice in the twenty-first century. They also prompt a deeper engagement with past materials as a crucial means of transmission, as I will explore in relation to an artwork created by the Minneconjou Lakota man Standing Bear at the turn of the twentieth century. (See also Dylan Miner's discussion of pipes and pipelines in this volume.)

The issues I've highlighted connect to a broader tendency evident throughout the varied eco-critical, ontological, new materialist, and post-humanist turns, to embrace Indigenous philosophical precepts as radical insights about a world shared with nonhumans (with or without due credit). The aims of this essay depart from past efforts, my own included, to address the colonial dynamics of claiming such perspectives as "new" within a European intellectual genealogy.[9] Métis scholar and artist Zoe Todd, for one, told of attending a talk by Latour on the topic of climate change in 2013. She waited for him to acknowledge Indigenous thinkers' "millennia of engagement with sentient environments, with cosmologies that enmesh people into complex relationships between themselves and *all* relations, and with climates and atmospheres as important points of organization and action." The moment never came. Todd memorably concluded that "'ontology' is just another word for colonialism."[10] In light of NoDAPL's unprecedented visibility, I build on such insights about *whether* Native cosmologies are named and *who* is speaking about them to ask *how* they are integrated with ongoing processes of dispossession and decolonization. From global biennials to activist networks to art history conferences, "all our relations" may enter broader conversations about ecology as a political force or an ameliorative balm, depending on the degree to which the prayer remains enmeshed in a specific terrain of struggle. Put another way, more rigorous attention is needed to the *means of survival* by which philosophical alternatives to colonial-capitalist exploitation have arrived in the present. Art historians may be particularly well positioned to address the crucial role of material culture in transmitting distinct environmental knowledges across violent historical ruptures. Such an inquiry, however, demands unsettling disciplinary temporal and spatial boundaries—especially those attached to the American Revolution and so-called closure of the frontier—that locate colonialism in a past prior to national cohesion. "All our relations" persists on occupied ground.

Standing Bear's Battlefield

To give shape to the broad issues I've introduced, I will consider the role of one powerful object in diffusing Lakota principles of interconnectedness between Indian Removal and NoDAPL. Around 1899 at Pine Ridge Reservation, Standing Bear created a pictorial account of the events leading up to and including the Battle of the Little Bighorn of 1876 (fig. 5). He drew the images in pencil and painted them with watercolor on a six-foot square of muslin. They were created from memory and collectively verified by Oglala Lakota peers. Standing Bear's work belongs to a much larger archive of late nineteenth-century Plains graphic arts and an associated multivocal literature on which my own story depends. The muslin is unusual, however, for the degree to which it interweaves multiple episodes of ceremony and battle in a moment of crisis.

In one sense, the object is a material distillation of the broad upheavals—human and nonhuman—occurring on the plains in the final decades of the nineteenth century. Here we might consider "the work of art as an ecological object," to borrow a phrase from a fellow contributor to this volume, James Nisbet.[11] Still, when ecology first developed as a discourse of natural science during the artist's lifetime, it precluded those cultural and technological dimensions that Standing Bear harnessed to bind humans, animals, and rivers.[12] Furthermore, the muslin's objecthood is complicated by Indigenous philosophies and protocols described by Sherry Farrell Racette: it possesses its "own life force" and is capable of "nudging memory, calling for a story."[13] With a gaze calibrated by NoDAPL's

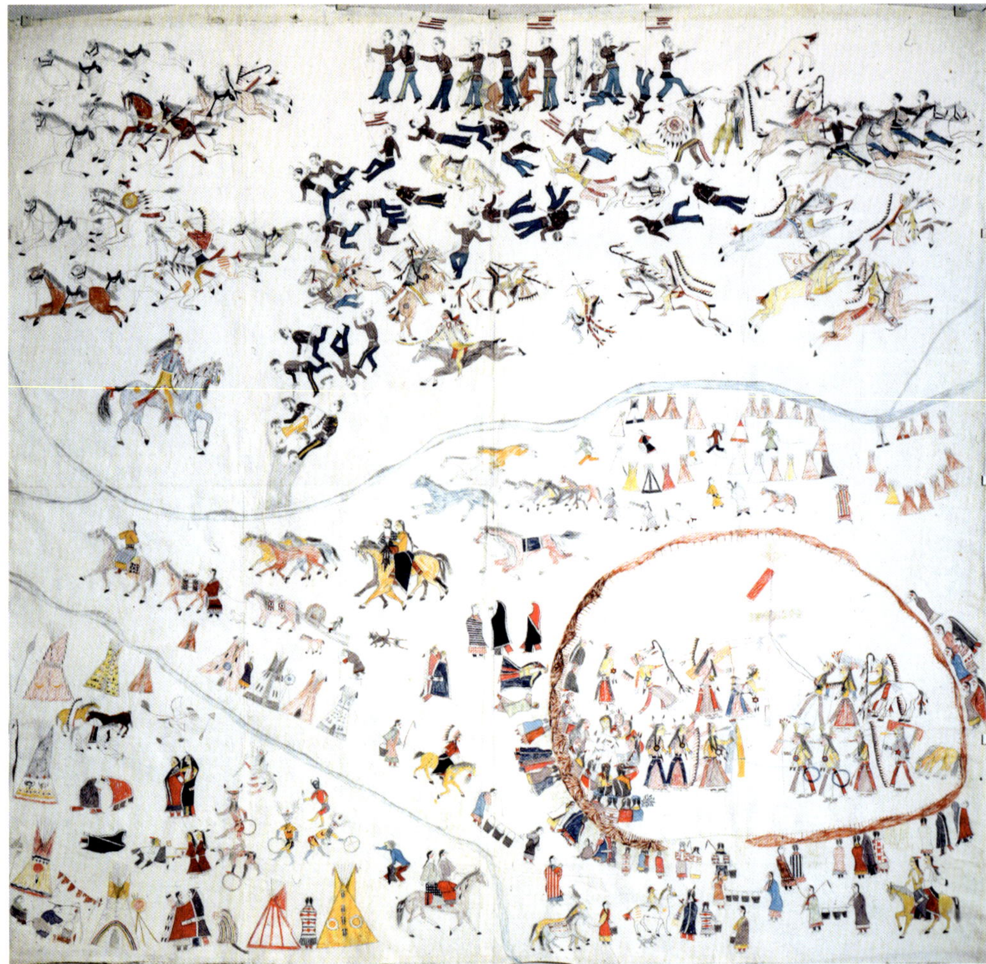

Fig. 5. Standing Bear (Mato Najin), (Minneconjou Lakota, 1859–1933), *Events Leading to the Battle of the Little Big Horn*, c. 1899. Muslin, pencil, and red, blue, yellow, green, and black pigment, 72 × 72 in. (182.88 × 182.88 cm). Foundation for the Preservation of American Indian Art and Culture, Saint Augustine's Indian Center, Chicago. Gift of Dorothy C. and L. S. Raisch

own proliferating archive of prayer and battle, we can see how the very material concentrates power amid colonial rupture to anticipate a future (fig. 6). Standing Bear's muslin models the survival of "all our relations" through a potent blend of history-telling, embodied resistance, and spiritual renewal that is as pressing in the time of NoDAPL as it was during the artist's life. In many ways, it can function as a teacher in relation to the eco-art-historical challenge I've highlighted.

My own retrospective efforts are prompted by a number of scholars and activists who have insisted on a historical approach to NoDAPL that emphasizes

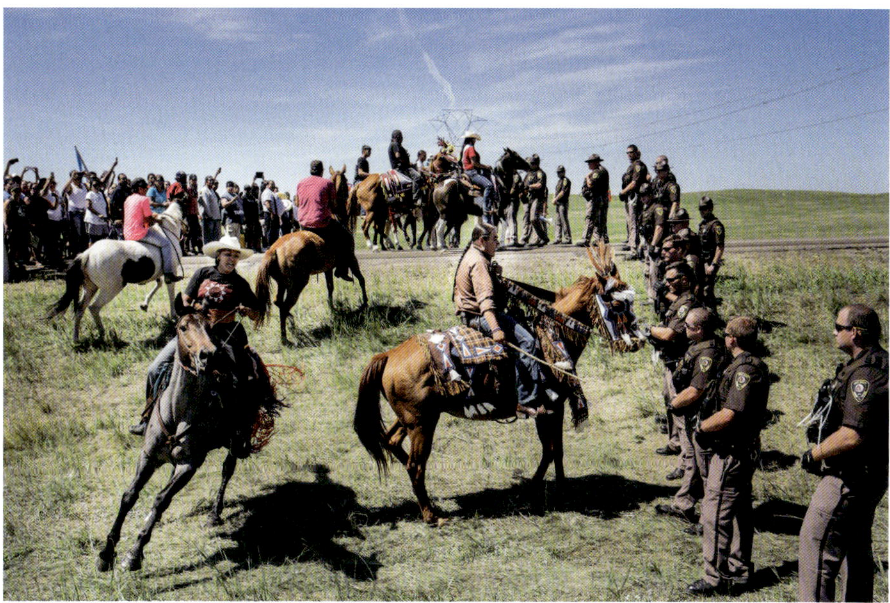

Fig. 6. Riders from the Standing Rock, Rosebud, and Lower Brule Lakota reservations approach a police line that formed between a group of protesters and the entrance to the Dakota Access Pipeline construction site, 2017.

continuity with the events of Indian Removal. The Sicangu Lakota historian Nick Estes, for one, writes: "Like our ancestors' wars of the nineteenth century, our current war is also defensive—it is to protect water and land from inevitable spoliation in the name of profit."[14] Winona LaDuke, Ojibwa activist and director of Honor the Earth, an organization that raises awareness and funding for Indigenous environmental justice, likewise stated baldly: "The Indian wars are far from over out here."[15] In the fall of 2016, a group of scholars in New York City created the #StandingRockSyllabus, an online educational resource examining the historical, cultural, and political dimensions of NoDAPL.[16] It opens with a map made by Anishinaabe architect Elsa Hoover, which relates the episodic history of Oceti Sakowin dispossession to the path of the now-completed Dakota Access Pipeline (fig. 7). Gradations from white to black indicate the shrinking legal boundaries of Native land due to treaties that the United States government negotiated and then systematically violated beginning in 1851.

Especially relevant to the story at hand is the dispossession that occurred between the years 1868 and 1876–77. The Treaty of Fort Laramie (1868) was meant to protect the verdant region known as *He Sapa*, or the Black Hills of present-day South Dakota, a sacred center to the people of Oceti Sakowin,

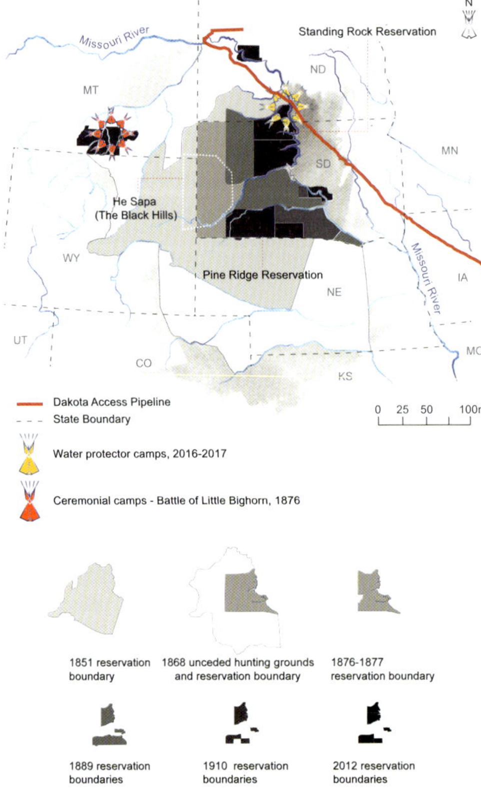

Fig. 7. Elsa Hoover, *Map of Oceti Sakowin Oyate Territory and Treaty Boundaries, 1851–present*. Created for the NYC Stands with Standing Rock Collective, "#StandingRockSyllabus," 2016, https://nycstandswithstandingrock.wordpress.com/standingrocksyllabus/. The version reproduced here was customized to illuminate the essay.

from incursions by non-Natives. In 1874, General George Armstrong Custer supervised the largest of the nineteenth-century federal surveys mapping western topographies for the purposes of military and industrial expansion. He reported "lumber sufficient for all time to come" and "gold in paying quantities" in the Black Hills.[17] Responding to public petitions for the forced expulsion of Native Americans, President Ulysses S. Grant cancelled treaty obligations in the Indian Appropriations Act of 1876 and annexed the coveted land for mining in the Black Hills Act of 1877.[18] These actions foreshadowed President Donald Trump's executive green light on the contested final Dakota Access Pipeline permit in January 2017.[19] So, too, did they set the stage for past and present acts of resistance. The great battle between the US cavalry and Lakota, Dakota, and allied Northern Cheyenne and Arapaho forces in the summer of 1876 occurred beside the Little Bighorn River in Montana, on land that Oceti Sakowin leaders had not agreed to relinquish to the United States. Likewise, the Dakota Access Pipeline snakes for miles across *unceded* hunting grounds, shown in the white on the map.[20]

Born in 1859, Standing Bear bore intimate witness to the history abstracted on the #StandingRockSyllabus map. When he was seventeen years old, he took part in the Battle of the Little Bighorn and witnessed the ceremonies that preceded it. He was among the first Lakota men to travel with Buffalo Bill Cody's Wild West Show to Europe in 1887, 1889, and 1890. While convalescing from an injury abroad during his final trip, he lost his wife and possibly their daughter in a massacre of Lakota men, women, and children by US cavalry at Wounded Knee. Standing Bear married his Austrian nurse, a talented linguist named Louise Rieneck. They returned to live among the Oglala Lakota of Pine Ridge Reservation. The couple participated in the new cash economy by farming, ranching, making caskets, and providing medical services for others in the community.[21] Standing Bear also completed four known large-scale works on muslin and countless drawings on paper before his death in 1933. His oral account, along with additional drawings of the Little Bighorn and other events of historical and ceremonial significance, was published in *Black Elk Speaks*, a classic text on Lakota spirituality and history, in 1932.[22]

Key aspects of Standing Bear's transformed life are captured in *The Visit* (2006), an homage to his creative, spiritual, and historical vision made by his great-grandson, the artist Arthur Amiotte (fig. 8). At the center of the collage

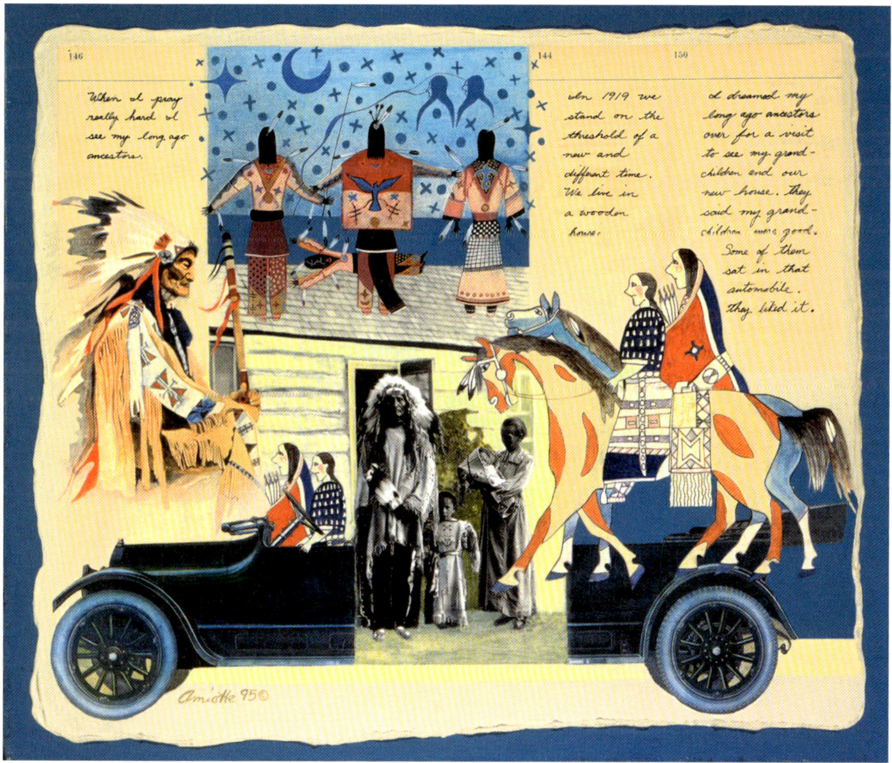

Fig. 8. Arthur Amiotte (b. 1942), *The Visit*, 1995. Collage, 20 × 24 in. (50.8 × 61 cm). Buffalo Bill Center of the West, Cody, Wyoming. Gift of Mrs. Cornelius Vanderbilt Whitney (17.95)

appears an archival photograph of Standing Bear in full regalia next to Louise in a calico dress and two of their three children. They stand in front of a well-appointed wooden house. The surrounding text and drawings depict a visit from Standing Bear's ancestors during a dream: "Some of them sat in that automobile. They liked it." Interactions between spiritual visions and new technologies likewise informed his great-grandfather's historically-minded work, albeit without the puns on "horsepower."[23]

Standing Bear's rendering of the Battle of the Little Bighorn was probably commissioned by the white artist Elbridge Ayer Burbank, who wrote that he "was eager to get the Indians' account of the Custer Massacre" during his trip to paint portraits of Lakota people in 1899.[24] The battle scenes continue a Plains graphic tradition in which men recorded events of individual bravery and collective importance on animal-hide shirts, shields, drums, tipis, and pictographic historical records known as winter counts (fig. 9). More unusual is Standing Bear's choice to flank the battle with animal dreamer society dances (lower left) and the Sun Dance (lower right) that preceded it, for ceremonial scenes have no deep precedent in tribal annals. Janet Berlo suggests that three commissioned drawings on paper by the Sans Arc Lakota man Black Hawk in 1880 may be the first to depict the Sun Dance. She attributes the appearance of such imagery to a new auto-ethnographic impulse born of crisis on the plains.[25] The visual repertoire of Lakota artists expanded when they were forcibly contained on reservations, where they suffered unprecedented material and spiritual hardship. Notably, the first federal ban on sun dancing was issued in 1883. The official "Code of Indian Offenses" targeted ceremonies that involved the redistribution of material goods to the community, which violated the logic of private capitalist accumulation that drove Indian Removal and assimilation policy. Some Lakota people nonetheless continued to dance and gift covertly. Standing Bear's family was unusually prosperous and earned a reputation for great generosity.[26]

The shift from hide to cloth and paper marked another site of negotiation between two markedly different systems of valuing the beyond-human world. Skins were more than a dead ground upon which anthropocentric histories were inscribed. Animals were spiritual intermediaries in the events whose memory they hosted. Given their importance to every aspect of plains cultures, Kiowa writer and artist N. Scott Momaday has likened the US government's orchestrated decimation of buffalo herds as a "deicide."[27] Standing Bear joined countless other Native artists who used manufactured pens, pencils, paints, paper, and cloth procured at

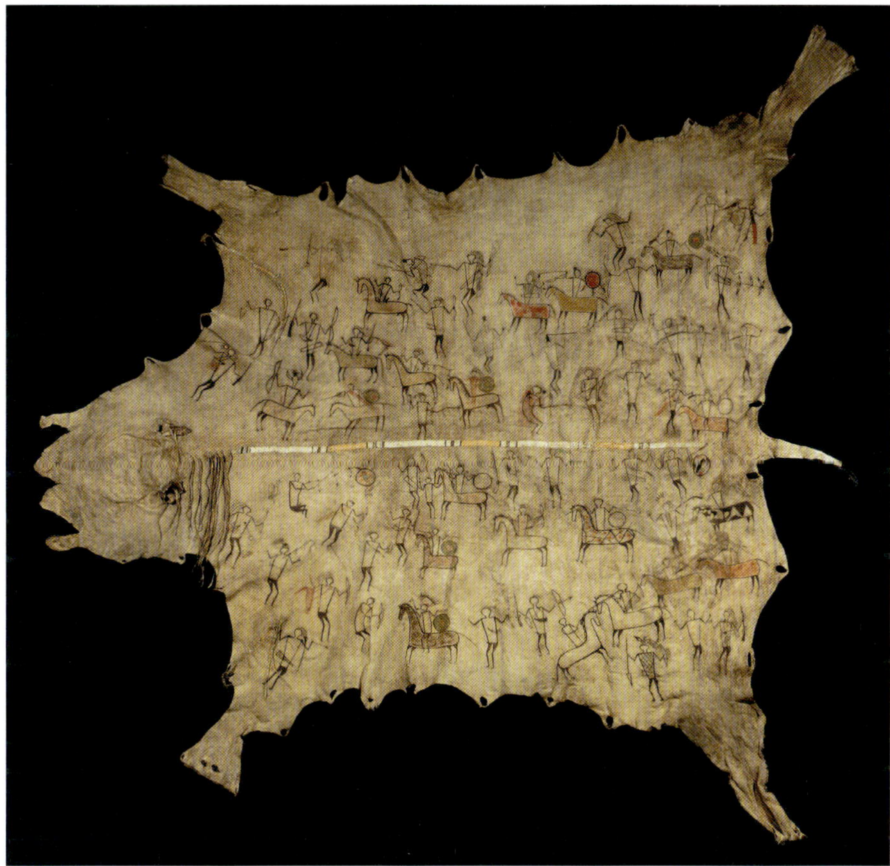

Fig. 9. Pictographic robe, Sioux, c. 1780–1825. Bison skin, 11 3/4 × 102 × 94 in. (30 × 259.1 × 238.8 cm). Peabody Museum of Archaeology and Ethnology, Harvard University, Cambridge. Gift of the heirs of David Kimball (99-12-10/53121)

reservation trading posts, military prisons, and boarding schools, throughout the nineteenth century. Whether by choice or necessity, those who replaced the uneven contours of animal bodies with neat rectangles of paper or cloth were participating in the capitalist revaluation of their environments. Many such objects left the reservation altogether, sold for needed cash to traders, tourists, or collectors.[28] Standing Bear's work thus reconstituted the most sacred activities of the tribe for consumption by the very cultural outsiders responsible for their disruption.

But the muslin affected Lakota people and aided the continuation of distinctly Lakota values as well. Amiotte's interviews with his grandmother, Christina Standing Bear (1894–1987), revealed that Standing Bear's artistic process included hosting social gatherings in the family's cabin. The furniture was pushed aside. Guests sat on the floor, smoked pipes, and enjoyed a generous feast while the artist unrolled his yet-unfinished work. A process of verification and storytelling among his age mates would continue late into the night.[29] As art historian Marilee Jantzer-White has underscored, "Meanings were crafted in a nexus of relationships that stressed both pictorial and oral traditions."[30] Notwithstanding their physical departure, artworks remained knit into the cultural fabric of Lakota life through the vestiges of the stories they prompted.

The visual-spiritual dimensions of the muslin also powerfully reframe a unilateral narrative of frontier closure and capitalist assimilation. To discuss these elements, I am indebted to Father Peter J. Powell's detailed scholarship on specific figures and scenes; interpretations of form are mine. The animal-dreamer society dances depicted by Standing Bear took place during a multitribal gathering on the Rosebud Creek prior to the battle. Here, sacred powers bestowed upon humans by animal guardians who visited them in dreams were publicly displayed and tested. Four black-tailed deer and elk dreamers carry sacred hoops that concentrate the power of everything that is *wakan*, or sacred, as expressed in the Lakota phrase *Wakan Tanka*, "the great mysterious."[31] One elk dreamer raises a hoop with a mirror at center to protect himself from a challenger shooting unseen missives. The mirror reflects the bright light of the sun, chief of Wakan Tanka, and exhibits the power to detect and deter ill will.[32] Eagle feathers, horns, and star and cloud symbols adorn the dreamers' headdresses. Such signs, gifted by guardian spirits, were reproduced on clothing and belongings as marks for personal distinction and protection against danger.[33]

The power of these sacred gifts was again tested during the Battle of the Little Bighorn. The details of the four battle scenes that Standing Bear has condensed into a single tableau are recounted elsewhere and are beyond the scope of this essay.[34] I will mention only that the famous last stand of Custer and his command is represented by the relatively ordered line of upright figures at the top of the muslin. The flag-bearing cavalrymen are mainly distinguished from one another by their relative states of demise. In contrast, Standing Bear lavished detail on the decoration of Indigenous persons and horses. Each is "clothed in mystery and power."[35] These tangible marks alert us to the spiritual guardianship that bolstered human agency during the conflict. Their "active power" in turn enlivens industrial cloth and the social contexts from which the object calls forth stories.[36]

At the heart of the muslin (and the matter) is a representation of the Sun Dance lodge, a giant bower of tree branches, animal hides, and tipi poles, with an entrance facing the sunrise. The Sun Dance is held during four days at midsummer when *Unci Maka*, Grandmother Earth, has nurtured plants and animals to maturity. Amiotte, a ritual participant himself, writes:

> In the mythic beginning of the Lakota world, its sacred and temporal dimensions were one, and the Lakota still recognizes himself as a microcosmic reflection of that macrocosm. If he can live in concert with the holy rhythm of that which causes all life to move, he is then assisting in the ongoing process of creation. To maintain his participation in this process, he needs annually to make the journey to the Center of the World, which is the place of his beginning and the origin of all things. There he can renew his relation with the sacred rhythm in the ceremony known as the Sun Dance.[37]

The particular event of 1876 was hosted by the famous Hunkpapa Lakota chief and leader of the resistance, Sitting Bull. He is pictured on the far right with his white horse in full regalia, preparing to offer a sacrifice of flesh and blood to the Sun. Two other men are shown attached by the flesh of their chest to the central pole made of cottonwood.[38] Sometimes denigrated by colonizers as a form of torture, the giving of flesh and blood joins human to the tree, the earth in which it is planted, and the sky toward which it reaches, in a recapitulation of Lakota origins. Amiotte explains, "Inyan, the original rock of the universe . . . opened himself to release his blood which flowed and spread around him in a great disc to form Maka, the Earth."[39] It is while dancing with bloodied arms that Sitting Bull received a prophetic vision of blue-coated soldiers raining from the sky. Standing Bear shows that the premonition was fulfilled during the Battle of the Little Big Horn. The soldiers cascade downhill, or perhaps, given the absence of topography, from the heavens.

The Sun Dance lodge circle—a place of origin and return—guides the entire composition. This "emblem of eternity" and spiritual wholeness is repeated in the tipi camp, in dreamers' hoops and warriors' shields.[40] Standing Bear's use of the circle calls to mind winter counts, Lakota calendars in which pictographic representations of a single important event of each year are arranged in a spiral

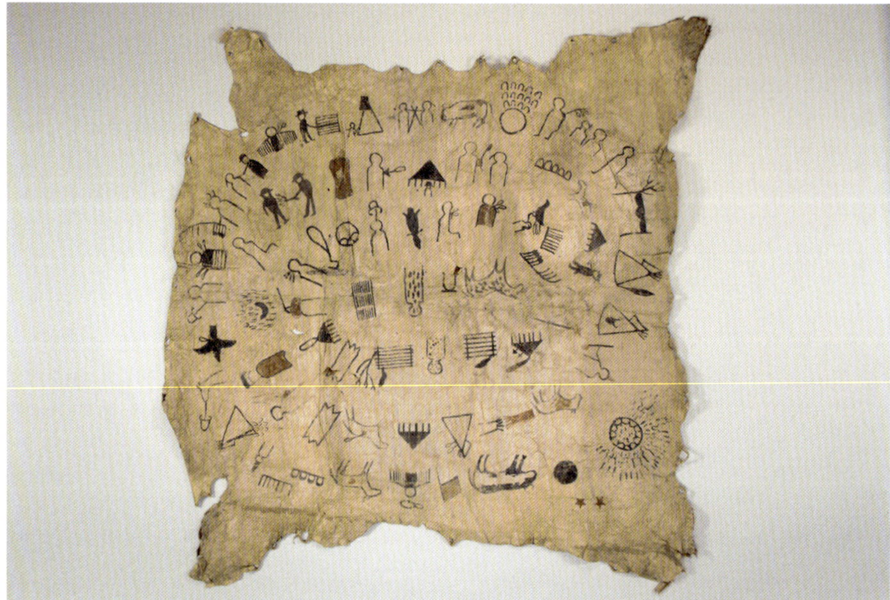

Fig. 10. Lone Dog (Shunka Ishnala), (Nakota [Yankton Sioux]), *Winter Count*, c. 1871. Painted buffalo hide, 102 × 81 ¹/₂ in. (259 × 207 cm). National Museum of the American Indian, Cultural Resource Center. National Museum of the American Indian, Smithsonian Institution (Catalog # 1/617). Photo by NMAI Photo Services

(fig. 10). These mnemonic devices prompt count keepers to forge a relationship between past and present during oratory. As James R. Walker, a physician at Pine Ridge Indian who recorded Lakota peoples' accounts of cultural practices between 1896 and 1914, summarized, "The past is preceded, accompanied, and followed by an ever present, sacred dimension which is outside the realm of human time. . . . The integration of these aspects of history into the telling of the winters was an important duty of the count keeper."[41] Likewise, annual journeys back to the center pattern a nonlinear temporality in which sacred sources of power at once withstand and affect the unfolding of particular events. Taken as a whole, Standing Bear's work clarifies how ceremony powerfully affects human history and its retelling. The animal dreamers' dances legitimized individual gifts of spiritual guardianship; the Sun Dance renewed collective relations to earth and sky and foretold victory; the Battle of the Little Bighorn brought these regenerative and protective forces to bear on a crucial historical-political juncture. Finally, the muslin helps to ensure their transmission, prompting new past-present stories in winters to come.

And what of *Mni Wiconi*, water is life? Viewers familiar with canonical images of the Western landscape by Timothy O'Sullivan, Albert Bierstadt, Thomas Moran, and others will be struck here by the near lack of topographic detail. Notably absent is the horizon line, the compositional element that typically grants viewers a sense of mastery over a vast pictured terrain. Land, which federal survey photographs, paintings, and maps prepared to be objectified, owned, conserved, settled, tilled, mined, or drilled, is not made available as a representation. Only the sinuous parallel lines of the Rosebud and Little Bighorn rivers stand in for physical geography. When asked about the rivers in his great-grandfather's work, Amiotte stressed that his Lakota ancestors had "maps in their heads of the vast territory of the plains," including the locations and names of rivers needed to make good camping decisions.[42] Standing Bear demonstrated a clear grasp of Euro-American cartographic conventions by drawing a map of the battlefield upon request in 1907.[43] Yet the idiosyncratic configuration of the rivers on the muslin indicate that grids and measurements did not interest the artist here. It is neither a landscape nor a map. Instead, rivers appear as dynamic elements that counter the static leanings of the square cloth. They provide a secondary, organic frame around the Sun Dance lodge, creating lines of energy that course to the edges of the muslin. Rivers are also the boundaries that demarcate and unite episodes of ceremony and battle into a compositional and spiritual whole. Lanniko L. Lee of the Oceti Sakowin collective Oak Lake Writers Society described rivers as Earth arteries, "life-giving and healing forces coursing through *Unci Maka*, Grandmother Earth." They are "part of a larger expression of our relationship to everything that is."[44]

Mirrored Shields

Standing Bear's muslin shows that the prayer of interconnectedness, *Mitákuye Oyás'iŋ*, "all our relations," did not transcend the violence of Indian Removal. Rather, it provided a powerful framework for affecting, interpreting, and withstanding colonial ruptures that were then, as they are now, unfinished. As NoDAPL gathered force in 2016, a group of five artists formed the Winter Count collective to create works "in offering to the water protectors, the land and the water."[45] Founding artist Cannupa Hanska Luger, a member of the Mandan, Hidatsa, and Arikara Nation who was born at Standing Rock, distributed mirrored shields made out of Masonite and foil to those on the NoDAPL frontlines

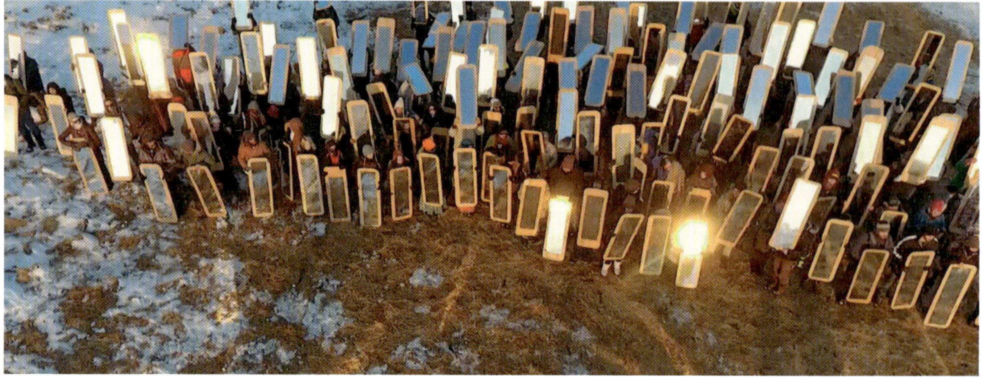

Fig. 11. Rory Wakemup (b. 1976), photo of mirror shields conceived by artist Cannupa Hanska Luger. Water protectors at Oceti Sakowin camp near Standing Rock, North Dakota, 2016

(fig. 11).[46] They reflected back lines of militarized North Dakota police, who appeared like historical reenactors in their very own frontier drama. Authorities in riot gear aimed rubber bullets and water cannons as if to reprise the actions of nineteenth-century cavalrymen who advanced across the land before them. The mirrors thus captured a real-time image of violence unfolding again on the plains. Yet they also concentrated the light and power of the sun to deflect physical and spiritual harm, like the elk dreamer's shield drawn by Standing Bear more than a century earlier. Across the "separation, negativity, and disruption" of ongoing colonization, Luger's protective armament and Standing Bear's prayerful battlefield reflect one another.[47]

I am grateful to Christopher P. Heuer, Rebecca Zorach, and all the organizers and participants involved in the Clark Art Institute conference, "Ecologies, Agents, Terrains," for generating this timely conversation. I thank artists Arthur Amiotte and Cannupa Hanska Luger for generously sharing materials and perspectives. This essay has benefited greatly from Elsa Hoover's cartographic talents. Father Peter J. Powell's scholarship and support were invaluable, as was Kristine Ronan's feedback. Finally, my enduring gratitude goes to Janet Catherine Berlo for including me in her network of relations.

1. A version of the prayer was published in Catherine de Zegher, "arc are ark arm art . . . act!," in *The 18th Biennale of Sydney: all our relations*, ed. Catherine de Zegher and Gerald McMaster (Sydney:

Biennale of Sydney, 2012), 104. See also Winona LaDuke, *All Our Relations: Native Struggles for Land and Life* (Cambridge: South End Press, 1999).

2. Gerald McMaster, "*Ntotemuk*: Commonalities among Great Differences," in *The 18th Biennale of Sydney*, 307. The catalogue also included a reprint of Bruno Latour, "An Attempt at a 'Compositionist Manifesto'," 65–77.

3. Gerald McMaster and Catherine de Zegher, "all our relations," in ibid., 49.

4. Mark Watson, "'Centring the Indigenous,' Postcommodity's Trans-Indigenous Relational Art," *Third Text* 29, no. 3 (2015): 141–54, http://dx.doi.org/10.1080/09528822.2015.1076209 (all websites cited in this essay were accessed November 12, 2017).

5. Kathryn Akipa et al., "Reflections on Mnisose after Lewis and Clark: A Dialogue between Members of the Oak Lake Writers' Society Held at The Birdsong Inn and Guest House, Java, South Dakota, February 12, 2005," in *This Stretch of the River*, ed. Phillip Howe and Kimberly TallBear (Sioux Falls: Pine Hill Press, 2006), 82, 85.

6. See the official website for Idle No More: http://www.idlenomore.ca. On the rise of the global climate justice movement, see Yates McKee, "Art and the Ends of Environmentalism: From Biosphere to the Right to Survival," in *Nongovernmental Politics*, ed. Michel Feher (New York: Zone Books, 2007), 539–83.

7. Nika Knight, "Activists Around the World Take #NoDAPL Fight to the Banks," *Common Dreams*, December 1, 2016, https://www.commondreams.org/news/2016/12/01/activists-around-world-take-nodapl-fight-banks.

8. One arrested participant, Rebecca Zimmerman Hornstein, explains her reasoning: "Whether we say *Wni Miconi* in Lakota or *Va'u Mayim ahd Nefesh* in Hebrew, we follow the Water Protectors because we know the truth all who have survived have known: Water is Life [*sic*]." The incorrect spelling of *Mni Wiconi* is to my point. See "Here's Why I Was Arrested as a Rabbi-in-Training in Solidarity with Standing Rock," *Jewschool: Progressive Jews & Views*, November 7, 2016, https://jewschool.com/2016/11/77979/heres-why-i-took-action-as-a-jew-in-solidarity-with-standing-rock.

9. The following is only a partial list of the scholars who have sought to critique or extend these "turns" in relation to Indigenous arts: Richard William Hill, "The Malice and Benevolence of Inanimate Objects: Jimmie Durham's Anti-Architecture," in *A Matter of Life and Death and Singing*, ed. Anders Kreuger (Antwerp: MUHKA, 2012), 75–83; Richard William Hill, "The Question of Agency in the Art and Writing of Jimmie Durham" (PhD diss., Middlesex University, 2010); Jessica L. Horton and Janet Catherine Berlo, "Beyond the Mirror: Indigenous Ecologies and 'New Materialisms' in Contemporary Art," *Third Text* 27, no. 1 (2013): 17–28; Jessica L. Horton, "Ojibwa *Tableaux Vivants*: George Catlin, Robert Houle, and Transcultural Materialism," *Art History* 39 (February 2016): 124–51; Kim TallBear, "An Indigenous Reflection on Working Beyond the Human/

Not Human," *GLQ: A Journal of Lesbian and Gay Studies* 21, nos. 2–3 (June 2015): 230–35; Zoe Todd, "Indigenizing the Anthropocene," in *Art in the Anthropocene: Encounters among Aesthetics, Politics, Environments and Epistemologies,* ed. Heather Davis and Etienne Turpin (London: Open Humanities Press, 2015): 241–54.

10. Todd also urged that "the current push to challenge the Euro-Western ontological split between nature and culture not obscure the concurrent, ongoing radical questioning and disruption of racism and colonialism." See Zoe Todd, "An Indigenous Feminist's Take on the Ontological Turn: 'ontology' is just another word for colonialism," October 24, 2014, https://zoestodd.com/2014/10/24/an-indigenous-feminists-take-on-the-ontological-turn-ontology-is-just-another-word-for-colonialism. An expanded scholarly essay with the same title was published in the *Journal of Historical Sociology* 29 (March 2016): 4–22.

11. James Nisbet, *Ecologies, Environments, and Energy Systems in Art of the 1960s and 1970s* (Cambridge: MIT Press, 2014), 3.

12. Ibid., 4–5.

13. Sherry Farrell Racette, "Encoded Knowledge: Memory and Objects in Contemporary Native American Art," in *Manifestations: New Native Art Criticism,* ed. Nancy Mithlo (Santa Fe: Museum of Contemporary Native Arts, 2011), 41.

14. Nick Estes, "Fighting for Our Lives: #NoDAPL in Historical Context," *The Red Nation,* September 18, 2016, https://therednation.org/2016/09/18/fighting-for-our-lives-nodapl-in-context.

15. Quoted in Amy Goodman, "Native American Activist Winona LaDuke at Standing Rock: It's Time to Move on from Fossil Fuels," Democracy Now!, Sept. 12, 2016, https://www.democracynow.org/2016/9/12/native_american_activist_winona_laduke.

16. See https://nycstandswithstandingrock.wordpress.com/standingrocksyllabus.

17. G. A. Custer, "The Black Hills: Official Report of General Custer News of the Expedition up to August 15th," *St. Paul Press,* August 23, 1874, reprinted in Herbert Krause and Gary D. Olson, eds., *Prelude to Glory: A Newspaper Accounting of Custer's 1874 Expedition to The Black Hills* (Sioux Falls: Brevet Press, 1974), 246. For more on the importance of the Black Hills to Oceti Sakowin history and thought, as well as relevant historical treaties, see Craig Howe, Lydia Whirlwind Soldier, and Lanniko L. Lee, eds., *He Sapa Woihanble: Black Hills Dream* (St. Paul, Minn.: Living Justice Press, 2011).

18. For a broader history of Oceti Sakowin anticolonial struggles, see Jeffrey Ostler, *The Plains Sioux and U.S. Colonialism from Lewis and Clark to Wounded Knee* (Cambridge: Cambridge University Press, 2004).

19. "Trump Signs Dakota Pipeline Orders," *Associated Press,* January 24, 2017, https://www.nytimes.com/video/us/politics/100000004891031/trump-signs-dakota-pipeline-orders.html.

20. Estes, "Fighting for Our Lives: #NoDAPL in Historical Context."

21. Louis S. Warren, "Prelude: The Life of Standing Bear," in Arthur Amiotte, Louis S. Warren, and Janet Catherine Berlo, *Transformation and Continuity in Lakota Culture: The Collages of Arthur Amiotte, 1988–2014* (Pierre: South Dakota State Historical Society Press, 2014), 3–5.

22. John G. Neihardt, *Black Elk Speaks* (1932; Lincoln: University of Nebraska Press, 2014). An inventory of all known Standing Bear works appears in in Amiotte, Warren, and Berlo, *Transformation and Continuity in Lakota Culture*, 23.

23. The work is discussed in Janet Catherine Berlo, "Giving Voice to the Ancestors through Art: Hybridity, Memory, and Imagination in Arthur Amiotte's Collage Series," in Amiotte, Warren, and Berlo, *Transformation and Continuity in Lakota Culture*, 54.

24. Father Peter J. Powell, "Sacrifice Transformed into Victory: Standing Bear Portrays Sitting Bull's Sun Dance and the Final Summer of Lakota Freedom," in *Visions of the People: A Pictorial History of Plains Indian Life*, ed. Evan M. Maurer, exh. cat. (Minneapolis: Minneapolis Institute of Arts, 1993), 82; Elbridge Ayer Burbank, *Burbank among the Indians*, ed. Frank J. Taylor (1944; Harvard Diggins Library and Caxton Press, 1972).

25. Janet Catherine Berlo, *Spirit Beings and Sun Dancers: Black Hawk's Vision of the Lakota World* (New York: Braziller, 2000), 40, 18.

26. Janet Catherine Berlo and Arthur Amiotte, "Generosity, Trade, and Reciprocity among the Lakota: Three Moments in Time," in *Plains Indian Art of the Early Reservation Era: The Donald Danforth Jr. Collection at the Saint Louis Art Museum*, ed. Jill Ahlberg Yohe and Janet Catherine Berlo (St. Louis: St. Louis Art Museum, 2016), 32, 48–50.

27. N. Scott Momaday, *Way to Rainy Mountain* (Albuquerque: University of New Mexico Press, 1969), 10.

28. See Janet Catherine Berlo, "Drawing and Being Drawn In: The Late Nineteenth-Century Plains Graphic Artist and the Intercultural Encounter," in *Plains Indian Drawings, 1865–1935: Pages from a Visual History*, ed. Janet Catherine Berlo (New York: Harry N. Abrams, 1996), 12–18, and other essays in that volume for an overview.

29. Arthur Amiotte, "A Journey of Discovery: Standing Bear's Artwork," in Amiotte, Warren, and Berlo, *Transformation and Continuity in Lakota Culture*, 14.

30. Marilee Jantzer-White, "Narrative and Landscape in the Drawings of Etahdleuh Doanmoe," in *Plains Indian Drawings, 1865–1935*, 51.

31. William K. Powers, *Oglala Religion* (Lincoln: University of Nebraska Press, 1975), 45–47.

32. Powell, "Sacrifice Transformed into Victory," 85. See also Clark Wissler, "Societies and Ceremonial Associations in the Oglala Division of the Teton-Dakota," *Anthropological Papers of the American Museum of Natural History* 11, Societies of the Plains Indians (New York: The American

Museum of Natural History, 1916), 87–88.

33. Helen H. Blish, *A Pictographic History of the Oglala Sioux* (Lincoln: University of Nebraska Press, 1967), 63.

34. Sandra L. Brizée-Bowen, *For All to See: The Little Bighorn Battle in Plains Indian Art* (Spokane: Arthur H. Clark Company, 2003), 143–57; Powell, "Sacrifice Transformed into Victory"; Rodney G. Thomas, *Rubbing Out Long Hair (Pehin Hanska Kasota): The American Indian Story of the Little Big Horn in Art and Word* (Spanaway, Wash.: Elk Plain Press, 2009), 183–97.

35. Blish, *A Pictographic History of the Oglala Sioux*, 83.

36. Ibid., 62.

37. Arthur Amiotte, "The Lakota Sun Dance: Historical and Contemporary Perspectives," in *Sioux Indian Religion*, ed. Raymond J. DeMallie and Douglas R. Parks (Norman: University of Oklahoma Press, 1987), 46.

38. Powell, "Sacrifice Transformed into Victory," 91–92.

39. Amiotte, "The Lakota Sun Dance," 50.

40. Vine Deloria Jr., *Singing for a Spirit: A Portrait of the Dakota Sioux* (Santa Fe: Clear Light Publishing, 1999), 33.

41. James R. Walker, *Lakota Society*, ed. Raymond J. DeMallie (Lincoln: University of Nebraska Press, 1982), 113.

42. Arthur Amiotte, conversation with the author, May 1, 2017.

43. This map accompanied an interview between Eli S. Ricker and Standing Bear on March 12, 1907, in Manderson, South Dakota. The annotations are by Ricker. See Michael N. Donahue, *Drawing Battle Lines: The Map Testimony of Custer's Last Fight* (El Segundo, Calif.: Upton and Sons, 2009), 184.

44. Quoted in Oak Lake Writers, "Reflections on Mnisose after Lewis and Clark," in *This Stretch of the River*, 79.

45. The current artists are Cannupa Hanska Luger, Dylan Mclaughlin, Ginger Dunnill, Merritt Johnson, and Nicholas Galanin. See their first short video work, *We Are in Crisis*, 2016, viewable and downloadable for free on Vimeo: https://vimeo.com/187762675. Winter Count is conceived as an open-ended series of collaborations that will continue to incorporate new partners (Cannupa Hanska Luger, conversation with the author, May 2, 2017).

46. Luger would like to thank Jack Becker from Forecast Public Art for helping bring Mirror Shields to Standing Rock, North Dakota, along with Rory Wakemup at All My Relations Arts in Minneapolis, Minnesota, who facilitated a workshop, hosting Luger as guest artist for the Mirror Shield Project (Cannupa Hanska Luger, email to the author, May 9, 2017). For more information, see the artist's website: http://www.cannupahanska.com. See also Carolina A. Miranda, "The

Artist Who Made Protestors' Mirrored Shields Says the 'Struggle Porn' Media Miss Point of Standing Rock," *Los Angeles Times*, January 12, 2017, http://www.latimes.com/entertainment/arts/ miranda/la-et-cam-cannupa-hanska-luger-20170112-story.html. For more on contemporary art and activism during and beyond NoDAPL, see T.J. Demos, "The Great Transition: The Arts and Radical System Change," *e-flux Architecture*, April 12, 2017, http://www.e-flux.com/architecture/ accumulation/122305/the-great-transition-the-arts-and-radical-system-change.

47. McMaster and de Zegher, "all our relations," 49.

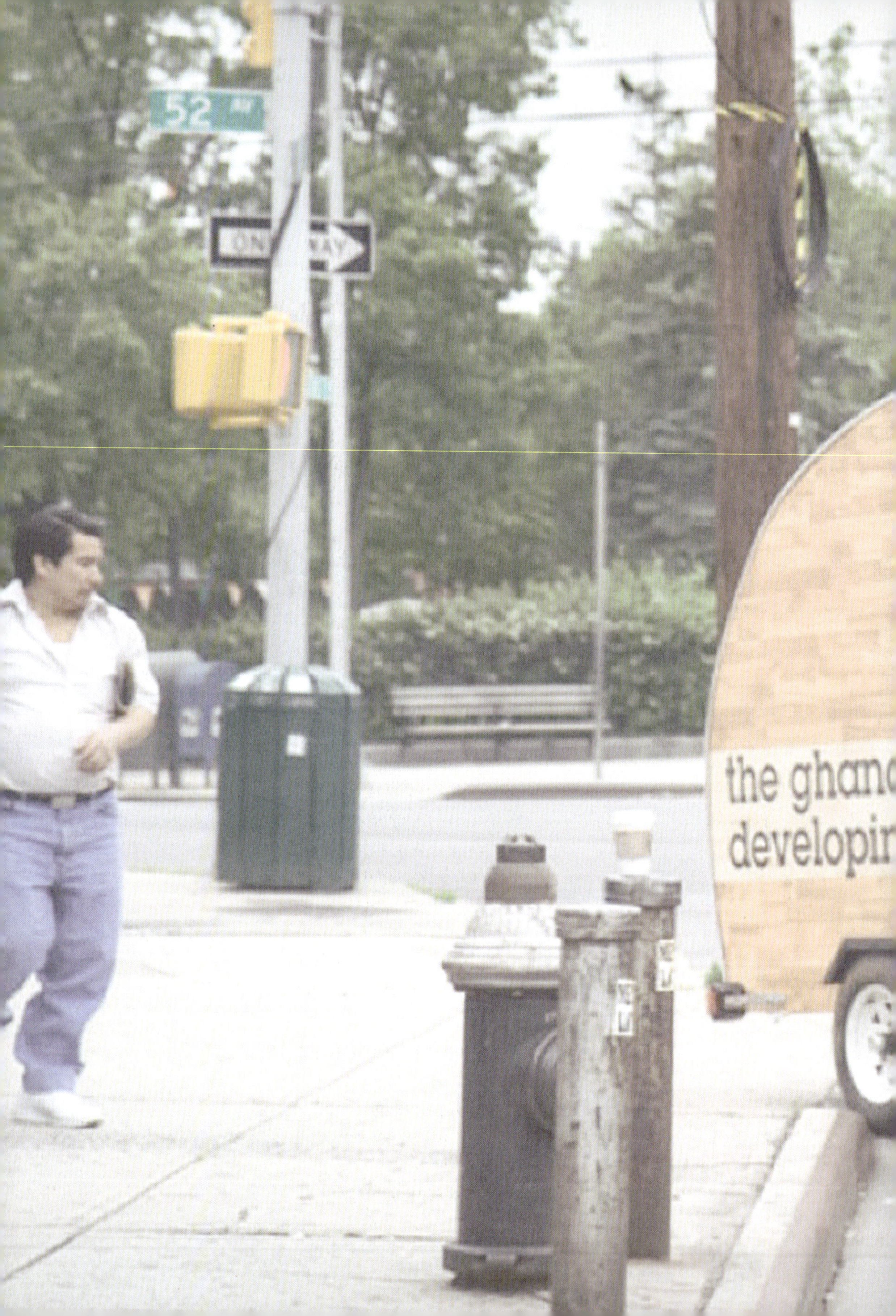
52
ONE WAY
the ghan
developin

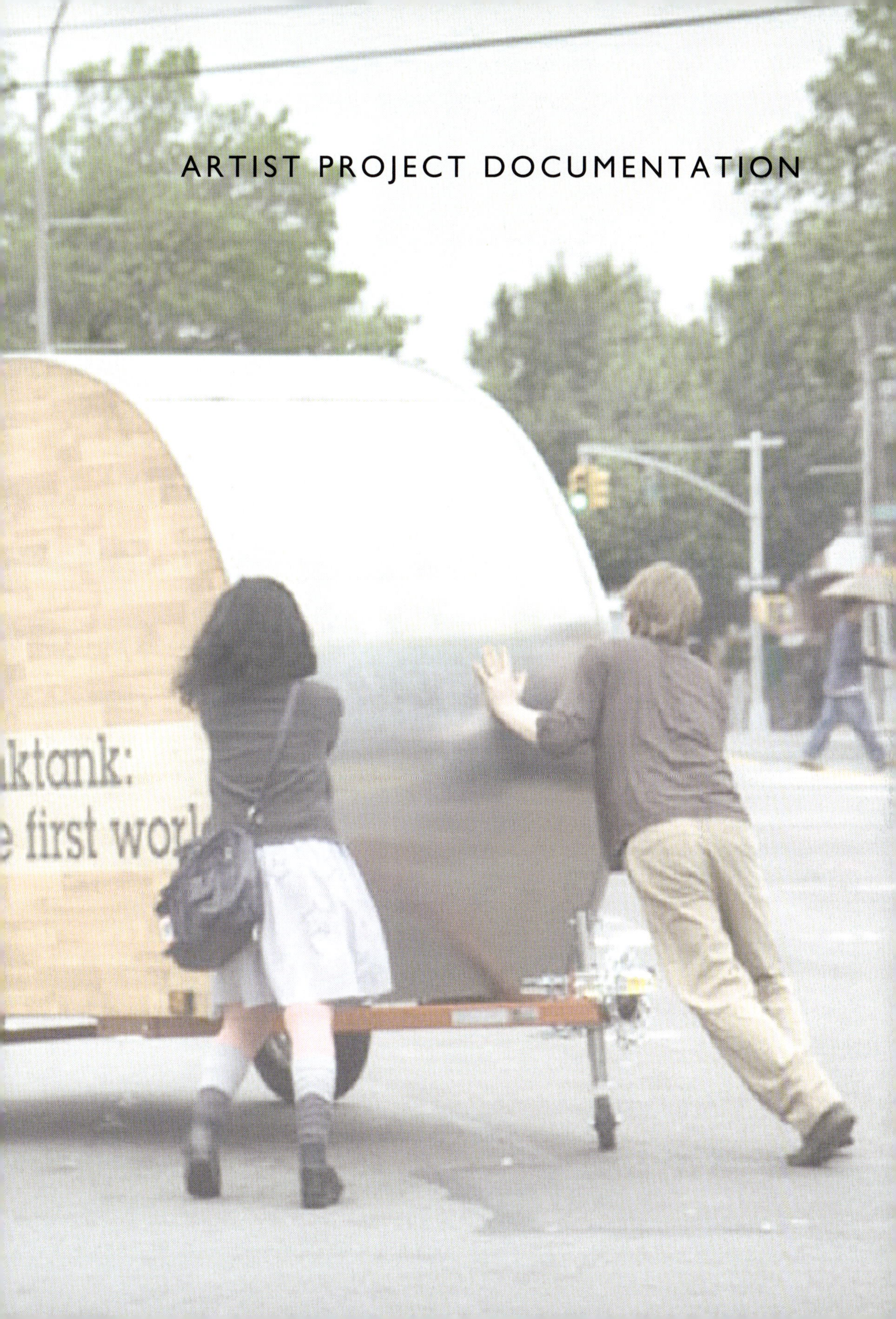
ARTIST PROJECT DOCUMENTATION

Talking About the Man in the Moon, Combating Climate Change with Art

Ghana ThinkTank, Sonnet Coggins, and Terence Washington

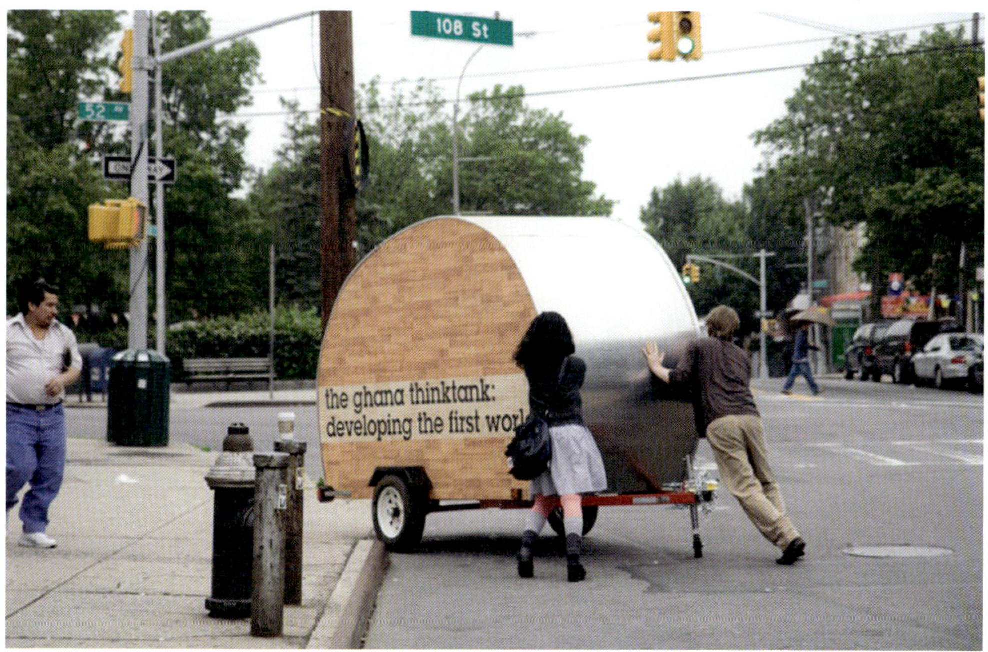

Fig. 1 (and detail, pp. 94–95). The Ghana ThinkTank teardrop trailer on its maiden voyage, Corona, Queens, New York, 2010

The mission of the Ghana ThinkTank (GTT) is to develop the "First World."

During the 1990s, each of the three core members of Ghana ThinkTank (John Ewing, Carmen Montoya, and Christopher Robbins) worked on the fringes of international development and saw how the wrong solutions to the wrong problems could—even with the best intentions—cause more harm than good. Ghana ThinkTank began as a response to the hubris and paternalism of international development models that often assume that "White is right" and "West is best," discounting the wealth of knowledge of people living in other parts of the world.

In 2006, we founded the Ghana ThinkTank. Our goal was to flip this power dynamic through art-based interventions. We began the process by setting up a simple dichotomy: powerful/powerless, First World/Third World. We then flipped that assumed power imbalance, asking the "powerful," or "First World," participants to seek help from the "powerless," or "Third World," participants. We started by collecting problems in the so-called First World, and then sent them to think tanks in the so-called Developing World to be solved by a network of citizen think tanks.

We found that asking for help immediately elevated the "Third World" think-tank members to the level of resource and acknowledged that they could make an important contribution. Our vow to the think tanks: implement their solutions whether they strike us as brilliant or impractical.

Ghana ThinkTank creates an intercultural mirroring process. As the problems collected in a community are compiled, an image of that community begins to emerge. Consider it a portrait in discontent. Participants are able to view the problems and learn about problems they didn't realize existed in their community or connect with the experiences of others who share the same problems. After the problems are sent to the think tanks, which then return their analyses, participants once again get a sense of what they "look like," this time through the eyes of others. Finally, as we all come together again to implement solutions, we see ourselves again, as resourceful—"game," as they say, to make a change.

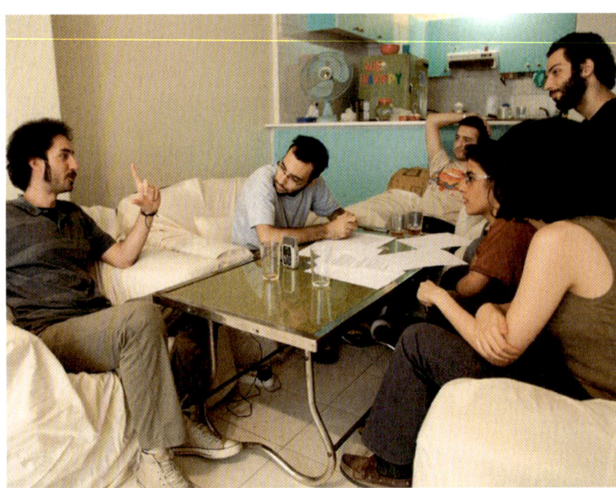

Fig. 2. The think tank in Tehran, Iran, 2009

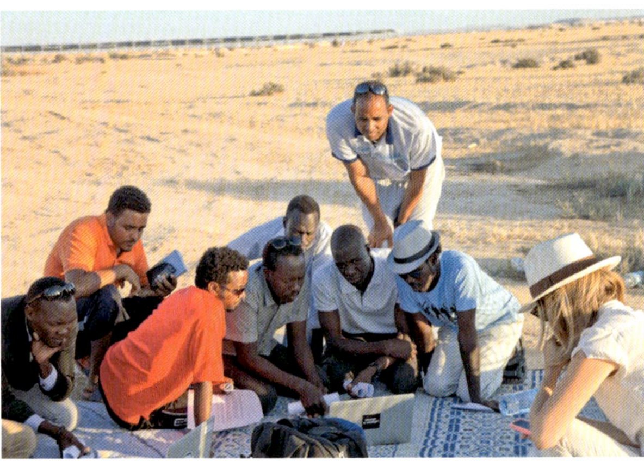

Fig. 3. The Sudanese think tank. Israeli internment camp, Negev Desert, Israel, 2014

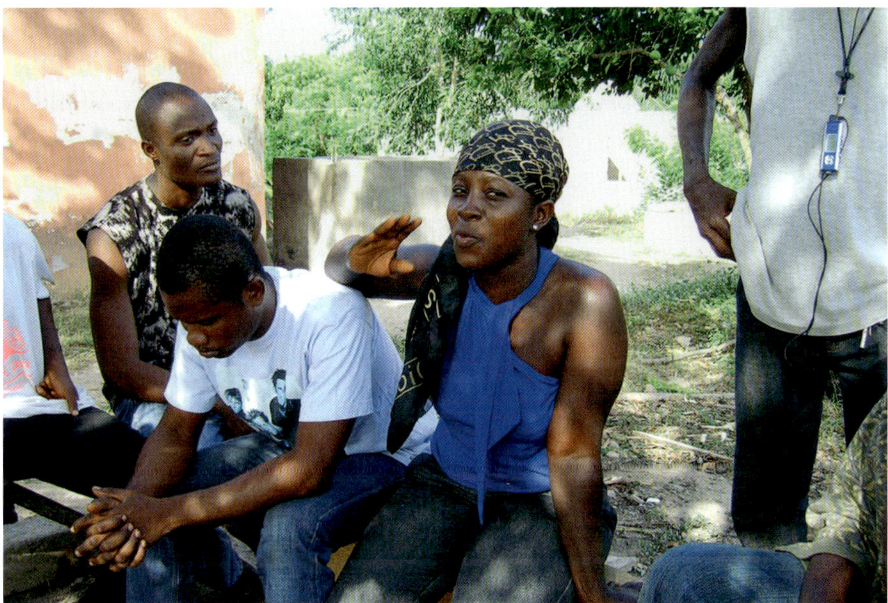

Fig. 4. The think tank in Kokrobitey, Ghana, 2006

The first think tanks were set up in Ghana, Cuba, and El Salvador. In the decade since, the international network of think tanks has expanded to include:

- an artist collective living in Tehran, Iran
- a group of medical students in Gaza
- Sudanese refugees seeking asylum in Israel
- incarcerated teenage girls in the United States
- a team of bike mechanics in Ghana
- a radical rural radio station in El Salvador
- recently deported immigrants in Tijuana, Mexico
- Lifepatch—a citizen initiative in art, science, and technology, in Jogyakarta, Indonesia
- a group of artists, designers, and artisans in Morocco

Coggins and Washington invited Ghana ThinkTank to work with the Williams College Museum of Art (WCMA) as part of Confronting Climate Change, an initiative at Williams committed to "[making] anthropogenic climate change a campus-wide theme of inquiry" for the 2016–17 school year. The effort to confront climate change consisted mainly of public talks and seminars and new course offerings, but we wanted to ensure that art was included among the modes of inquiry undertaken by the college. Ghana ThinkTank's work captured WCMA's imagination in part because it is, by design, intensely anthropocentric: its concern is people and how we relate to one another. Even more importantly, GTT's method is designed to throw a spotlight on ideological blind spots and to encourage participants to embrace discomfort caused by such a bald look at the underpinnings of our culture. By weathering the discomfort and engaging in face-to-face conversations with members of our publics, we began to perceive and to think about WCMA and Williams—and the people within and outside those institutions—much more critically. At WCMA, we had to reconsider how we operate and become more comfortable with uncertainty as we facilitated GTT's activities. That sort of reflection is a function of working with art, which embraces the questioning of its premises. Of all the elements of Confronting Climate Change on campus, WCMA's collaboration with GTT was the only one that called attention to the nature and quality of the College's collective looking at this critical issue of our time.

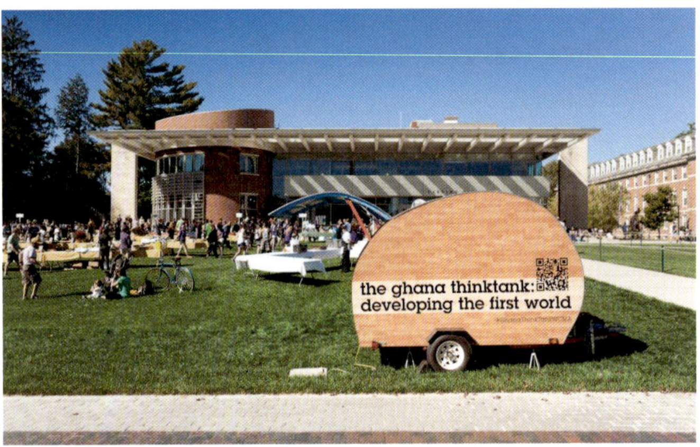

Fig. 5. The newly restored teardrop trailer collecting problems in front of Paresky Center, Williams College, Williamstown, Massachusetts, 2016

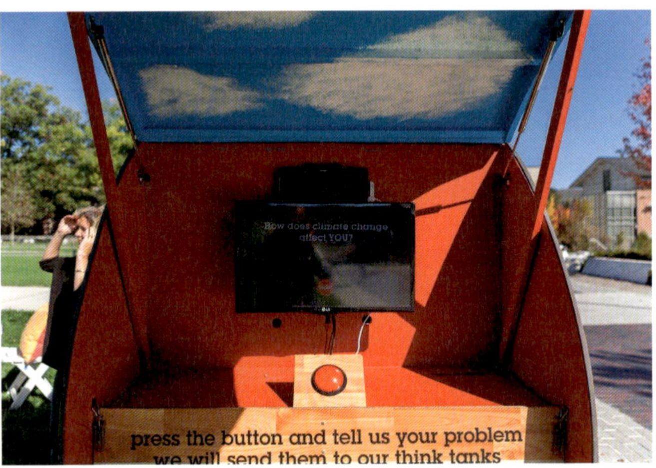

Fig. 6. Got a problem? Press the big red button! Williams College, Williamstown, Massachusetts, 2016

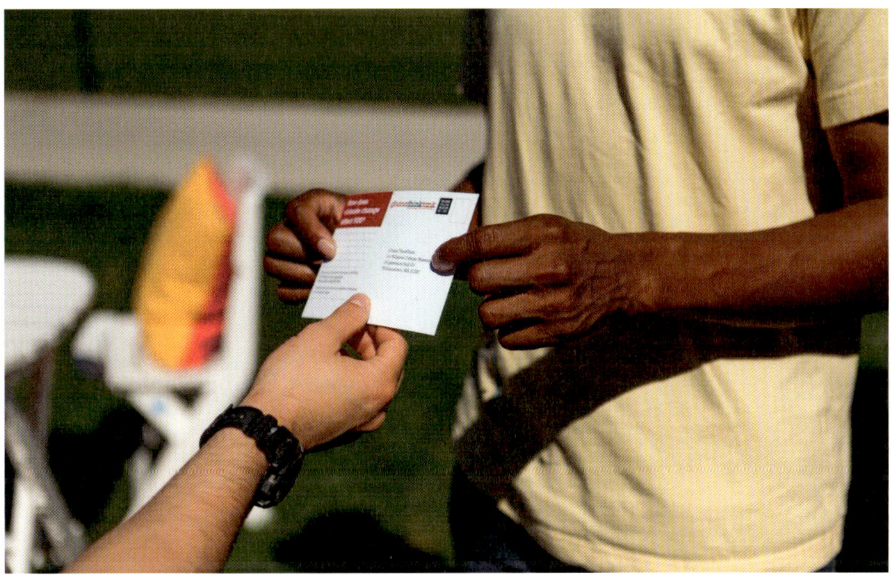

Fig. 7. Terence Washington, Action Team co-leader, presenting a card to a student at Williams College, Williamstown, Massachusetts, 2016

GTT and WCMA engaged in a yearlong collaboration in which problems related to climate change were collected in the Berkshires and sent to think tanks in Indonesia and Morocco, two countries already grappling with the day-to-day realities of climate change.

Using a customized teardrop trailer, Ghana ThinkTank and the members of the Williams College Action Team traveled throughout the Williams campus and the surrounding communities, asking: "How does climate change affect you?"

The trailer was equipped with an automated video dropbox allowing participants to record messages to the think tanks.

People who were a little shy or wanted time to craft their response could participate by filling out a "problem card."

Responses ranged from the personal to the societal, from silly to serious:

- Party/drinking culture is unsustainable with recycling, especially when it comes to picking up their beer cans/bottles.
- I feel so blessed to live in a place where my soul is fed by northern winters. So the lack of beautiful snow is deeply affecting my psyche—which seems trivial!
- We live in a *right now* generation and we need to meditate on our future generation and the impact it will have on them.

- I feel incapable of making accurate calculations about the consequences my choices have on the planet on a daily basis.
- I worry that my beach house will be flooded.
- Basically destroyed my parents' farm.
- Warmer winters with lack of snow affects amount of water—causes shortages. Warmer weather doesn't kill ticks, bugs, etc. Can cause more Lyme disease—is it safe to go outside?

Out of the over two hundred problems collected, we worked with WCMA to select eight to send to the think tanks.

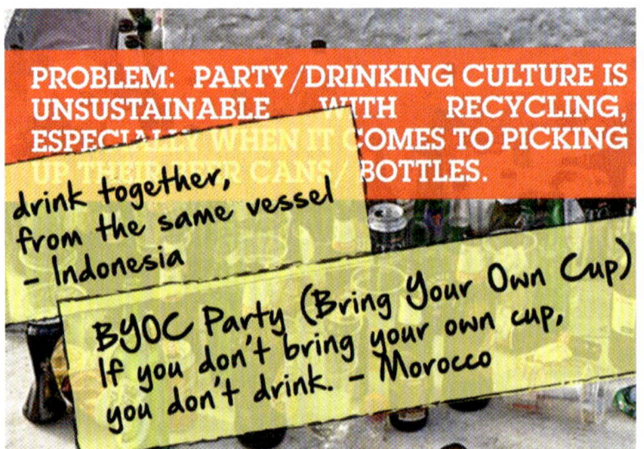

Fig. 8. Think tanks in Indonesia and Morocco respond to problems collected in Williamstown.

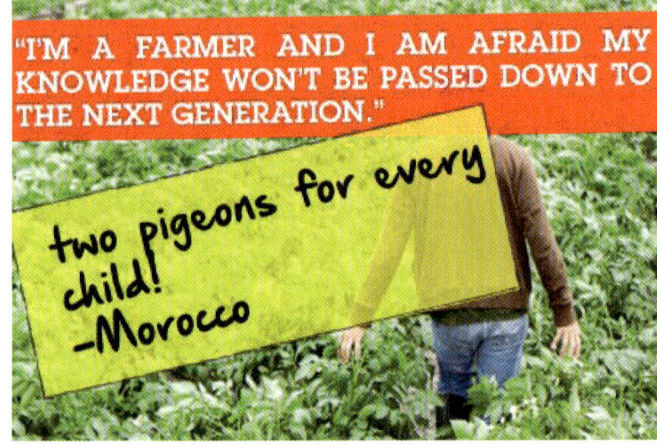

Fig. 9. The Moroccan think tank responds to the problem of disappearing knowledge.

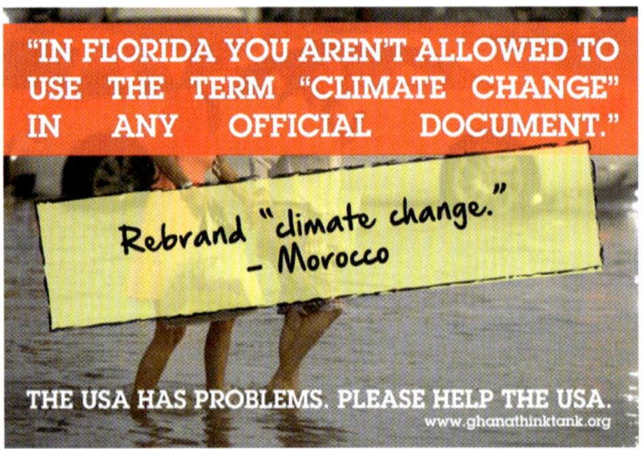

Fig. 10. The Moroccan think tank responds to the problem of censorship around climate change.

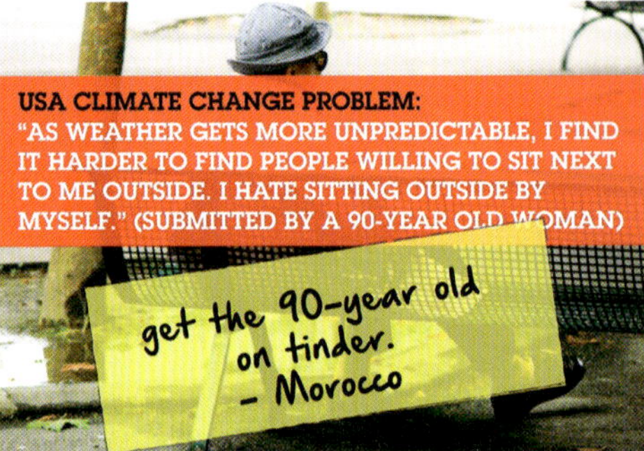

Fig. 11. The Moroccan think tank believes in using technology to combat the social isolation caused by climate change.

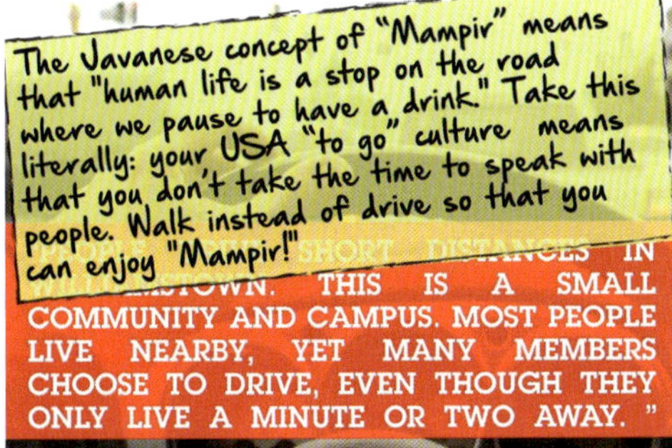

Fig. 12. The Indonesian think tank responds to US car culture.

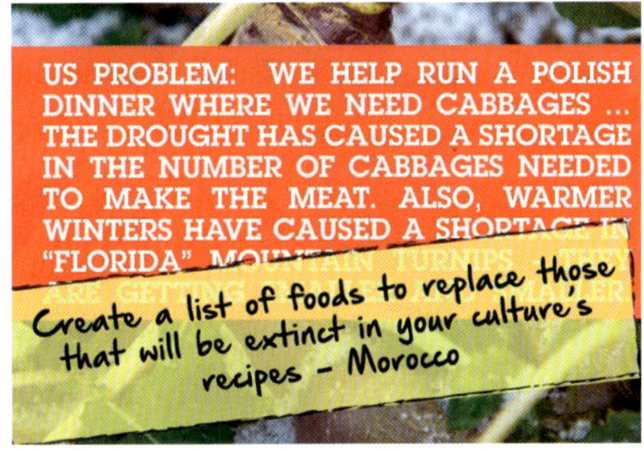

Fig. 13. The Moroccan think tank responds to the shift in culinary choices caused by climate change.

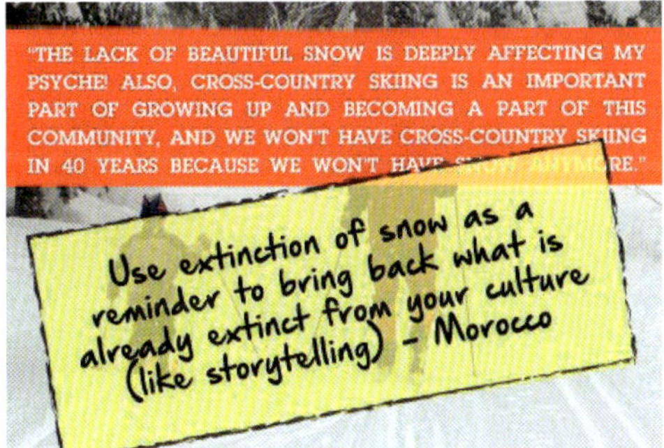

Fig. 14. The Moroccan think tank prompts broad reflection on what has been lost due to shifts in human culture.

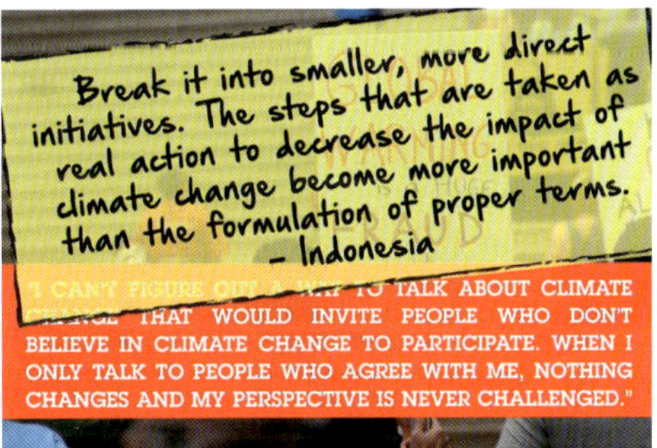

Fig. 15. The Indonesian think tank reminds Americans that actions speak louder than words.

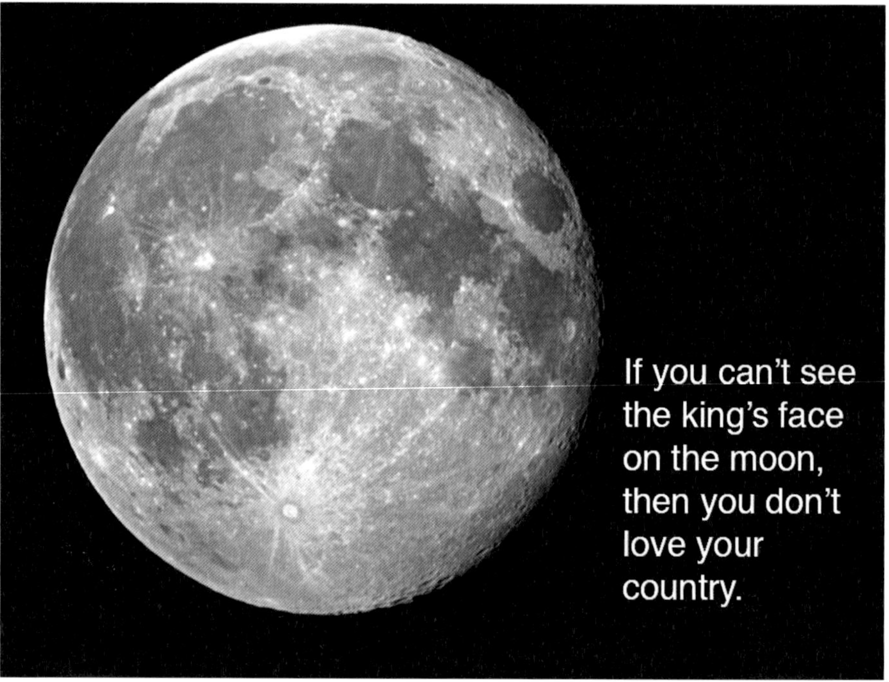

Fig. 16. The Moroccan think tank uses allegory to help explain the complexity of climate change communication.

This was the first time we were able to bring think tanks to the host community, and this created an opportunity for face-to-face clarification of ideas and a deeper conversation about solutions than ever before. For example, "In Florida," one of the problems stated, "you aren't allowed to use the term 'climate change' in any official document." Obviously, the prohibition of certain terms affects the character of debate on the issue in the state government. At face value, Morocco's solution was quite straightforward: rebrand climate change. But as they provided more detail, we began to realize that what they were suggesting was not a cynical or strategic update of language, but a consideration of what is sacrosanct, unspoken, or triggering in the almost tribal beliefs around climate change today.

To illustrate this distinction, the think tank in Morocco talked about a story from the 1950s. In 1953, when King Mohammed V was deposed to Madagascar, many Moroccan citizens believed that they could see his face in the moon, proof for them that he was still looking out for them, even after French colonial interference. As one think tank member put it, "It is a very very very terrible thing even today to doubt that his face was on the moon." While the members of the think tank do not believe the story, their grandparents do, and it is still a sacrosanct issue. How can one address such an issue: something that is clearly factual to one group of people, while laughably dubious to others?

The think tank members offered the following story. Decades later, they recalled a Moroccan television program—a skit show something like *Saturday Night Live*—that found a way to address this divide of belief. A man appeared on an ersatz interview show dressed as King Mohammed V. At one point, the interviewer asked if the king really believed that the United States had landed on the moon, or if it was just a Stanley Kubrick fabrication, as many people say. The man dressed as the king responded that of course this is not true. "Moroccans, as we all know, were the first people ever to go to the moon."

This example contrasted two national stories—stories some people believe are fairy tales—and tied humor and sarcasm to nationalist myth-making as a way to begin a conversation between people who do not share beliefs about the basic tenets of that conversation.

The Moroccan think tank was proposing a parallel between climate change and the story of the moon king. Climate change belief has become something of a tribal signifier in the United States; one's beliefs about climate change define important aspects of identity. The think tank was asking us to consider how we could talk about climate change when the term itself is sacrosanct to some, and triggering to others. How can "believers" and "deniers" speak about climate change when its very existence is, to some, a false premise?

Indonesia's solution: "Break it into smaller, more direct initiatives. The steps that are taken as real action to decrease the impact of climate change become more important than the formulation of proper terms." The Indonesian

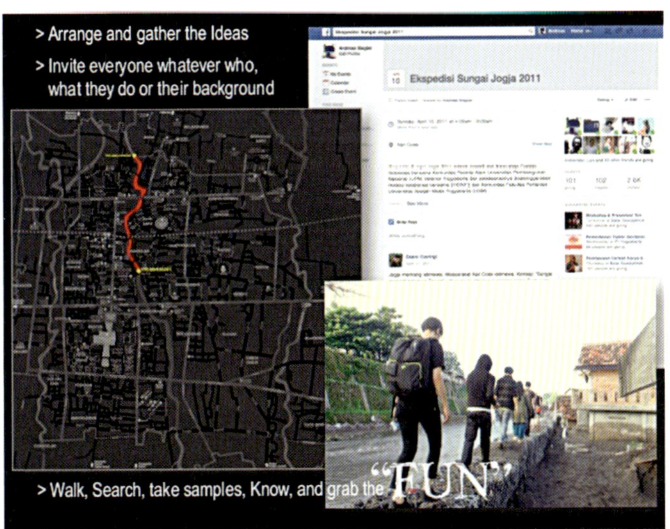

Fig. 17. The Indonesian think tank reminded Americans that climate change activism can be fun.

think tank offered some more details in process (and in politics) by describing a river project they began in Jogyakarta, Indonesia. The think tank discovered that the Jogyakarta River, which provided water for cleaning, fishing, and drinking for many villages, had become incredibly polluted, and that the Indonesian government was largely responsible. Straightforward publicizing and questioning of the government's behavior was not an option in a political climate as controlled and tense as Indonesia's. The think tank's nonprofit status could have been revoked, or much worse. In the past, political activists have been imprisoned and beaten for peaceful political protests.

Since the think tank could not simply report on the pollution of the river, they organized science lessons and river walks in which children tested plants and water samples from the river. This was a way to bury the lede and publicize damaging government policy while seeming to focus on harmless, photogenic activities. They drew parallels between their river project and our problem with discourse, urging us to focus less on the language around climate change (if "climate change" itself is a problematic term for some, then don't use it), and instead target behaviors and actions that point to specific recognizable impacts.

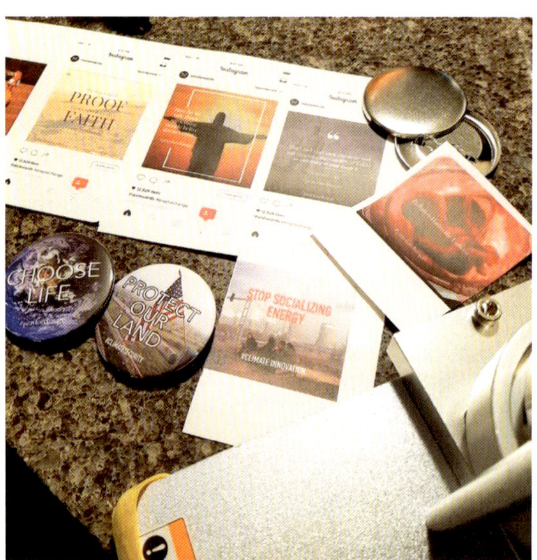

Fig. 18. Ghana ThinkTank's climate change messaging incorporating right-wing themes.

Taken together, we have the Indonesian think tank asking us to "thin slice" climate change by looking at specific impacts and aspects of the debate. And we have the Moroccan think tank exhorting us to use humor and self-deprecation as a way to acknowledge that our own liberal, progressive belief systems are probably not the best way to connect with beliefs of typically conservative climate-change skeptics.

How did GTT and WCMA apply the lessons from the think tanks? We began by trying to understand climate change from belief systems other than our own, so we immersed ourselves in media of the right and center-right (including the Drudge Report, the Ricochet Podcast, and the National Review) and interviewed people who do not believe climate change is caused by human activity on the planet. We considered what it could mean to "rebrand" climate change and drew heavily from typical American corporate marketing strategies, creating slogans and printing them on items such as drink coozies and wearables like T-shirts, ball caps, and buttons.

We are bleeding-heart lefties, so this can get pretty uncomfortable! The goal is to inhabit *their* political views, not our own, to make our points. This phase of the project has become liberals teaching liberals how to talk about climate change according to the belief systems of conservatives. While this sometimes takes the form of written primers on conservative talking points that can be used to discuss climate change, we illustrated the idea with language and images that create a cognitive dissonance—pairing "Choose Life," an anti-abortion slogan, with a picture of the Earth, for example.

We asked people for help making climate-change buttons with right-wing or anti-abortion slogans—and they did it. And by thinking through the stakes of trying to utilize political rhetoric with

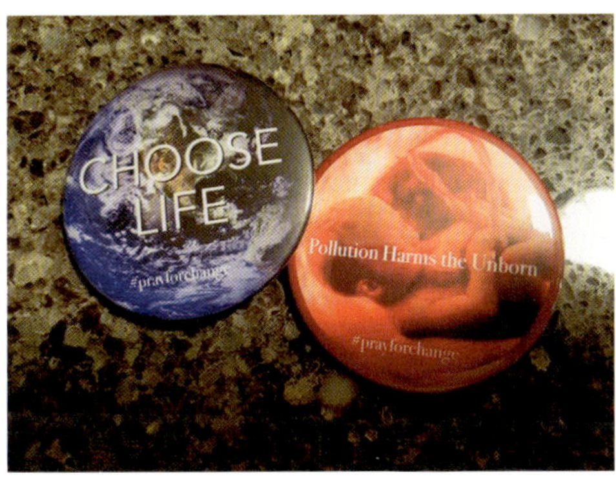

Fig. 19. Climate change buttons incorporating right-wing themes.

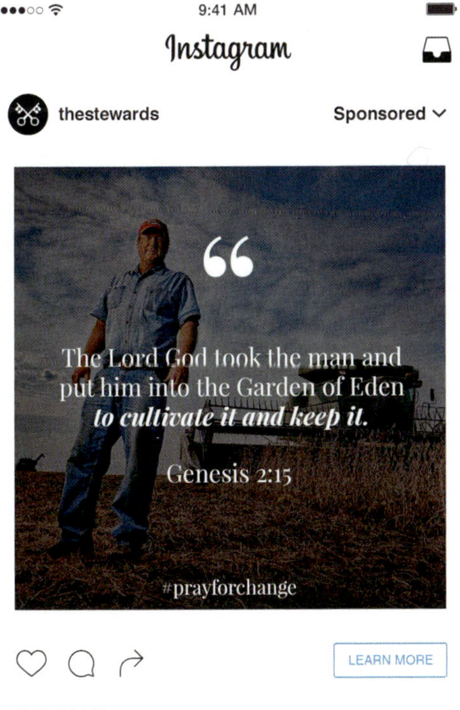

Fig. 20. Ghana ThinkTank delved into right-wing social media to try to understand their perspectives.

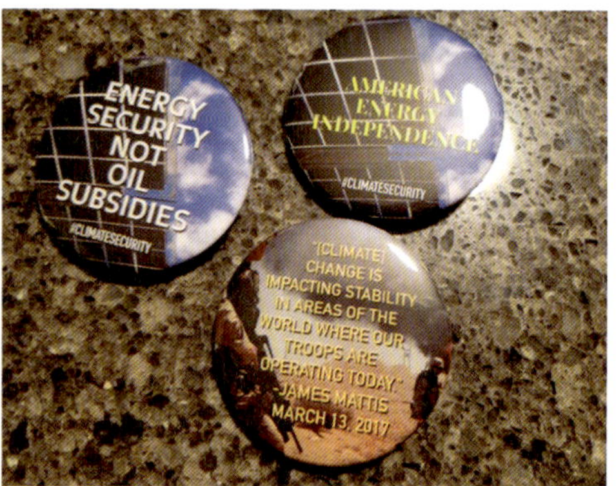

Fig. 21. Several climate change buttons incorporating right-wing themes were created using ideas generated at a workshop during the "Ecologies, Agents, Terrains" conference at the Clark

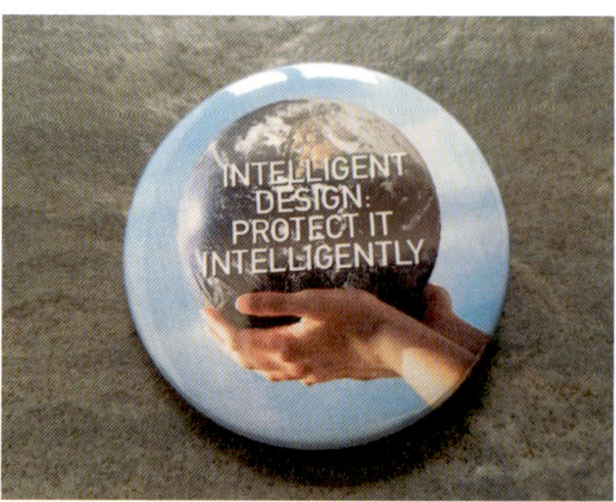

Fig. 22. A climate change button incorporating a right-wing theme

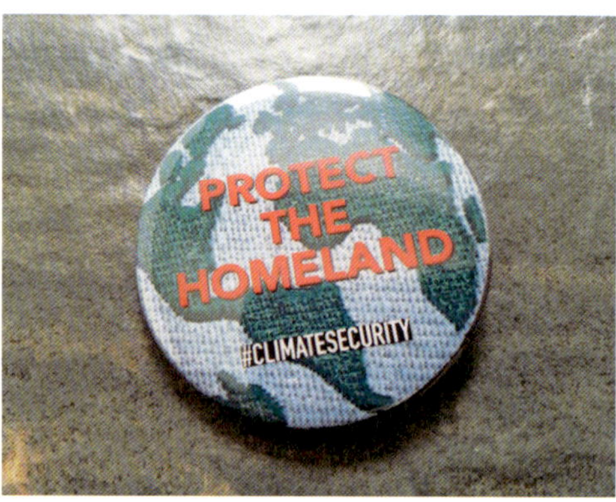

Fig. 23. A climate change button incorporating the theme of homeland security

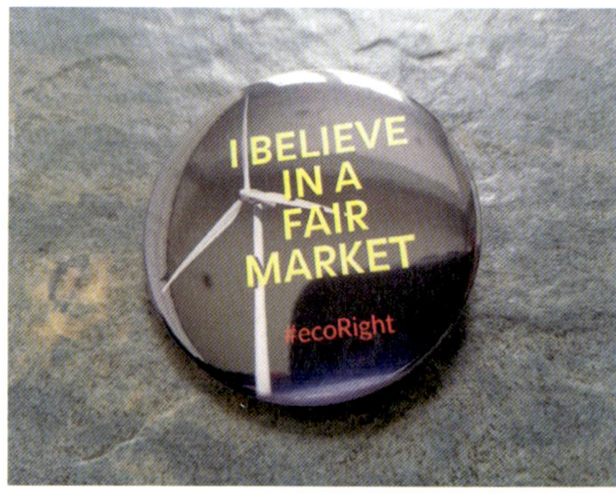

Fig. 24. A climate change button incorporating the theme of free market capitalism

Fig. 25. A climate change button incorporating the theme of free market capitalism

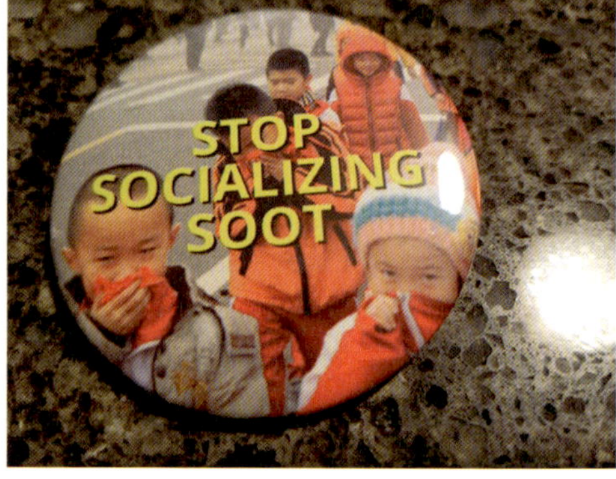

Fig. 26. A climate change button incorporating multiple right-wing perspectives

which they didn't agree, they helped lay the groundwork for confronting climate change by tackling the more fundamental issue of communication. Making the buttons was only one of several actions that took WCMA out of its comfort zone into a realm of decentralized, unscripted, and often disruptive activities. Other parts of the college's efforts to confront climate change—among them, seminars, public talks, and new course offerings—tended to have like-minded individuals conversing with one another. The project with GTT, by contrast, forced everyone who encountered it to deal with our differences. From having conversations with people who didn't believe in climate change to researching political positions opposed to our own, we were asked to consider difference as a possible starting point on a path toward deeper connection with those around us.

There are certainly risks in repurposing concepts that fly in the face of the ideals we hold dear. Will climate change action built on free market principles continue to help the US government opt out of direct support for its citizens in need? Will national security narratives further jingoistic tendencies? Must we stop protecting a woman's right to choose in order to convince more people that we are destroying our planet?

More to the point, is this campaign truly a distillation of the think tanks' solutions? A relationship with a grandparent was at stake in denying the king's face was on the moon. Incorporating a politically touchy issue into science projects with children is very different from wrapping it in the flesh of unborn fetuses, though in both instances the think tanks place importance on the optics of their arguments with respect to who they aim to persuade. In seeking to execute the directive of the Other, we are crafting language that sticks in our throats. Are we inadvertently endorsing causes we do not believe in, hoping that it will help promote a cause we do support? Does what we have made allow us to understand anything at all about the worldview of climate change deniers?

The challenge is how to maintain the humor, fun, and effectiveness of communicating with ideological opponents while illuminating the problematics of the power play inherent in the exchange. We are continuing to hone this work into other ways of thinking and to devise effective strategies for reaching across the divide.

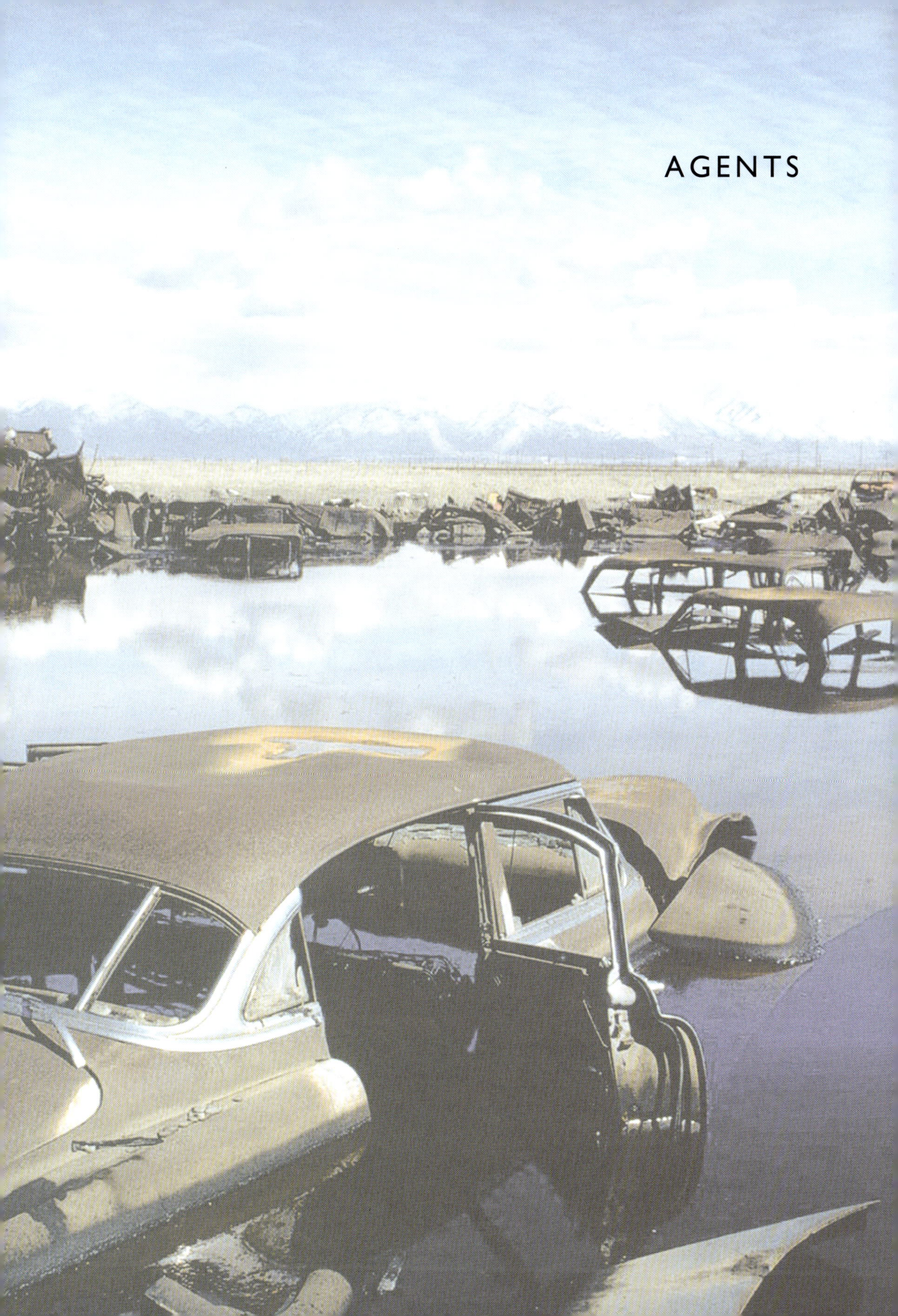
AGENTS

Premodern Geosphere: Nature's Workshop, Treasure House, and Deep Time

Robert Felfe

Song for Coal, an art project by Nick Crowe and Ian Rawlinson, was presented at the Yorkshire Sculpture Park in 2015 (fig. 1). The presentation combined a video installation in an eighteenth-century neo-Gothic chapel with the performance of a chorale, specifically arranged for this occasion.[1] Within the ornamental structure of a flamboyant rose window, the video installation unfolds a kaleidoscope of fragments culled from the iconographies of coal and its relevance for culture. It connects the carboniferous era of natural history, the origin of coal and the mineral's depositories, and its role as the basic resource for the industrial culture of whole

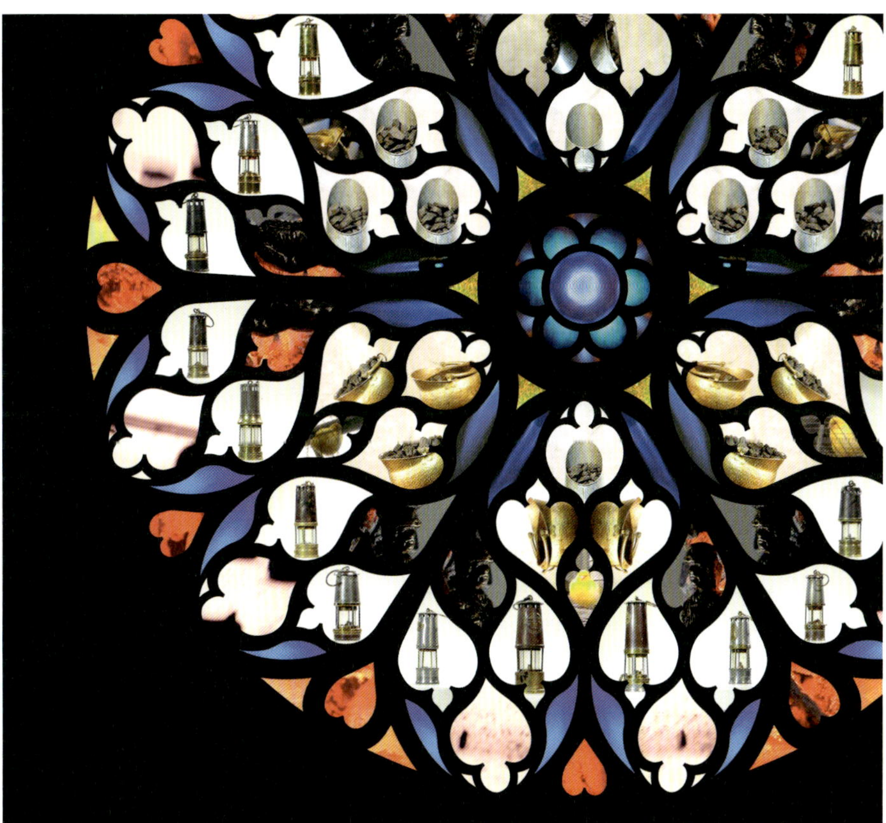

Fig. 1. Nick Crowe and Ian Rawlinson (British, b. 1968 and b. 1963), still from *Song for Coal*, 2015. 4k video installation, 10 minutes. Commissioned by Yorkshire Sculpture Park, Wakefield, England

regions. And it reflects the ongoing, and even increasing, importance of coal as a source of energy, and the relevance of this constellation for global climate change, including real problems as well as apocalyptic scenarios.

At first sight, the work may appear to harmonize a history not least of exploitation, social conflicts, and massive ecological problems in an inadequate way. Individual motifs from coal's cultural history are sampled and set to music. Visually organized as a decorative pattern integrated to a sacred architecture and ceremonially affirmed by the religious form of choral song, the piece may strike some viewers as dubious sublimation of a difficult history. Yet, this solemnly celebrated transcendence makes sense. It echoes several partly buried aspects of early modern relationships between the fine arts and nature without highlighting them explicitly; they may even be unintentional. In recovering these connecting strands, the piece provides insight into how profoundly research and knowledge specifically about the Earth has been intertwined with art and art history. And this may open up further perspectives for the work of contemporary artists.

Fossils and the Art of Nature

It is well known that, on the one hand, early modern art and art theory assumed Nature had specific potentials for image making. One of the examples most frequently quoted can be found in Leon Battista Alberti's *Libro della pittura* (1437) and contains a description of the images of centaurs and the heads of kings painted in stone by Nature herself.[2] On the other hand, such conceptions were of equal importance in natural history.

This is especially true for discussions of such curious phenomena as dendrites or those figured stones that are today considered to be the fossil remains of living beings. These debates remained controversial until the eighteenth century. For a long time these natural things provoked contradictory interpretations and genetic explanations.[3] Concepts such as that of Nature as artist or the *ludi naturae* provided the backdrop for a broad spectrum of interpretations.[4] Their particular scientifically creative potential, however, was not limited to this fairly general *topos* or allegorical concept. Yet within the scope of these phenomena, concrete image-making procedures were used and tested as models in explaining these natural images.[5]

In his *Musaeum Metallicum*, the Bologna-based collector and scholar Ulisse Aldrovandi presented, as one among various other stony images from nature, the admirable figure of a fish that "playful nature had printed precisely in

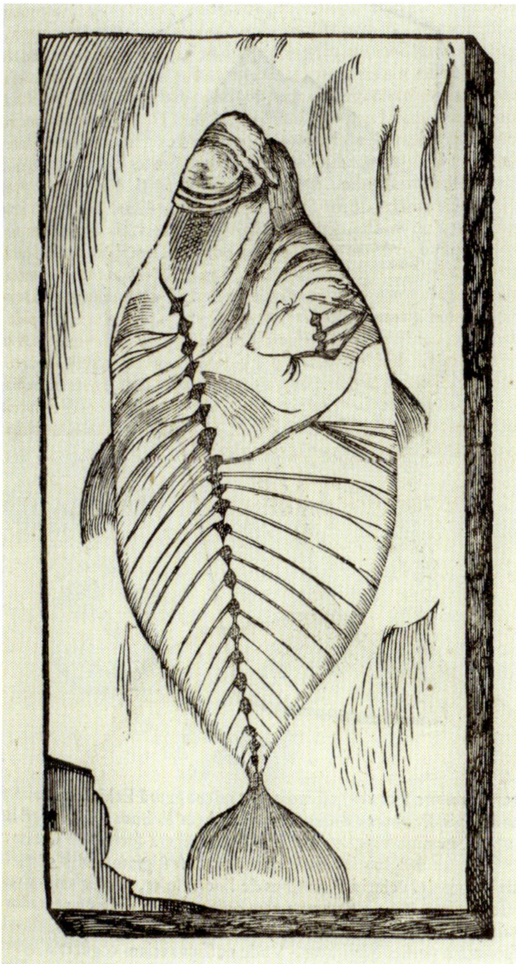

Fig. 2. Illustration in Ulisse Aldrovandi, *Vlyssis Aldrovandi patricii Bononiensis Musaeum metallicum in libros IIII distributum* (Bologna, 1648), p. 453. The Henry E. Huntington Library and Art Gallery, San Marino, California (RB 761992)

stone" (fig. 2).[6] That the image is supposed to have been printed is by no means trivial. Instead, the technological specificity substantiates hypothetical reflections regarding its origin. For example, a fossilized fish is described by Aldrovandi as though it had been made with extreme precision using a paintbrush: "penicillo delineatae."[7]

When talking about marble, the same author distinguishes between dashed-off animal creatures and those plants that he describes as extremely finely painted: "elegantissimae picta."[8] In another passage, he mentions vegetable figures composed of such subtly drawn lines that the eye could hardly distinguish them.[9]

Particularly bold speculations about the concrete genesis of such images in stone can be found in Michele Mercati's *Metallotheca Vaticana*. The original text and the majority of the elaborate copperplate engravings date from around 1580.[10] Yet it was only in 1717 that the work was printed with occasional critical annotations, and it then became one of the standard reference works of mineralogical literature and collecting. Several passages of this publication make it clear that the collector of *naturalia* considered Nature's image-making potentials as by far surpassing the quality of techniques and media humans employed in the making of art. Using a particularly delicate dendrite as an example, the author shows that, contrary to any doubts about Nature's perfect workmanship, evidently such a rich diversity of shapes could not have been arrived at by artificial means but had to have been produced by Nature herself (fig. 3).

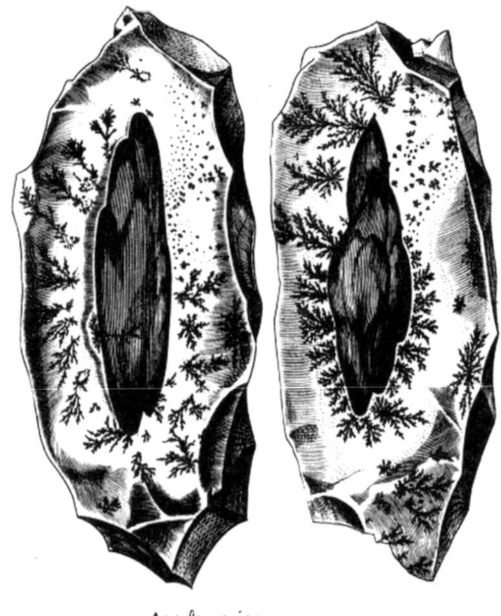

Fig. 3. Illustration in Michele Mercati, *Metallotheca Vaticana Michaelis Mercati* (Rome, 1719), p. 272

Whereas, according to the author, artificial painting produced only copies of things, which are nothing but shadows on a surface, Nature had also added *soliditas*—density, solidity, and thickness—to its painting on stone, while also establishing particular relationships between individual parts.[11]

This aspect is further elaborated in the description of fossils, as, for instance, three petrified fish in a block of black slate as they were often found near Eisleben in Germany. The lustrous golden-metallic animal bodies in black stone are described as a relief of superimposed layers of painted tablets.[12] In this case, the author evokes a mixed media artifact that had no corresponding real existence in contemporary art practice, in order to give the reader a hypothetical idea of such a thing's visible qualities. And inevitably, this sort of description suggests a fictional yet concrete artisanal procedure as a model of a conceivable process of generation.

Scholars and collectors in this field of research observed a correspondence of shape and color in the material of the figured stones, which human endeavor hardly ever managed to achieve in the arts. Or, to put it differently: Nature was seen to employ an art technology, which incorporated painting and sculpture in one, combining at the core of substances the distribution of color and the gestation of bodily shapes. In comparison with painting and sculpture, Nature, according to this argument, surpassed both because of its ability for endogenous construction of form. And this was certainly beyond the scope of any art discipline.

Especially in this variation of the *Paragone*, the traditional competition between arts or individual artists, Nature had a tendency to have the advantage over the human artist.[13] But this was not the only outcome of the widespread adaptation of visual arts and their practice by naturalists. In describing natural phenomena as artworks, concrete visual arts procedures became the terrain for a collective thought experiment many naturalists involved in premodern Earth sciences contributed to. Around 1600 and as part of this ongoing discourse connected with visual arts and their techniques, naturalists such as Ferrante Imperato and Fabio Colonna combined considerations about the formation of specific petrifactions with speculations on a historical dimension of these things. But they focused not primarily on drawing, printmaking, or painted tablets, but on procedures of casting and pouring.[14]

Bernard Palissy: Artificial Stone, Casts from Life, and the Potter as Ecologist

A particularly interesting figure in the context of early modern connections between art and Earth sciences is Bernard Palissy, painter on glass, potter, and garden architect.[15] As an artist, he was held in high esteem for his so-called *rustiques figulines* (fig. 4). These polychrome ceramic sculptures are casts from nature. Their negative shapes were cast directly from the bodies of the respective animals or parts of plants. Subsequently, a ceramic material was poured into these molds in order to produce artificial bodies as exact substitutes for the preceding living objects. In a final stage, colored glazes were applied and then the casts were burned one last time.[16] Animal casts especially required the killing of the formerly living being before taking the mold. In the next step, the dead bodies had to be incinerated within the mold, in order to get as pure a negative shape as possible.

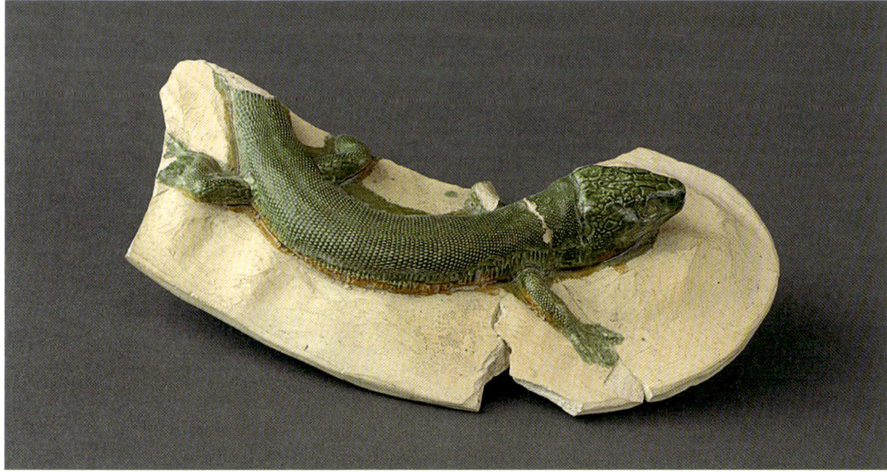

Fig. 4. Bernard Palissy (French, 1509–1590), *Rustique figuline of a Lizard*, about 1560. Earthenware with colored glaze. Musée Nationale de la Renaissance, Écouen (EP871a)

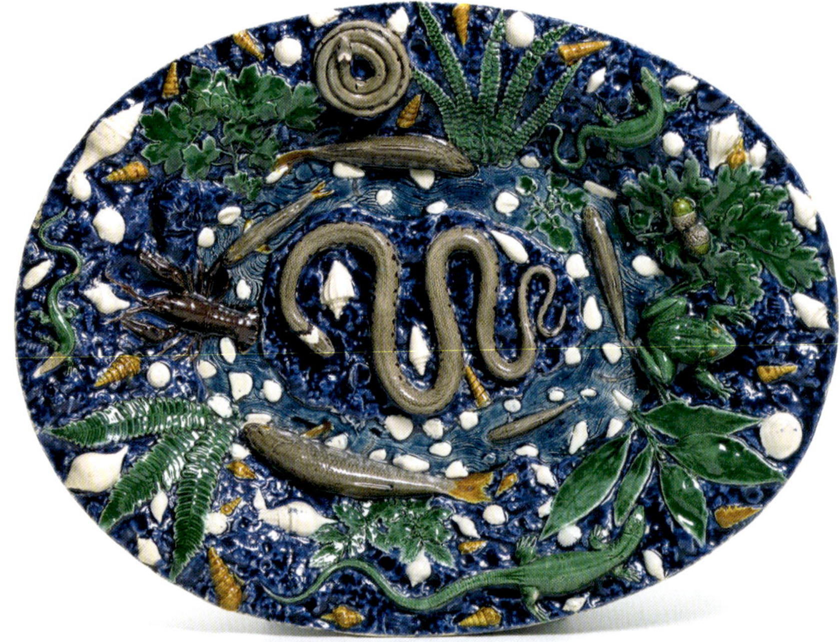

Fig. 5. Bernard Palissy, *Dish with rustiques figulines*, 1565–85. Earthenware with colored glaze. Victoria & Albert Museum, London (5476-1859)

Detailed descriptions of similar techniques quite explicitly relate the procedure as a coherent process of killing, burial, complete decomposition, and final re-creation. So, the technology of making casts from nature could be understood as the artificial realization of a metabolic cycle, culminating in a body that was at one and the same time a quasi-living being and imperishable.[17] The striking effect of suggestive illusionism was primarily the result of the detailed modeling of a lifelike body. In addition, the bodies' postures often appear as though they had been suddenly arrested in mid-motion and as if this locomotion could proceed again at any moment.

In many cases, these individual sculptures were mounted on large platters, plates, or jugs (fig. 5). In combination with these vessels, the casts from nature evoked micro landscapes, with a suggestion of water—the bank of a brook or pond, for instance. These splendid vessels in the shape of artificial habitats were in great demand, primarily at princely courts where they might be used at table or kept as collector's items in the Kunstkammer.[18]

Bernard Palissy's sustained interest in the geosphere manifests itself in several perspectives. On the one hand, it provided the conceptual framework for his art of pottery, encompassing the materials he worked with as well as the iconography of his works. On the other hand, we have a considerable body of Palissy's writings, in which he noted down and published his own observations of natural phenomena with far-reaching hypotheses about the mineral buildup, hydrologic balance, and the fertility of the Earth.[19]

There are two ways in which Palissy considered his work as potter to be analogous to the creation of natural forms, especially as regards scale formation: first, the composition of different clays could be regarded as imitating the material compound out of which all forms in nature were formed. By about 1548, he had developed his so-called *pierre jaspis*. These ceramics were characterized by textures on the surface similar to those in the stone of a *jaspis*. Palissy described these streaks and blotches in the natural stone as figures, images, and damasks that were very pleasurable to look at.[20] And he conceived of the design of the interior walls of an artificial grotto as covered with a glaze that imitated exactly such textures, in order to please our imagination.[21] In many pieces, these exterior patterns correspond to the interior structure of the whole piece and resulted from the working principle of compound clays. This technology and design imitated the veins and marbling effects of natural stone as well as a plethora of potential shapes, which manifested themselves within it.[22]

After having invented these *jaspis* ceramics, the life-casting technique in the *rustiques figulines* was a second mode of artificial mimesis. In this case, the primary intention of art was not to imitate mineralogical processes but individual living creatures from the realms of animals and plants. Even if both facets of mimesis were not necessarily combined in every single piece of the *rustiques figulines*, they are obviously connected in the more complex works, above all, in the artificial grottoes.[23] Here the *art de terre* moves continuously between these two poles: there is, on the one hand, the demonstration of the materials' potential, made visible by the imitation of the stones' interior structures. And, on the other hand, the art of pottery channels the clay's substance to take on the shape of animals and plants, culminating in a highly suggestive verisimilitude to living beings, accomplished by means of the aesthetic qualities of the glazed surface. Soil and stone as points of departure for this art were by no means regarded simply as raw material. Instead, they were an active principle in themselves and a complex source of causes which the potter adapts and manipulates. In the ostensibly living plants and animals in his *rustiques figulines*, the lowly natural realm of the *mineralia* evolves into the higher realms of *vegetabilia* and *animalia*.

Palissy, as far as we know, was involved in the design and construction of two artificial grottoes with numerous *rustiques figulines* as sculptural elements. He first planned one such grotto for the Duc Anne de Montmorency in Écouen around 1556, but the project was never finished.[24] Between 1567 and 1572, he installed a second grotto for Catherine de' Medici in the royal gardens in the Tuileries in Paris. During the newly erupting conflicts of the religious war within the following years, the self-professed Huguenot was captured several times before he died in the Bastille in 1590.

In the grotto ensembles, as Palissy envisions them in his writing, *rustiques figulines* would populate an artificial wilderness, which is celebrated as a milieu of the Earth's primordial fertility. The rooms would be lavishly furnished with water basins and fountains, and the water in these subterranean rooms evokes the condition of mineralogical processes as well as an abundant organic growth. Corals, sculpted vegetation, a multitude of animals cast from life, and living animals that enter in order to admire the artworks suggest a very prolific habitat uniting various specimens from all three realms of nature.[25] An additional function of the water would be to keep food and drinks chilled while also being served as a beverage and to be mixed with the wine.[26] Palissy himself implied that fertility and nutrition were not just inherent iconographical aspects of his grotto design, but he also connected them directly with the intended use of such places as sites for festive banquets. It is hard to say to what extent this function was being put to use. But we have evidence of diplomatic ceremonies in the 1570s that included ballet performances as well as banquets, some of which were staged in the garden of the Tuileries, where Palissy's grotto was one of the attractions. While France suffered the upheavals of confessional conflict, Catherine de' Medici enacted the mythical figure of Cybele or Ceres as a nurturing mother of France in these celebrations.[27]

Palissy himself saw his art as intrinsically related to soil fertility and its improvement as crucial parameters of French economy and culture. This topic was an essential part of the dynastic and national self-image at the time. In this view, France's territory and soil were blessed with exceptional fecundity, and it was believed that they yielded a unique abundance of produce and harvests without requiring the investment of labor. And it was further part of this self-mythologizing that the power and wealth of crown and kingdom originated in no small degree in the rulers' ancestral ties to Mother France and her presumed natural copiousness.[28] Palissy, however, did not take it for granted that these agricultural products simply appeared like gifts from Nature rather than as the result of labor. This might have been an additional reason for Catherine de' Medici to commission him with the grotto for the Tuileries in an attempt to compensate for not belonging to the ancestral line rooted in that generous, motherly Nature.

But beyond the concrete national and political dimension of these goods, he embedded his art in a larger natural philosophical context. In his own writings, especially the *Discours admirable* of 1580, Palissy describes his art as part of a comprehensive ecology.[29] The book begins with the description of the hydrologic circulation, and how it should be used in irrigation systems for gardens and fields, and it includes extensive passages about the nature, virtues, and transformations of minerals. According to Palissy, these formed the basis for all civilization. The unique position of the *arts de terre* within this complex situation was to work in direct analogy to these basic natural processes, and in creating such complex artworks as his artificial grottoes, this art embodies a fragile balance between culture and a fundamentally dynamic Nature characterized by incessant consumption and augmentation, decline, generation, and reshaping.

The Architecture of the Earth

Notwithstanding the obvious differences between explanations of the figured stones in analogy to artworks and Palissy's art of pottery,[30] both shared concepts of nature as something highly active, productive, and maybe even creative. Connected to the two strands of close relationships between art and the thinking about the Earth discussed so far, there is a third nexus. But here the geosphere is seen primarily as an artwork, which means as a manifestation and a more or less passive object of various actions, forces, and effects.

In the decades after 1600, the natural history of the Earth gained a new temporal weight in European thinking. Speculation about fossils was no longer limited to the process of their formation as image-like appearances. From the early seventeenth century, scientists considered how divergent geological environments could have emerged: what might have caused the various forms of the Earth's surface, from flat plains to high mountain regions? These questions required thinkers to consider historical temporality, not only the time scale required by Nature to generate forms.[31] The above-mentioned Fabio Colonna, for instance, linked his thoughts about petrifaction explicitly with the idea that these stony remains might once have been submerged and hidden in the earth for an unimaginably long time, so they should be seen as testimonies to an extremely distant historical past.[32] This idea of a decidedly extended time span is not found in Palissy.

Initially, mythical concepts informed and framed this historical time with the cornerstones of biblical history: the Creation, the Deluge, and the Apocalypse. Very soon, however, this discourse surrounding the Earth's natural history gained a momentum, which extended and ultimately destroyed this framework. Besides natural historical methods of research, particular analogies and core metaphors played an important role. They provided compatible connections to the fine arts and fundamentally influenced the cultural design of geological knowledge, far beyond the circle of experts and researchers.

In this case, they were mainly architectural metaphors. From the sixteenth to the eighteenth century, the more or less specified imagery of the Earth as an architectonic construction coexisted with the widely held concept of the Earth as a living female body. Thoroughly sexualized, this anthropomorphic idea was primarily used to explain the fertility of the soil in general and the existence of living beings as the offspring of this big mother, generated in the viscera of her body.[33] In many sources, this motherly organism overlaps with the idea of a *natura ludens* who produces, besides other things, pictorial images of crustaceans, fish, etc., as in the above-mentioned interpretations of fossils.

Writers from antiquity, such as Plato, Aristotle, and Cicero, had passed on different versions of the analogy between architecture and the Earth, primarily in order to declare the sublunar world in general to be part of the cosmic order, organized by a divine power.[34] The Renaissance naturalist Conrad Gessner revered the great Architect when he emphatically described the magnificence of the alpine mountains;[35] but it seems that specifically in the second half of the seventeenth century, this metaphor became crucial as a leitmotif in geological speculations. In this context, John Ray turned the analogy between the Earth and architecture into an argument ex-negativo against any strictly atomistic natural philosophy:

> For if this concourse of Atomes could make a whole World, why may it not sometimes make, and why hath it not somewhere or other in the Earth made a Temple, or a Gallery, or a Portico, or a House, or a City? which yet it is so far from doing, and every Man so far from believing, that should any one of us be cast, suppose, upon a desolate Island, and find there a magnificent Palace artificially contriv'd according to the exact Rules of Architecture, and curiosly adorn'd and furnish'd, it would

> never once enter into his Head, that this was done by an Earthquake,
> or the fortuitous shuffling together of its component Materials; or that
> it had stood there ever since the Construction of the World, or first
> cohæsion of Atomes; but would presently conclude that there had
> been some intelligent Architect there, the effect of whose art and
> Skill it was.[36]

Beyond a general polemic rejecting all opinions suspected of deism, atheism, or some strands of hermeticism, metaphorical speech about buildings and their parts made it possible to think of the Earth as a fundamentally tectonic order. It could be seen as a system of horizontal "floors" and vertically supporting parts, as well as different rooms—caves, for instance—which many authors assumed were veining the entire Earth's body in a system of basements and catacombs.[37]

One of this metaphor's main achievements was the transformation of the geosphere with all its irregular shapes, the frequently overwhelming relations of scale and undiscovered regions, into an artificial and rigorously ordered context. More than other art forms, architecture embodied the regularity of measurements and proportion, functionality, symbolic qualities, and a relatively high level of durability. Applying these features even to high mountain ranges prefigured concrete models of geologic processes, and it was strategically effective for the cultural and scientific appropriation of regions largely uncontrolled by civilization up until the late nineteenth century. The above-mentioned ideas of a quasi-architectonic system of concavities within the Earth had a profound impact on seventeenth-century debates about earthquakes and landfalls. And the way in which in 1695, a writer like John Woodward described the big flood primarily as a violent surge of water out of vast subterranean caverns is an example of how fundamentally architectonic imagery could influence the development of models for geophysical processes.[38]

Late examples for this long-lasting connection can be found in the writings of John Ruskin and Eugène Emmanuel Viollet-le-Duc. The French architect, designer, and curator of monuments imagined the geosphere, and particularly the mountains, as constructions based on the geometry of crystalline structures and their tectonic performance.[39] The art critic and writer John Ruskin interpreted the visible shapes of mountains as the results of geological processes and as being congruent with aesthetic rules. Conversely these natural shapes, according to Ruskin, offered the prototypes for many artificially made forms, specifically those of architecture and its ornaments.[40] Both Ruskin and Viollet-le-Duc were autodidacts in geosciences, but they used their abilities as very well-trained draftsmen in different ways as methods of analysis and speculation.[41]

Perfect Building versus Ruin and the Deep Time of Natural History

Metaphors and models of the Earth as architectural work often implied the characteristic ambivalence of a perfect, integral building, on the one hand, and a ruin, maybe even broken up into a heap of fragments, on the other. Both options opened up fundamentally different perspectives to the present world, and these architectural metaphors' antithetical implications can be traced back to the center of debates in early modern Earth sciences. Mountains' irregular and weathered appearances seemed to provide strong evidence in favor of seeing the Earth as an enormous ruin. And such an interpretation posed a serious challenge to an understanding of the whole of nature as a well-organized and purposeful creation.

One of the most prominent voices in this connection was Thomas Burnet. In his cosmological speculation *Telluris Theoria Sacra* of 1681, he proclaimed the current condition of the entire Earth a pitiful state of ruin.[42] Burnet views this maximum of disorder and decay as cosmologically tied into a cyclical process, as it is visualized in the frontispiece of his book (fig. 6). The biblical chaos had been succeeded by an impeccable state of initial Creation, which was subsequently destroyed by the Deluge. And only the Apocalypse's world fire would deliver it from its current state of decay. According to Burnet, this would be superseded by a new phase of

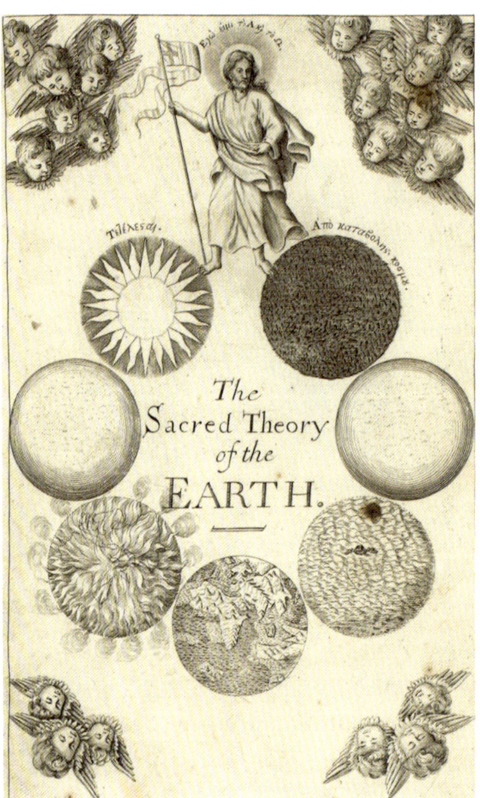

Fig. 6. Frontispiece in Thomas Burnet, *The Sacred Theory of the Earth* (London, 1684). The Henry E. Huntington Library and Art Gallery, San Marino, California (RB 601426)

perfection, until the Earth's natural existence culminates in a metamorphosis into a star. The previous order of Creation could then only be intuited based on fragments and detritus.

Mountains were the most poignant manifestation of this state of ruin, because they so obviously contradicted any idea of order. In the aesthetic pleasure Burnet takes in looking at these heaps of rubble, we can already discern an intimation of the philosophical category of the sublime, established in the late eighteenth century by Edmund Burke and Immanuel Kant.[43] But, nevertheless, Burnet's emphasis is on the pure absence of order, beauty, and any counsel, without a positive turn.[44] Burnet's metaphor of the ruin transforms the Earth into a monument of a lost divine order. In the eye of divine providence, this ruin is a transitory period, but still this state offers no escape, either for nature or for human history.

This radically negative manifestation of the Earth was vehemently rejected by authors such as the above-mentioned John Woodward and John Ray or by Johan Jakob Scheuchzer in Zurich.[45] These opponents were also inclined to use architectural metaphors. In the face of mountains, rocks, and chasms, the apparent facts of irregularity, disproportion, and disarray could evidently not be denied, and these phenomena could not be readily understood as an orderly context, integrated into a well-organized entirety.

Even for this challenge, architecture supplied an aesthetic trick that geological sciences adapted. Thus, in the middle of the seventeenth century, the Neapolitan Jesuit Daniello Bartoli, for instance, came up with a virtuoso reinterpretation of the evident disarray and lack of proportion of the Earth's surface. Phenomena such as mountains should be seen as a new art of architectonic composition whose very appeal resided in the fact that under the ostensible lack of order and norm, art was concealing itself.[46] And he emphasized this very concealment as evidence of a divine architect's particularly skillful craftsmanship. This reinterpretation was implicitly based on actually existing varieties of early modern architecture.

Without giving exact examples, Bartoli refers to artificial ruins that had been designed for Mannerist and Baroque chateaus, often in combination with grottoes and sharing their rustic outfit.[47] Around 1700, the above-mentioned Woodward and Scheuchzer pursued Bartoli's argument for evident disarray as the highest art form and thereby directly contradicted Burnet and his idea of the present Earth as a ruin and pile of debris.[48] They rejected Burnet's opinion with a fair amount of scorn: Burnet did not appear to be able, so they claimed, to recognize in his mind's eye, and contrary to outward appearances, the Creator's particularly masterly art and the sublime order of Nature. Yet in this masked art of architecture, the present Earth was no ruin at all, but a complete new construction which had emerged after the Deluge.

The debates about the Earth as an actual or artificial ruin and, as such, a completely new construction, revolved primarily around various historical perspectives. Burnet's cycle was aimed chiefly at a hermeneutics of nature. It remains within the strictly defined and closed framework of a Christian plan of salvation. Woodward and Scheuchzer's version of the present Earth as a new building, by contrast, signaled an open-ended, interconnected history of Earth and civilization. Having been designed for human purposes after the Deluge, this divine architecture of the Earth is by far more promising for progressive scientific research, territorial development, and industrial exploitation.

Irrespective of these differences in the use of architectural metaphors for the Earth, an elective affinity was established in the seventeenth century, epistemically informing universal history as well as the geological sciences. Those who were interested in minerals, and especially those who tried to explain the origin of fossils, often considered their work as being analogous to the work of antiquarians and later archaeologists.[49] One of the most noted statements along those lines is by Robert Hooke, the renowned microscopist and curator of the Royal Society's Collection in London. He wrote around 1675:

> These are the greatest and most lasting Monuments of Antiquity, which, in all probability, will far antedate all the most ancient Monuments of the world, even the very Pyramids, Obelisks, Mummys, Hieroglyphics, and Coins, and will afford more information in Natural History than those others put together will in Civil.[50]

Scheuchzer used this analogy not just verbally but in the context of arranging a collection of pictorial materials for book projects about minerals and petrifacts.[51] Part of this collection includes some drawings of idyllic ruin landscapes, on top of which the crude fragments of individual stone crystals have been placed in a trompe l'oeil manner—as though there existed a real, maybe even natural, connection between the ruined buildings of antiquity and the accretion of stones. Other pages of these albums incorporate drawings and prints, cut out from contemporary publications (fig. 7). One of the most impressive collages shows an atmo-

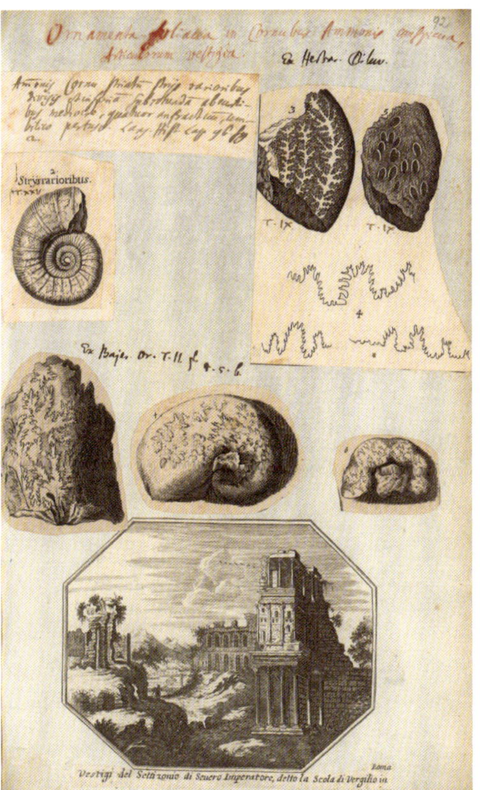

Fig. 7. Collage with fragments of fossil ammonites and Roman ruins in Johann Jakob Scheuchzer, *Icones pro lexico diluviano*, (c. 1715–30), fol. 92. Zentralbibliothek Zürich, MsZ VIII 21 a–d

spheric scenery of ancient Roman ruins surrounded by printed fragments of various ammonites, some of them distinguished by rich patterns of very subtly articulated zigzag lines.

Here the gesture of showing something and the visual argument point in another direction: regard these stones—in this case, fragments of ammonites—as witnesses from Nature's past, in the same way in which you look at antique Rome's ruins and fragments as precious witnesses of a past time in history.

Yet Hooke, Scheuchzer, and other collectors and researchers from the seventeenth century onward assumed quite self-confidently that their evidence of natural history, as it manifested itself in the shape of material remnants, would transmit information about the past not only more directly but also more reliably. They were also convinced that these constituted a body of tradition with a further reach into the past than any linguistic documents. Defining itself as archaeology, the natural history of the Earth appears to have first jettisoned its ties to language as a means of tradition before discovering a deep time that was no longer tied to the time of myths and human history.

In the traditional history of sciences, the constitution of an objective history of nature, independent of man, is one of the groundbreaking revolutionary changes. Cultural history is also aware of the fact that this process also entailed a certain destabilization of cultural self-images and thus proved to be one of the narcissistic humiliations within the Western history of becoming subjects. But today it should also be considered from an almost opposite premise. In the face of a nature that is gravely affected by human societies, what is at stake today is to think of both as a shared history: "humanity-in-nature" and "nature-in-humanity." Under this premise we can look back to the early modern times and find surprisingly alternative traces. Certainly, the visual arts of the early modern times don't provide answers to the ecological crises of the present. But for a long time, they were a very prolific site where collectors, artists, and naturalists deliberated about natural processes and the way in which the histories of Nature and culture were intertwined.

Song for Coal by Crowe and Rawlinson responds to some of the loose ends of this history, even if there are no explicit links. The piece is a profuse collection of heterogeneous documents. On the visual level, the combination of pictorial footage evokes time travel in quick motion, back and forth between the recent industrial present and the lush vegetal growth of the carbon era. Every single motif is an abruptly fragmented sequence. Coherence arises merely from their succession and the effected narrative associations. Another kind of relationship between the bits is defined by the ornamental rose window. On this level, the orchestration doesn't address the subjective process of connecting the individual motifs. Here, all of them appear simultaneously in manifold reiterations as elements of a strictly concentric whole, which in its symmetry embodies the totality of an order of permanent existence.

The artwork addresses not just episodes of a connected history of nature and human culture in the region but also particular principles, which have structured the thinking and knowledge about this relationship. The kaleidoscopic choreography is remarkably consistent in arranging a balance of contradictory moments: the undulating rhythm of alternating movie images seems to (re)vitalize the flamboyant ornament which, however, ultimately remains a static pattern. These sequences find their center of gravity in the initial burst of vegetal life, and they illuminate the stony grid of architectural décor until they fade away.

Yes, the whole piece is a kind of requiem—but not in the way it might seem to be at first sight. The chapel as location, the chorale, and especially the rose window with its Christological symbolism evoke a perspective of belief and salvation. But the installation refuses to affirm such a promise. On the contrary, it insists on the history of fossil fuels as a crucial and most problematic tradition in the ecology of industrial cultures. *Song for Coal* is a strange and hybrid combination: in some ways, it echoes the early modern culture of curiosity as well as Romantic traditions. The artwork opens up a setting of sheer contemplation, and here the tension between a suggestive beauty of forms and colors and sublime ideas of nature and history offers no solution and no escape. The obviously artificial and highly synthetic character of the piece not only reflects but mimics a permanent, breathless investment of labor, invention, and technical knowhow, while it appropriates nature almost completely, glorifies yearned-for pockets of untouched wilderness, but so far fails to organize alternative ecologies. The adaptation of ornamental formalism and the aura of religious certainties might be seen as anachronisms. But their use also extrapolates one of the most consistent and profound levels of critical reflection—maybe as necessary as political activism and art as intervention.

1. For further information, see http://works.croweandrawlinson.net/Song-for-Coal (accessed December 12, 2017). I cordially thank the artists for being in conversation about the project since 2013. See also Nick Crowe and Ian Rawlinson, "Song for Coal," *Kritische Berichte: Zeitschrift für Kunst- und Kulturwissenschaften* 3 (2013): 43–57.

2. "Ipsam denique naturam pingendo delectari manifestum est. Videmus enim naturam ut saepe in marmoribus hippocentauros regumque barbatas facies effigiet." Leon Battista Alberti, "De Pictura– Die Malkunst," in *Das Standbild. Die Malkunst. Grundlagen der Malerei*, ed. Oskar Bätschmann (Darmstadt: Darmstadt Wissenschaftliche Buchgesellschaft, 2000), 244–45; Horst Woldemar Janson, "The 'Image Made by Chance,'" in *Renaissance Thought: Essays in Honor of Erwin Panofsky*, vol. 1, ed. Millard Meiss, *De artibus opuscula* 40 (New York: New York University Press, 1961), 254–66.

3. See Martin J. S. Rudwick, *The Meaning of Fossils: Episodes in the History of Palaeontology* (Chicago: University of Chicago Press, 1972).

4. For the *topos* of *ludi naturae*, see Paula Findlen, "Jokes of Nature and Jokes of Knowledge. The Playfulness of Scientific Discourse in Early Modern Europe," *Renaissance Quarterly* 43, nos. 1–2 (1990): 292–328; as a crucial concept in the Kunstkammer, see Horst Bredekamp, *Antikensehnsucht und Maschinenglauben. Die Geschichte der Kunstkammer und die Zukunft der Kunstgeschichte* (Berlin: Wagenbach, 1993), 63–76; with focus on wonder and curiositas as an intellectual passion, see Lorraine Daston and Katherine Park, *Wonders and the Order of Nature, 1150–1750* (New York: Zone Books, 1998), 255–301.

5. See Robert Felfe, *Naturform und bildnerische Prozesse. Elemente einer Wissensgeschichte in der Kunst des 16. und 17. Jahrhunderts* (Berlin and Boston: DeGruyter, 2015), 113–62.

6. Ulisse Aldrovandi, *Musaeum metallicum in Libros IIII distributum* […] (Bologna, 1648), 453.

7. "Verum debemus admirari pulchrum naturae ludentis in his lapidibus spectaculum, dum in his

variorum animantium icones adeò accuratè effigiat, ut penicillo delineatae esse vidantur." Ibid., 101.

8. "Aliud fragmentum Marmoris varijs animalibus à natura maculatum exhibemus in alia tabella delineatum: id circo dicitur Marmor aliud polymorphites: cum in illo effigies multae quadrupedum, & avium intueri liceat. / Rursus maiori admiratione tenemur, quando i[n]tuemer Marmora ab Opifice Dei Natura, arbusculis elegantissimae picta." Ibid., 763.

9. "Nos autem damus iconem Marmoris lividi, & albi, in quo arbusculae, & herbae tam exilibus lineis fuerunt à Natura designatae, ut vix oculis comprehendi possent. Deinde per lineam rectam tam eleganter constructae, ut artificio quodam laboratae esse viderentur" (ibid., 763).

10. Michele Mercati, *Metallotheca Vaticana Opus Posthumum . . .* , ed. Giuseppe Maria Lancisi (Rome, 1717); for information about this publication, see Alix Cooper, "The Museum and the Book. The Metallotheca and the History of an Encyclopaedic Natural History in Early Modern Italy," *Journal of the History of Collection* 7, no. 1 (1995): 1–23.

11. "Sanè negarent à Natura perfectas esse, nisi doceret ipsa, non posse ab arte fieri. Ars effigiem rerum velut umbram in superficie sistit. Ipsa in hoc lapide picturae soliditatem addit, omnemque partium situm persequitur." Mercati, *Metallotheca Vaticana*, 272.

12. "Hunc vero de hoc figmenta ludentis Naturae recenseri debent. Crustas enim, quae ex lapide facile disparantur, ipsa sibi pro tabellis pictorum instituit, imagines animalium eis superinducens, non aliis usa coloribus, quam lapidis qualitas concedit. Cum aerosus lapis, ac bituminosus sit, aureas pyritae micas ita disponit, ut delineamenta animalium omnino reddantur. Neque commodius accidere potuit, ut ea perspici possent, in altro lapide auri fulgore scintilante." Ibid., 319f..

13. Robert Felfe, "Figurationen im Gestein und die Koproduktivität von Kunst und Natur," in *Paragone als Mitstreit*, ed. Joris van Gastel, Yannis Hadjinicolaou, and Markus Rath (Berlin: Akademie Verlag, 2014), 153–75.

14. See Felfe, *Naturform und bildnerische Prozesse*, 121–33.

15. For the comprehensive monograph, see Leonard N. Amico, *Bernard Palissy: In Search of Earthly Paradise* (Paris and New York: Flammarion, 1996); see also the biography by Jean-Pierre Poirier, *Bernard Palissy. Le secret des émaux* (Paris: Pygmalion, 2008).

16. For the procedure and techniques, see further Andrea Klier, *Fixierte Natur: Naturabgüße und Wachseffiges im 16. Jahrhundert* (Berlin: Reimer, 2004), 90–117.

17. For this aspect with focus on metal casts from life, see Robert Felfe, "Naturabgüsse— künstliche Zeugung und Kreisläufe des Lebens," *Zeitschrift für Kunst- und Kulturwissenschaften* 3 (2012): 11–35.

18. See *Arcimboldo, 1526–1593 (Kunsthistorisches Museum, Wien)*, exh. cat., ed. Sylvia Ferino-Pagden (Milan and Vienna: Skira, 2008), 201–3.

19. Bernard Palissy, *Discours admirables de la nature des eaux et fontaines, tant naturelles qu'artificielles* [. . .] (Paris: Le Jeune, 1580), in *Bernard Palissy. Œuvres complètes*, ed. Marie-Madeleine Fragonard et al., 2nd ed. (Paris: Champion, 2010), 241–573. A brief summary of Palissy's writing on geology

is found in H. R. Thompson, "The Geographical and Geological Observations of Bernard Palissy the Potter," *Annals of Science* 10, no. 2 (1954): 149–65; more detail in the commentary of Reinhart Dittmann, *Naturerkenntnis und Kunstschaffen. Die Discours admirables von Bernard Palissy. Übersetzung und Kommentar* (Berlin and Boston: De Gruyter, 2016).

20. ". . . figures, ydees, ou damasquinees en ladite pierre de jaspis." Bernard Palissy, *Recepte véritable* (1563), in *Bernard Palissy. Œuvres complètes*, 152–53.

21. Ibid., 165.

22. In a passage of Palissy's dialogue about the architecture of artificial grottoes, the inventor of such a work declares: "Il [l'œuvre R.F.] est plus étrange que vous ne cuydez. Car les venes, figures & labeurs qui apparoissent par dehors, sont aussi par le dedans incorporés." Bernard Palissy, *Architecture et ordonnance de la grotte rustique* [. . .], in *Bernard Palissy. Œuvres complètes*, 79.

23. The description of the "four cabinets" as well as the "four green cabinets" in the *Recepte veritable* give the best evidence to the conceptual relevance of these two poles in their connectedness. See *Bernard Palissy. Œuvres complètes*, 163–78.

24. The above-mentioned publications *Architecture et ordonnance de la grotte rustique and Récepte veritable*, both printed in 1563 in La Rochelle, refer directly to this project.

25. "Ce premier rocher donc, qui sera au cabinet du costé du vent de Nord, sera fait de terre cuite, insculpee et esmaillee [...] Note donc qu'au bas et pied du rocher, il y aura un fossé naturel, ou receptacle d'eau qui tiendra autant en longueur comme ledit rocher. [...] Aussi y aura plusieurs branches de coral, duquel les racines seront tout au pied du rocher, à fin que ledits couraux ayent l'apparence d'avoir creu dedans ledit fossé. [...] et tout le residu du haut du rocher, sera ainsi biais, tortue, bossu, ayant un nombre d'espece d'herbe, et de mousses insculpees, qui coustumierement croissent és rochers et lieux humide [...] et au dessus desdites mousses et herbes, il y aura un grand nombre de serpents, aspics, viperes, langrotes et lizers, qui ramperont le long du rocher, les uns en haut, les autres de travers, et les autres descendans en bas, tenans et faisans plusieurs gestes, et plaisans contoumemens, et tous lesdits animaux seront insculpez et esmaillez si pres de la nature, que les autres lizers naturels et serpents, les viendront souvent admirer . . ." *Bernard Palissy. Œuvres complètes*, 168–69.

26. A little later in the same passage follows: "Aussi audit rocher sera formé quelque espèce de buffet, pour tenir les verres et coupes de ceux qui banquetteront dans le cabinet. Et par un même moyen seront formés audit rocher certaines parquets et petit réceptacles pour faire refraîchir le vin pendant le repas, lesquels réceptacles auront toujours l'eau froide, à cause que quand ils seront pleins à la mesure ordonnée de leur de leur grandeur, la superfluité de l'eau tomberadedans le fossé, et ainsi l'eau sera toujours vive dedans ledits réceptacles. Aussi audit cabinet y aura de semble étoffe que la rocher, laquelle sera assise aussi sur un rocher, et sera la dite table en façon ovale, étant émaillée, enrichie et colorée de divers couleurs d'émail qui luiront comme un cristallin. Et ceux, qui seront

assis pour banqueter en ladite table pourront mettre de l'eau de l'eau vive en leur vin sans sortir audit cabinet . . ." Ibid., 169.

27. Ewa Kociszewska, "War and Seduction in Cybele's Garden: Contextualizing the *Ballet des Polonais*," *Renaissance Quarterly* 65, no. 3 (2012): 809–63, esp. 839–42.

28. Rebecca Zorach, *Blood, Milk, Ink, Gold: Abundance and Excess in the French Renaissance* (Chicago: University of Chicago Press, 2005), 124.

29. Robert Felfe, "Vom künstlichen Leben niederer Tiere. Eine vergessene Ökologie mitten im Europa der Frühen Neuzeit," in *Andere Ökologien*, ed. Iris Därmann and Stephan Zandt (Paderborn: Wilhelm Fink, 2017), 135–60.

30. Indeed, Palissy was one of the early writers who strictly declared an organic origin of petrifactions and has to be seen in that regard as an opponent of the explanations of fossils as Nature's artworks. This was one reason for the enthusiastic reference, for instance, by Georges-Louis Leclerc, Comte de Buffon, in the mid-eighteenth century: "Un potier de terre, qui ne savait ni latin, ni grec fut le premier, vers la fin du XVIe siècle, qui osa dire dans Paris et à la face de tous les docteurs que les coquilles fossiles étaient de véritable coquilles déposées autrefois par la mer dans les lieux où elles se trouvaient alors [. . .] C'est Bernard Palissy, saintongeais, aussi grand physicien que la Nature seule en puisse former un." Poirier, *Bernard Palissy*, 10–11.

31. Primarily from a perspective of the history of sciences: Martin J. S. Rudwick, *Earth's Deep History: How It Was Discovered and Why It Matters* (Chicago and London: University of Chicago Press, 2014), 9–54; David R. Oldroyd, *Thinking about the Earth: A History of Ideas in Geology* (London: Athlone, 1996); and with a focus on the implications for the cultural history: Paolo Rossi, *The Dark Abyss of Time: The History of the Earth and the History of Nations from Hook to Vico* (Chicago: University of Chicago Press, 1984).

32. Colonna characterized them as "immemorabili tempore ab hominibus deiectis." Fabio Colonna, *Aquatilium et terrestrium aliquot animalium, aliorumque naturalium rerum observationes* (Rome, 1616), 46.

33. Palissy again is only one example for this coexistence. He drew extensively on the figure of the Earth as a big mother, but he was also a protagonist of Earth's architecture: as an artist, he plays with this imagery in his artificial grottoes, and in his *Discours admirables*, for instance, he directly blends the ideas of veins and vessels inside the Earth with that of subterranean vaults. *Bernard Palissy. Œuvres complètes*, 275.

34. Of course, we find the analogy between the world and a building and/or the idea of God as a divine architect in many writings since antiquity, as, for example, in Plato (*Timaeus* 28c–29a), Aristotle (*Physics* II.5.196b), and Cicero (*De natura deorum* II.89). But it seems that in the seventeenth century, this analogy and metaphor were adopted as a concrete model for geological speculation.

35. Conrad Gessner, *Libellus de lacte, et operibus lactariis, philologus pariter ac medicus. Cum epistola ad Jacobum Avienum de montium admiratione . . .* (Zurich, 1541), 2–2v.

36. The logic in this twisted variation of an architectonic metaphor is: to deny that the Earth necessarily must be the creation of an intelligent divine being, and to see it instead as the mere effect of the random movements of material, would be as reasonable as to deny the art of an architect as the indisputable origin of a building and its complex order. Ray published this argument in his *Wisdom of God Manifested in the Works of the Creation*, for the first time in 1691; quoted here after the 3rd edition (London, 1701), 40.

37. Most influential in this context: Athanasius Kircher, *Mundus subterraneus*, 2 vols. (Amsterdam: Jansson & Weyerstraten, 1665). See "Sogni di caverne et caverne da sogni. Realtà et finzione scientesche tra Shakespeare a Kircher," in *La Montagna. Arte, scienza, mito da Dürer a Warhol*, exh. cat., Musco di Arte Moderna, Rovereto, ed. Gabriella Belli, Paola Giacomoni, and Anna Ottani Cavina (Milan: Skira, 2003), 117–29. Further examples for the pictorial imagination of such an architecture, especially of the inner parts of the Earth, are the many fantastic grotto landscapes by painters such as Abraham van Cuylenburgh and Wilhelm von Bemmel.

38. John Woodward, *An Essay toward a Natural History of the Earth and Terrestrial Bodies, especially Minerals: as also of the Sea, Rivers and Springs. With an account of the Universal Deluge, and of the Effects it had upon the Earth* (London: R. Wilkin, 1695).

39. See Eugène Emmanuel Viollet-le-Duc, *Le massif du Mont Blanc. Étude sur la constitution géodésique et géologique sur ses transformations et sur l'état ancien et moderne de ses glaciers* (Paris, 1876).

40. See John Ruskin, *Modern Painters*, vol. IV, part V, *Of Mountain Beauty* (Sunnyside, Orpington: George Allen, 1888); John Ruskin, *The Stones of Venice*, vol. III (Sunnyside, Orpington: George Allen, 1897), 222ff.

41. For the geological studies by Ruskin and Viollet-le-Duc, see Jan von Brevern, *Blicke von Nirgendwo. Geologie in Bildern bei Ruskin, Viollet-le-Duc und Civiale* (Paderborn: W. Fink, 2012).

42. Thomas Burnet, *Telluris Theoria sacra* [...] (London: Typis R.N. impensis Gualt. Kettilby, 1681). See Stephen Jay Gould, *Time's Arrow, Time's Cycle: Myth and Metaphor in the Discovery of Geological Time* (Cambridge: Harvard University Press, 1987), 21–59.

43. Edmund Burke, *A Philosophical Enquiry into the Origin of Our Ideas of the Sublime and the Beautiful* (London: R. and J. Dodsley, 1757); Immanuel Kant, *Die Kritik der Urteilskraft* (1798).

44. Burnet writes in chapter XI, "Concerning the Mountains of the Earth": "And yet these Mountains we are speaking of, to confess the truth, are nothing but great ruines; but such as show certain magnificence in Nature; as from old Temples and broken Amphitheaters of the Romans we collect the greatness of that people." And: "It will be good, to observe farther, that these Mountains are plac'd in no order one with another, that can either respect use or beauty; And if you consider

them singly, they do not consist of any proportion of parts that is referrable to any design, or that hath the least footsteps of Art or Counsel. There is nothing in Nature more shapeless and ill-figur'd than an old rock or Mountain, and all that variety that is among them, is but the various modes of irregularity." Thomas Burnet, *The Sacred Theory of the Earth* (London: R. Norton, for Walter Kettilby, 1684), 110 and 114.

45. Besides Woodward's *An Essay toward a Natural History of the Earth* (1695) and Ray's *Wisdom of God* (1691), the following should be mentioned here: John Ray, *Three Physico-Theological Discourses: Concerning I. The Primitive Chaos, and the Creation of the World. II. The General Deluge, Its Causes and Effects. III. The Dissolution of the World, and Future Conflagration. Wherein are largely Discussed the Production and Use of Mountains* [...] (London, 1693); Johann Jakob Scheuchzer, *Beschreibung der Natur-Geschichten des Schweizerlands*, 3 parts (Zürich, 1706–8); Scheuchzer came back to that topic in his publications about the history of the Earth, most extensively in the *Helvetiae historia naturalis oder Naturhistorie des Schweitzerlandes*, 3 vols. (1716–18) and the *Physica Sacra* (1731–35).

46. See, above all, chapter 8, "Il mondo con nuovo Ordine d'Architettura Scomposto, e per cio piu artificiosamente composto," in Daniello Bartoli, *La recreazione del savio in discorso con la Natura e con Dio* (Rome, 1659), 111–23.

47. Bartoli wrote: "Souviemmi d'hauer veduto in vn palagio die ricreatione d'vun Principe, fra le altre bellissime, vna particolar camera tutta finta a capriccio di rouine, con vn nuouo stile d'Architettura, che ben potrebbe chiamarsi, l'Ordine Scomposto, e da adoperarui non meno ingegno, e guidicio, che ne gli altri; dovendosi dare vnita al dissipato, gratia al deforme, regola allo sconcio, simmetria allo sconcertato, e arte al caso." Ibid., 115–16.

48. Scheuchzer, *Beschreibung der Natur-Geschichten des Schweizerlands*, part 3, 180.

49. Alain Schnapp, *The Discovery of the Past: The Origins of Archaeology* (London: British Museum Press, 1996); *L'antichità del mondo. Fossili, Alfabeti, Rovine*, exh. cat., Museo di Palazzo Poggi and Biblioteca Universitaria, Bologna, ed. Walter Tega (Bologna: Compositori, 2002); Rossi, *The Dark Abyss of Time*.

50. Robert Hooke, *Lectures and Discourses of Earthquakes* [. . .] (London: Richard Waller, 1705), 335.

51. The author planned two illustrated lexica: *Lexicon mineralogicum* and *Lexicon diluvianum*; the latter included all fossils that Scheuchzer interpreted as formerly living beings and testimonies for the biblical flood. Four separate volumes contain a collection of images as material for the illustrations. They are today in the Zentral Bibliothek Zürich, as *Icones pro Lexico mineralogico* (MsZ VIII 19e) and *Icones pro Lexico diluviano* (MsZ VIII b–d).

Gichi-mookomaanan miinawaa Gichi-maazhigaa-aabkook //
From Big Knives to Big Pipelines

Dylan Miner

This is a story about images and their meaning. This is a story about stories and a story about beings. It is about pipes and pipelines. It is about oil and not about oil paintings. It is fragmented and disjointed. It is a needed intervention for our fossil-fuel-addicted society.

This story, however brief, is about the ways that colonialism and capitalism—as intertwined and immutable—continue to extract so-called resources, while enacting violence against Indigenous peoples and simultaneously Indigenous ways of being. It is about how images—and the humans who create them—participate in and reproduce these violent and unwieldy processes. It is about images and stories as living beings.

Most importantly, this story, which masquerades as a chapter in a book on the history of art, is about *mookomaanan* (the Anishinaabemowin- or Ojibwe-language word for "knives") and pipes—both those ceremonial pipes that communicate with the ancestors and spirits and those pipes that transport the bodies of dead beings and whose oil destroys the earth.

The Anishinaabemowin word for medicine is *mshkiki*, a word that some have translated as "strength of the earth." Yet, on the heels of the violence enacted at Standing Rock and during many centuries of settler colonialism, not to mention the apocalyptic futures that climate change lays bare, I wonder how we heal ourselves and the Land, when those *mshkikiwan* disappear.

Through this brief chapter, and in its former iteration as a lecture, I have only begun thinking through and talking about knives and pipes and, therefore, these written words are only preliminary. But, like any story, it is not fixed and, as such, we can without a doubt shift and transform and shape the narrative in ways that direct us toward better and more sustainable futures, ones that are always intimately tied to the past.

Dibaajimowinan // Stories

The words that appear on this page and the ideas they communicate are a simple *dibaajimowin*, or narrative; they are not an *aadizookaan*, or sacred story. This is a crucial, yet difficult, distinction. I have heard *aadizookaanag* described in many ways, which includes traditional or sacred stories; they are sometimes referred to as myths or legends, although many Indigenous people are not fond of the ways that these two concepts diminish the importance of the *aadizookaanag*.

I have also been told that the *aadizookaanag* are those stories that are so significant that they become living and sentient beings and know that they are being told. For many, the belief that some stories—the exquisite accumulation of words strung together to create multidimensional meaning—are living is a marvelous, yet troublesome proposition for those whose ontology is firmly positioned in the rationalist epistemologies of Western ways of being.

Here on Turtle Island, those Indigenous lands of North America, the *aadizookaanag* are stories, *who* are also living beings. These stories // beings become alive through the process of being told. As human animals, we tell these stories into beings. As both a historian of art and an artist myself, I am particularly interested in those stories // beings we call art.

But the words on this page and the story it communicates is not a sacred story. It is an accessible narrative. It is *dibaajimowin*. However, I wonder that if this anticolonial and anticapitalist story is told in a good way, it too will know it is being told and, in turn, become a sentient being. Can all our stories become beings? Is all this knowledge sacred?

As artists and creators—as art historians—how do we braid together our precious words like the strands of *wiingashk* // sweetgrass? How do we make beings from our stories? How do we prevent the ongoing ecological destruction of Indigenous territories and the spirits that inhabit them? Over the past year, as I have watched the increasing violence against Indigenous, Black, Latinx, immigrant, trans, queer, and female bodies and communities, I wonder how better understanding the history of art—and telling stories about it—facilitates the dismantling of systems that are intimately linked with art. By thinking about knives and pipelines and John Berger, I hope to offer this humble *dibaajimowin* // narrative as possible seeds whose sowing, harvesting, and dissemination are beyond my own control.

Bezhigo-mookomaan // One knife

Maybe it is my academic lineage and kinship, having studied under Marxist art historian David Craven, but I have always been drawn to art historian John Berger, whose book and BBC television program *Ways of Seeing* were both funda-

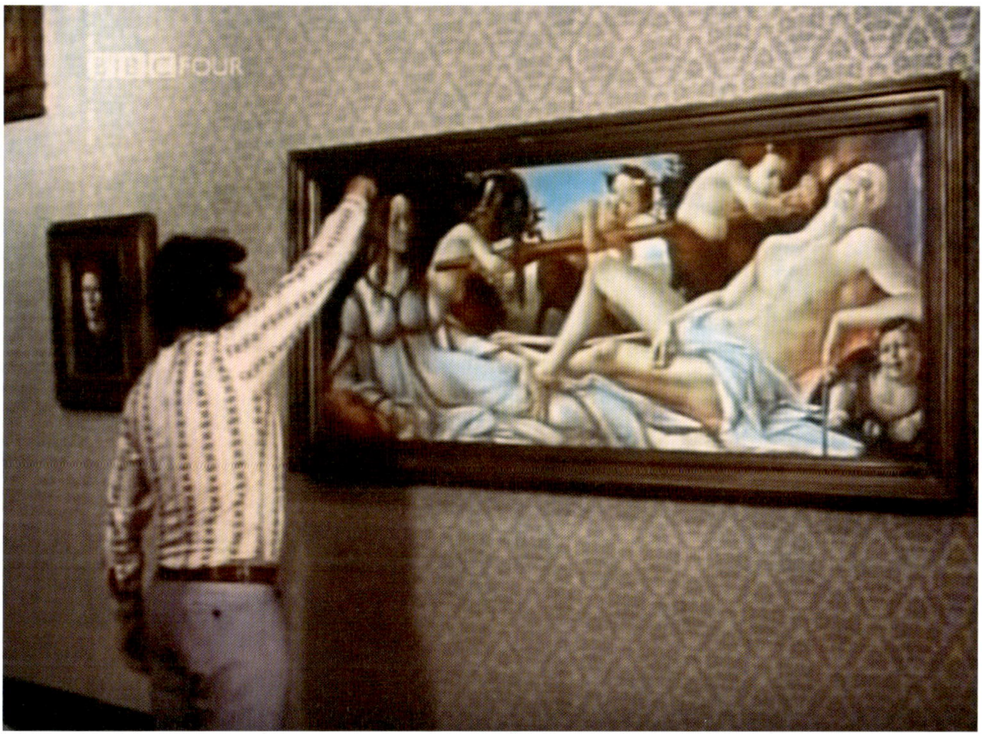

Fig. 1. John Berger (British, 1926–2017), *Ways of Seeing,* still from "Episode 1," aired January 8, 1972, BBC Two

mentally important and overly simplistic. At the beginning of the four-part BBC program from 1972, Berger systematically removes a red utility knife from his back pocket. Wearing blue pants and a striped shirt with a butterfly collar, hair oddly messy—clearly a cool dude in 1970s England—Berger methodically cuts through the canvas of Sandro Botticelli's *Venus and Mars* (c. 1483; fig. 1).

Berger's *mookomaan,* or knife, travels clockwise in a series of four straight lines around the face of Venus in what, I reckon, could only be a reproduction of Botticelli's masterwork. As someone who has been chastised countless times by museum guards and docents for getting too close to paintings, I viscerally cringe as Berger's knife slices through oil paint, and linseed oil, and canvas, to remove the head of Venus.

As an art historian, albeit a historian of the arts of the Americas, I cannot decolonize the thousands of Western paintings and sculptures in my mental archive. As Berger cuts, I immediately think to myself "Ceci n'est pas une pipe"

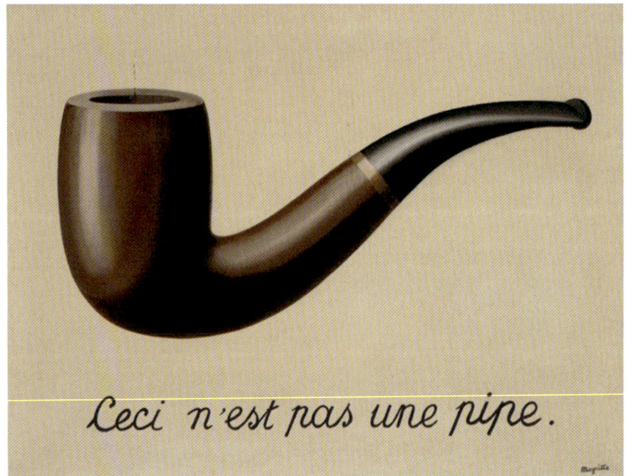

Fig. 2. René Magritte (Belgian, 1898–1967), *The Treachery of Images*, 1928–29. Oil on canvas, 23 ³/₄ × 31 ¹⁵/₁₆ × 1 in. (60.3 × 81.1 × 2.5 cm). Los Angeles County Museum of Art. Purchased with funds provided by the Mr. and Mrs. William Preston Harrison Collection (78.7). © 2017 C. Herscovici / Artists Rights Society (ARS), New York

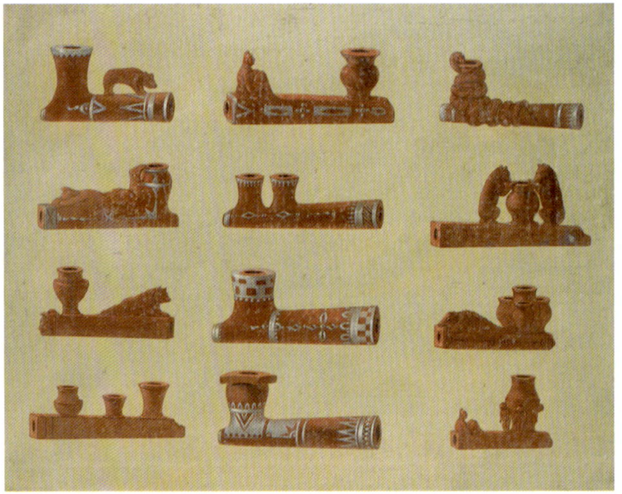

Fig. 3. George Catlin (American, 1796–1872), *Portfolio of Pipes*, 1852. Cardboard, 17 ¹/₂ × 22 ³/₄ in. (44.5 × 57.8 cm). British Museum, London. Purchased by the Trustees of the Christy Collection, 1882 (Am2006, Ptg.26)

(This is not a pipe), and my mind quickly goes to René Magritte's *La trahison des images* (*The Treachery of Images*, 1928–29; fig. 2). If Magritte's pipe is not a pipe, then Berger's Botticelli is neither Venus nor Botticelli. Just as Berger hopes I will, I start to decipher the distinction between a work and its reproduction. I quickly think about the intimate relationship between art and artifice. But, maybe I shouldn't care. Or should I?

In my mind, Magritte's Surrealist pipe—or rather, following the logic that Berger establishes, mental images of digital reproductions of photographs of paintings of pipes—transforms and becomes George Catlin's *Portfolio of Pipes* (1852; fig. 3). Catlin (1796–1872) was the quintessential colonialist American painter, whose nineteenth-century paintings participated in a sort of salvage ethnology. According to Catlin himself, his work was intended "to rescue from oblivion their primitive looks and customs." Founding director of the National Museum of the American Indian W. Richard West (Southern Cheyenne) notes that Catlin is "a cultural P. T. Barnum, a crass huckster trading on other people's lives and life ways." As the Smithsonian notes of his legacy, "Today Catlin's Indian Gallery is recognized as a great cultural treasure, offering rare insight into native cultures and a crucial chapter in American history."[1]

I care little about Catlin as an artist, but in addition to painting "primitive looks and customs," he also painted pipes—the sacred ones that are smoked in ceremonies or used to mark significant events. He painted the pipes whose smoke communicates with the spirits and the ancestors and with the Creator.

In an obviously settler-colonial tradition that cannot be invented—as one might say on social media, you can't make this stuff up—the reddish brown, fine-grained sedimentary rock used to make pipe bowls, a material that I might call *miskopwaaganasin*, or red pipestone, is commonly known as catlinite. It is named after the artist who "discovered" it. Catlin painted nineteenth-century Indigenous people and their practices, and now the red pipestone used by many Indigenous peoples and communities bears his name.

As for me, I am interested in Catlin solely because he painted pipes and participated in salvage ethnology, believing that his work as an artist was "to rescue from oblivion their primitive looks and customs."[2] Botticelli's *Venus and Mars* is housed in the National Gallery in London and recognized as a true work of art; Catlin's portfolio of pipes is located in the British Museum, a work of cultural history.

But as I write, don't forget that John Berger's *Ways of Seeing* is still playing, even if our minds are drifting across a series of image-based discourses. Nonetheless, I drift further away from Berger and his violent engagement with Botticelli's painting. I move beyond Catlin's paintings and migrate toward those paintings that Swiss artist Peter Rindisbacher (1806–1834) created of what he called "half-castes" around Red River, Manitoba (fig. 4). These images were painted around the same time that my *gichi-gichi-aanikoobijigan* (grandfather's great-grandmother) was born in Red River.

Rindisbacher painted lots of people smoking pipes. That is to say, he painted lots of Indigenous people smoking pipes. He painted Métis voyageurs smoking small clay pipes in their Hudson's Bay Company canoe. He painted a Métis woman smoking a long pipe while carrying a baby in a *dikinaagan // * cradle board. He painted Indigenous folks smoking outside in a variety of environments and people smoking inside teepees. Rindisbacher loved painting people and their pipes. He even painted a self-portrait of himself smoking a pipe. During autumn 2016, at the height of the resistance to the Dakota Access Pipeline (DAPL) and associated issues at Standing Rock, I employed this image as source material to

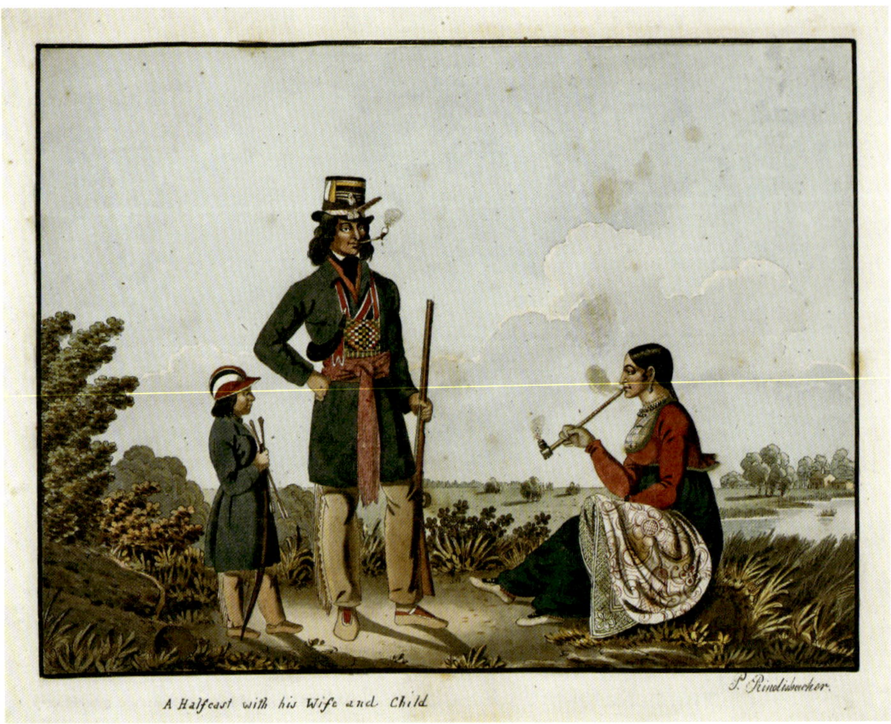

Fig. 4. Peter Rindisbacher (Swiss, 1806–1834), *A Half-cast with His Wife and Child*, c. 1825. Watercolor, ink on paper, 6 ½ × 8 ½ in. (16.5 × 21.6 cm). Winnipeg Art Gallery, Winnipeg, Manitoba, Canada. Collection of the Winnipeg Art Gallery; acquired with financial assistance from the National Museums of Canada (G-82-215). Photo by Ernest Mayer

quickly create an anti-DAPL meme. The text of the image read: "The only pipeline that I support doesn't transport oil."

At this point, and I hope you are still with me, I imagine pipes and ceremony and, then, I go immediately to pipelines and the intimate relationship between extraction and the ongoing dispossession of Indigenous peoples of this hemisphere. I think about the Dakota Access Pipeline and fossil fuel extraction as contemporary Indian Removal Acts. The discovery of oil in Oklahoma, what was called the Indian Territory for much of the nineteenth century, was linked to extralegal dispossession of Indigenous land bases. In this story, we must remember that President Donald Trump desires to be Andrew Jackson. Trump tweeted, his unofficial form of presidential communication, about Andrew Jackson in a way that demonstrated a form of colonial amnesia and revisionist historical memory. For Indigenous people, the linkages that Trump makes to Jackson are not coincidental. After all, it was Jackson who initiated the Indian Removal Act on May 28, 1830, and it was Trump who signed an executive order on January 24, 2017, only a few days after entering office, approving the completion of the Dakota Access Pipeline.

But if you have forgotten—and I think I have at this point in the story—that as I write, I am still watching John Berger's *Ways of Seeing* and Berger's voice-of-God narration interrupts the sound of the knife slicing through Botticelli's canvas. The sound of the knife punctuates my own thoughts and slices them, as well. I no longer care about Botticelli or Europe or even art history, as a discipline.

Rather, in this moment watching *Ways of Seeing*—and in this durational moment that I write this story down—Berger and his words become the impetus for me to think through an anticolonial art history and bring Berger's own Western Marxism forward forty-five years while simultaneously linking it backward to time immemorial and engaging it with the uniquely North American variant of settler-colonialism and an Indigenous studies perspective. In his obituary for the BBC, Will Gompertz writes that Berger "had the eye of [an] artist, intellect of an academic, and charisma of a born performer. He was though, above all, a writer and story teller. He enriched our lives with his novels, poetry and criticism. He showed us how to see, not as individuals, but together."[3] But Berger's thoughts were inextricably tied to British and Western Marxisms, unable to fully integrate non-Western ontologies.

To borrow from Berger himself: "Tonight it isn't so much the paintings themselves which I want to consider, as the way we now see them. Now in the second half of the twentieth century, because we see these paintings as nobody saw them before. If we discover why this is so, we shall also discover something about ourselves and the situation in which we are living."[4]

Only a few seconds into this four-part series, the narrator speaks and asks us—the audience—to consider how we understand the process of vision. Berger, as both voice-of-God and protagonist, as both critic and poet, asks us to "discover" why we see these paintings like no one has before, discovering something about ourselves in the process. By doing so, and evoking the language of *discovery*, Berger evokes the same colonial process of claiming that his critique potentially lays bare.

I am less interested in *discovery* per se than in merging Berger's ideological critique of capitalism with the potentiality that Indigenous ontologies have to challenge the omnipotence of capitalist violence. I am more invested in dismantling institutional extraction than I am with academic exploration. From Berger, however, I learned to revel in the disavowal of disinterest. If images have agency to act upon us in certain ways, why should we not reciprocally engage with them from partisan positions that are, at the least, not impartial.

Both Berger and I are, I think, disinterested in the paintings themselves. Rather, Berger wants us to question some of the assumptions we have about European painting, a tradition that he notes died around 1900. Berger, and many of his peers on the Left, recognized that the periodization of European painting intimately coincides with the age of empire and the expansion of capitalism. Unlike painting, though, colonialism has not ended. As DAPL so horrifically illuminates, colonialism continues in an unfettered, if contested, trajectory.

Niizho-mookomaanan // Two knives

Botticelli's *Venus and Mars* is conveniently housed in the National Gallery, London, which is significant for Berger's story—less for mine (but significant in the ways that colonial institutions extracted cultural history, in a way similar to how the extraction industry does so today).

I recall as an undergraduate art student, back before I had children, falling asleep through many of the long and boring lectures on Renaissance paintings. Even today, I wonder how and why this story exists in this publication. I wonder why it was previously given as a talk at the Clark, in dialogue with many renowned art historians. I wonder if these words even have resonance in a publication distributed by Yale University Press, primarily for other art historians and those professionals embedded in high art institutions.

As an art student, as I still do today, I often wondered how art historians could do such violence to images by rendering them—how do you say—boring. During a typical lecture, with the lights dimmed to near darkness, the hum of the slide projector-turned-digital projector only served as the music to the art historians' lullaby. If Berger's knife was a provocation, then the art history lecture was a grievance.

I never met John Berger in real life, but in my viewing of a digital projection of a video cassette of a 1970s BBC television series, I knew that John Berger rocked a butterfly collar and that he had little concern for the necessary distance between a work of art and its viewer. He was willing to take up a knife and, even if only disfiguring a reproduction, destroy a work that others held in high regard.

Each time I watch the opening scene of *Ways of Seeing*, and it has been many dozens at this point, I smile as if Berger's knife literally undoes the economic and colonial legacy that is objectified in the history of Renaissance painting. How many times have I fantasized about doing exactly what he does? Berger's knife and words and image served to dismantle—or at least illuminate—those institutions of oppression (heteropatriarchy, class divisions, sexism, racism, colonialism, etc.) that I also wanted to smash. I cannot help but think about Berger's knife, as both metaphor and symbol, for his work as an art historian. Berger's writing, like the knife, was similarly sharp.

Like Berger, I also wield a utility knife, though mine is not red. Mine is black and silver—the pocket knife I have today is black—and, like Berger, I too remove it from my pocket before I cut into priceless objects. But my *mookomaan* does work dissimilar to that of Berger's knife. My knife, however, does not slice canvas to remove and isolate the heads within canonical masterworks housed in one of the greatest museums in the world whose collections were pillaged through European colonial expansion.

No, my *mookomaan,* or knife, is not an analytical tool to understand Benjaminian theory, "the work of art in the age of mechanical reproduction" or "the work of art in the age of technological reproducibility," if I'd rather cite its more recent translation.[5]

My knife, however, does serve a similar function in that it pierces through the outer bark of the birch tree to harvest *wiigwaas,* the Anishinaabemowin word for birch bark. My *mookomaan* is both theoretical and practical. It links what I do in the academy with what I do in the bush.

With my left hand, I gently remove *asemaa* (tobacco) from my pocket and offer this *asemaa* to the ancestors and to the tree. I conjure the spirits with my attempt at a song before making a small and delicate incision, testing if this particular *wiigwaasaatig* // birch tree is ready to share its bark. If the time is right, I make a vertical incision down the tree. Next, I slowly insert the tips of my fingers, feeling the moisture under the bark, and gently begin to remove the outer bark from the *wiigwaasaatig,* making sure not to damage the tree. If the time is right, and this should only be done at the precise moment during the year, the *wiigwaas* removes itself. It creates a thunderous boom, echoing the sounds of a late-summer storm as it peels itself off the tree. With moistened fingers, the sweet scent, likened only to a late-season watermelon, permeates the air, and I think of trees, and Land, and ancestors. I think of the generations who have harvested bark to make canoes and *makakoon* // baskets and structures. If this process is done properly, the tree will scar, but it will survive.

When harvesting—and throughout life—I wield a *mookomaanens,* a small knife. Small knives are precious and intimate. They do work that *gichi-mookomaanan* cannot do.

Like Berger, my knife does its work in an esteemed site of social and cultural importance. In Anishinaabemowin, the lingua franca of the Great Lakes Indigenous world, the term for an American or a white person is *gichi-mookomaan.* Literally, the term translates as someone who carries a big knife. In an Indigenous worldview, colonial agents carried, and wielded, big knives in their assault on Indigenous sovereignties, epistemologies, and ontologies. I am certain that not much has changed. Thinking about this today, I am still convinced that, in the sentences above, I should have used the present tense of the verb "to carry" and "to wield," but this is one of the dilemmas of English, and most European languages—it creates a linearity of verb tenses: past, present, future.

As carriers of small knives, both Berger and I challenge the *gichi-mookomaaniimowin* that are the capitalist, colonial, and heteropatriarchal ontologies. Our knives are both small knives.

Gichi-maazhigaa'aabkook // Big pipelines

If *gichi-mookomaanan* is used to describe those who throughout the colonial period wielded the power of settler-colonialism, it is possible that our *aanikoobijiganag*—a word that simultaneously means "descendants" and "ancestors"—will call those who benefit from this moment in time the *gichi-maazhigaa'aabkook* // big pipelines. If early colonialism was a violent task wielded by the weapons of war, today's colonial project is maintained through state-sanctioned and market-based weaponry. But these are similarly used to dismantle Indigenous sovereignty and relationships to Land. These weapons are not better; they are only contemporary weaponized practices intent on appropriating Indigenous lands and enacting genocide against Native peoples.

As David Blackmon wrote for *Forbes* in April 2017:

> DAPL has already begun to improve the economics of drilling for and producing oil from the Bakken Shale, whose rig count has begun to rise over the last few months. And while the aggressive and often-violent protesters who spent half a year opposing the project's completion would never admit it, DAPL is also already improving the safety of moving Bakken crude out of the basin to be sold and refined.[6]

While I would disagree with Blackmon's accounts of the Water Protectors as "aggressive and often-violent," we can nonetheless see that the Indian Wars continue. This is not about the safety of moving oil, but rather the ontological and epistemological desire to even do so. There is also the epidemic of Missing and Murdered Indigenous Women, Girls, Trans, and Two-Spirits (MMIWGTTS, but often shortened to MMIW) and the relationship between sexual and other forms of violence to the extraction industry.

In Canada, a nation-state where Indigenous issues are more visible than in the United States, yet where Indigenous peoples consider themselves living in apartheid-like conditions, Native communities are supposed to have "free, prior, and informed consent" before mineral extraction occurs. Yet, as we saw in early 2017, Prime Minister Justin Trudeau said about Indigenous peoples—particularly in reference to the Musqueam, Squamish, and Tsleil-Waututh nations who oppose pipelines—"No, they don't have a veto." Trudeau subsequently approved the Trans Mountain Pipeline. Current pipeline projects under development to move shale gas include Energy Transfer Partners LP's (ETP) Rover, TransCanada Corp's Leach Xpress, and Williams Cos Inc.'s Atlantic Sunrise. Extractive industries, their relationship to the ongoing appropriation of Indigenous lands, and the creation of new pipelines to move gas and oil is one of the most pressing environmental and political issues today. Of course, Indigenous resistance will not likely stop.

We have gone from Big Knives to Big Pipelines. Or maybe, we are in an era of both Big Knives and Big Pipelines // *Gichi-mookomaanan miinawaa Gichi-maazhigaa-aabkook.*

If John Berger taught me to read oil paintings to understand the machinations of capitalism as well as the functions of the cis-gendered male gaze, it is our task to read oil and the machinations of settler-colonialism. As Eve Tuck and K. Wayne Yang so forcefully write, "Decolonization brings about the repatriation of Indigenous land and life; it is not a metaphor for other things we want to do to improve our societies and schools."[7] Decolonization is not a metaphor.

In the Great Lakes, where I make my home and where my paternal ancestors fought with the British against the *Gichi-mookomaanan* and were forced to the other side of the lakes and across the newly established geopolitical border, we face the potential oil spill from Enbridge Line 5, an aging pipeline that was built in 1953. The pipeline moves oil from western Canada through Wisconsin, across the Straits of Mackinac and to Sarnia, Ontario. Anishinaabekwe activist Vanessa

Gray has brought attention to the ecological violence enacted against citizens of Aamjiwnaang First Nation and their home in Canada's Chemical Valley.

The struggles against pipelines and mineral extraction is not a new one, but Indigenous peoples are in the most sacred fight and ones linked to sovereignty. Again, decolonization is not a metaphor. The economics of colonial extraction continues full force. The logics of settler-coloniality are unrepentant.

I wield a *mookomaanens* and use it accordingly.

1. "Catlin Virtual Exhibition," George Catlin and His Indian Gallery, https://2.americanart.si.edu/exhibitions/online/catlin/highlights.html.

2. George Catlin, quoted in ibid.

3. Will Gompertz, "John Berger, Art Critic and Author of *Ways of Seeing*, Dies," *BBC News*, January 2, 2017, www.bbc.com/news/entertainment-arts-38492516.

4. John Berger, *Ways of Seeing*, episode 1, aired January 8, 1972, on BBC Two, https://youtu.be/0pDE4VX_9Kk.

5. Walter Benjamin, *Gesammelte Schriften*, 7 vols., ed. Rolf Tiedemann and Hermann Schweppenhauser (Frankfurt am Main: Suhrkamp Verlag, 1972–89); for biographical information and bibliography in English, see https://plato.stanford.edu/entries/benjamin (accessed November 15, 2017).

6. David Blackmon, "Gov. Cuomo Proves Pipeline Politics Aren't Limited To DAPL," *Forbes*, April 24, 2017, www.forbes.com/sites/davidblackmon/2017/04/24/gov-cuomo-proves-pipeline-politics-arent-limited-to-dapl/.

7. Eve Tuck and K. Wayne Yang, "Decolonization is Not a Metaphor," *Decolonization: Indigeneity, Education, & Society* 1, no. 1 (2012).

"Welcome to My Volcano": New Materialism, Art History, and Their Others

Rebecca Zorach

Art history—which has always thought about materials—has watched with interest the turn toward "matter" in literary and cultural studies. Or at least some of art history has. As Huey Copeland puts it, the "supposed theoretical innovations" of new materialisms "not only echo the preoccupations and procedures of aesthetic inquiry but also suggest the relevance of art-historical methods for producing interdisciplinary accounts of the world's continual unfolding and reconfiguring."[1] Whatever the label given to the material turn—here I will use "new materialism" as a catchall—it may prompt a bit of cynicism from those of us who have been thinking about matter for a long time. Certainly, it provides art historians with some additional theoretical context for positing strong versions of nonhuman agency and exploring the ways in which that adjusts our understanding of human agency. Equally, it seems to confirm some of what art history has always known. But is this confirmation justified? Would not an incisive theoretical intervention around questions of matter instead *unsettle* our preconceptions? It would seem that art history might in fact sit somewhat uneasily with the more strictly "ecological" implications of new materialist thinking, invested as we are in preserving a different distinction, that between nonhuman things that *humans have made* and nonhuman things *that are part of nature.*

Definitions of "art" in early modern Europe—via Giorgio Vasari, the originary site of art history—would encourage the blurring of this boundary, too. Among many historical and cultural alternatives for thinking about matter, the historical European idea of "art" from which the modern discipline of art history derives is deeply intertwined with the question of the agency of the nonhuman—sometimes allied with it, sometimes opposing it, as in questions of idolatry, but almost always thinking with it.[2] Idols and idolatry constitute an obvious site for thinking about the agency of nonhuman beings—in this case troubling—of artifacts whose blurring of boundaries makes their existence an accusation, their excessive effectiveness consciously presented as *not*-art.

In addition to questions of the liveliness of art objects, the question of the agency of "nature" undergirds European definitions of art. For Alberti, for Leonardo, half-formed shapes found in rocks or in trunks of trees, or moss on moist stone walls, served as the emergent art that spurred artists to produce their own works. In Europe through the early modern period, Nature—often personified—was not something outside, out "there"; not landscape, but a force. When art imitated nature, it imitated nature's actions as much as its appearance. In the sixteenth century, a notion of "art" as fine art emerged in dialogue with nature in the context of conjoined processes of religious upheaval and colonial expansion. In conversations with Gabriele Paleotti, the Bolognese cardinal charged with developing an account of the Catholic Counter-Reformation position on holy images, the sixteenth-century Italian naturalist Ulisse Aldrovandi proposed an Aristotelian position in which art imitates nature, not just in the products of nature but also in the processes of nature. This was not mere metaphor, but a view of art and nature as holding parallel purposes. Art's relationship to nature is more complex in this reading than if we think of nature purely as *subject matter of art*. If nature was a force inside all living beings, it might even extend to the products of human labor. Aldrovandi wrote several letters to Paleotti responding to draft chapters of his *Discorso sopra le immagini sacre e profane* (Discourse on sacred and profane images). In one he writes, "Art is an image and vestige of nature; but nature is a living exemplar and just as art does whatever it does for some end, thus with nature as well, all it does, it does with some end."[3] It is not just that they both have goals, not even just that they have similar goals. "Painting," he writes, "should be the true imitation of natural things. And such is the family relationship and consistency between nature and art, that if nature should perform the work of art, it would not do it any differently. Similarly, if art should perform the work of nature, it would do it no differently than Nature does."[4]

Echoes of this parallelism and cooperation also appear in contemporary new materialist texts. Jane Bennett's *Vibrant Matter*, for example, suggests the generative possibilities that emerge when we dispense with ideological divisions between humans and nonhumans, whether artifacts or nonhuman natural beings. If these critical tendencies might intervene forcefully in an urgent political moment—the situation of severe environmental damage, climate change, and their attendant crises—all the better. The optimism of *Vibrant Matter* goes in this direction. For Bennett, the "political project"—not merely a philosophical position—of her book is "to encourage more intelligent and sustainable engagements with vibrant matter and lively things." She asks, "Why advocate the vibrancy of matter? Because my hunch is that the image of dead or thoroughly instrumentalized matter feeds human hubris and our earth-destroying fantasies of conquest and consumption."[5]

But as with any critique of humanism, including those that came from a linguistic as opposed to a material direction, we have to pose the question—perhaps even more urgently, now: What about those people not yet, or no longer or not again, allowed to claim membership in the "human"? The critique of humanism risks remaining embedded in its assumptions, the idea of nonhuman agency simply reinsulating a universalized (unmarked) human position—taking for granted what Sylvia Wynter describes as the "overrepresentation" of a particular formation of "the human" (Man2, the white bourgeois colonial subject) as the full extent of humanness.[6]

Where do humans who have been the object of the murderous historical process of dehumanization fit into the revivifying of "matter"? Simply returning to sixteenth-century Aristotelian thinking can show us how "nature" was employed in other, more troubling ways. Earlier, I mentioned that the historical European idea of "art" from which the modern discipline of art history derives is deeply intertwined with the question of the agency of the nonhuman. It is also intertwined with the question of the otherly-human. Aldrovandi's text presents the appealing possibility of enhancing respect for Nature by imagining "her" as an artist. Two decades before Aldrovandi corresponded with Paleotti, the Spanish priest Juan Gines de Sepúlveda derived justification from Aristotle for the enslavement of Indigenous inhabitants of the Americas by Europeans. Sepúlveda wrote: "But that some among them seem to be ingenious at some art form [*artificia*], this is no argument that they possess human prudence, since we see small creatures such as bees and spiders fabricating works [*opera*] that no human industry could properly imitate."[7] His argument sweeps aside the architectural accomplishments of the Aztecs and Inca as signs not of human prudence but of natural necessity. To be defined as human, for Sepúlveda, ordered artifactual or architectural making was *not enough*. Characterized by servility, in Sepúlveda's view, the inhabitants of the Americas *do not* demonstrate human freedom in their architectural accomplishments, and therefore are properly dominated by Europeans.

Aristotle's account of "natural" slavery in the *Politics* itself depends on ideas about craft and artifice. Aristotle poses his views as an argument against the idea that the state of slavery is only a matter of art, artificial, deriving from convention. He accepts that there is slavery that is not natural, but insists that some people are not just born in slavery but are slaves by nature, and his primary rationale for this is awkwardly analogical, symptomatic of an inability to actually clinch his argument: the soul rules the body by nature, he says, and wherever there is a similar divide between men, the "lower sort" are slaves by nature. At the same time, he acknowledges, this divide would be easier to discern if human bodies differed from one another as much as those of ordinary humans differ from "statues of the gods." Statues, here, appear as such successful stand-ins for the gods that they constitute a self-evident hierarchy with humans—a distinct superiority.[8]

Slaves number among the "instruments" of their owners and of the arts they perform, but they are living instruments. Invoking a fantasy of instruments that are themselves animated, Aristotle notes that if they were, if tools could act on their own, slaves would be unnecessary:

> Now instruments are of various sorts; some are living, others lifeless; in the rudder, the pilot of a ship has a lifeless, in the look-out man, a living instrument; for in the arts a servant is a kind of instrument . . . . And so, in the arrangement of the family, a slave is a living possession, and property a number of such instruments; and the servant is himself an instrument which takes precedence of all other instruments. For if every instrument could accomplish its own work, obeying or anticipating the will of others, like the statues of Daedalus . . . if, in like manner, the shuttle would weave and the plectrum touch the lyre without a hand to guide them, chief workmen would not want servants, nor masters slaves.[9]

From this perspective, the making of wondrous artifacts cannot establish the human rights of the maker—the right of the maker to humanness. The question gets resolved in a feat of circular reasoning underpinned by violence. The less-than-fully-human can be an animated thing and a maker of other things at the same time. The natural right of the relationship of master and servant is constituted, "naturally," by the mere existence of the relationship itself. Property, and specifically the ownership of humans, defines not only the position of master but even, potentially (as for Sepúlveda), the legitimately human.

The colonial history and history of enslavement that I indicate with the synecdoche of Sepúlveda and Aristotle must be considered whenever we claim to be breaking down boundaries between the human and the nonhuman. Not least because the people targeted by abusive definitions of the human also had rich and complex positions on the relationship between humans and the world of living and nonliving things. Considering the origins of new materialist thinking, Janet

Berlo and Jessica L. Horton take a critical view of recent scholarly interest in matter that critiques the divide between subject and object. As they note, this divide in the first instance "authorized the foundational capitalist imperative to own and control nature." They write, further, "we are concerned with those humans who are too often left out of the conversation. Indigenous scholars and scholars of the Indigenous will attest to the survival of alternative intellectual traditions in which the liveliness of matter is grasped as quite ordinary, both inside, and at the fringes of, European modernity."[10] In the essay I quoted at the outset, Huey Copeland also points out that "in the name of universal values and transcendent theoretical schemas," new materialist discourses risk abetting white supremacy, as when the editors of one anthology sweep aside, in a single gesture, "fashionable constructivist approaches and identity politics."[11] Kyla Wazana Tompkins writes: "I, alongside many others, worry and am cynical about how the nonwhite or otherwise minoritarian subjects and indeed history itself, haunt the edges of certain veins within New Materialist thought, sometimes explicitly as the cause of previous intellectual movements that undermine or critique facticity in favor of discourse and sometimes subtly when minoritarian life appears as the ideologically undertheorized yet exemplary object of the New Materialism itself."[12]

Thus, the stakes of new materialism have to involve questions of European colonial logics that set up divides between the human and the nonhuman that refused humanness to a large majority of humans. They need to account for how that situation creates the conditions within which the new materialism itself fails to acknowledge that the "liveliness of matter" has a history outside European philosophical tradition. But I am also interested in a related problem of new materialism—one that is also a consequence of these erasures. The claim that work like Bennett's may be political is not trivial or uninteresting, but as taken up in the academy, it can look like just one more of theory's seemingly relentless veerings away from any initially promising engagement with pressing political claims. What happens when theory, or art, seeks to cultivate in humans a respect for, an aesthetic preoccupation with, nonhuman agency? Presenting a picture of powerful nonhuman forces could suggest a political project that encourages humility, receptivity, or quiescence rather than hubris and instrumentality in human dealings with the nonhuman world. The description of nonhuman liveliness could be absolutely warranted as an ethical redescription and critique of ideology and still dangerously misjudge the needs of the current moment. Certainly, there is a pleasure (and pleasure is not wrong) in relinquishing instrumentality, as in the case of modern artists who relinquished skill and control, allowing chance or the medium to chart the course of their work—yet as often as not, remaining secure in their subject positions. But the glamor of nonhuman agency casts the white liberal academic subject a bit too much in the role of the spectator, aestheticizing restraint as a technique of the individual self—a view that would never cross the collective "mind" of the industries and political formations that are the worst contributors to pollution and global warming. Who is understood as the audience for the subtle encouragement to abandon instrumental attitudes toward nature; who can and should actually hear this argument?

A similar set of problems emerges in Amanda Boetzkes's book *The Ethics of Earth Art*, in which she makes the case in Heideggerian terms for a phenomenology of "earth art," art that brings elemental qualities of the Earth into play. Boetzkes establishes a useful corpus of earth art and argues for its capacity to make ecological interventions by redirecting viewers' consciousness to the elemental properties of the Earth. Her work echoes both the opportunities and the problems of new materialism (without being avowedly "new materialist"). She makes a distinction between art projects that take action to remediate environmental harms (whose contours are in turn implicitly constrained by those harms), and those that operate on a phenomenological level to encourage a receptive attitude toward the elements. Boetzkes writes: "In the works considered here, the earth is not a closed system that can be balanced, restored, studied, and effectively reintegrated into an 'eco-friendly' global capitalism. Instead, the artworks mediate contact with elemental forces that overwhelm the senses and confound the stability of one's perceptual apparatus." She echoes concerns about overemphasis on human agency in pointing out that "reclamation" projects "risk being complicit with a sociopolitical order responsible for pollution and the overzealous harvesting of resources." The artists she emphasizes in *The Ethics of Earth Art* "see their role as cultivating a different attitude or stance toward natural activity that acknowledges its existence beyond the parameters of human control."[13] This suggests an experience of art as a reckoning with radical alterity.

Boetzkes's work resonates productively with new materialist theory in her suggestion that artworks can orient us toward nonhuman forces to reframe our perceptions of and attitudes toward the nonhuman world, adjusting our conceptions of agency. These might be spaces that surround the viewer with elemental stimuli, or works that use the body as a medium (not humanizing nature or idealizing the body, but distorting it, rendering it "alien"). The approach Boetzkes

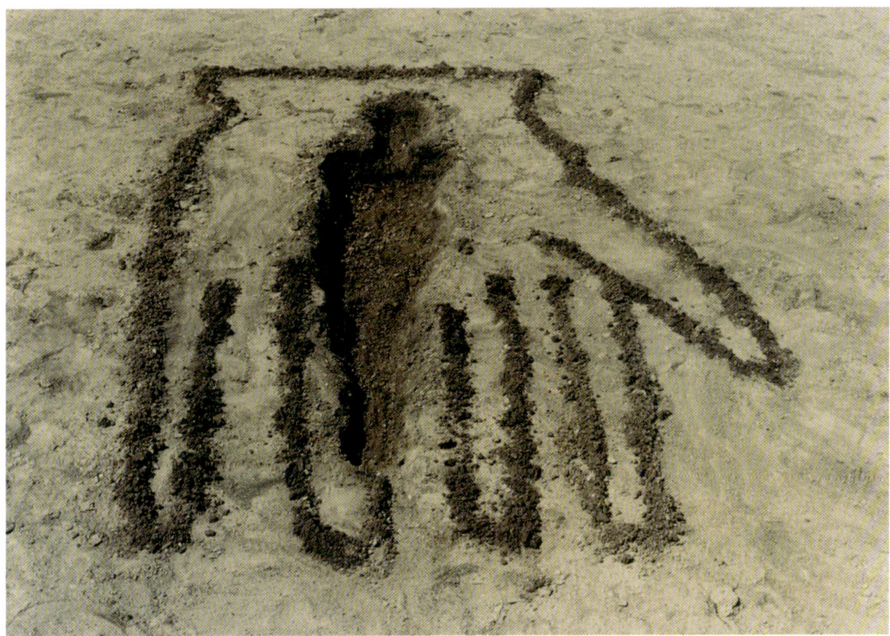

Fig. 1. Ana Mendieta (Cuban American, 1948–1985), *Incantation a Olokun-Yemayá*, 1977. Photograph. Galerie Lelong, New York. © The Estate of Ana Mendieta Collection, LLC. Courtesy Galerie Lelong & Co.

takes centers fundamentally on the phenomenology of the viewer's experience. In her view, these artworks cultivate in their viewers an attitude of receptivity to the earth's withholding.

This position resonates with the problem of quiescence that I described above with respect to Bennett's argument; Boetzkes's approach, however appealing, cannot account for collectivity, or for difference (including cultural difference) among viewers or makers. For example, Boetzkes finds a prime example in the work of Ana Mendieta, in particular her *siluetas*, body sculptures (often excavated or imprinted forms of a stylized female body) situated in landscapes. In Mendieta's *Incantacion to Olokun-Yemayá* (1977; fig. 1), it would seem that the giant hand (made of piled-up dark sand) that "holds" the body imprint belongs to one or both of two powerful Yoruba water *orishas*, Olokun and Yemayá (Olokun, who governs the depths of the oceans, is the mother or grandmother of Yemayá, who represents rivers and beaches). What does it mean for a Cuban artist to invoke Yoruba water deities? This question is, perhaps necessarily, absent from Boetzkes's account of the piece. What would be required to delve fully into the import of these deities, the "incantation" to them, the regard for them, in

Mendieta's work? It cannot, I would suggest, be derived from an approach that rests exclusively on a universalized understanding of the viewer's experience.

I'm therefore suggesting that the quiescence and individualism of new materialism and related critical approaches encourage forms of frugality that allow the question of power to drop out. With it, then, we might lose questions of conflict, the laboring body, political struggle, the economics of the art world, cultural identity, gender, and racial justice. Can ecopoetical forms be equal to the need to *assume* agency, to take action against harms caused by other humans to humans and nonhumans alike? And what would that agency look like? From the point of view of some of these issues, Jinthana Haritaworn writes: "If we are interested in recovering things and beings that are continually rendered disposable as a result of colonial capitalism and cis-heteropatriarchy, why not start with anti-colonial accounts of the world that have a long history of resisting both human and non-human erasure?" This "would have the potential to tackle anthropocentrism and dehumanization simultaneously, as relational rather than competing or analogous paradigms."[14] In the remainder of this essay, I want to address some examples of such "anti-colonial accounts" found in contemporary artistic practices that address ecologies, which I understand in the capacious sense indicated by Félix Guattari's "three ecologies": ecologies of the natural world, social life, and consciousness.[15]

Rebecca Belmore's powerful video installation, *Fountain*, is one example. Presented at the Venice Biennale of 2005, *Fountain* comprises a video projected in a darkened room against a wall of running water. The video begins with a camera sweeping across a beach littered with debris. Fire surges up in one spot. The artist struggles, nearly submerged in a body of dark water against a dark sky, as if trying to escape something that is pulling her under the waves (fig. 2). She *labors* with a bucket, which she seems to be trying to fill, grunting with the seemingly futile effort, the water working with and against her body. Finally, she pulls it up out of the water, onto the shore, and throws the water at the camera: it turns blood red (fig. 3).

Belmore is Anishinaabe Canadian. Rather than attempt to read specifically "Indigenous" meanings into her work, I want to think about a kind of universalizing call an Indigenous position might be making possible in it. Water may be ubiquitous and universal, but in this piece, it is violent; it does not, or does not only, withdraw itself from consciousness, but floods it. The artist's body labors against it, and it is that labor, that effort, that forms the center of this work. In several ways, the piece is structurally similar to Belmore's video installation of a

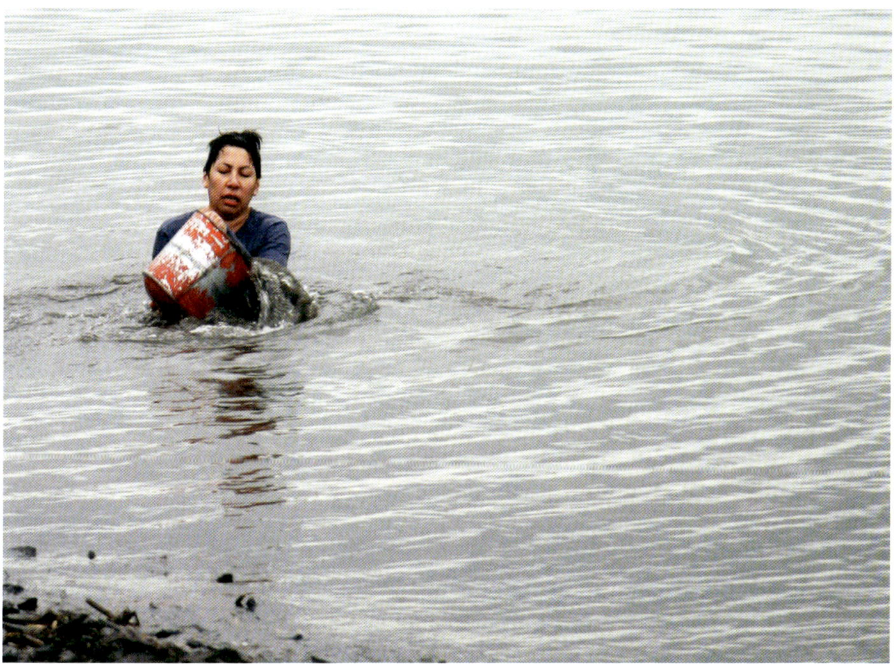

Fig. 2. Rebecca Belmore (Anishinaabe Canadian, b. 1960), still from *Fountain*, 2005. Courtesy of the artist and the Morris and Helen Belkin Art Gallery. Photography by José Ramón González

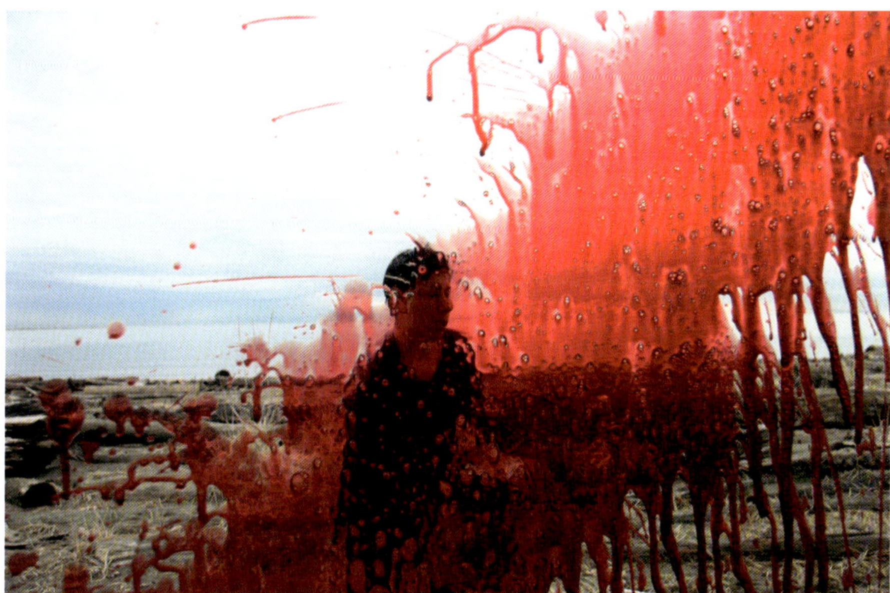

Fig. 3. Rebecca Belmore, still from *Fountain*, 2005. Courtesy of the artist and the Morris and Helen Belkin Art Gallery. Photography by José Ramón González

few years earlier, *The Named and the Unnamed* (2002), and a discussion of the earlier piece may provide some additional texture to my account of *Fountain*. *The Named and the Unnamed* likewise presents a performance in which Belmore struggles against an external and internal force; each is constituted by a video, projected on an unconventional viewing surface: a wall of streaming water in the case of *Fountain*, a wall of lightbulbs in the case of *The Named and the Unnamed*.

The Named and the Unnamed records a 2002 performance called *Vigil* in which Belmore marked the names and fates of disappeared women in Vancouver. Over the preceding twenty years, hundreds of women in Vancouver, and elsewhere in British Columbia, had disappeared. The missing women were disproportionately Indigenous Canadians.[16] Many were sex workers and/or drug users. Many turned out to be among the victims of serial killer Robert Pickton, who was finally arrested in 2002 and prosecuted.[17]

Belmore has a bucket of water at the opening of *Vigil*, too. She pours most of its contents on the ground near a telephone pole in a Vancouver alley and scrubs. Scrubs *hard*. Later, she solicits a volunteer to light votive candles, and begins shouting names: each one the first name of a missing woman, each one written on her arm. For each one, she draws yellow flowers, alone or in clumps, through her teeth, spits out the petals (fig. 4). When she's done she puts on a red dress, drinks from the bucket, wipes her face with the water. She starts nailing the red dress to the telephone pole, then ripping it away. First just a single nail. She tears the dress easily. Then, many nails. We read grim lines of struggle on her face. When she tries again to wrest herself and the dress from the battalion of nails holding it in place, tearing her dress, trying to rip it, the fabric is tough; it won't rip. It won't rip. It's as if she's ripping herself away from a captor with determination, with terror. Finally, she pulls the dress, except for one caught fragment, free—and begins again, nailing it and tearing it away. She's trying to escape, and she's trying to get the dress to tear—at once fleeing and enacting violence. As the dress is ripped to shreds, as there is less and less dress to nail and to pull apart, she is forced into an ever more intimate proximity to the pole. She has to hug herself close to it. The hammer and nails are very close: there's hardly room to wind up, hardly room to swing. Women observing look serious—grim, even; they clutch themselves tensely and look away, look back. A man walks by, stops, and stares.

Belmore conjures a collective through the rhyme of the nailing and ripping gestures with the litany of names and the lighting of candles. The conditions of performance are such that the audience has to remain, passive, *im*passive, nec-

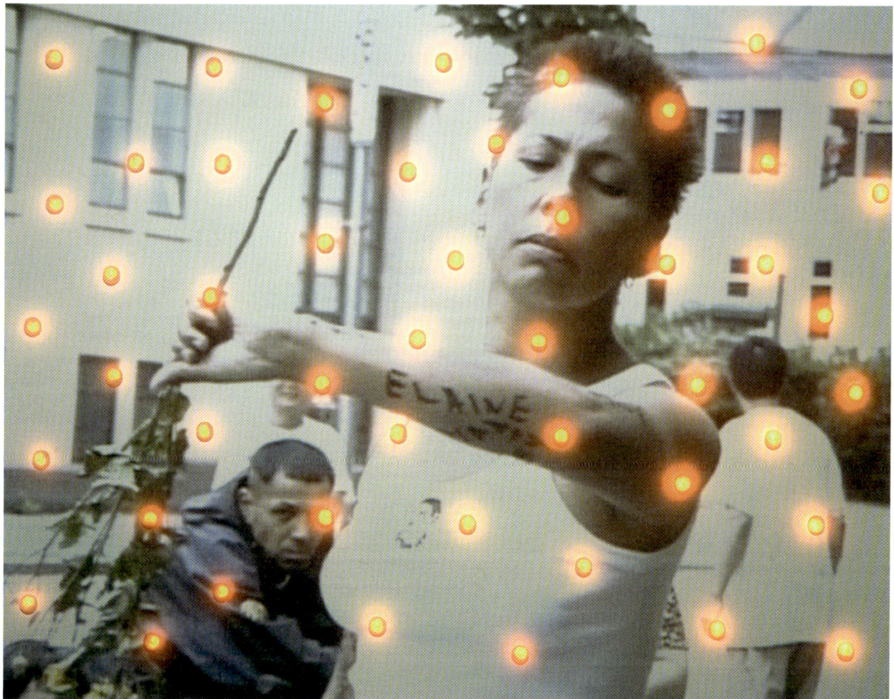

Fig. 4. Rebecca Belmore, still from *The Named and the Unnamed*, 2002. Video installation, 38 minutes 25 seconds. Courtesy of the Morris and Helen Belkin Art Gallery

essarily complicit in this staging of violence: for the performance to be, you and all your fellow audience members together must *let* it happen as the artist *makes* it happen. And that is uncomfortable. The event's very "artness" makes it impossible to intervene; the conventions of art are assimilated to passivity in the face of violent acts and social injustice. As, finally, Belmore struggles for a shred of dress to nail, her actions are reduced to a frustrated parody of the rules of this game: she takes a piece of dress and catches it half-heartedly on already embedded nails.

Fountain presents a similar kind of struggle—the effort to free herself from a force that the performer herself is conjuring—without the obvious context of the crowd, of social interaction. Yet water itself is suggestive of things that link human beings together. About *Fountain*, Belmore said: "I think *Fountain* is on one level a very simple piece, because it's just addressing this idea of water, and you know the bottom line is as human beings we all need water, and I think the future of water is something that we should think about, as a planet, as a planet of human beings."[18] Water, whether as ocean, hurricane, glacier, also represents the elemental forces, and their insistent withdrawal from our consciousness, that Boetzkes invokes. But in *Fountain* it also foregrounds the stark intensity of struggles for survival. Nature is not always nice.

The question of intrahuman relationality is one I will take up in the next section of this essay, but there are a few things I want to retain from the way *Fountain* recapitulates aesthetic elements of *The Named and the Unnamed*. The wall of water marks a significant change with respect to the wall of lightbulbs. First, a contrast: the wall of lightbulbs repels the viewer, making it hard to look, while the water attracts—you *want* to be close to the water, even to touch it, and by making you approach, the water puts you almost inside the work—inside the projection. Second, the violence of *Vigil* illuminates the violence of *Fountain*, implying just how dangerous *and* vital water can be. Finally, there is the self-imposed, laborious struggle that the performer undertakes in each, in which she is unable to fully free herself from a violent force because it is at least partly through her own agency that she is subjected to it. Work, understood as actual labor and not just "the artwork," is a key figure in Belmore's oeuvre. In "Rebecca Belmore: Art and the Object of Performance," Jessica Bradley quotes Belmore on her mother's and grandmother's "work hands": "I can see their hands touching hide, cloth, and bead, creating colour, beauty: work hands. I look at my hands and I am aware of their hands. That is how I wish to work."[19]

The obvious reading of "named and unnamed" is the victims whose names are known and the ones whose names are not. But if we take the two parts of the title as names for the two parts of the performance, the serial, ritual form and the more improvised, violent one, we might read the "named" as the naming, and the "unnamed" as the unspecified collectivity that is called into being and called out by the performance and its several iterations. That is, the viewers are called to experience their own passivity in the face of performance as a representation of their own complacency and comfortable ignorance. Many nails together are much more powerful than any single nail alone. This power can be used through action or through inaction. The structure of the viewing situation finds itself brilliantly represented in the form and content of the work itself.

The Named and the Unnamed redirects us to the body of the artist in *Fountain*, the labor and the violence that her body undergoes. In *Fountain*, "nature" is not romanticized. The artist's body labors against it, though at the same time with it. We are mostly water; we labor against ourselves. The perverse intimacy of this struggle suggests consideration of our entanglements with the Earth, with the elements, as actor and acted-upon, dangerous and endangered. How can we continue to exist as we are in a world in which the human presence, writ large, can be equated with harm? Philosophical recognition of the ways in which we overlap with other lives and beings might work toward alleviating human pressure on fragile ecologies. But collective action is also needed: a fundamental transformation of current definitions of the human to enable peaceful shared resistance against the acts of our own species.

Indeed, a key question that *The Named and the Unnamed* raises—which *Fountain* does not address directly—is that of collectivity. For a piece sensitive to the nonhuman in which human collectivity is also central, I turn to *Triangle Trade*, a 2017 collaborative short film by Jérôme Havre, Cauleen Smith, and Camille Turner. It begins with water too, with efforts to escape the water and find oneself on land. I say "oneself," awkwardly, because I'm talking about a puppet, not a person. The swimming figure who lugs himself up onto the shore—or seems to, since he's manipulated by puppeteers—is one of three puppet avatars of the creators of the film that alternately assume responsibility for the surreal narrative, each in solitude within an exquisitely desolate landscape. The artifice is apparent, the work it takes to animate the scene, as human hands—working hands, I might say, that are firm, tender, attentive—manipulate the puppets.

The wet, hot, icy world in which the puppets find themselves serially is made of the same kind of stuff they are: papier maché, heavy corrugated paper, tulle, sequins, plaster, sheets of colored plastic. Messy, chaotic, visually and aurally arresting, foregrounding the artifice needed to produce it, the piece allows us no illusion that these awkward, endearing protagonists are in full, autonomous control of themselves. And yet, as the shredded blue plastic sheets of water spit the "Jérôme" puppet out onto the shore, as the puppet seems to heave himself up, once, twice, three times, from the sand, I feel the breath expand in my own lungs. Someone moves the puppet and the puppet moves me.

From his aloneness, "Jérôme's" interior voice questions (in French) what it means to be part of a community. In the film, the three puppets are African diasporic subjects, isolated from one another, holding both a troubled relationship to the physical landscape of the "New World" and a surreal relationship to survival.[20] They find themselves in landscapes that are bejeweled but impassive and alienating. "I don't mean to be ungrateful, but this is not what I was expecting," the "Camille" puppet keens as she wanders in an icy landscape. "Am I the only one?" she wonders. "Where is everybody?" The "Cauleen" puppet perches at the edge of

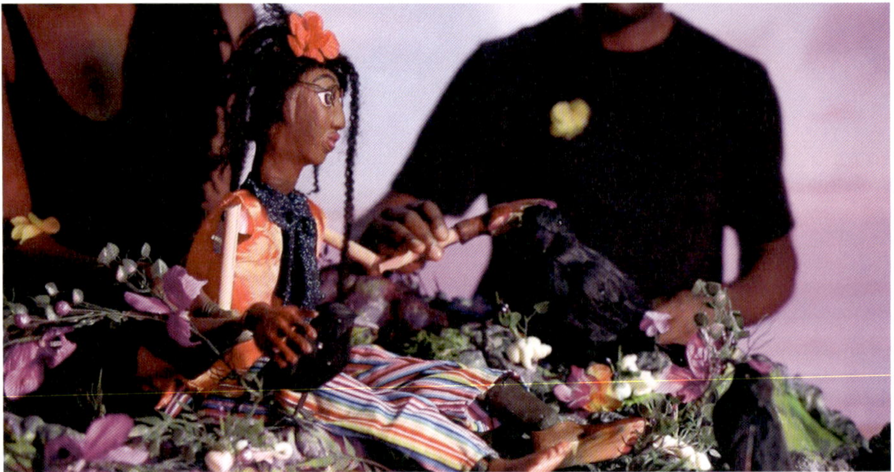

Fig. 5. Jérôme Havre (French Canadian, b. 1972), Cauleen Smith (American, b. 1967), and Camille Turner (Canadian, b. 1967), still from *Triangle Trade*, 2017. Film, 15 minutes

a volcano (fig. 5). Amidst these landscapes, the volcano serves as a space radically outside the violence of property. As Smith explained it in *Artforum*: "really, the only place you can arrive at and settle in without doing harm is at a lava berg."[21]

As "Cauleen" sits beside the volcano, a high-pitched voice intones an echoing chant of welcome:

> I just watch the Earth make itself. The Earth owns herself. I just choose to live on her. Welcome to my volcano. Her most feral and free emissions. This volcano belongs to the earth. . . . Welcome to my volcano: infertile, glassy, opaque, black, new and eternal. Everyone, everyone is welcome here. You have to be able to give it or leave it. If the lava oozes over the dotted line, do you give it? Do I leave it? Who can have it? Who needs it?[22]

This figure positions herself in an alert, watchful awe. Maintaining its autonomy, the volcano resonates with the independent voice of the Earth that appears in another work by Smith, *Songs for Earth and Folk*. In 2013, the Chicago Film Archive commissioned this ten-minute piece, which Smith created from footage in the archive, working with the multigenre, unclassifiable rock band the Eternals, led by Damon Locks. The Eternals' soundtrack is the first thing you notice about *Songs for Earth and Folk*: a high-pitched buzz, a lower drone, and a desultory

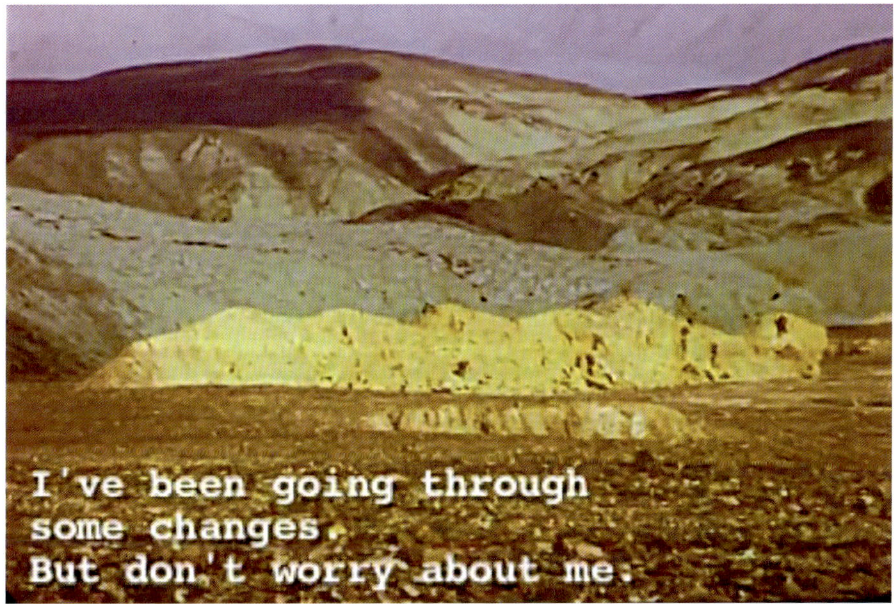

Fig. 6. Cauleen Smith, still from *Songs for Earth and Folk*, 2013. Film, 10 minutes

scrape, scrape, scrape of a drumstick across a metal bell. The camera pans across a cracked desert landscape. Earth speaks in a typewriter font: "Earth: I've been going through some changes. But don't worry about me" (fig. 6). The edge of a sandbank collapses, bit by bit, breaking up again and again into cascades of sand as the synthesizer embarks on a deep, frantically accelerating, repetitive motif, the sound of filmic foreboding. "I've been thinking that it's time," Earth's words read—pause—"so very time"—pause—"for you to leave." The title *Folk* hovers a moment over scenes of rapidly moving machines, then disappears. It seems as if Folk has nothing to say. For two minutes, we see busy scenes of human activity: a film reeling, an oil rig drilling, air traffic controllers at work. The same frantic synth motif plays. Then: "Sorry," Folk says, devastatingly obtuse to Earth's needs. "Did you say something?" (fig. 7).

The film pursues its course for about six more minutes, a dialogue between an Earth in all its majesty, devastation, and change, and a Folk blindly in love with its own hubris. The sounds and images, by turns jangly and lyrical, conclude with the "End" titles of all the films that served as source material. *Triangle Trade* ends differently, a quieter apocalypse. The figures slowly make their way toward one an-other—a destination they cannot know at the outset—and cluster together in the

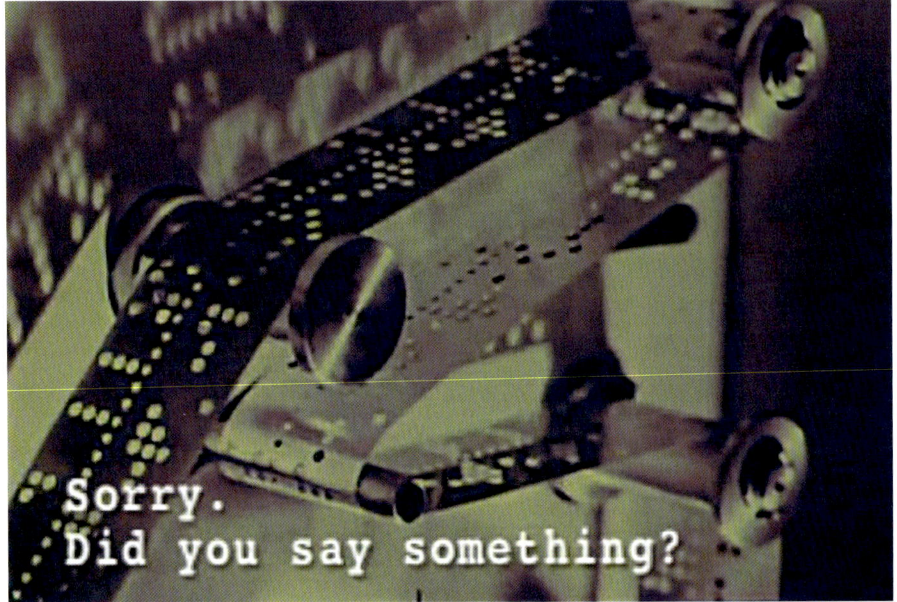

Fig. 7. Cauleen Smith, still from *Songs for Earth and Folk*, 2013. Film, 10 minutes

shadow of the volcano. The title *Triangle Trade* alludes to the historical triangle trade that brought enslaved Africans to the Americas and exported crops produced in the Americas to Europe. But it also evokes the "triangle" of three collaborators and their representatives in the film. Speaking about the project in an interview with Christopher Borrelli, Cauleen Smith described this symbolic relationship: "Who owns North America? Native Americans. There's nowhere to go where you're not a part of a colonial project. A volcano is the only uncontested land."[23] The volcano's danger and undesirability make it perversely attractive. The radical outsideness and aloneness of the impassive volcano dismantles ideas about land as property that cannot escape entanglement with the abusive dehumanization of human populations. But community shapes itself at the edges through a shared relationship to danger. Alongside a final eruption of the volcano, in muddy, ropey spurts and pink bubbles, the three puppets devise quiet ways to encounter one another (fig. 8). As Smith put it: "It was an important challenge to create *Triangle Trade* together without necessarily agreeing on what time or space we were in. I think that's an interesting lesson on how to get along with people in general. You may not all have agreements on where, and when, and who we are."[24]

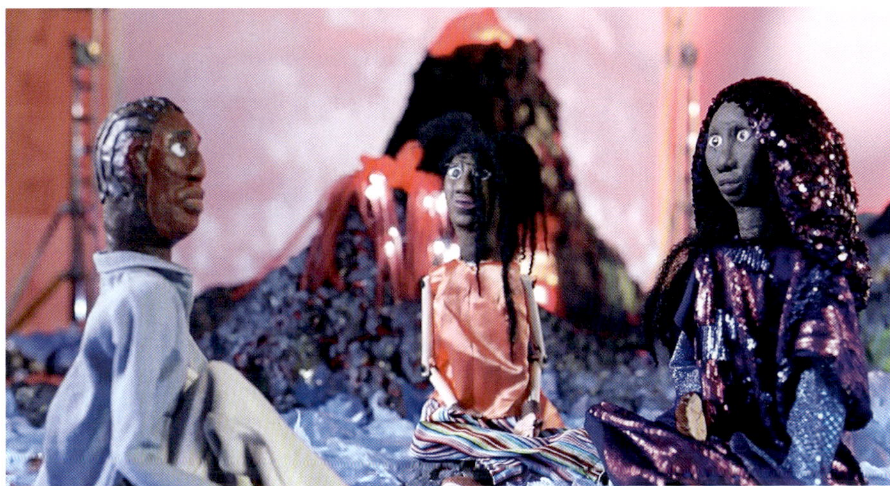

Fig. 8. Jérôme Havre, Cauleen Smith, and Camille Turner, still from *Triangle Trade*, 2017. Film, 15 minutes

In Patricia Williams's 1991 *The Alchemy of Race and Rights*, the legal scholar conjoined the claims of nonhumans with the claims of racially marked "others." She addressed critical legal studies (CLS) in the throes of its deconstruction of the legal discourse of "rights." From the perspective of CLS, the establishment of rights was problematic because it took for granted the ideology of liberal individualism as the basis for defining personhood, and could even be counterproductive as an instrument toward progressive political goals. This can be hard to hear, Williams notes, for those—African Americans in particular—who have nurtured an imagination of the power of "rights" as they struggled toward them for centuries. As she notes, "The making of something out of nothing"—that is, the imagination and coming to fruition of "rights"—"took immense alchemical fire—the fusion of a whole nation and the kindling of several generations."[25] She suggests instead that the goal, for a critical legal studies that would be alive to the crucial relationship of race and rights, should be

> not to discard rights but to see through or past them so that they reflect a larger definition of privacy and property: so that privacy is turned from exclusion based on self-regard into regard for another's fragile, mysterious autonomy; and so that property regains its ancient connotation of being a reflection of the universal self. . . . In discarding rights

> altogether, one discards a symbol too deeply enmeshed in the psyche
> of the oppressed to lose without trauma and much resistance. Instead,
> society must give them away. Unlock them from reification by giving
> them to slaves. Give them to trees. Give them to cows. Give them to
> history. Give them to rivers and rocks. Give to all of society's objects
> and untouchables the rights of privacy, integrity, and self-assertion; give
> them distance and respect. Flood them with the animating spirit that
> rights mythology fires in this country's most oppressed psyches, and
> wash away the shrouds of inanimate-object status, so that we may
> say not that we own gold but that a luminous golden spirit owns us.[26]

Today, in discussions around new materialism, the term "agency" stands in for "rights," but similar risks emerge, a risk that the call to relinquish destructive human agency might become a call to relinquish struggle itself in the face of danger. And this would be a particularly dangerous risk to Indigenous people, Third World people, people of color. But for Williams, the attribution of rights to nonhumans need not obstruct, indeed could run parallel to, the carving out of the fullness of those rights for African Americans. Contained within Williams's proposition is the idea that animating nonhuman others could have the corresponding effect of disentangling "regard for another's fragile, mysterious autonomy" from property-based notions of personhood—from the colonial legacy represented earlier in this essay by Sepúlveda. The call to relinquish "rights" cannot be placed as a demand on those who aspire to them by those who securely have them. Nor should the call to relinquish agency in favor of "matter" be placed on those rightfully seeking nothing short of revolution. And artists who see these issues with special clarity because of the ways their own communities are endangered have the most to teach us all—that we might heed the warning of danger, the insistence on labor, the call to collective action, and even finally the affectionate intimacy with the nonhuman that these works whisper insistently.

For help with this essay, direct or indirect, I wish to thank Rebecca Belmore, Huey Copeland, Chelsea Frazier, Christopher P. Heuer, Christina Kiriakos, Samantha Page, Cauleen Smith, Julian Yates, and students in two iterations of my Art, Ecology, and Politics class.
1. Huey Copeland, "Tending-toward-Blackness," *October* 156 (Spring 2016): 141–44.

2. W. J. T. Mitchell, *What Do Pictures Want? The Lives and Loves of Images* (Chicago: University of Chicago Press, 2006); Michael Wayne Cole and Rebecca Zorach, *The Idol in the Age of Art: Objects, Devotions, and the Early Modern World* (Burlington, VT: Ashgate, 2009).

3. "All'Illmo et Rmo Mons.e. Ils.e Cardinale Paleotti. Vlisse Aldro.di.," Biblioteca Universitaria di Bologna (BUB), Aldrovandi ms. 6, vol. II, fol. 129r, v.

4. "Auuertimenti del Dottore Aldrouandi sopra le pitture mostrifiche et prodigiose. All' Ill.mo et R.mo Mons. Il Cardinal Paleotti Sig. et Pron. suo Colend.mo.," BUB Aldrovandi ms. 6, vol. II, fol. 97v.

5. Jane Bennett, *Vibrant Matter: A Political Ecology of Things* (Durham: Duke University Press, 2009), viii–ix.

6. Sylvia Wynter, "Unsettling the Coloniality of Being/Power/Truth/Freedom. Towards the Human, After Man, Its Overrepresentation—An Argument," *New Centennial Review* 3, no. 3 (2003): 257–337.

7. "Nam quod eorum nonnulli ingeniosi esse videntur ad artificia quaedam, nullum est id prudentiae humanioris argumentum, cum bestiolas quasdam opera fabricare videamus, ut apes et araneas, quae nulla humana industria satis queat imitari." Angel Losada, *Juan Gines de Sepulveda através de su "Epistolario" y nuevos documentos* (Madrid: Consejo Superior de Investigaciones Científicas, 1949).

8. Aristotle, *Politics*, Book I, part V.

9. Aristotle, *Politics*, Book I, part IV.

10. Janet Berlo and Jessica L. Horton, "Beyond the Mirror: Indigenous Ecologies and 'New Materialisms' in Contemporary Art," *Third Text* 27, no. 1 (January 2013): 17–18.

11. Diana H. Coole and Samantha Frost, eds., *New Materialisms: Ontology, Agency, and Politics* (Durham: Duke University Press, 2010), 19; cited in Copeland, "Tending-toward-Blackness," 142.

12. Kyla Wazana Tompkins, "New Materialisms," *Lateral* 5, no.1 (2016), http://csalateral.org/issue/5-1/forum-alt-humanities-new-materialist-philosophy-tompkins (accessed November 15, 2017).

13. Amanda Boetzkes, *The Ethics of Earth Art* (Minneapolis: University of Minnesota Press, 2010), 13–14.

14. Jinthana Haritaworn, "Decolonizing the Non/Human," in "Theorizing Queer Inhumanisms," special issue, *GLQ: A Journal of Gay and Lesbian Studies* 21, nos. 2–3 (June 2015): 213. Haritaworn and others in this issue of *GLQ* point to the serious—possibly even constitutive—gaps with respect to race in the academy's mainstream critiques of humanism.

15. Félix Guattari, *The Three Ecologies*, trans. Ian Pindar and Paul Sutton (London: Athlone Press, 2000).

16. As Amnesty International points out, "Sixteen of the missing women are Indigenous, a number far in excess of the proportion of Indigenous women living in Vancouver." (The number refers to 16 of 60 women just in Vancouver.) See Amnesty International, *Canada: Stolen Sisters. A Human*

Rights Response to Discrimination and Violence against Indigenous Women in Canada (2004), 14, https://www.amnesty.ca/sites/amnesty/files/amr200032004enstolensisters.pdf (accessed November 15, 2017).

17. For a detailed account of this project by a sociologist, see Maggie Tate, "Re-presenting Invisibility: Ghostly Aesthetics in Rebecca Belmore's *Vigil* and *The Named and the Unnamed,*" *Visual Studies* 30, no. 1 (2015): 20–31.

18. Elisha Burrows, "Rebecca Belmore: Fountain," documentary, 2011, https://vimeo.com/18764906 (accessed November 15, 2017).

19. Jessica Bradley, "Rebecca Belmore: Art and the Object of Performance," in *Rebecca Belmore: Fountain,* exh. cat. (Kamloops, BC: Kamloops Art Gallery, 2005), 43.

20. Smith said in an interview: "These works [land art] did push me even closer toward trying to understand my own relationship to the land, being the descendant of captive Africans, and being cargoed onto the North American continent—a land that was inhabited and stewarded by a people who endured obscene genocide. The work that I am making right now is attempting to reconcile the kind of dislocation that comes from actually not having any kind of homeland at all—from being a people who made ourselves in the fires of survival in the 'New World'." Cauleen Smith, interview with Carolyn Lazard, *Mousse Magazine,* http://mousemagazine.it/cauleen-smith-carolyn-lazard-2016.

21. "Cauleen Smith," *Artforum,* October 10, 2017, https://www.artforum.com/words/id=71562 (accessed December 5, 2017).

22. *Triangle Trade* (2017), dir. Jérôme Havre, Cauleen Smith, Camille Turner.

23. Christopher Borrelli, "The Complicated Exodus of Art World Star Cauleen Smith," http://www.chicagotribune.com/entertainment/ct-ae-cauleen-smith-0820-20170819-column.html (accessed November 15, 2017).

24. "Cauleen Smith," *Artforum.*

25. Patricia Williams, *The Alchemy of Race and Rights* (Cambridge: Harvard University Press, 1992), 163.

26. Williams, *Alchemy,* 165.

Thinking Red, Wounds, and Fungi in Wangechi Mutu's Eco-Art

Chelsea Mikael Frazier

With Wangechi Mutu's 2004 piece *One Hundred Lavish Months of Bushwhack* (fig. 1), we enter a world of blackish cloud-like gloom. The cloud grows into a lighter gray, giving way to a spotlighted protagonist—commanding our gaze with her size and elaborate bodily adornments. Curled animal-printed horns frame our protagonist's head while a skirt of flora or of exaggerated pubic hair gesticulates around her waist. The skirt bears an uncanny resemblance to what might be either vegetation or fungal spores emerging from the bottom of the plane. It remains unclear if the skirt has a vitality of its own, or if the protagonist's dancelike gesture—with bent elbows and a raised heel—is responsible for the skirt's movement. While a small motorcycle functions as a decorative ankle bracelet on the raised foot, three other small motorcycles seem to take the place of where the lowered foot might be—that is, if it wasn't a mass of splattered red blood. Similar splatters—emanating from yet another small motorcycle—crown the figure's head, and the vibrancy of the red and the sites of what appear to be wounds indicate both dazzle and danger for the viewer. But danger from whom and what? Where we might find hands, the figure wears (or is composed of) hippopotamus mouths. This is possibly a reference to a voracious yet vegetarian

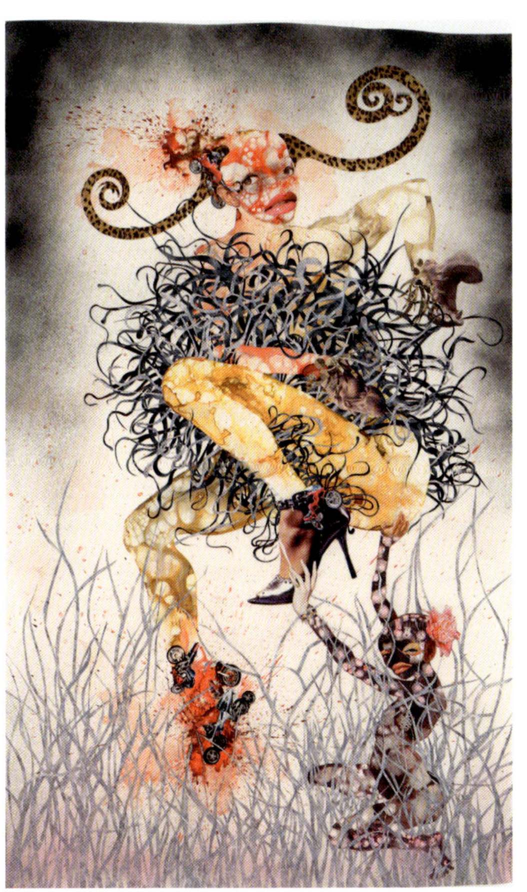

Fig. 1. Wangechi Mutu (Kenyan, b. 1972), *One Hundred Lavish Months of Bushwhack*, 2004. Cut-and-paste printed paper with watercolor, synthetic polymer paint, and pressure-sensitive stickers on Mylar, 68 ¹/₂ × 42 in. (174 × 106.7 cm). The Museum of Modern Art, New York, NY. Fund for the Twenty-First Century (99.2005)

appetite—as hippos are very hungry, if misunderstood, herbivores.[1] Her very skin or cat-suit, in its paled pinkish-yellowish-brownish coloring, takes on the hues and appearances of fungi catalyzing the decay of various organisms. And after absorbing all these competing and intricately stitched-together symbols, our eyes are finally free to settle on a smaller and much darker figure, enmeshed in the grayed gloom of the background—ornamented in floral and supporting the weight of the striking protagonist. The obvious, if simple, question is: what exactly are we looking at?

Art and its histories have long held the potential for transforming ways of knowing and thinking, disrupting fixity, and radically confronting hegemonic intellectual traditions. As eco-criticism and eco-theory's epistemologies continue to contend with their uneven conceptualizations of the interconnectivity of race, gender, coloniality, and ecological crisis, a guiding question for this essay is: What is the *function* of Black art and its epistemologies in a time of ecological crisis? Or, more to the point of this engagement with Wangechi Mutu's art: What kinds of problems or questions rise from eco-theory's epistemologies when we place occluded *black-fem* bodies at the center?

This essay carries two primary preoccupations regarding Brooklyn-based, Nairobi-born Wangechi Mutu's ecological critique. First, it examines how Mutu employs a strategic use of the color red and many pools and splatters of bright red (blood) to illuminate the interrelated ecological wounds of several kinds of bodies—human bodies, bodies of land, and certain political bodies. In the 2014 volume *Prismatic Ecology*, editor Jeffrey Jerome Cohen critiques the predominance of "greenness" in the environmental humanities and widens the scope and spectrum of colors through which we discern ecological thinking. This essay's focus on red builds on the invitation by Cohen and others to intentionally expand ecological discourse beyond the notion of "greenness." For all its innovation, however, and despite the volume's focus on discourses of animality, post-humanism, violence, and color, this essay is also a direct response to *Prismatic Ecology*'s missed opportunity to engage a sustained dialogue about the fundamental role of race, implicit racism, and racialized violence in ecology's epistemological formations.[2]

Second, this essay probes the way Mutu enacts fungal imagery by heavily layering images and materials that have largely come to simultaneously signify grotesquery, excessiveness, surprise, and beauty.[3] These centered "excessive" images and significations include but are not limited to nonwhite bodies, non-male bodies, severed limbs, a mosaic of iridescent hues, and highly glamorized physical terrains. Centering nonwhite, non-male bodies, and fungus and doing it through art that is challenging, complex, and at times ambiguous provides an entry point to reconfigure our understandings of mainstream environmental discourse's limited potential for confronting and addressing the roots of our ecological crisis.

To pinpoint "mainstream environmental discourse," we can turn to the mission statements and talking points of powerful environmental organizations, which in turn offer instructive examples of these limitations. Some of these organizations include the Nature Conservancy, Conservation International, the World Wildlife Fund, and the Global Environment Facility, among others. They all spotlight their concern with "inclusion" and "diversity" and a commitment to protecting and holding "all" and "everyone" accountable for finding solutions. For example, Conservation International maintains that "for nearly 30 years, Conservation International (CI) has been protecting nature for the benefit of all." They go on to explain that

> we're taking more from nature than nature can give. We're weakening the Earth's ability to provide the clean air, fresh water and food we depend on. In short, we're creating a crisis. We can end this crisis. . . . Conservation International works at every level, from remote villages to the offices of presidents and CEOs, to find these solutions. Our work is moving societies toward healthier, more sustainable development paths—so that we don't use up today what we're going to need tomorrow.[4]

Yet another environmental organization with global reach, the Nature Conservancy maintains that "the mission of The Nature Conservancy is to conserve the lands and waters on which all life depends" and that their "vision is a world where the diversity of life thrives, and people act to conserve nature for its own sake and its ability to fulfill our needs and enrich our lives."[5] Both missions and visions of the Nature Conservancy and Conservation International insist on a "we" and an "all" that presume a monolithic relationship to and understanding of the ways environmental degradation is experienced. Though these organizations claim to be invested in the fight to build a healthier world for all lands and forms of life on the planet and though they make mention of their "diverse" staffs and partnerships

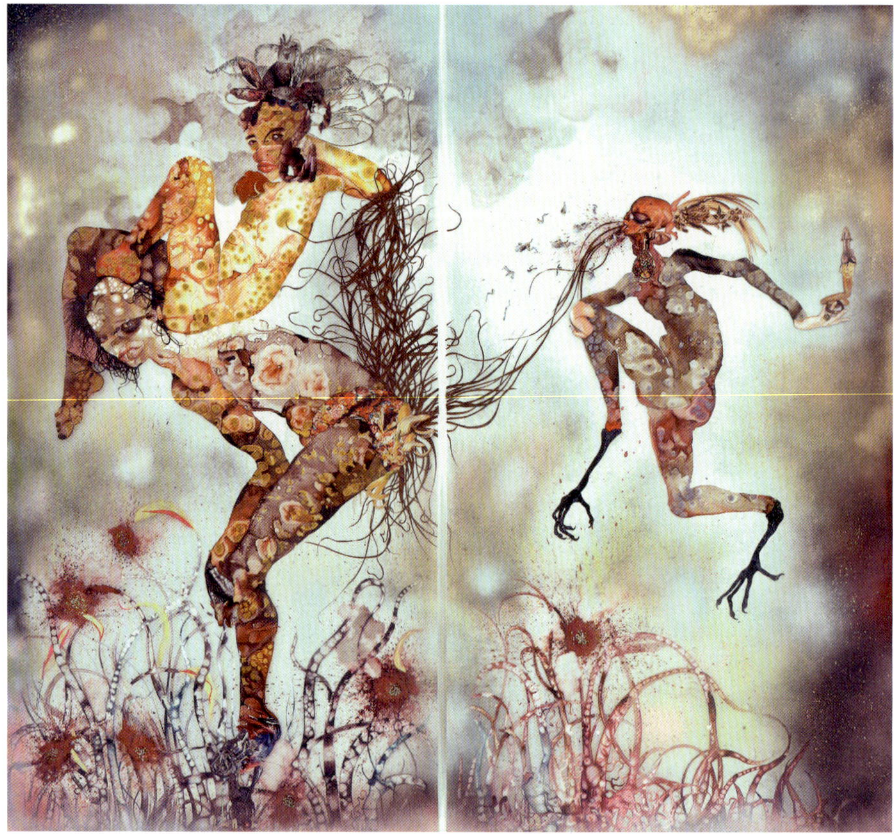

Fig. 2. Wangechi Mutu, *Your Story, My Curse*, 2006. Ink, acrylic, and collage on Mylar, 101 ¹/₂ × 109 inches (257.8 × 276.8 cm). Norton Museum of American Art, West Palm Beach, Florida. Purchase, acquired through the generosity of the Contemporary and Modern Art Council of the Norton Museum of Art and Deaccession Funds, 2016.2a-b

with "indigenous and local" communities, they make absolutely no mention of challenging or dismantling the violent White, colonial cis-heterocapitalist logics that continue to underpin ecological imbalance.

This is where Mutu's intellectual and artistic contributions can be especially illuminating. Her work—through her interviews, her essay, "The Power of Earth in My Work," and her collage paintings, *One Hundred Lavish Months of Bushwhack* and *Your Story, My Curse* (2006; fig. 2)—helps us to see what might otherwise be obscured or sidelined in mainstream environmental discourse. Across her oeuvre, Mutu spotlights several kinds of bodies—particularly *black-fem* bodies—that are (at best) only cursorily represented in ecological/environmental discourse. While not prescriptive or even moralizing, Mutu offers a lens through which we can comprehend the ways our current ecological crisis is rooted in (ongoing) colonial histories and violence that mainstream environmental discourse remains incapable of or unconcerned with acknowledging. In turn, I argue that by enacting red (blood) and fungal imagery, Mutu's work offers a method of questioning and comprehension that (1) simultaneously visualizes the ecologically wounded grotesqueries that emerge as a result of White cis-heterocapitalist colonial histories, violences, and logics; and (2) affirms alternative "excessive" metrics of beauty and being conjured by vulnerable and maligned ecological subjects "in the Anthropocene."[6]

Thinking with Fungi and Black Femininity

Mutu is arguably one of the most prominent living artist-intellectuals to repeatedly and consistently center *black-fem* subjects and bodies in her conceptualizations of our troubled earth ethics.[7] An interrelated, but less-discussed feature of her work has been Mutu's preoccupation with visualizing fungi (recall the mottled skin of the main figure in *Bushwhack*). In an interview, when asked specifically about the role mushrooms and fungus play in her paintings, Mutu responded:

> Mushrooms are mysterious because they pop up in the forest, the way toadstools emerge in European fairy folktales. Fungus was one of those things that played into my sense of the grotesque but they reference so many different things. . . . I thought they were almost like a migrant culture that exists in the most decrepit parts of the city, and what emerges are these fascinating people and interactions. They're also in-between, in that they're not really plants. In some cases fungus is actually closer to animal because they eat food. They don't make food, which is one of the big separations between the plant and animal kingdoms. Also the way they reproduce is closer to the most basic and primitive animals, a sort of asexual sporing. I like the idea that they are a little alien family found in the middle of these two massive kingdoms.[8]

Several of Mutu's points about fungus beg our attention. First, she names the element of surprise or unexpectedness associated with the emergence of mushrooms; not only in the way they "pop up in the forest" but also in the way—though over-associated with British folklore—they "pop up" in her own work. This follows a recognizable pattern in Mutu's catalogue, whereby she references principal themes in Western portraiture, but often in ways that destabilize or repurpose their logics.[9]

Mutu also illuminates fungi's ability to survive in the most hostile conditions. As she notes, this sets the scene for compelling and specific interactions between organisms that can often go unnoticed and under-affirmed because of their intimacy with decrepitness, danger, or decay. Further, Mutu instructs us on the challenges of fungi classification. The organisms that we easily classify are the ones that fit neatly into the plant or animal kingdoms. Fungi, however—understood to be distinct from both kingdoms only in recent history—exist in excess of these normative classifications. Finally, Mutu highlights fungal reproduction. Reproduction represents yet another paradigmatic way we classify organisms. Her quote references asexual sporing and the association of such sporing with primitivity. Though she highlights only asexual sporing here, fungi reproduce in five distinct ways—four more than the narrative of heteronormative sexual reproduction we routinely attribute to many plants and most animals.[10]

The above characteristics, coupled with Mutu's consistent fixation on visualizing *black-fem* subjectivity, help us to understand the ways "matter and meaning"[11] shift when *black-fem* bodies and fungal bodies are juxtaposed or collapsed onto each other. Mutu fills the frame of her decadent canvases with the spore, fruit, rust, and smut visual cues collapsed onto *black-fem* bodies. In doing this, Mutu encourages our focus on the processes by which both organisms—*black-fems* and fungi—forged within this planet's most hostile terrains, pop up suddenly and in seemingly unexpected places in ecological discourse.

Upon further investigation, though mushrooms (the fruiting body of a fungus) make themselves known in obvious ways above ground, they are always part of a deeper network of fungi playing an essential role in stabilizing the ecosystem. As Paul Stamets explains, by being "myco-magicians, disassembling large organic molecules into simpler forms, which in turn nourish other members of the ecological community," fungi function primarily as "the interface organisms between life and death."[12] Across the Black diaspora, when considering the systemic overexposure to death and disease that *black-fem* subjects experience, describing them as "the interface organisms between life and death" functions as a particularly tragic and yet appropriately precise descriptor as well;[13] especially if we acknowledge the fact that Black and *black-fem* subjects—as they withstand systemic overexposure to death and disease—function as the necro-political scapegoats that, in the words of Achille Mbembé, "constitute the *nomos* of the political space in which we still live."[14]

Before moving into a close read of Mutu's painting and writings, *black-*

fem as a descriptor requires clarification. The purpose of using the term *black-fem* throughout this essay (as opposed to "Black woman" or "Black female," which appears much more frequently in the Black feminist intellectual tradition) is two-fold. First, it is meant to describe a variety of "affectable" Black subjectivities forged through the connective tissue of White, cis-heterocapitalist colonial logics.[15] Second, the term is meant to mark the liminal spaces between the *distinct* (and not to be conflated) categories of Black woman, Black female, and Black (queer) femme.[16] In the close readings that follow, this language critiques the assumed central subject of Black feminism—the Black (heteronormative, heterosexual, and/or homonormative) woman. Furthermore, *black-fem* marks and considers the intricacies of a broader range of feminine subjectivities with which Black feminism—as a political/ecological project—must be concerned.[17]

Mutu's investments in both (Black) feminism and ecological ethics appear most clearly when naming the intellectual foremothers that have shaped her political consciousness. Citing both Black feminist theorist Michele Wallace[18] and Nobel Peace Prize–winning environmental activist Wangari Maathai[19] as strong influences, it comes as no surprise that after recently winning the esteemed 2017 Anderson Ranch National Artist Award, Wangechi Mutu took the opportunity to insist:

> Art is my way of speaking about things that are *unspeakable*, it is my truest voice and my strongest form of resistance. It is such a privilege to be recognized in these times for doing what I most love doing, it gives my work more urgency. I know we can do better for one another and for our Earth, and I am deeply committed to using creative means to bring attention to violence and inequality against women and to the parallel destruction of our Earth.[20]

Her remarks succinctly capture her most urgent political concerns that recur in her interviews, statements, and activist and creative work.

The Function of Black Feminist Eco-Art (?)

Situating Mutu as a Black feminist eco-artist/critic alongside a trajectory of contemporary Black feminist thinkers allows us to better comprehend the West's desperate reactionary impulses, to acknowledge and confront the irresolvability of its violences, and through the "gift" of *black-fem* wounds, look *through* (not adjacent to or on the margins of) Man's apprehension of the World right into a Black feminist elsewhere.

The wounds rendered across her work speak to Mutu's notion that "women's bodies are particularly vulnerable to the whims of changing movements, governments, and social norms. They're like sensitivity charts—they indicate how a society feels about itself."[21] So for Mutu, Black women—even as they are camouflaged under the normative gender category of "women" in Mutu's statement—chart society's prescriptions of itself, despite universalizing narratives that speak otherwise. Further, Mutu's work destabilizes normative understandings of Black female-ness and Black woman-ness rooted in a cis-heteronormativity that Arielle A. Concolio has explained "relies upon a biological authenticity of sex and gender that produces the trans/cis and the homo/hetero binaries."[22] Mutu's paintings and writing also undermine the erroneous notion that Black feminist art and critique are relevant solely for Black (female/women) subjects. Given the violence and inequality against women and paralleled destruction of our Earth that Mutu highlights, I contend that her work situates *black-fem* bodies—and all the trauma and triumph they bear—as repositories of critique of the broader societies in which they exist. Though Mutu does not flag Blackness in her Anderson Ranch statement specifically, in almost all her interviews and statements, Blackness, Black femininity, and the Black female body are recurrent and centered fixations. To name the cis-heterocapitalist colonial paradigms that plague mainstream environmental discourse, and the necessity of a Black feminist critique that helps us to unearth those paradigms, the environmental organizations discussed earlier in the essay continue to offer apt examples.

At first glance, it might seem ungenerous and even unfair to accuse an environmental organization of being enmeshed in cis-heterocapitalist logics, particularly because environmental ethics are presumed to be relevant for everybody, and diversity and inclusion rhetoric has long been a feature in the mission statements of top environmental organizations. These large and wealthy institutions have accomplished a great deal in the way of preserving and protecting the biodiversity in vulnerable areas around the globe, raising enough funds to purchase and protect land that would otherwise be used in more exploitative ways, and have made efforts to ensure that the work they do is relevant and transparent to the numerous families and individuals that donate their money to their causes and projects.

In their fight against changing climates and environmental degradation, however, they continue to be unaware of, unable to, or unwilling to address some central problems with their efforts. While these organizations have made significant strides in branding climate change, environmental awareness, and greenness into the Western imagination, they have relied on conceptual frames that leave the root causes of environmental degradation unnamed—thereby creating a narrative of climate change and its effects that does little to hold colonial histories and the West's monopoly of material resources accountable. They reduce understandings of race and gender to biological markers of "otherness," measured against an implicit though unnamed White, cis-heterocapitalist subject. Under this conception of otherness as biologically marked, they can then make calls in their mission statements and press releases for the belated inclusion and incorporation of some gendered, raced, and Indigenous bodies and cultural practices into their offices and efforts[23] without disrupting the ways that material resources around the globe and in their offices are funneled primarily to White cis-heterocapitalist subjects. Concurrently, these organizations remain ill equipped to confront the intrinsic material inequities that not only derive from colonial histories but also exacerbate increasingly detrimental impacts on the environment.[24]

Eco-critics like Jeffrey Myer and Sarah Jaquette Ray have noted that cis-heterocapitalist colonial logics dictate that the most paramount relationship one can have with land, space, and all the materials in it is to own it and use it for one's own self-interested benefit.[25] This self-interested benefit usually comes at the cost of others (Indigenous folks, flora, and fauna) with differing relationships to land. What measures the strength of these organizations is their ability to acquire capital and purchase land for the "preservation" of wildlife, "conservation" of national parks, and "assistance" of certain groups of people in ways that have come to signify and mark the mainstream environmental ethics to which we "should" all universally aspire. As a result, global environmental organizations and their leaders—which are in many ways responsible for authoring and reinforcing the ethics of mainstream environmental discourse—recapitulate yet leave unnamed evolved manifestations of the very cis-heterocapitalist colonial logics that underpin the ecological crises they both benefit from and claim to fight.

These insights become discernible with the help of scholars invested in outlining the functions of Black (feminist studies) critique and, indeed, this critique is indispensable to an effective and more comprehensive eco-criticism. In her essay, "The Idea of Black Culture," Black feminist theorist Hortense Spillers closes in on her definition(s) of Black diasporic culture as both "*statement* and *counterstatement,* that would both undo alienation and constitute its own standpoint." As she further elucidates its function in our post-Obama present, she asserts "that black culture, having imagined itself as an *alternative* statement, as a *counter*statement to American culture/civilization, or Western culture/civilization, more generally speaking, identifies the cultural vocation as the space of 'contradiction, indictment, and the refusal'."[26] It is here that Spillers outlines the chief function of Black diasporic culture—and the ways it opens up opportunities for counterstatements that see, name, and refuse the unnamed logics that reinforce the destructive force of the West.

According to Black-diaspora theorist Michelle Wright, however, even counter epistemologies within Black studies have a tendency to exclude Black women, Black queer and trans folks, and other Black subjects that are not heterosexual, cis-gendered, and male. In her book, *The Physics of Blackness*, popular understandings of Black identity often denote static definitions, which derive from epistemological understandings of Blackness that have become yoked to a Black linear progress narrative. This predominant narrative "implicitly reformulates that [Black] collective into an ever narrower and more homogeneous membership"[27] and often leaves the experiences, lives, and offerings of non-male, non-cis, and non-heterosexual black subjects unacknowledged, undetected, and therefore unspeakable. Wright takes up and problematizes the predominance of what she terms the Middle Passage Epistemology, its insistence on Blackness as a qualitative value (a "what") and the ways "Blackness, as a vaguely biological 'what,' takes on an eerie resemblance to those anti-Black discourses that first claimed Blacks were indeed a 'what'—a distinct sub-human species 'marked by nature,' as [Thomas] Jefferson opined."[28] This allows for certain bodies—even within Black studies discourse—to be reduced to biological markers of "otherness," measured against and controlled by an implicit though unnamed White, cis-heterocapitalist subject—a facet reflected in the ways that mainstream environmental discourse makes sense of race, gender, and indigeneity.

This point relates to and underscores eco-critic Jeffrey Myers's reading of *Notes on Virginia* in his book, *Converging Stories: Race, Ecology, and Environmental Justice in American Literature*.[29] Concerning Jefferson's *Notes*, Myers exposes the text for its articulation of a racial-ecological hegemony whereby the security of the industrial Anglo-American empire is hinged upon the control, utilization, and exploitation of "all elements of the natural world," including bodies of land, flora and fauna, and Black and native people.[30] Extrapolating from Wright and Myers, their arguments about Jefferson's *Notes* demonstrate the problematic implications of understanding Blackness as a vaguely biological "what." If Blackness and other markers of "difference" (including queerness, femaleness, trans-ness, indigeneity, etc.) are understood as a vaguely biological otherness rather than onto-epistemological societal positions, mainstream ecological discourse can make calls for the inclusion of these excluded others in the fight for environmental protection without tending to the processes by which they were conscripted into ecologically vulnerable societal positions in the first place.

Rather than naming Blackness as a "biological what" in her essay, "Toward a Black Feminist Poethics," Denise Ferreira Da Silva—building on another of Spillers's works, "Mama's Baby, Papa's Maybe: An American Grammar Book"—explains Blackness as an onto-epistemological formation. This definition of Blackness is usually rendered invisible under predominant frameworks for understanding power, capital accumulation, "post"-colonial violence and its attendant ecological damage. Instead, Da Silva's account of Blackness is constructed for the purpose of challenging the "authorized and justified total violence (of the police and the courts), to reclaim, to demand the restoration of the total value the colonial architectures have enabled capital to expropriate from native lands and enslaved Black (and African) labor."[31] It is also crucial for Da Silva to begin with racialized slavery in order to highlight the processes by which slavery—and our lack of attention to its ongoing economic effects—produces many of the material inequalities with which we now find ourselves grappling desperately and anxiously. Da Silva continues:

> Beginning with slavery is crucial precisely because a most profitable effect of the tools of the scientific reason, which produce the Category of Blackness, is precisely the occlusion of the relationship between the enslaved labor and the owners as a sort of juridic arrangement that does not belong in capitalist relations, which are mediated by contract—and which it does not capture through the juridic concept of property. For in the same statement that articulates how slavery allows for the expropriations of the total value produced by chattel labor, Karl Marx disavows any consideration of how enslaved labor, as producer of surplus value that is the blood-nourishing capital, participates in the accumulation of capital.[32]

Here, Da Silva makes clear what is usually rendered invisible under predominant frameworks for understanding power and the effects of colonization by producing an account of capitalist space-making that explicitly names the West's reliance on enslaved Black labor and exploited African bodies of land. Da Silva discerns a bio/necro-political relationship where Black blood onto-epistemologically nourishes capital, and capital, in turn, nourishes environmental degradation.

The colonial history Mutu offers in her essay "The Power of Earth in My Work" punctuates Da Silva's point. Mutu details the history of Gikuyu people in Kenya being violently displaced from lands they had owned for almost a thousand years and interned by the British in "labor camps, barbed-wire villages, and prisons." This internment came as a result of British desires for an expanded colonial empire embedded in the ideal climate and sumptuous agricultural soils that characterized Kenyan bodies of land in the late 1880s. Furthermore, as scholar-activists like the late Wangari Maathai have noted, a result of colonial invasion and capitalist-driven (post)-colonial instability in Kenya has been deforestation and a significant loss of usable soil. This continues to trouble Kenya's material and political landscape and many other formerly colonized bodies of land throughout Africa that have suffered paralleled fates.[33]

As Mutu and Da Silva show, Black (African) bodies and Black (African) blood became and continue to be a fundamental salve through which environmental degradation is sustained. This degradation is propagated within the confines of "colonial architectures," which included racialized slavery and colonial internment/imprisonment. Da Silva's insights also outline the reasons why the relationship between the *black-fem* subjectivity and world/Earth ethics are impoverished. Most frameworks that critique power and capital, including Marxism, occlude (because of the disavowal of slave labor and colonial total violence) the ability to think, let alone speak, the function of the *black-fem* subject. This comes out even more clearly when Da Silva writes:

> Toward a Black Feminist Poethics, with Hortense Spillers, we must face slavery "as high crimes against the flesh, as the person of African females and African males registered the wounding" and "think of the Flesh, as a primary narrative." That wounded flesh, the inscriptions of the calculated violence, registers what the Category of Blackness hides, living-dead capital profiting from expropriated productive capacity of enslaved bodies and native lands. Her confronting question, questions

> Time and the World it sustains. Framed in a position that refuses the
> World of Man, pre-posed by (before and toward) man born in the
> world, the Feminist Black (racial) Critic becomes in material affectability
> (relationality, contingency, immediacy). With the gift, the black feminist
> Poet moves on ignoring the past and future, the old and new, asking the
> question of the World, toward the End of the Subject's apprehension
> of it, interrupts the desperate reaction—of the questioned.[34]

Da Silva's declarations here provide a blueprint for my reading of Mutu's enactment of red and fungal imagery as a method of questioning and comprehension that acknowledges *black-fem* bodies as wounded by living-dead capital, as evidence of primary and ongoing high crimes, and as harbingers of more-than-Worldly transformation. Da Silva draws on Spillers to recognize Black woundedness as a standpoint and mode of knowledge that registers the racialized violences that Blackness obscures within and through colonial architectures. Most crucially, however, Da Silva explains a method—a "gift"—by which the Black feminist eco-critic questions the very structure of the "World of Man."

Reading Mutu's Red and Wounds

Reductive stereotypes that bolster understandings of race and gender as biological "otherness" organize hierarchical social relationships and touch nearly every aspect of modern society. Eco-theory is no exception, and in *One Hundred Lavish Months of Bushwhack*, the title alone, as well as a cursory glance at the beguiling protagonist, recalls stereotypes about Blackness and femininity—stereotypes that obscure our ability to discern the ways that race, gender, and environmental pollution reinforce one another. Mutu has spoken publicly about her disdain for stereotypes, but rather than "attacking stereotypes head-on" through her work, she explains her tendency to "mine stereotypes for their weak foundations and produce figures that are distillations of [her] own issues, beliefs, perceptions, and personal stereotypes."[35]

The striking term "bushwhack" invites several associations—one of the most relevant for this essay being stereotypes about African landscape. The dark gray that engulfs the centered protagonist in *Bushwhack* might be read as smog, acid rain, or other forms of ill-contained earthly pollution and immediately signals a bleak and ominous African terrain. Relatedly, a synonym for "bushwhacker" is "guerilla," and as Kenyan satirist Binyavanga Wainaina notes in his essay "How to

Write About Africa," it carries significant racialized, gendered, and material weight in pervasive imaginings of African life.[36] On the one hand, the painting could be read as a depiction of a stereotype that paints African fem-bodies (human bodies) as always victims of an unruly and aggressive African terrain (body of land): a land that is barren, scorched, ecologically degraded and sedimented in the past by uncivilized "bush" people or hyperviolent and destructive, power-mad guerillas.

But, on the other hand, etymological considerations of the term "bushwhacker" invite us to examine this work simultaneously as a recapitulation *and critique* of multilayered ideas and familiar tropes. If Africa as a privileged geographical reference point is considered alongside other spaces and times, "bushwhacker" can also refer to fighters in the American Civil War. Several recent monographs have been written exploring the ways in which bushwhacker ideals are intimately tied to constructions of White masculinity in the continental United States. Yet the protagonist's feminine adornments—a high-heeled shoe, pink lipstick, a thickly embellished skirt, and what appears to be either exposed shapely legs or skin-tight bottoms—suggest that the figure is feminine-identified. The implications behind "bushwhack" or "bushwhacker" here can of course be read as a benign description of travel through dense landscape of flora and fauna, but from an academic perspective, the invoking of "bushwhack" in the title invites references to Western notions of Whiteness, guerrilla warfare, and violence wrought by colonial ideals. The polyvalent, yet almost always masculine, notions of "bushwhacker" also ask the viewer to question what symbolic and material "colonial architectures"[38] our protagonist is battling. These colonial architectures include but are not limited to the toxic White masculinity detailed in the historical monographs listed below,[39] as well as the toxic Black masculinity, essentialist stereotypes about uncivilized African-fem bodies, and decontextualized narratives about African bodies of land satirized under Wainaina's critique of stereotypical Western writings about Africa.

In addition to the title registering a battle or violence of some kind, the red of the protagonist's wounds guides the viewer's overwhelmed eye in *Bushwhack*. Cut-and-pasted printed paper is infused with Mutu's signature use of watercolor, synthetic polymer paint, and pressure-sensitive stickers on "transparentized" paper; the panoply of materials wrestles for our attention until red—which could either be ink or paint—beckons us, focusing our attention on a wound on the left side of the protagonist's head. This wound has transformed the body's material into a mass of blood splatters, and yet their bodily gestures are not attempting to tend to or cover presumed trauma. The brightness of the red calls to mind images of fresh blood spilled, signaling new pain, new violence, and new traumas suffered. The time and cause of the wounds, however, are entirely up for debate, but wounds this protagonist has sustained may also result from the fact that in order to facilitate colonial, capitalist space-making, *black-fem* bodies—as Nicole Fleetwood has explained—must continue to be hypervisible and rendered "excessive" so as to justify their violent state-sanctioned containment.[40]

The exact causes remain irresolvable—suggesting the simultaneity of multiple causes—but what is certain is that the gravity of the wounds we witness in this piece are undeniable. Yet our protagonist's face does not convey anguish. Instead, the figure wears an expression that might best be described as a placid side-eye—variations of which can be found on several figures in Mutu's oeuvre. (The "side-eye" is a colloquial term that originated within Black diasporic culture and describes a collection of facial expressions and gestures that subtly convey or disclose sentiments of dissatisfaction, discomfort, or contempt from within the confines of a highly surveilled and/or dangerous physical position.) Given the history of Black women's highly surveilled physical positions and exposure to vulnerability within settler-colonial landscapes, plantations, prisons, White houses, and other colonial structures, it makes sense that *black-fem* subjects have conjured gestures that allow them to express themselves, protect themselves by averting their gazes, and communicate with other knowing subjects all while maintaining enough relative safety to survive.

Fungal Flesh and Feeling

Mutu's use of the side-eye continues into her 2006 piece *Your Story, My Curse* (fig. 2). In this diptych, three figures take center stage, and discerning who or what might be the protagonist is much more of a challenge. In literary criticism, identifying the protagonist is important work. The main character shapes the reader's concerns, marks whom the reader might identify with, and often guides the direction(s) of the reader's empathy. Identification and empathy are difficult to place and process in this diptych. On the left side, we see two figures—a larger one enmeshed in the bottom of the plane, bent at the waist, with a slightly curved back signaling what appears to be a very uncomfortable position. Her eyes shoot the viewer a side-eye, but this one does not retain the same knowing glance as the protagonist in *Bushwhack*. The side-eyes of this figure in *Your Story* appear to be pleading with the viewer—begging for an empathy that cannot be afforded from within the logics of her confinement. By contrast, the slightly smaller figure that sits atop her does not appear bothered at all. With her buttocks and back floating, she rests her legs nonchalantly on top of the lowered figure. She also wears a side-eye, but hers retains the placidity discussed earlier, daring the viewer to question what could be read as an exploitative relationship between the two—as she is literally using the lowered figure's entire body as a recliner.

While the reclining figure relaxes atop the lowered one, her foot seems to be balding the lowered figure's head while her own head is adorned with an elaborate, amalgamated crown of birds, fish heads, gold twine, and silvery feathers. Protruding from the lowered figure's bent lower body are brown flora or perhaps spores that spiral upward, supporting the weight of the seated figure. But the brown spores also grow outward into the right diptych, appearing to be nourishing a much smaller centered figure—no less monstrous than the figures to the left—outfitted with what could be read as the legs-splayed, carefree gait of an innocent and oblivious young child. The skin of all three figures retains a multicolored, spongy glow intensely reminiscent of earthly fungus of many varieties. Though the vegetation in Mutu's work is often read as flora, thinking about the entire image as representative of fungus deepens our reading of the relationships between the figures.

In both *One Hundred Lavish Months of Bushwhack* and *Your Story, My Curse,* what can be read as fungal flesh maps onto all the figures Mutu renders, inviting questions about how she achieves the visualization of mottled fungal flesh that resembles these simple yet bewildering organisms. Her inventive use of materials includes ink and mylar—crucial elements of her controlled yet spontaneous process. When asked how her figures come into being and how they retain the mottled flesh that calls fungal imagery to mind, Mutu has explained:

> That happens within the lines that I want the drawing to be in. But if it pools beyond a certain point, it creates a river and sometimes you don't know where it will go. It might go from the belly down to the knee and if you leave the work for five hours, when you come back, you realize the knee has turned into two legs or something. . . . Most of the work in my show, "Yo•n•I," at the Victoria Miro Gallery in London this year was overpoured so that it could become what it wanted to be in the end. I call it "determining." I allow the chemical and natural qualities of the material to decide how it wants to lay on the paper.

For example, in "A dragon kiss always ends in ashes," the figure was almost perfectly placed on the paper and when I came back, her face had opened up. So this dragon or serpent that she's kissing actually created itself overnight. That kind of thing is important because being an artist wouldn't be interesting if I knew everything. I'm intuiting some of the stuff I'm working on, absorbing from the culture, and I haven't processed it. So I'm far more likely to be honest and unedited. If I know everything about the result, I might as well be doing graphic design. Also, you can get really good at your own thing and you start making work that bores you, and when you're bored with your work, then people get bored with it too. So I try to keep this element of surprise. I don't know and understand everything, even things that I care about, *so I want to know what this process can teach me about life, about the work and about myself.*[41]

Mutu's enactment of fungus as a mode of understanding even comes out in her creative process—particularly because of the way her methods encourage unexpectedness and surprise while helping her to understand things about life that she might not otherwise know. When asked how a central idea or aesthetic in one of her collages comes to be, Mutu has explained a process that she calls "determining." In this process, though she is the mastermind of her vision, the figures that emerge from her unique process retain the agency to come together in surprising and edifying ways. By utilizing (not producing) the materials at their disposal—much like fungi use other organisms and materials to nourish and bring themselves into being—Mutu's fems and other figures use available materials to constitute their existence. The combination of her intuition, command of materials, and humble curiosity allows Mutu to assist her protagonists in authoring their own enigmatic presence.

Though discerning the protagonist in *Your Story, My Curse* is difficult, we might settle on the lowered figure, particularly because her relationship seems to ground and connect the other two figures in the diptych. She is connected and likely of service to what appears to be the more privileged figure that reclines on her. Her body and the materials that protrude from her where her genitalia might be are literally nourishing the child-like figure that skips playfully behind her. Her legs are enmeshed into spore-like materials that protrude from the ground beneath her, and though bloodied wounds aren't fastened to the three centered humanoid figures themselves, bloodied woundedness seems to agitate the material at the bottom of the plane. Interestingly, the largest figure is literally embedded in the materials at the bottom of the diptych. Though the other figures are connected to this material by virtue of the lower figure on the left, her proximity to the dulled, brownish red is much more intimate.

In this piece, Mutu collapses human bodies and fungal bodies; *Your Story, My Curse* can be read as a visualization of how critical *black-fems* are to the stabilization of extant structures of power and the damage those structures cause to our shared material resources. The skin of her protagonists usually is read as diseased, mottled flesh, which is incredibly generative for thinking through public and women's health, but also thinking of *black-fem* flesh as fungus or as living decay enables other perspectives as well.[42] First, it draws attention to the ways that we overlook *black-fem* contributions in environmental conversations precisely because of the processes of gendering and racialization that continue to instrumentalize *black-fems*. Second, it draws attention to the ways in which *black-fems*, like fungi, stabilize the global ecosystem. Because of their role as harbingers of transformation, fungi are the earth's chief "recyclers" of organic (and some inorganic) material. These points require our reflection, especially as we contend with the fact that ideas about fungi within the early sciences have led to gross misrepresentations, general lack of knowledge, and unhelpful assumptions that persist to this day. We have a robust and growing knowledge of the harm stereotypes have on people, but we pay less attention to other kinds of organisms, maligned in the Western cultural imagination,[43] that play an irreplaceable role in managing waste and decay on the planet, and that might, as Paul Stamets insists, offer keys to stabilizing our increasingly damaged earth.

In *Your Story, My Curse* specifically, but also in many other works, Mutu displaces familiar optical euphemisms[44] for Black femininity (Black breasts, Black buttocks, Black genitals) to make room for alternative optical-euphemisms of Black femininity (gaudy fashion, animality, or enmeshment in earthly material such as bananas, soil, trees, flora, fungus), which bring the non-distinctions between different material bodies into focus. The wound-induced vulnerability that derives from various mechanisms of environmentally degrading colonial architectures in *Your Story, My Curse* makes clear the indispensability of routinely occluded *black-fem* bodies to the stabilization of the economic and material order on Earth, the multiple functions *black-fems* miraculously and painfully perform (including mothering while serving privileged others, for example), and the routine wounds and intensified exposure to environmental toxicity to which *black-fems* are routinely subjected because of their onto-epistemological functions in the Western order of the World.

Repurposing Woundedness

Though the previous readings and the ones that follow are expressly critical, they do not advance any correctives or definitive claims for capturing the exact or authentic meanings behind Mutu's work. The readings offered are meant to follow Mutu's visual and methodological cues to understand the anti-Black and anti-feminine violence that is often obscured within mainstream environmental discourse. Though Mutu has repeatedly marked her concern for Black women in numerous interviews, as Sarah Jane Cervenak has observed, Mutu has also expressed her frustration with people reducing the figures in her work merely to depictions of Black women. This essay (close) reads and engages Mutu alongside a Black feminist intellectual tradition that insistently reconfigures standpoints that have upheld the "World of Man" and its racialized colonial logics. That said, the arguments offered are not meant to mark woundedness and challenges to survival as markers of disempowerment. Instead, it has been my contention that Mutu's fantastic fungi, seductive reds, and splattered wounds create, to borrow language from Spillers, a "space of contradiction, indictment, and the refusal"[47] of wounds as inherently disempowering.

Though earlier discussions of *Bushwhack* gestured toward discursive and material violence, when highlighting the connotation behind "lavish," yet another reading of *Bushwhack* emerges. Mutu makes repeated allusions to female genitalia, whether it is the exaggerated pubic hair in *Bushwhack* or the title of her show at the Victoria Miro Gallery in London, *Yo•n•I*, which can be read, of course, as "you and I" or as "yoni." Similarly, reading *One Hundred Lavish Months of Bushwhack* as a reflection of an extended period of playful self-induced erotic pleasure (the lavish whacking of one's bush) is both compelling and in line with the queer femme empowerment themes Mutu advances across her oeuvre and activism.

Layering the reading further, the protagonist's wounds at her head and foot in *One Hundred Lavish Months of Bushwhack* can easily be read as adornments. The blood at the head is proudly displayed like a crown, and the blood at the foot, which might normatively be understood as a hindrance to mobility, invites our considerations of non-ableist modes of being in the world. While wounded and/or disabled, it is hard to argue that this protagonist is disempowered or lacks agency. Mutu—refusing the ableist sensibilities that proliferate in environmental discourse[48]—turns the normative logics of woundedness-as-disempowerment on its head. The central figure's gesture does not stop at relative safety or mere survival; the protagonist's side-eye instead opens up to an awkward yet elegant bodily expression that could be dancing, fighting, or some combination of the two. The image refuses a definitive reading, but that refusal illuminates the agential yet precarious space between victim and aggressor when certain bodies fall prey to racialized and gendered ecological wounding processes.

To close, I offer some open-ended thoughts to consider about the nature of power, its relationship to certain bodies, and how we conceptualize earthly damage. Elsewhere Mutu has noted: "Violent incidences are often fastened to images of privilege in my drawings. . . . There is this tiny percentage of people who live like emperors because elsewhere blood is being shed."[49] It is with these insights in mind that we might finally turn our attention to the easily unnoticed smaller figure in the lower right corner of *One Hundred Lavish Months of Bushwhack*. If the larger figure weren't confounding enough, the smaller figure brings even more questions into view.

The relationship between the two figures in *One Hundred Lavish Months of Bushwhack* is unclear—but the fact that the darker figure seems to be serving the lighter-skinned figure calls to mind centuries of depictions of White supremacy and Black inferiority.[50]

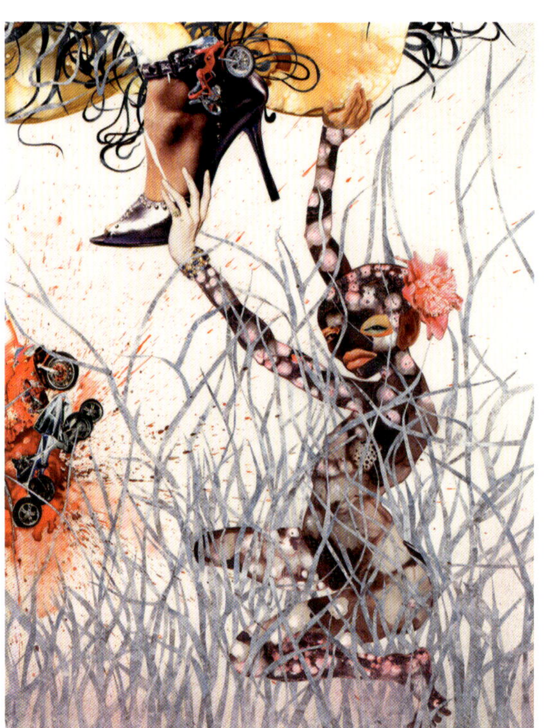

Fig. 3. Wangechi Mutu, *One Hundred Lavish Months of Bushwhack* (detail), 2004. Cut-and-paste printed paper with watercolor, synthetic polymer paint, and pressure-sensitive stickers on Mylar. 68 ½ × 42 in. (174 × 106.7 cm). Courtesy of the Artist. The Museum of Modern Art, New York, NY. Fund for the Twenty-First Century (99.2005)

In the images of Black servitude throughout the Western art historical canon (figs. 4–9), a White supremacist hierarchy is inextricably linked to Black and Brown exploitation and servitude in addition to a subdued (and therefore exploitable) physical landscape. In Mutu's pieces, however—particularly in *Bushwhack*—we are left to wonder about whether this re-signified relationship is voluntary or mandatory. Is the relationship racialized, exploitative, or mutually beneficial? Which figures and organisms constitute vulnerability, and who is vulnerable to what? The smaller figure could be a victim of the larger one—positioned literally underneath the larger figure's white-skinned foot—but the larger figure is the one that has or is currently sustaining serious wounds. The size and space between the two figures invites us to wonder whether or not the smaller figure is just slightly avoiding being stepped on by alerting the larger figure to their marginalized presence, or, by contrast, we might wonder if the smaller figure is supporting the larger figure from a position of disguised or camouflaged safety, hidden away from the amalgam of earthly damage I discussed earlier.

One of the most dazzling features of Mutu's work is that the relationships between various bodies and materials are intentionally left ambiguous and allow the viewers' racial/gender/spatial politics to (however uncomfortably) make up their own mind. To begin the essay, I asked: "What kinds of problems or questions rise from eco-theory's epistemologies when we place occluded *black-fem* bodies at the center?" In light of our difficulty to conceive of *black-fem* bodies at the center of most epistemologies—especially ecological ones—Mutu speaks wounded bodies. She makes visible amalgams of racialization and gendering that conceal colonial engravings on exploited Black bodies and bodies of land malformed into ecologically *degraded* and *degrading* "blood nourishing" capital.[51]

To pose a concluding question: if most epistemologies can't speak *black-fem* subjects despite the centrality of their woundedness to the destruction of earth, how might we continue to mine Black feminist art, not for resolutions to poorly conceptualized problems, but for better understandings of our hopeful, yet damaged presents?

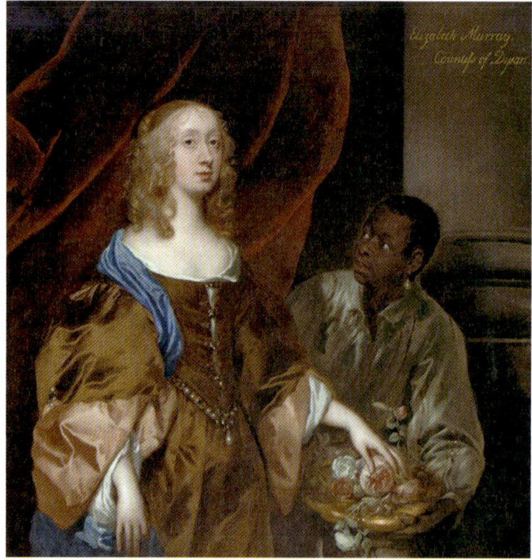

Fig. 4. Peter Lely (German, 1618–1680), *Elizabeth Murray, Lady Tollemache, later Countess of Dysart and Duchess of Lauderdale with a Black Servant*, 1651. Ham House, London

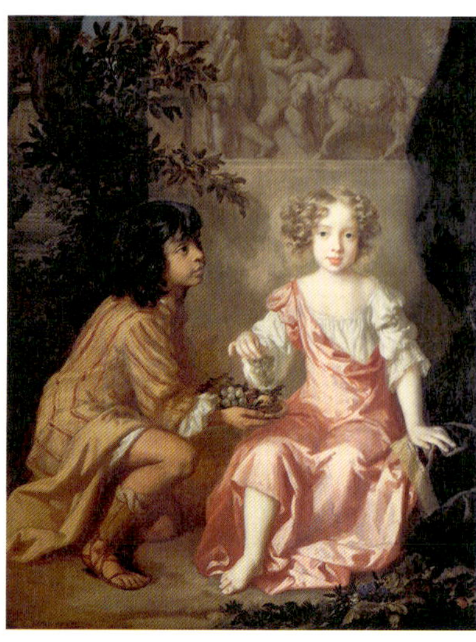

Fig. 5. Peter Lely, *Lady Charlotte Fitzroy (1664–1719), later Countess of Lichfield*, 17th century. Oil on canvas, 50 × 40 in. (127 × 101.6 cm). York Museums Trust (York Art Gallery), England

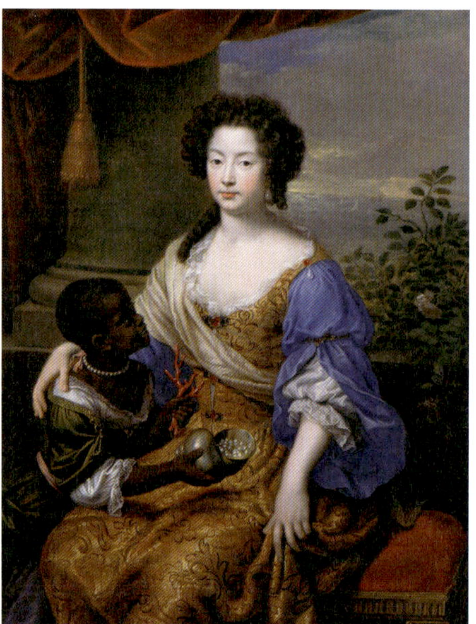

Fig. 6. Pierre Mignard (French, 1612–1695), *Louise de Kéroualle, Duchess of Portsmouth*, 1682. Oil on canvas, 47 ¹/₂ × 37 ¹/₂ in. (120.7 × 95.3 cm). National Portrait Gallery, London. Purchased 1878 (NPG 497). © National Portrait Gallery, London

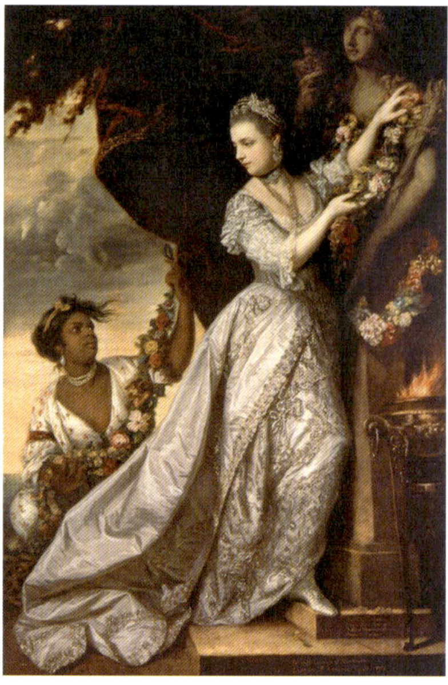

Fig. 7. Sir Joshua Reynolds (English, 1723–1792), *Lady Elizabeth Keppel*, 1761. Oil on canvas, 57 ¹/₂ × 92 ⁷/₈ in. (146.1 × 235.9 cm). From the Woburn Abbey Collection, Woburn Abbey, England

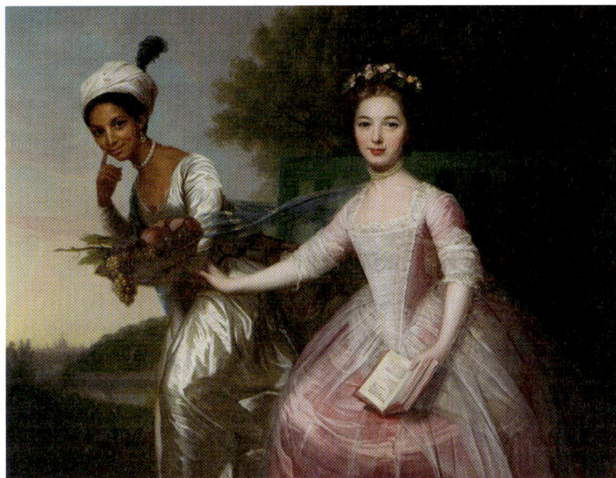

Fig. 8. Attributed to Johann Zoffany (German, 1733–1810), *Portrait of Dido Elizabeth Belle Lindsay (1761–1804) and Her Cousin Lady Elizabeth Murray (1760–1825)*, c. 1778. Oil on canvas. Scone Palace, Scotland

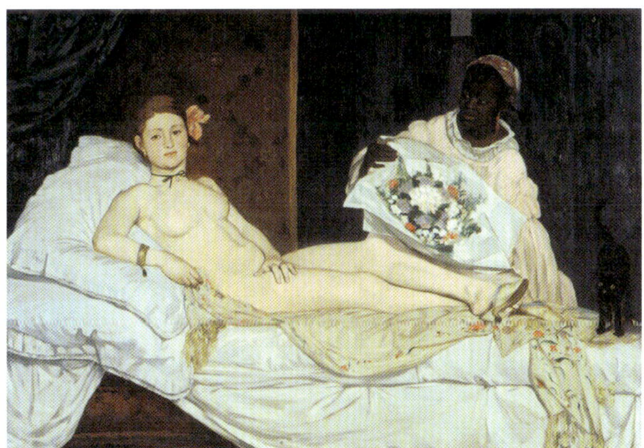

Fig. 9. Édouard Manet (French, 1832–1883), *Olympia*, 1863–65. Oil on canvas, 51 $^3/_8$ × 74 $^3/_4$ in. (130.5 × 189.9 cm). Musée d'Orsay, Paris

I would like to thank Michelle Wright, Huey Copeland, Theodore Foster, Chad Infante, R. J. Eldridge, Rene Rougeau, Fushcia Hoover, Lauren Miller, and Lace Burwell for the invaluable challenges, insights, and questions they offered to help with the development of this piece.

1. Dibloni Ollo Theophile et al., "Feeding Habits of Hippopotamus Amphibius and Carrying Capacity in the Biosphere Reserve of 'Mare aux Hippopotames' in the South-Sudanian Zone of Burkina Faso," *Pakistan Journal of Zoology* 44, no. 2 (2012): 1–14.

2. Jeffrey Jerome Cohen, ed., *Prismatic Ecology: Ecotheory beyond Green* (Minneapolis: University of Minnesota Press, 2014).

3. The idea of "excessiveness"—particularly with regard to Black female subjectivity—draws from Nicole R. Fleetwood, *Troubling Vision: Performance, Visuality, and Blackness* (Chicago: University of Chicago Press, 2011).

4. "About Us," *Conservation International,* http://www.conservation.org/about/Pages/default.aspx (accessed November 16, 2017).

5. "Vision & Mission | The Nature Conservancy," https://www.nature.org/about-us/vision-mission/index.htm (accessed November 16, 2017).

6. Alan C. Braddock and Renée Ater, "Art in the Anthropocene," *American Art* 28, no. 3 (September 1, 2014): 2. The term "Anthropocene" has been widely debated in recent years and has spawned many terms, including the "capitalocene," "plantationocene," and "chthulucene." I leave these debates bracketed in this essay and mark that my use of the term generally aligns with what Braddock and Ater explain as "the growing scientific consensus that Earth has entered a new geological epoch, the Anthropocene, distinguished from the preceding Holocene by the fact that humans since the nineteenth century have become the primary drivers of environmental change on a planetary scale."

7. This focus is very explicitly reflected in the mission of Mutu's organization Africa's Out!—geared toward the support and empowerment of African LGBTQ folks and "those who have been ostracized because of their color, ethnicity, gender, or sexual orientation," "About Us," *Africa's Out!,* http://africasout.com/aboutus (accessed November 16, 2017).

8. Robert Enright, "Resonant Surgeries: The Collaged World of Wangechi Mutu," *Border Crossings* 105 (February 2008): 25, http://bordercrossingsmag.com/article/resonant-surgeries-the-collaged-world-of-wangechi-mutu (accessed November 16, 2017). Also "About Us," *Africa's Out!*

9. For another discussion of mushroom symbols as representations of both trauma and healing, see Ann Cvetkovich's "Sexual Trauma/Queer Memory: Incest, Lesbianism and Therapeutic Culture," in *Incest and the Literary Imagination,* ed. Elizabeth Barnes (Gainesville: University Press of Florida, 2002), 329–57. For Cvetkovich, mushrooms figure prominently, as does the idea of reclaiming something productive (queerness and healing) from traumatic abuse (childhood sexual abuse).

10. For more on fungal reproduction, see Roy Watling, *Fungi,* ed. Jonathan Elphick (Washington, DC: Smithsonian Books, 2003), 10.

11. Language here references ideas advanced in Karen Barad's *Meeting the Universe Halfway: Quantum Physics and the Entanglement of Matter and Meaning* (Durham: Duke University Press, 2007).

12. Paul Stamets, *Mycelium Running: How Mushrooms Can Help Save the World* (Berkeley: Ten Speed Press, 2005), 1.

13. For a brief overview of the health disparities suffered by Black women in the United States from an environmental justice perspective, see Erin Switalski, "The Toxic Assault on Black Women's Health," *Women's Voices for the Earth*, August 3, 2016, http://www.womensvoices.org/2016/08/03/toxic-assault-on-black-womens-health. See also Jackie Ricciardi, "Too Many Black Women Die From Breast Cancer. Why?," *BU Today*, April 24, 2017, http://www.bu.edu/today/2017/black-women-breast-cancer-research. See also Zahra Barnes, "8 Health Conditions That Disproportionately Affect Black Women," *SELF*, http://www.self.com/story/black-women-health-conditions (all accessed November 16, 2017). For an overview of Kenyan women's health vulnerabilities, see Dr. Waithera Karim-Sesay, *Don't Sleep African Women: Powerlessness and HIV/AIDS Vulnerability Among Kenyan Women* (Pittsburgh: RoseDog Books, 2011). See also "Environmental Health Perspectives—Modern Environmental Health Hazards: A Public Health Issue of Increasing Significance in Africa," https://ehp.niehs.nih.gov/0800126 (accessed November 16, 2017).

14. Achille Mbembé and Libby Meintjes, "Necropolitics," *Public Culture* 15, no. 1 (March 25, 2003): 11–40. Mbembé's elucidation of necro-politics not only explains why the death of some subjects continues to remain routine, but also helps to explain why in a cis-heterocapitalist society, trans women of color, for example, are murdered every twenty-nine hours. See Addison Rose Vincent, "State of Emergency Continues for Trans Women of Color," *Huffington Post*, August 13, 2015, http://www.huffingtonpost.com/addison-rose-vincent/the-state-of-emergency-co_b_7981580.html (accessed November 16, 2017)

15. See Denise Ferreira Da Silva, *Toward a Global Idea of Race* (Minneapolis: University of Minnesota Press, 2007).

16. The term *black-fem* has been significantly influenced by Zakiyyah Jackson's offerings throughout the Black Feminist Futures Symposium conference at Northwestern University in 2016, where she advanced several critiques of the under-theorizations and imprecise conceptualizations of *black queer/femme-ness* within Black studies and queer-of-color critique. In addition, the term *black-fem* materialized as a result of several conversations with my colleague Brittnay Proctor that challenged my (re)formulations of gendered language. See Proctor's theorization of "the Black feminine bottom," in Brittnay Proctor, "Performing Black Masculine Alterity via Black Women's Enfleshed Sex Work: The Ohio Players *Skin Tight* (1974)," in "The Anoriginal Force of Black Performance", symposium held at Northwestern University, Evanston, Illinois, February 8, 2017. Further, for a discussion of the paradoxes, erasures, and necessities of "femme-visibility," see Amber Jamilla Musser, "Queering the Pinup: History, Femmes, and Brooklyn," *GLQ: A Journal of Lesbian and Gay Studies* 22, no. 1

(January 2016): 55–80.

17. I am indebted to conversations with Sarah Jane Cervenak and Jennifer Nash for my clarity around this point about the "assumed subjects" of Black studies and/or Black feminist studies.

18. Deborah Willis, "Wangechi Mutu (Oral History)," *Bomb Magazine*, February 28, 2014, http://bombmagazine.org/article/1000052/wangechi-mutu (accessed November 16, 2017).

19. Benjy Hansen-Bundy, "A Fantastic Journey into the Mind of Collage Artist Wangechi Mutu," *Mother Jones*, http://www.motherjones.com/media/2013/10/interview-collage-artist-wangechi-mutu-fantastic-journey (accessed November 16, 2017).

20. Sarah Cascone, "Wangechi Mutu Wins Anderson Ranch's National Artist Award " *Artnet News*, April 11, 2017, https://news.artnet.com/art-world/anderson-ranch-national-artist-award-wangechi-mutu-921149 (accessed November 16, 2017).

21. Lauri Firstenberg, "Perverse Anthropology: The Photomontage of Wangechi Mutu, A Conversation with Lauri Firstenberg," in *Looking Both Ways: Art of the Contemporary African Diaspora*, ed. Laurie Ann Farrell (Ghent, Belgium: Snoeck Publishers, 2004), 137–43.

22. Arielle A. Concilio, "Pedro Lemebel and the Translatxrsation: On a Genderqueer Translation Praxis," *TSQ: Transgender Studies Quarterly* 3, nos. 3–4 (November 1, 2016): 464.

23. See Sandra Cyr's piece, "The Relevance of Diversity," *Philanthropy Journal*, August 7, 2017, https://pj.news.chass.ncsu.edu/2017/08/07/the-relevance-of-diversity/, for an example of the ways that large environmental organizations narrate the necessity and relevance of belated inclusion in their organizations.

24. Though unnamed, the normalization of the White cis-heterocapitalist subject is even reflected within the histories of leadership of these organizations and the current leadership. Though there are a handful of women, gay and lesbian, and nonwhite people that can be found in their boards, offices, and labs, *all* of those that hold the most power over decision-making and command the highest salaries within the Nature Conservancy, Conservation International, the World Wildlife Fund, and the Global Environment Facility are cis-gendered, (presumably) heterosexual White men with histories of working with other large corporations.

25. See Sarah Jaquette Ray, *The Ecological Other: Environmental Exclusion in American Culture* (Tucson: University of Arizona Press, 2013), 9, for a discussion of "nature as nation-building."

26. Hortense J. Spillers, "The Idea of Black Culture," *CR: The New Centennial Review* 6, no. 3 (2007): 7–28.

27. Michelle M. Wright, *Physics of Blackness: Beyond the Middle Passage Epistemology* (Minneapolis: University of Minnesota Press, 2015), 25.

28. Ibid.

29. Jeffrey Myers, *Converging Stories: Race, Ecology, and Environmental Justice in American Literature* (Athens: University of Georgia Press, 2005).

30. Ibid., 114.

31. Denise Ferreira Da Silva, "Toward a Black Feminist Poethics," *The Black Scholar* 44, no. 2 (June 1, 2014): 82.

32. Ibid., 83.

33. For a narrative that details the ongoing colonial assault on various environments in Kenya, see Wangari Maathai, *Unbowed: A Memoir*, repr. ed. (New York: Anchor, 2007).

34. Da Silva, "Toward a Black Feminist Poethics," 91.

35. Firstenberg, "Perverse Anthropology," 143.

36. See "How to Write about Africa," *Granta Magazine*, January 19, 2006, https://granta.com/how-to-write-about-africa. In this essay, Binyavanga Wainaina satirically exposes the stereotypes that dominate the popular imagination about Africa—including the term "guerilla," a synonym for "bushwhacker."

37. Joseph Beilein Jr., *Bushwhackers: Guerrilla Warfare, Manhood, and the Household in Civil War Missouri* (Ashland, Ohio: Kent State University Press, 2016); Matthew C. Hulbert, *The Ghosts of Guerilla Memory: How Civil War Bushwhackers Became Gunslingers in the American West* (Athens: University of Georgia Press, 2016); Matthew M. Stith, *Extreme Civil War: Guerilla Warfare, Environment, and Race on the Trans-Mississippi Frontier* (Baton Rouge: Louisiana State University Press, 2016); Larry Wood, *Bushwhacker Belles: The Sisters, Wives, and Girlfriends of the Missouri Guerrillas* (Gretna, La.: Pelican Publishing Company, 2016).

38. Da Silva, "Toward a Black Feminist Poethics," 82.

39. See note 37.

40. Nicole R. Fleetwood, "Excess Flesh: Black Performing Hypervisibility," in *Troubling Vision: Performance, Visuality, and Blackness* (Chicago: University of Chicago Press, 2011).

41. Enright, "Resonant Surgeries."

42. Ibid. and Trevor Schoonmaker, *Wangechi Mutu: A Fantastic Journey*, exh. cat. (Durham: Duke University Press, 2013), for discussions of the mottled skin of Mutu's protagonists as disease.

43. According to mycologist Roy Watling, though there are millions of species of fungi, mycologists are aware of only about little more than 15 percent of the population. In Watling's *Fungi*, he explains that "the reasons for the lack of scientific knowledge of fungi compared with groups such as mammals, fish, birds and flowering plants originate with the early naturalists. They usually considered the fungi to be connected with the devil, and studying them at all was frowned upon by the church, right up to the 19th century, when the rest of natural history was blossoming. As a result of this taboo, scientific understanding of fungi, and especially their classification, has been hindered so much that it is no exaggeration to say that it lags 100 years behind that of many organisms. Thankfully, this unfortunate state of affairs is now rapidly changing as biologists appreciate the importance of these remarkable organisms and are searching for them in previously unexpired habitat" (p. 19).

44. I conjured the term "optical euphemism" to refer to reductive, visual placeholders that reinforce stereotypical understandings of various subjects—in this case, *black-fem* subjects.

45. Sarah Jane Cervenak, "Like Blood or Blossom: Wangechi Mutu's Resistant Harvests," *Feminist Studies* 42, no. 2 (2016): 398.

46. Da Silva, "Toward a Black Feminist Poethics." For more extended discussions of "Man's" apprehension of the "World," see Alexander G. Weheliye, *Habeas Viscus: Racializing Assemblages, Biopolitics, and Black Feminist Theories of the Human* (Durham: Duke University Press, 2014). Furthermore, Weheliye's work builds on and departs from Sylvia Wynter's "Unsettling the Coloniality of Being/Power/Truth/Freedom: Towards the Human, After Man, Its Overrepresentation—An Argument," *CR: The New Centennial Review* 3, no. 3 (2003): 257–337.

47. Spillers, "The Idea of Black Culture," 19.

48. See Ray, *The Ecological Other,* for a critique of ableism in the environmental movement, environmental studies, and eco-criticism.

49. Firstenberg, "Perverse Anthropology," 142.

50. Critical conversations with art historian Huey Copeland added significant texture and nuance to my understanding of the visualization of Black servitude throughout the Western art historical canon. See Copeland's "Flow and Arrest," *Small Axe* 19, no. 348 (November 1, 2015): 205–24.

51. Da Silva, "Toward a Black Feminist Poethics."

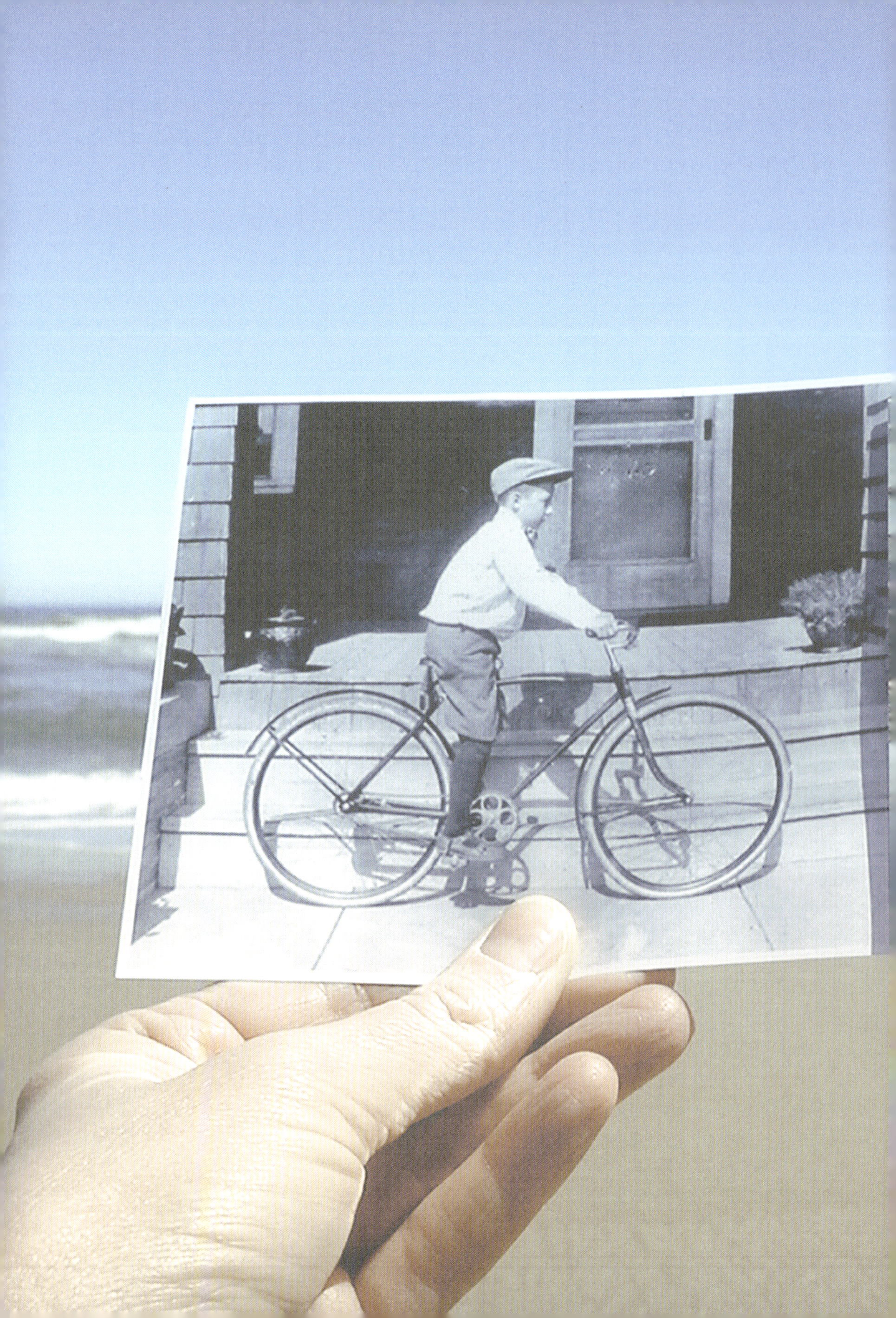

NOTES ON A PERFORMANCE-IN-PROGRESS

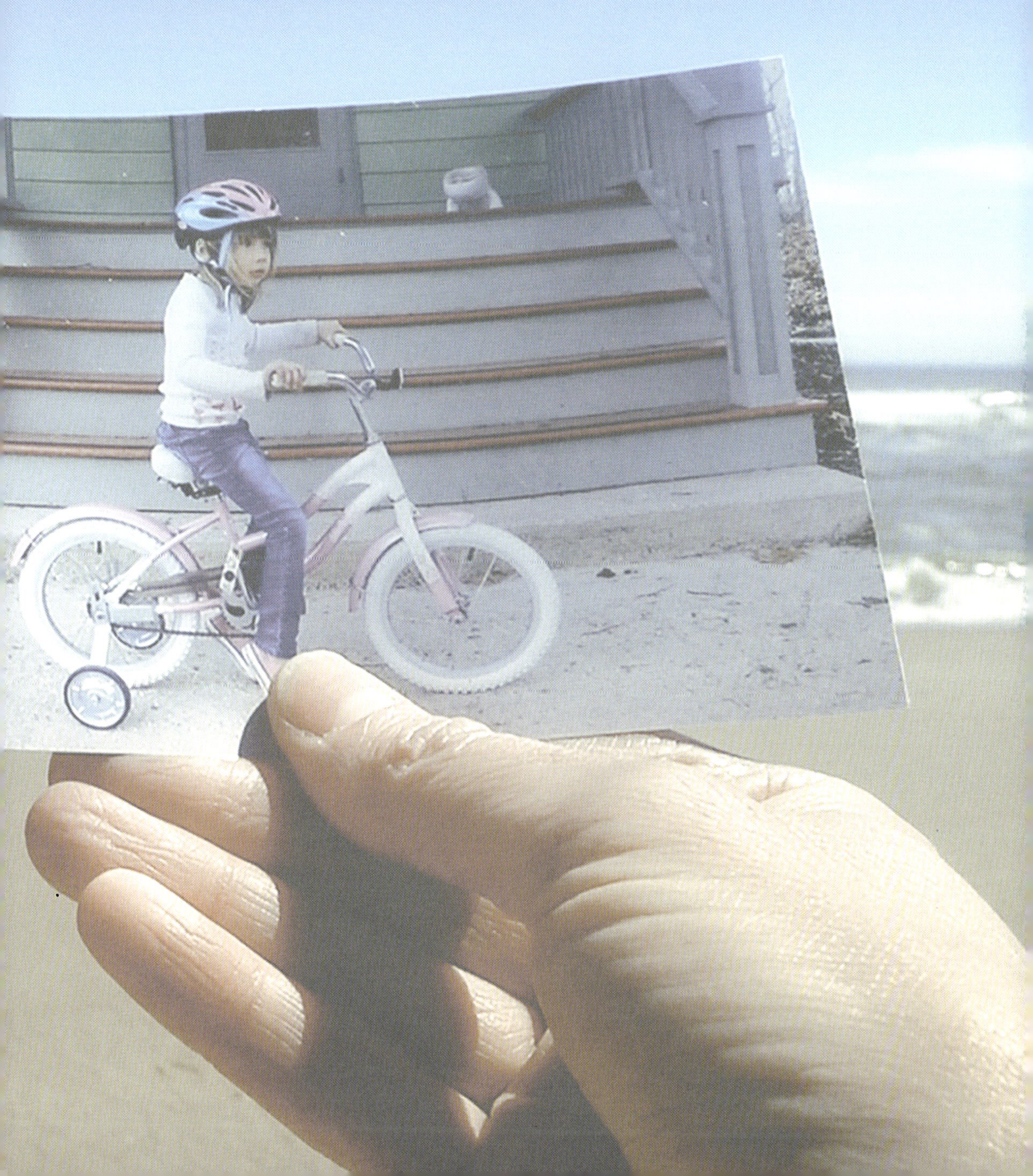

My Electric Genealogy

Sarah Kanouse

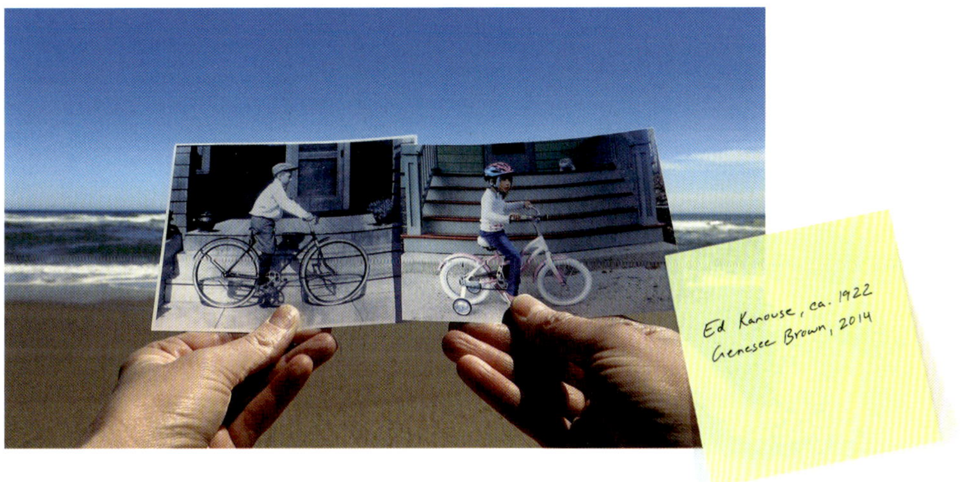

My grandfather would have been ninety-nine the year my daughter was born.

They share an odd century, but just barely. He, born ten years into the twentieth; she, nine years after its not-yet-apocalyptic end. I float two-thirds of the way between them: the Kanouse reproductive rhythm seemingly calibrated in precise thirty-three-year cycles, like a brood of undiscovered cicadas.

Poised on opposite shores of that oceanic expanse we call the twentieth century, they will never see each other's faces, but mirror images they are all the same.

My grandfather was born during what textbooks call the "Second Industrial Revolution"—that period of rapid change in electricity, chemistry, agriculture, and transportation from the end of the American Civil War until the middle of the twentieth century. Cars replaced trains. Farms got by without farmers. Working families abandoned tenements for single family homes. My grandfather loved electricity. His passion for the intricacies of energy—generating it, moving it, using it—may have exceeded all other passions in his life. He missed the great discoveries, but focused on their implementation.

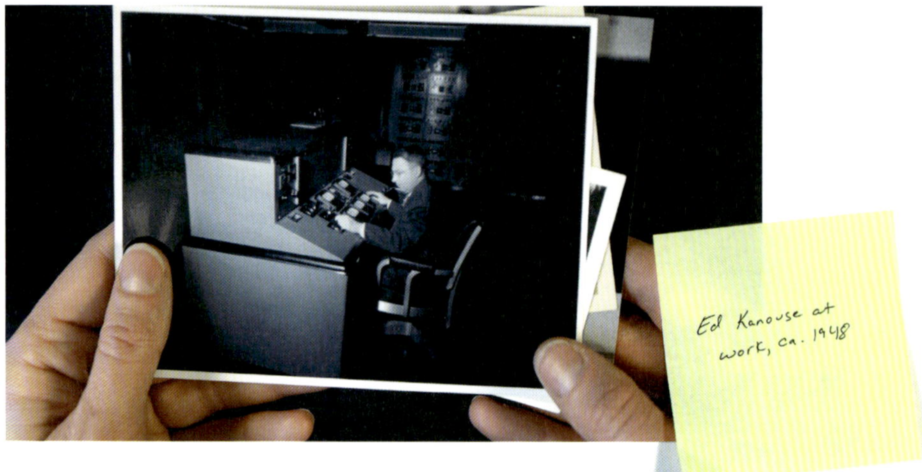

My grandfather specialized in transmission: the art of moving enormous amounts of electricity across vast desert distances. He started working for the Los Angeles Department of Water and Power (LADWP) in the testing labs and worked his way up. The spider-vein network of lines he designed, planned, and administered fueled an ever more voracious California lifestyle: the radios of the 1930s; the TVs of the '40s; the air conditioners of the '50s; the all-electric kitchens of the '60s; and the Jacuzzi tubs and heated pools of the '70s. By the time he became the department's general manager in 1968, the utility had to remind its sticker-shocked customers, "It's not just a light bill anymore."[1]

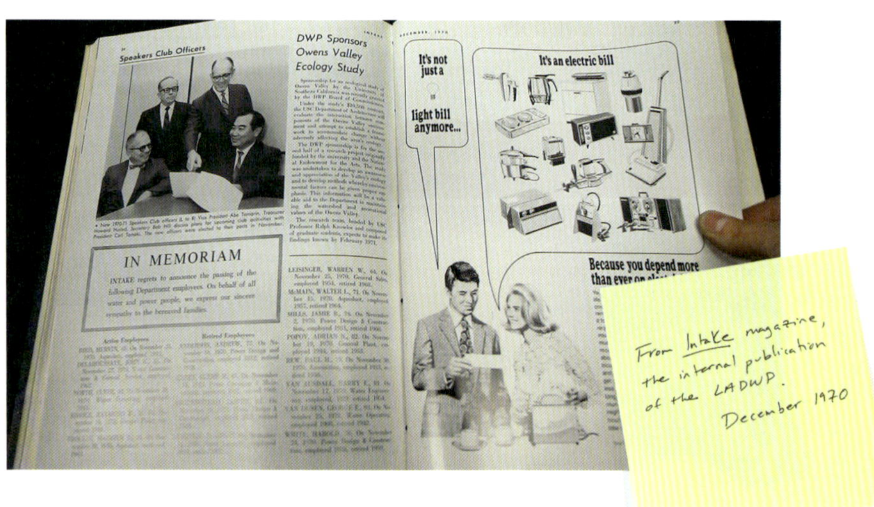

It's not just a light bill anymore.

Like long-distance water, long-distance energy insulated human senses from the extremities of desert life. LA's development jumped coastal mountains and sprawled into the hot inland valleys where I grew up.

Between my grandfather's birth and my daughter's, LA's population grew twelvefold. Between my grandfather's birth and my daughter's, the earth got hotter by one degree.

It's not just a light bill any more.

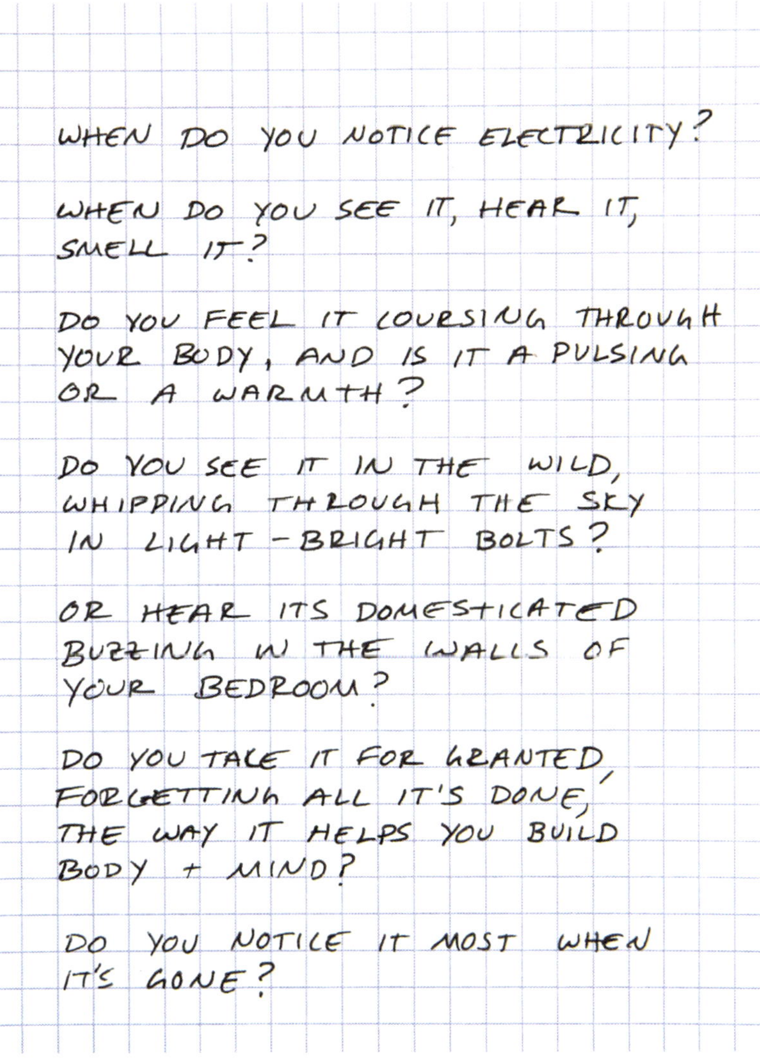

Sometime in my teens, my grandfather rallied from his long, but not slow, decline. I already identified as an artist, and somehow that information stuck with him when little else could anymore. During one of the visits that terrifies me to contemplate—even the best days smelling of urine and death—he said he had something important to show me. Slowly turning, he retrieved a box from the wheeled table beside the club chair where he spent his days. He fumbled the lid off and exhaled deeply at the sight of the contents. A stack of 8 x 10 photographs came out, each capturing a single high-voltage transmission tower in sharp black and white. He had taken them all and proudly talked me through each image. The specifics of the design decisions seemed hazy to him, or maybe I've forgotten details I didn't understand to begin with. What struck me was my grandfather's experience of these objects' aesthetic force. "This one is just . . . so . . . beautiful," he'd exclaim. I smiled, indulging an old man his moment, and tried to see the beauty in the images that he did.[2]

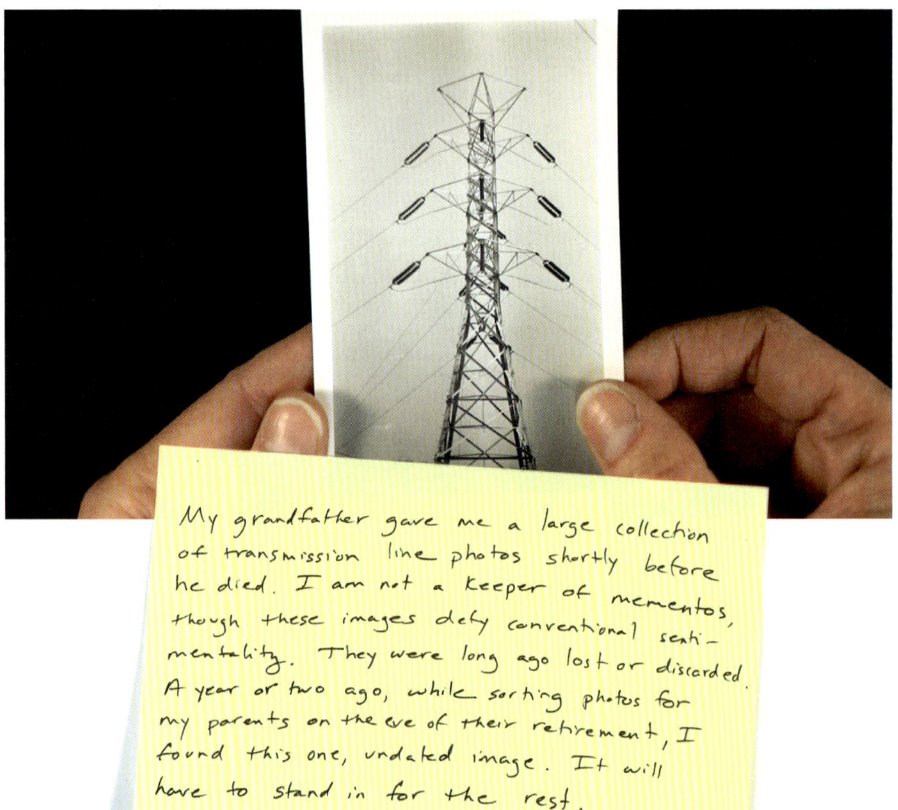

Today, it is difficult to understand the impact of electricity on what we now think of as daily life. Like the Internet this century, electricity brought radical change in the organization of work, recreation, and home. Seasonal and geographical patterns of daylight no longer governed the rhythms of human activities, which industrialization had already accelerated. For my grandfather's generation, electricity carried an affective and aesthetic force beyond its mere utility. This excess of meaning registered in turn-of-the-century slang we still use today. Energetic people are called "live wires" or "dynamos," after the first industrial generators. To "feel electric" means to be socially, or sexually, aroused. Many of the first public displays of electric lighting were installed as much for pleasure, consumption, and spectacle as for utility. World's Fairs delivered fantastic lightscapes that inspired illuminated thoroughfares and entertainment zones in cities across the country. Patterns of mobility quickly reoriented around zones of street lighting and the automobile. Headlights and tail lights added to the newfound brightness of night.[3] Electric signage soon followed, commodifying the newly accessible evening public spaces with advertising and providing some of the most iconic and nostalgia-drenched images of twentieth-century petro-modernity.[4]

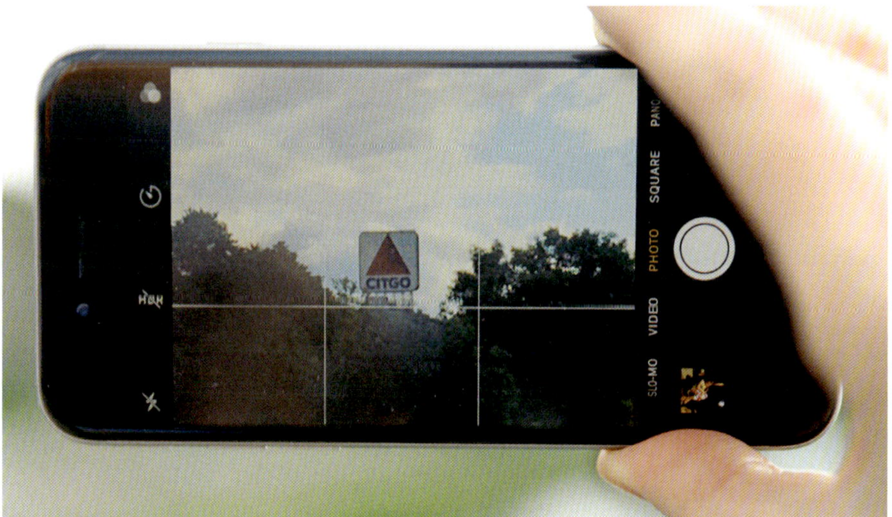

Infrastructures enable, shape, and constrain life at any given historical moment. They are relational and not immanent: we make them, and they make us. Alan Liu has argued that over the course of a century in which American lives unfolded in organizations of ever greater intricacy and reach, the experience of infrastructure has become "operationally, the experience of culture" itself.[5] Deborah Cowen notes that infrastructures are "systems engineered to order social and natural worlds."[6] For that reason, they occupy a central position within many contemporary political conflicts, from port and road occupations to the Flint water crisis to pipeline construction on sovereign Indigenous land. The political nature of infrastructure is also personal for Ruth Wilson Gilmore and Clayton Rosati, who describe an "infrastructure of feeling," in which technology, matter, and space form the "tangible, material conditions within which . . . our social emotions are developed, felt, and communicated."[7] For Lauren Berlant, infrastructure is "the living mediation of what organizes life: the lifeworld of structure."[8]

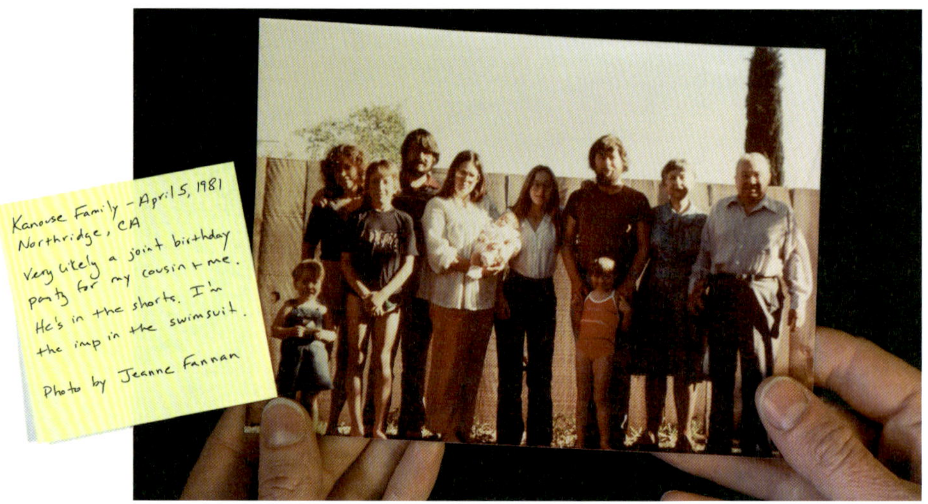

This project is an invitation to both *feel* and *think* with infrastructure. It's about conflicting notions of the future, uncertain filiations, and different ways of assembling the past. It is reparative, but it is also critical.[9] In it, I hope to queer the environmental history of my family even at the moment of its first and fragmentary writing. By "queer," I mean to establish another "horizon of possibility" for my familiar family tree than the linear progression through generational begats: a "straight time" that leads inexorably to my child and a 406.75 ppm world.[10] By "queer," I mean to locate and compose a set of "improper" family relations arrayed against, or maybe residing inside, what we presume we know.

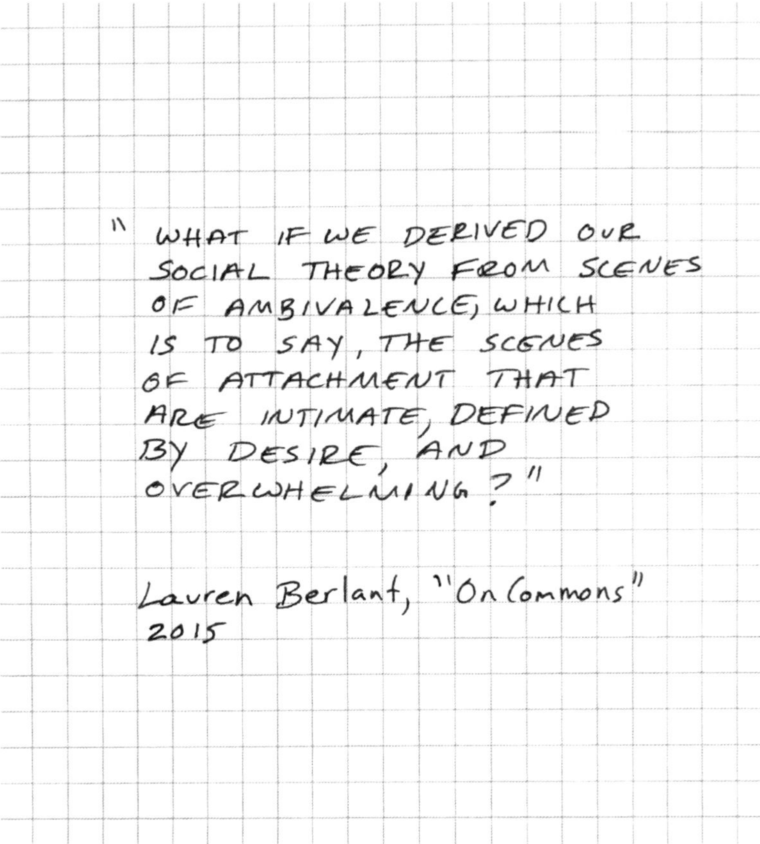

My grandfather gestated transmission towers, brought forth miles of cable, and nursed power plants into being. Like all parents, he could hardly fathom what he had birthed and who he was leaving behind. He made the desert buzz. In this queer infrastructural genealogy, I am kin not just with my human cousins or even other critters but also with the Victorville Switching Station, the Sylmar Converter Station, the Pacific DC Intertie, the Hoover Dam.[11] My tools in finding these relations are clumsy and my research skills imprecise. It is a performance of poor theory that "proceeds through appropriations and improvisations, through descriptions that do not leave what it describes unchanged." I ask you to remain open "to that which outpaces understanding."[12]

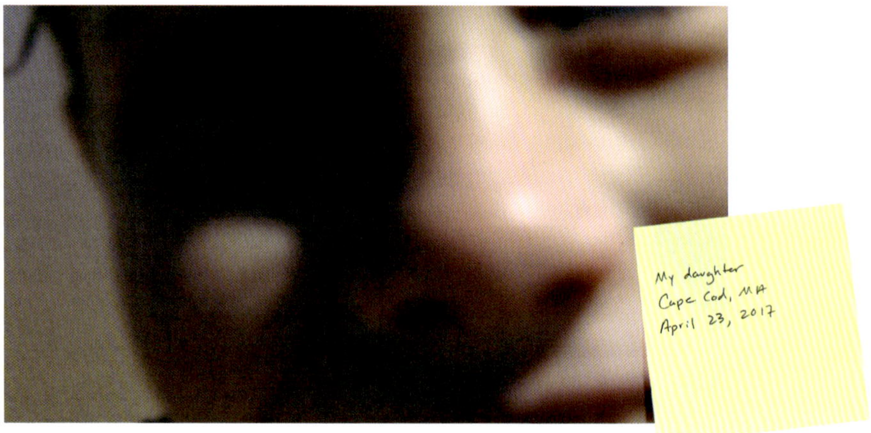

My grandfather would have been ninety-nine the year my daughter was born.

Instead, he died eighteen years earlier, when I was still in high school. The recorded milestones of my life, my parents', and his—the birthday parties and Christmases, the parade of school portraits, the heading-off-to-college, first relationship, first apartment, first job—these are so twentieth century. I can and cannot place my daughter in these pictures. The world where these normative rites of passage make any sense is being rearranged as I watch.

My daughter is growing, animate, but suspended. She is eight years old now, her short life marked by climate milestones as much as developmental ones. She turned five in the warmest year on record, and six, and then seven.[13] Her father and I hold our breath and buy her piano lessons. We talk to her about serious things—climate change, colonialism, racism. Most of the time she is curious: "Why did slavery happen, mommy?" Sometimes we overdo it: her face crumbles and she covers her ears. "Don't tell me how bad the future will be!"

I don't know what is coming, I tell my daughter, and me. I don't know that it'll be all bad. I don't know what it will be like at all. An emptiness where her future is concerned is preferable to the images of apocalypse that populate our collective environmental anxieties. I can't parent in a state of "sublime despair," so I cultivate an openness, a state of blankness, a possibility.[14] It doesn't come easily to me. I catch myself picturing her in college as I walk across some campus, wondering if her love of poetry will survive another decade identifying the features of informational texts. These inherited fantasies end with a wrenching feeling in my gut: Who knows if that world will still exist? Who knows?

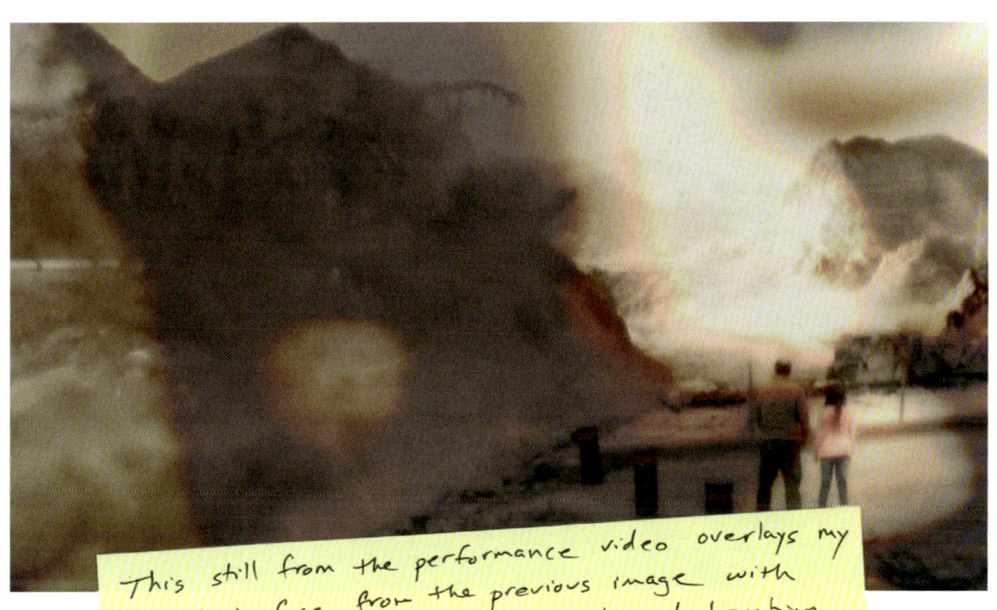

This still from the performance video overlays my daughter's face from the previous image with the aftermath of the spectacular destruction of Hoover Dam from the 2015 Warner Brothers disaster film "San Andreas". Moments before this Bierstadt-worthy tableau, the white girl in the foreground is rescued by Dr. Kim Park, a seismologist who seemed like a major character until abruptly dying a hero's death. His Asian-ness underscored by not one but two Korean surnames, he serves little function to the plot behind saving a white girl. Reproductive futurity is white—and deadly.

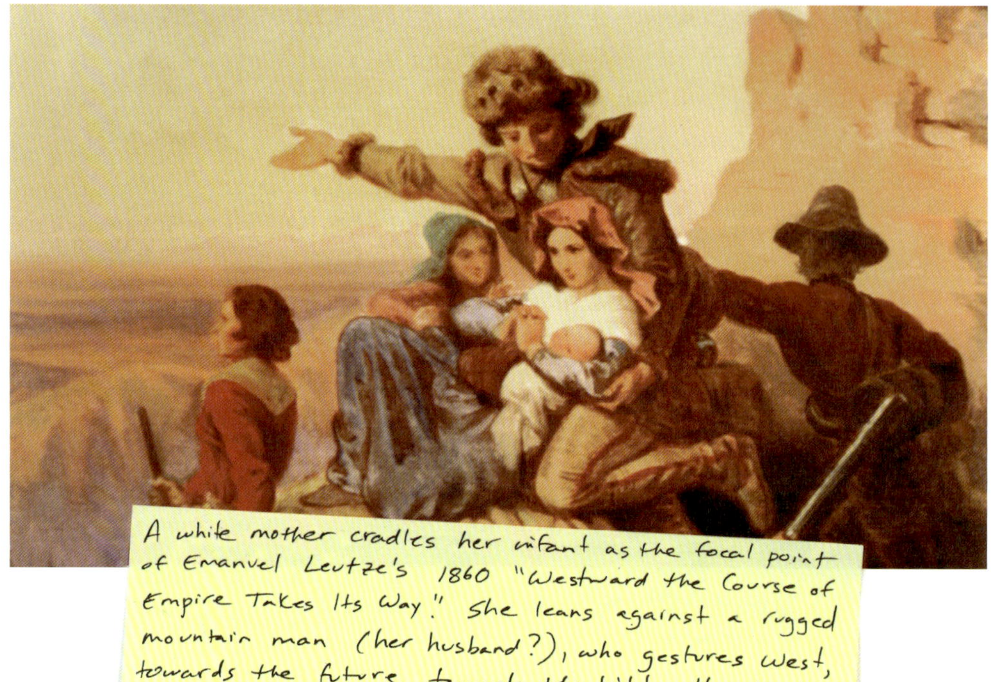

Elders at climate action meetings choke up when they see her and tell us, blinking back tears, that they testify, march, and blockade for her future. At these moments, I am both moved and alarmed. I am moved because, quite honestly, climate change went from abstract to intimate only when I had this child, and moments of feeling shared with a stranger are too rare. For the same reason, I am also alarmed. The symbol of child-as-future—only ever inhabited by those who look like *my* child—has been mobilized for all kinds of repressions.[15] *That* future is more about the reproduction of the present than the remaking of the world. The futures I can easily picture for her—the ones that resemble my own past—I know they foreclose the futures of others. Which is to say, they are no future at all. The world that now exists—the one that settler cultures so fear losing—is someone else's apocalypse, survived.[16]

Sustain what, for whom, for how long?

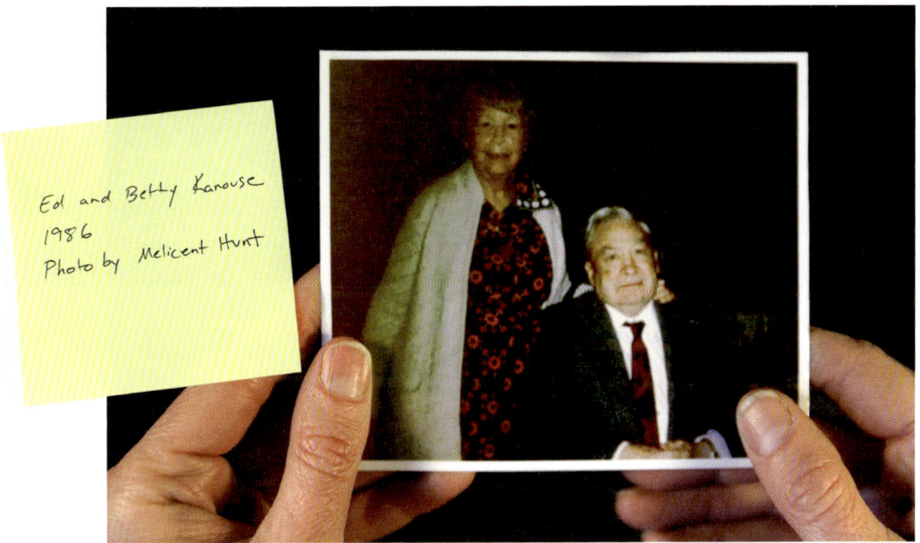

My grandfather passed away one year after the first intergovernmental report established that human activities were warming the planet. He was too far gone to notice, but I was both old enough and young enough to care. The next year was the Earth Summit in Rio de Janeiro and, tellingly, the 500th anniversary of Columbus's first colonial voyage.

At the Summit, Chile proposed the notion of "ecological debt." The word captures how the prosperity and development of the Global North was financed by hundreds of years of extraction, deforestation, land theft, and pollution in the Global South. The idea helped to reframe the debate surrounding poor countries' cash debts to the World Bank and the International Monetary Fund and set the stage for the alter-globalization movements of the 1990s and early 2000s, about the time I got involved in political struggle. It resurfaced a few years later in the debate over how to fairly distribute the sharp emissions cuts needed to limit global warming to a still suicidal, still genocidal two degrees.

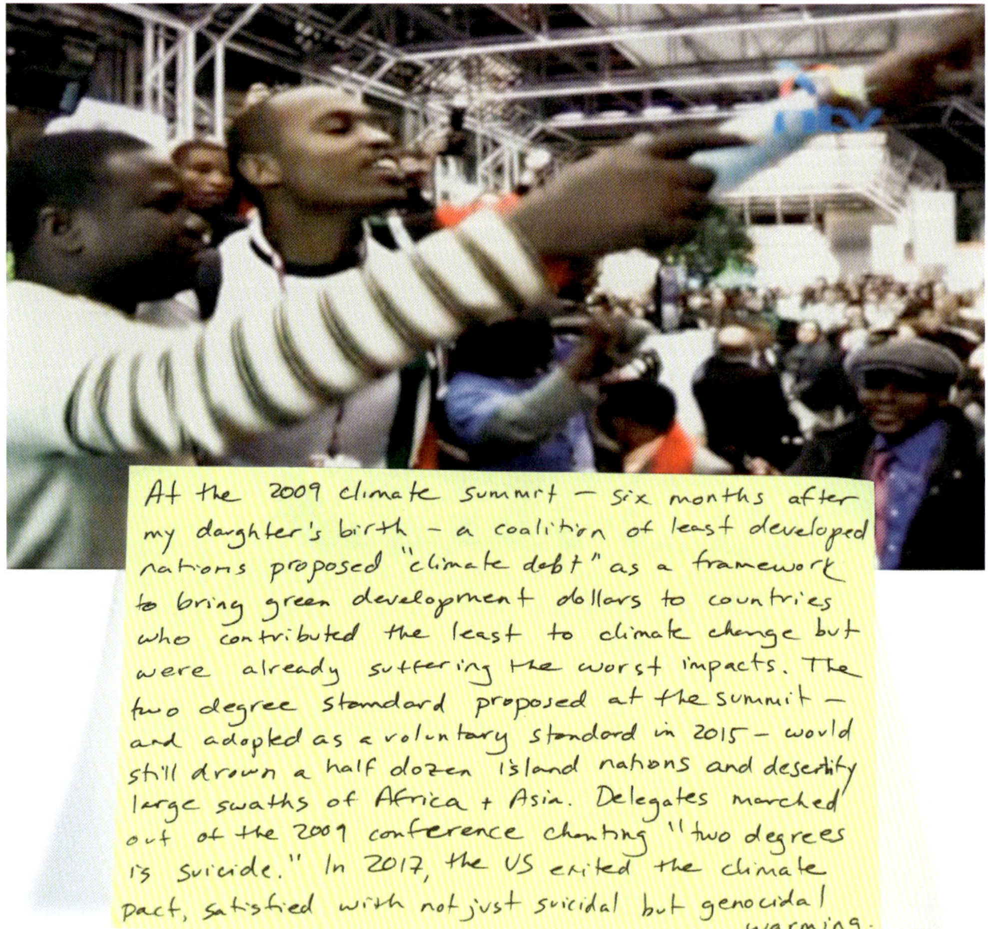

The scale of ecological debt defies all attempts at accounting it. How to place a value on the disappearance of a species? How to put a price on an entire way of life? Would doing so be an act of responsibility, or the definition of its limit? Placed in the wider scale of colonialism, it becomes clear that the ecological debt owed by the Global North and its settler colonies vastly exceeds the value of all unpaid loans held anywhere in the world.

"DEBT IS MUTUAL."

LIKE CURRENT ON AN OLD
TRANSMISSION LINE,

"CREDIT RUNS ONLY ONE WAY. BUT
DEBT RUNS IN EVERY DIRECTION,
SCATTERS, ESCAPES, SEEKS
REFUGE."

"THE DEBTOR SEEKS REFUGE
AMONG OTHER DEBTORS, ACQUIRES
DEBT FROM THEM, OFFERS
DEBT TO THEM. THE PLACE
OF REFUGE IS THE PLACE
TO WHICH YOU CAN ONLY OWE
MORE AND MORE BECAUSE
THERE IS NO CREDITOR, NO
PAYMENT POSSIBLE."

Stefano Harney + Fred Moten,
The Undercommons: Fugitive Planning
and Black Study (New York:
Minor Compositions, 2013), 61.

In other words, what do I owe on behalf of my grandfather? What will my daughter owe for me? From opposite shores of that oceanic expanse we call the twentieth century, they will never see each other's faces, but mirror images they are all the same.

Wendy Brown calls justice "a practice of responsible relations between generations."[17]

But my genealogy is also electric.

1. Although a municipal utility and not able to generate profit, the LADWP operated within a resolutely capitalist growth mindset. Financially independent from the city, it sought to keep prices low by maximizing average energy use throughout the day. To bolster domestic consumption, the LADWP sponsored appliance trade shows, financed air conditioning, took out "electric lifestyle" ads on the pages of the *LA Times*, and ran pro-electricity, anti-natural gas commercials on local TV. According to annual reports, under my grandfather's leadership, the LADWP reported $3–5 million of new, recurring revenue from increased power consumption, year after year. The "Great Acceleration" of Los Angeles outpaced that of most American cities, which, in turn, outpaced the rest of the world.

2. My grandfather's awe at images of transmission towers may be an extreme but illustrative example of the experience of the technological sublime. Coined by Perry Miller but more widely credited to Leo Marx, the term "technological sublime" refers to the impulse, originating in the late nineteenth century, to look toward both Nature and technology as the apotheosis of human experience, imbued with quasi-religious overtones. If the Classical sublime humbled the viewer before Nature, the technological sublime celebrated humanity's capacity to overcome the nature–culture binarism: each dam, suspension bridge, and new communications technology promises to usher in a new utopian era in which environmental limits and social tensions will be harmonized, beyond politics. David Nye argues that the technological sublime reached its greatest expression in the United States, where industrialization occurred alongside territorial expansion and technology become bound up on narratives of American exceptionalism. The electrification of the country in the late nineteenth and early twentieth centuries provides countless examples of the technological sublime cropping up in literature, music, slang, popular philosophy, civil ritual, and educational films. By the 1990s, my incomprehension of my grandfather's performance of wonder underscores how the sublime glow fades as new technologies become banal. See Perry Miller, *The Life of the Mind in America: From the Revolution to the Civil War* (New York: Harcourt, Brace & World, 1965); Leo Marx, *The Machine in the Garden* (New York: Oxford University Press, 1964); James W. Carey and John J. Quirk, "The Mythos of the Electronic Revolution," *American Scholar* 39, no. 2 (1970): 219–41; and David Nye, *The American Technological Sublime* (Cambridge: MIT Press, 1994).

3. My description of the cultural aspects of electrification and its effects on the experience of urban modernity draws on the work of David Nye, *Electrifying America: Social Meanings of a New Technology* (Cambridge: MIT Press, 1990), and Scott McQuire, *The Media City: Media, Architecture and Urban Space* (London: Sage Publications, 2008).

4. Though electric and petroleum cultures are often described separately, they are inextricably linked. Coal and natural gas are close material and technological cousins of crude oil. Indeed, the hydraulic fracturing used to pump what Stephanie LeMenager calls "tough oil" is also used to generate natural gas to burn for electricity. My grandfather's efforts to combat LA's notorious smog in the 1960s led

to the use of both natural gas and diesel fuel, rather than coal, in the city's steam plants. Cultural kinship can further be identified in the many monumental electric signs advertising various aspects of petro-modernity's most visible technology: the automobile. For more on tough oil and "petro-melancholia," see Stephanie LeMenager, *Living Oil: Petroleum Culture in the American Century* (Oxford and New York: Oxford University Press, 2014).

5. Alan Liu, drafts for *Against the Cultural Singularity* (book in progress), May 2, 2016, http://liu.english.ucsb.edu/drafts-for-against-the-cultural-singularity (accessed November 13, 2017).

6. Deborah Cowen, "Infrastructures of Empire and Resistance," Verso Blog, January 25, 2017, http://www.versobooks.com/blogs/3067-infrastructures-of-empire-and-resistance (accessed November 13, 2017).

7. Ruth Wilson Gilmore is working on a book on this topic and has offered tantalizing glimpses in several conference settings, including that cited in Trevor Paglen's influential 2008 catalogue essay "Experimental Geography: From Cultural Production to the Production of Space," republished in *Critical Landscapes: Art, Space, Politics*, ed. Emily Eliza Scott and Kirsten Swenson (Berkeley: University of California Press, 2015), 34–42. The quotation is taken from her collaborator Clayton Rosati's presentation "Infrastructures of Feeling: Media, Materialism, and Struggles for the Geography of Culture," PDF available at https://www.bgsu.edu/content/dam/BGSU/college-of-arts-and-sciences/ics/documents/InfrastructureofFeeling-Rosati.pdf (accessed November 13, 2017).

8. Lauren Berlant, "On Commons: Infrastructure for Troubling Times," *Environment and Planning D: Society and Space* 34, no. 3 (2016): 393–419.

9. Eve Kosofsky Sedgwick coined the term "reparative reading" to describe a mode of engagement with cultural texts that remains contingent and open to surprise. Such a position seeks less to unmask or expose the oppression lurking within an object of study than to cultivate the capacity to envision an otherwise. This move from what Sedgwick calls a drive to an affect entails a certain vulnerability that the defensive smartness of the conventionally critical or "paranoid" reading position forecloses. "Hope, often a fracturing, even a traumatic thing to experience, is among the energies by which the reparatively positioned reader tries to organize the fragments and part-objects she encounters or creates. Because the reader has room to realize that the future may be different from the present, it is also possible for her to entertain such profoundly painful, profoundly relieving, ethically crucial possibilities as that the past, in turn, could have happened differently from the way it actually did." Eve Kosofsky Sedgwick, *Touching Feeling: Affect, Pedagogy, Performativity* (Durham: Duke University Press, 2003), 146.

10. Building on Ernst Bloch's work on utopia, José Esteban Muñoz (*Cruising Utopia: The Then and There of Queer Futurity* [New York: New York University Press, 2009]) identifies queerness as a "horizon imbued with possibility" (p. 1), a perpetually "not-yet-here" (p. 12) that holds more radical potential for new forms of relationality and futurity than liberal, assimilationist homonormativity.

He also associates this queer utopianism with the practices of reparative reading identified above. Revisiting Stonewall-era gay culture, Muñoz intellectually "cruises" through public sex practices, installation art, queer poetry, movement ephemera, and dance clubs to argue that queerness is deeply invested in futurity, and that visions of the future—too long bound up with heterosexual reproduction—urgently need to be queered. Acknowledging the specificity of Muñoz's project, I take license to apply its methods and insights to the all-too-straight narrative of both my family-of-origin and my own day-to-day life.

11. Donna Haraway (*Staying with the Trouble: Making Kin in the Chthulucene* [Durham: Duke University Press, 2016]) has proposed non-natal, multispecies kin making as an ethico-political survival project urgently needed in light of the mass extinctions of the Anthropocene/Capitalocene. Enjoining her readers—who likely hail from the overconsuming classes of the world—to "Make Kin, Not Babies," her "purpose is to make 'kin' mean something other/more than entities tied by ancestry or genealogy. . . . Kin making is making persons, not necessarily as individuals or as humans" (pp. 101–2). Though her examples are largely biotic, she relates her delight in learning that "'relatives' in British English were originally 'logical relations' and only became 'family members' in the seventeenth century" (p. 103). Following Haraway, my project asks what relations of care—with matter, infrastructure, and the beings that are connected through it—are opened up by figuring the electric grid as kin in this sense.

12. Abbas Ackbar, *Poor Theory: Notes toward a Manifesto*, 2009. Originally formulated in conversation with David Theo Goldberg, a revised version of this open-ended manifesto was adopted by the University of California Irvine's Critical Theory Institute and subsequently posted online at https://www.yumpu.com/en/document/view/21808575/poor-theory-notes-toward-a-manifesto (accessed November 13, 2017). Like the manifesto, my own performance is in a constant state of evolution and becoming, its autobiographical nature allowing me to become intimate with both personal and professional vulnerabilities.

13. Justin Gillis, "Earth Sets a Temperature Record for the Third Straight Year," *New York Times*, January 18, 2017, https://www.nytimes.com/2017/01/18/science/earth-highest-temperature-record.html?_r=0 (accessed November 13, 2017).

14. Donna Haraway recognizes the emotional pain engendered by serious contemplation of and work to address climate change and its mass extinction. At the same time, she cautions against the "game over" mentality of some exhausted scientists and scholars that assumes that "only if things work do they matter" and that can shade slowly, or not so slowly, into a "politics of sublime indifference." *Staying with the Trouble*, 4.

15. Lee Edelman (*No Future* [Durham: Duke University Press, 2004]) identifies what he calls "reproductive futurism" as the symbolic regime in which "the Child has come to embody for us the telos of the social order and come to be seen as the one for whom that order is held in

perpetual trust" (p. 18). He goes on to identify the various ways in which the obligatory protection of children—always figured straight and white—has been mobilized to persecute gays and lesbians in particular, and, though underdeveloped in his polemic, women and people of color more broadly. Noting that futurism is a set of "fantasies [that] reproduce the past, through displacement, in the form of the future," he calls for a queer politics of radical negativity, "to insist that the future stop here" (p. 31). Scholars working on queer ecology have identified a similar dynamic in which queer sexuality is deemed not merely unnatural but something from which nature (also figured as straight and white) must be protected. Rather than abandoning nature or, as Edelman enjoins, the future, other scholars, such as Catriona Mortimer-Sandilands and Bruce Erickson (eds., *Queer Ecologies: Sex, Nature, Politics, Desire* [Bloomington: Indiana University Press, 2010]), and Stacey Alaimo (*Exposed: Environmental Politics and Pleasures in Posthuman Times* [Minneapolis: University of Minnesota Press, 2016]) have positioned queerness at the heart of nature, while José Esteban Muñoz (*Cruising Utopia*) explicitly describes his celebration of queer futurity as a direct response. While Edelman's description of the trap of reproductive futurism continues to resonate, ecological crises of the last fifteen years, as well as the resurgent right's simultaneous pursuit of pro-natal nativism and overt ecocide, have shown that it is really reproductive futurism that promises to deliver "no future" in short order.

16. "The dystopia of our ancestors" is how Neshnabé (Potawatomi) scholar-activist Kyle Powys Whyte characterizes the modern environment whose transformation was every bit as much part of the settler-colonial project of attempted extermination as broken treaties and boarding schools. He contrasts settler society's generalized dread of species loss—evoked by the omnipresent image of the polar bear—with an Indigenous facility (born of centuries of experience) of negotiating environmental transformation by renewing key relationships between humans, places, and other species. While what Daniel Wildcat calls "indigenous realism" may be key to human survival on a damaged planet, those of us embedded in settler societies must take care not to position traditional ecological knowledge as yet another resource to exploit for our benefit, erasing the bodies of actual Indigenous people and leaving political structures predicated on colonialism intact. See Kyle Powys White, "Our Ancestors' Dystopia Now: Indigenous Conservation and the Anthropocene," in *The Routledge Companion to Environmental Humanities*, ed. Ursula K. Heise, Jon Christensen, and Michelle Niemann (Oxford and New York: Routledge, 2017), 206–15; Daniel Wildcat, *Red Alert! Saving the Planet with Indigenous Knowledge* (Golden, Col.: Fulcrum Press, 2009). See also Eve Tuck and K. Wayne Yang, "Decolonization is not a metaphor," *Decolonization: Indigeneity, Education & Society* 1, no. 1 (2012): 1–40; Zoe Todd, "Indigenizing the Anthropocene," in *Art in the Anthropocene*, ed. Heather Davis and Etienne Turpin (London: Open Humanities Press, 2015), 241–54.

17. Wendy Brown, *Politics Out of History* (Princeton: Princeton University Press, 2001), 147.

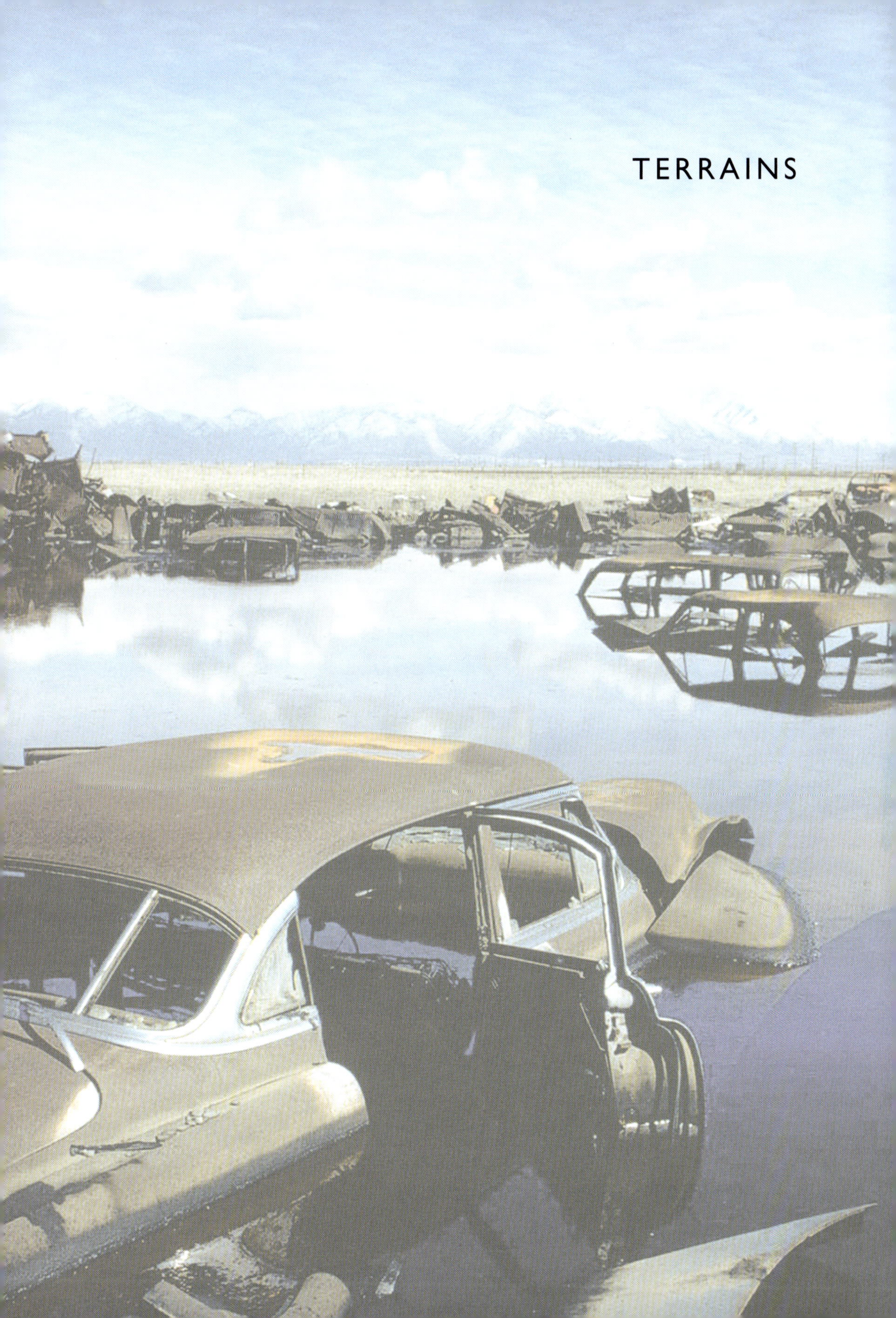
TERRAINS

Ecology, Ethics, and Aesthetics in Pliny the Elder's *Natural History*

Verity Platt

> *oikeiôsis* (Greek, from **οἰκεῖος**, "in or of the house"): appropriation, affinity, attraction, affection.
> —Henry G. Liddell and Robert Scott, *A Greek-English Lexicon* (1940)

> An affective disposition—the understanding of one's participation in a relational matrix that transcends traditional notions of social allegiances.
> —Daniel Richter, *Cosmopolis: Imagining Community in Late Classical Athens and the Early Roman Empire* (2011)

In the reception of Classical antiquity, distinctions between image and prototype, "art" and "nature," have been repeatedly mapped onto an anecdote related by the Roman author Pliny the Elder. In his *Natural History*, Pliny famously recounts how the Greek painters Zeuxis and Parrhasius took part in a contest of naturalistic skill: while Zeuxis's depiction of grapes manages to deceive birds, who try to peck at his painted fruit, Parrhasius's depiction of a linen panel deceives Zeuxis himself, who charges his competitor to "remove the cloth and reveal the painting."[1] Within the Western tradition, this quest for the "True Vine" or "Essential Copy" is rooted in a paradigmatic split between art and its objects—one in which the natural world serves as both model for and naïve judge of man's technical prowess, and in which art's seemingly self-annihilating goal is dependent upon a capacity to master and deceive.[2] In its complex reflections upon the nature of representation, Pliny's anecdote seems to reinforce distinctions between the sphere of human activity and that of the natural world. Tellingly, the birds fly *in scaenam*, "into a stage-building": when nonhuman forces make their presence felt within the theater of images, it is to crash straight into the insistent artifactuality and performativity of painting itself, the two-dimensional grapes forever beyond their reach.

This interpretation of the Zeuxis and Parrhasius tale helps explain why the art of Greece and Rome is so rarely associated with ecological thinking: after all, this is a visual tradition that is held to focus above all on the human body rather than its environment; that is concerned with the imitation and idealization of nature, rather than deference to or collaboration with it; that imposes form on matter in a celebration of the rationalizing power of human *technê*; and that in its rampant imperialism laid the groundwork for structures of power and practices of consumption that continue to imperil fragile ecosystems and communities today.[3] This is despite the fact that it is in the historiography of Classical art that eco-criticism is first prominently applied to the visual sphere, in the eighteenth-century scholar Johann Joachim Winckelmann's attempt to account for the "Greek miracle" by recourse to the particular qualities of landscape, climate, and political context in which Classical naturalism came into being.[4] In Winckelmann's 1764 *History of the Art of Antiquity*, it is the ancient Mediterranean itself that gives rise to the social, psychological, and environmental conditions—the "three ecologies," in Félix Guattari's phrase—in which the Classical style was forged.[5] Yet even here, the delicate ecological balance that generated the Classical aesthetic is conceived of as an accident of history, an "inimitable" world removed in space and time from the inevitable decline of the present day. Tellingly, where Classical culture does feature in cultural histories of environmentalism, it is in critiques of the literary pastoral, in all its fraught constructions of the "natural" as a space of nostalgia and poetic artifice.[6]

In Winckelmann's *History*, as elsewhere, the ancient world occupies a complex position as both pre-modern society and ancestral source, insulated from the anxieties of late capitalism yet cradle of the concepts and ambitions that would engender the Anthropocene.[7] As a stylistic concept, Classical naturalism encompasses many related contradictions: while underlining art's close resemblance to features of the environment, it simultaneously constructs nature as object of scrutiny and analysis, a separate sphere distinct from the rationalizing, civilizing, and idealizing enterprises of *homo faber* (Man the Maker).[8] When aligned with the Platonic concept of *mimêsis* (imitation), naturalism presupposes an ontological distinction between prototype and representation, opening up a chasm between nature and culture even as it celebrates parallels between the two. A relation of likeness necessarily presupposes a relation of difference—one that is deeply problematic for ecological approaches to the visual arts.

We must be wary, however, of reading antiquity as a straightforward forebear of later European preoccupations, projecting our own familiar models and concepts back onto the past.[9] While Pliny's anecdotes about ancient artists may have influenced the biographical tradition later spearheaded by Giorgio Vasari (in his 1550 *Lives of the Most Excellent Painters, Sculptors, and Architects*), inspiring both the content and generic conventions of the historiography of art, they nevertheless emerge from very different artistic, literary, and cultural frameworks.[10] This is particularly important for our approach to ancient thinking about the relationship between art and the environment. The *Natural History* may be a foundational text for the discipline of art history, but it is first and foremost an exuberant catalogue, exploration, and celebration of the material stuff of *natura*, driven by a complex and self-conscious ethical examination of humanity's relationship to the natural world. While the contest between Zeuxis and Parrhasius establishes a clear ontological difference between image and prototype, it nevertheless reasserts the insistent materiality of the object. Despite the virtuality of its representational content, the material artifact is contiguous with the sphere of both human and animal viewers, and is fabricated from the very stuff of the world it seeks to simulate. That Zeuxis, too, is deceived by the illusionistic power of painting is not simply a sign of his inferior skills as painter and viewer, but a reminder that men are also animals: the superior reason (*or ratio*) with which humans are endowed does not preclude them from being brought up short by the objecthood of their own creations. Here, as elsewhere in the *Natural History*, Pliny explores the nuances of man's relationship to a *natura* that serves as the passive object of inquiry and source of raw materials, on the one hand, and supremely intelligent agent and artist (*artifex*) in its own right, on the other.

In line with a materialist cosmology inflected by Hellenistic and Roman Stoicism, Pliny's *natura* (or its Greek equivalent *physis*) does not correspond in any straightforward way to later formulations of "Nature" (as opposed to "culture," or any number of structuralist binaries). Indeed, as Brooke Holmes has suggested, antiquity is arguably a period "before nature," especially a "capital *N*" Nature conceived as "a pernicious fiction standing in the way of a healthier relationship to the nonhuman world."[11] Pliny's *natura*, I contend, exists in dialogue with the Stoic concept of *oikeiôsis*—a principle of "self-care" derived from the Greek word *oikeios*, denoting that which "belongs to" or is "proper" for one's *oikos* (household).[12] *Oikeiôsis* can be translated as "appropriation" (as in my epigraph above), referring to each species' concern for its own well-being (or *physis*), but in its expanded sense it comes to express a notion of "affinity, attraction, affection" that is extended beyond one's immediate *oikos* to the broader clan, community, nation, and, indeed, to the entire inhabited world (the *oikoumenê*) of which one is part.[13] In the context of Stoic ethics, *oikeiôsis* is best understood (as Daniel Richter puts it) as "an affective disposition—the understanding of one's participation in a relational matrix that transcends traditional notions of social allegiances."[14] The anthropocentric (and anthropomorphizing) impulses of this position admit no need to apologize for a focus on the well-being of mankind, whose superior rationality (*ratio*) grants him authority over other species. Yet at the same time, the doctrine of *oikeiôsis* allows for the recognition that each and every living creature, whether human or nonhuman, begins from a similar position of self-concern—one to which *oikeiôsis* in its expanded sense must attend.[15]

The Greek term *oikos* lies at the root of the concept that in 1866 Ernst Haeckel termed Ökologie, and is thus closely bound to the emergence of ecological studies.[16] As the *Natural History* makes clear, the origins of Western art history demonstrate an awareness of the overlapping ecosystems—or circles of affinity and care—in which human artistic endeavor is situated. The ethical responsibilities, anxieties, and conflicts that this awareness entails reveal modes of ecological thinking that destabilize conventional ideas of what, exactly, Pliny has handed down to us, while demonstrating how an eco-critical approach to the historiography of art might help us to see the old and familiar in fresh light.

Aristotle's Mother

In Book 35 of the *Natural History*, Pliny reaches the climax of his history of painting with an extensive passage on the Greek painter Protogenes.[17] Known for his *impetus animi* (force of spirit) and *libido artis* (artistic capriciousness), Protogenes emerges from the pages of Pliny's encyclopedic enterprise as a surprising anti-hero whose humble lifestyle, workaholic tendencies, and reluctance to finish paintings echo the proclivities of the author himself.[18] He is also an artist whose fraught relationship to kingly power would provide an important model for early modern figures seeking to navigate the complexities of court and papal patronage (just as Pliny sought to manage shifting relationships with the Roman principate).[19] For Protogenes, painting in the fourth century BCE, the ultimate authority to negotiate was Alexander the Great, and Pliny relates how the artist was pressured by none other than the philosopher Aristotle (Alexander's tutor) to paint the achievements of Alexander "as belonging to history for all time."[20] Protogenes, however, rejected this invitation to produce a grand historical narrative—something along the lines, we might imagine, of the late Classical painting that inspired the famous *Alexander Mosaic* from Pompeii (fig. 1).[21] Instead, he chose to paint a portrait of Aristotle's mother, Phaestis.[22]

What might painting Aristotle's mother mean? And why might it be relevant to the role of Greco-Roman art within the longer history of eco-criticism?

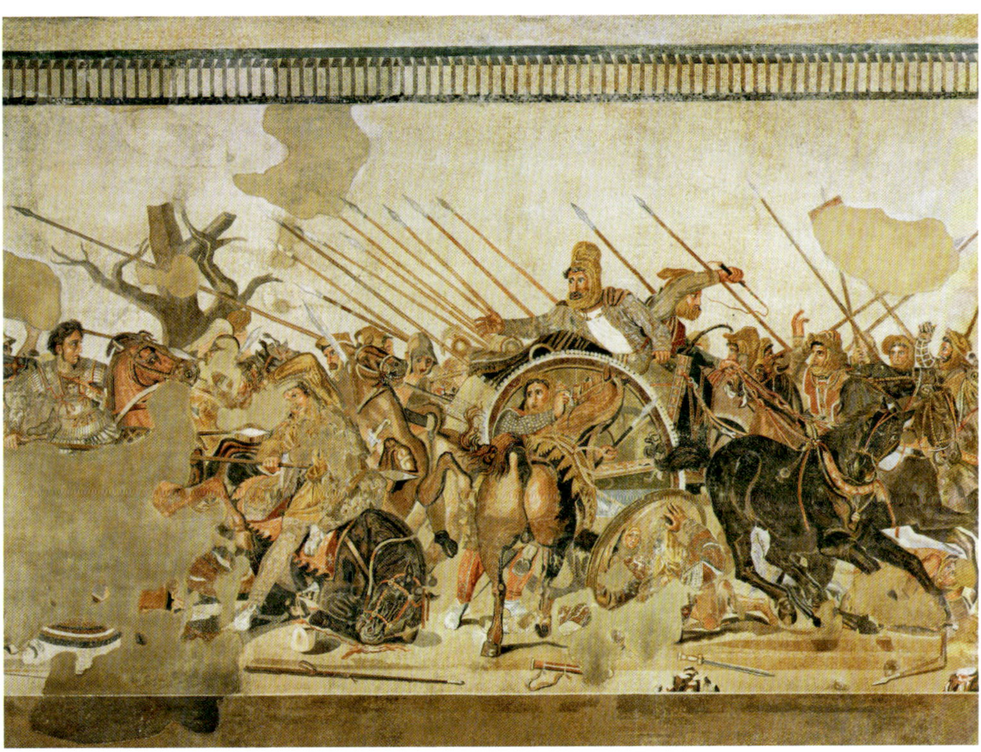

Fig. 1. The Alexander Mosaic, from the House of the Faun, Pompeii (VI.12.2), c. 100 BCE. 107 ⅛ × 202 in. (272 × 513 cm). Museo Archeologico Nazionale, Naples

Protogenes's response to Aristotle, I suggest, gestures toward ways of thinking about art making in antiquity that do not sit easily within dominant structures of power—neither the colonizing model of rulership embodied by Alexander nor the ontological hierarchies and scientific taxonomies of Aristotelianism. Indeed, the anecdote indicates that these two models are mutually complicit. Protogenes's response may be typical of his status as an outlier—a demonstration of his irrepressible *libido artis*. Yet it also points to alternative strategies of reading the *Natural History*, particularly Pliny's complex relationship with an author whose influence over the practice of natural science is strongly felt elsewhere in the text.

Portraits of philosophers are ubiquitous within the Classical tradition, including those of Aristotle (fig. 2).[23] An inscription on a (now headless) herm discovered in the Stoa of Attalos in the Athenian Agora claims that "Alexander set up this portrait of the divine Aristotle, the son of Nikomachos, fountain of all wisdom," suggesting a certain reciprocity in the commissioning of artworks by the young

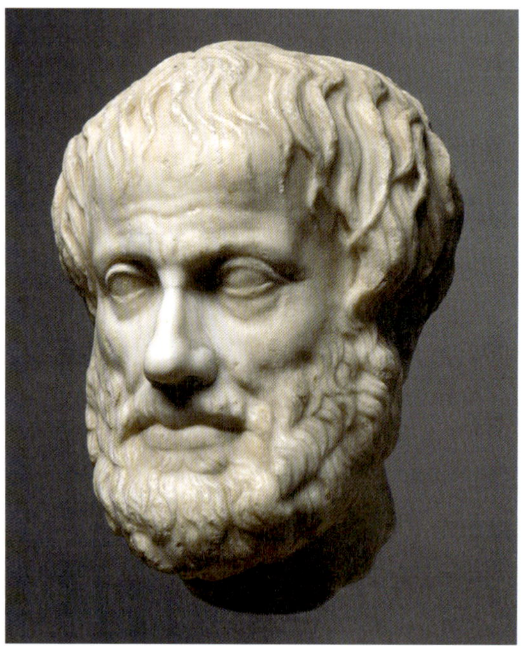

Fig. 2. Portrait of Aristotle, 1st–2nd century CE, Roman, after a Greek original c. 320 BCE. Marble, h. 12 in. (30.5 cm). Kunsthistorisches Museum Vienna (I 246)

king and his tutor.[24] Philosophers' mothers, however, are far less prominent. Aristotle refers to a "likeness" (*eikôn*) of Phaestis in his will, asking that the image (probably a statue) be dedicated to the goddess Demeter at Nemea following his death, but otherwise his mother is unattested within the history of Greek art.[25] Why, then, would Phaestis have been of interest to Pliny, and the tradition concerning Protogenes? The issue of parentage is a sensitive topic when it comes to Aristotle, who famously discusses the relative roles of male and female in his accounts of conception. In his *Physics* and *Generation of Animals*, the father is explicitly referred to as the "efficient cause" of the child (the provider of the *dynamis*—"power"), whereas the mother, who supplies the matter for generation rather than its agency or form, is effectively the child's "material cause."[26] In this sense, Phaestis is Aristotle's "material cause," a biological receptacle impressed with vital form, who in function and significance could not be more diametrically opposed to the model of masculine agency and historical causality offered by Alexander. In choosing Phaestis over Alexander for the subject of his painting, Protogenes not only rejects the political and ontological hierarchies of Aristotelianism, but actively celebrates the priority of matter, which is recast as generative, causal, and, by implication, constitutive of the very *natura* that is the focus of Pliny's *Natural History*.

It is tempting to see in Protogenes's willful act the response of a Luce Irigaray *avant la lettre*, a critique of Aristotelian formations of gender and power.[27] Tellingly, the painter does not look to the maternal origin of the subject matter Aristotle has proposed (that is, Alexander's mother, the Macedonian queen Olympias); rather, he looks to the maternal source of Aristotelian philosophy itself—to the role of the feminine as "prime matter" (*prôtê hulê*), that which (in Irigaray's words) "is both radically lacking in all power of *logos* and offers, unawares, an all-powerful soil in which the *logos* can grow."[28] While the philosopher encourages the painter to recognize the conditions of patronage that fund his artistic enterprise (the mighty "works" [*opera*] of Alexander), the painter turns instead to the unspoken material conditions that enable patriarchy, that maternal source that the master "does not say very much about . . . because he lacks words or because he wants to keep it to himself—because he cannot or does not want to talk about his relationship with her."[29]

What does it mean for a painting to draw attention to material causality in this way? Unsurprisingly, one does not find overtly feminist critiques of the Aristotelian division between form and matter within antiquity.[30] The ontological hierarchies of Aristotelianism, however, were very much up for debate, in part because of the increasing popularity of materialist cosmologies amongst adherents of Epicureanism and Stoicism during the Hellenistic period (that is, the third to first centuries BCE).[31] This is also the period in which the historiography of the visual arts was first developed as a genre by the (now lost) Greek authors who form Pliny's most important sources for Greek painting and sculpture.[32] Yet rather than reconstructing these sources and their intellectual agendas from the *Natural History* (a doomed project at the best of times), we might get farther by examining how Pliny's Protogenes anecdote relates to the far bigger project in which his history of Greek painting is embedded.[33]

The Art of Natural History

Although they are traditionally excerpted as a stand-alone "history of art," Books 33–37 of the *Natural History* form just one part of a comprehensive inquiry into matter itself.[34] As one can see from the table of contents in figure 3, Pliny's histories of statues, paintings, and gems emerge from his account of metals, pigments, and stones, which together form the mineral section of the work, following his accounts of cosmology, geography, animals (including humans), and plants.[35] As objects designed by humans in collaboration with natural materials, works of art are thus akin to cultivated crops, animal husbandry, and pharmaceutical remedies (*materia medica*). In this context, the visual arts exemplify just another form of skill, an *ars* (in Latin), or *technê* (in Greek), generated through the convergence of human and natural *ratio* (rational principle); indeed, metalwork and ceramics are included as such (alongside viticulture, medicine, sailing, and calendars) in the

Pliny the Elder's *Natural History*	Structure of the text, from Thomas R. Laehn, *Pliny's Defense of Empire*, p. 7.
Book 1	Index
Books 2-6	The Cosmos and the Geography of the World
Book 7	Man
Books 8-11	Animals
Books 12-19	Plants
Books 20-27	Medicines Derived from Plants
Books 28-32	Medicines Derived from Animals
Books 33-37	Metals and Minerals, with Sections on Sculpture and Painting

Fig. 3. Table showing structure of Pliny the Elder's *Natural History*. From Thomas R. Laehn, *Pliny's Defense of Empire* (London: Routledge, 2013)

climax to Book 7, Pliny's list of human *inventa* (discoveries).[36] The beginnings of art history—at least in the form that has survived for us from antiquity—are thus framed and conceived within a work of natural science that is deeply concerned with interactions between humans and their physical environment.

If the *Natural History* can be read as a proto-ecological text, what kind of ecology has it bequeathed us? Here, Protogenes's mischievous painting of Phaestis might provide us with a clue. *Naturalis historia*, for Pliny, certainly looks to the practice of natural science exemplified by Aristotle, based as it is in empirical observation of the natural world (*historia*, in Greek, means "inquiry" rather than our term "history").[37] Pliny, after all, famously met his end as a result of his burning desire to observe and record the eruption of Mount Vesuvius in 79 CE.[38] Yet although Aristotle's work on animals forms one of Pliny's major sources, the *Natural History* could never be described as a straightforwardly empiricist work of the Peripatetic school whose work Aristotle inspired, despite its enthusiastic use of sources by Aristotle and his pupils (including writings on plants and stones by Theophrastus, Aristotle's successor).[39] Pliny has often been criticized for his lack of scientific consistency, his seemingly eclectic, even random use of source materials, and his over-enthusiastic incorporation of *miracula*—marvels and paradoxes which tug at the boundaries of the rational.[40] It is in this very attention to the wonders of nature, however—in the holistic practice of what Mary Beagon calls a "terrestrial curiosity"—that a more ethically guided ecological form of thinking might actually be found.[41]

Rather than subscribing to an Aristotelian cosmology whereby form is prior to and supervenient upon matter (or a Platonic model in which the material world is merely an imperfect *mimêsis* of transcendent Forms), Pliny's approach conforms more closely to the pantheistic materialism of Stoicism.[42] Within this system, mind (or soul) is itself regarded as a form of matter, and the entirety of matter is understood as a vital, rational, integrated, and purposeful entity, infused with a motivating life force (*pneuma*). Reason (*ratio*) is not just the preserve of humanity, but permeates the whole of creation, so that *natura* is not just the product of intelligent design, but is herself the intelligent force that drives her own formation. As Pliny puts it, the *mundus* (world) is "at once the work of nature and nature herself": that is, *natura* can symbolize or draw attention to natural processes of becoming, at the same time as simply "being."[43]

Traditionally, scholars have looked for traces of a more "scientific" account of nature in Pliny, only to be disappointed when they fail to identify a consistent set of rational principles. Yet arguably it is in its very *in*consistencies that the *Natural History* plays out the complex and often conflicting ways in which humans relate to their environment. This tension is borne of the paradox that humanity is simultaneously part of nature, and yet capable of classifying, analyzing, and manipulating it to a degree that differentiates it from all other species. Certainly, Pliny shares with Aristotle the anthropocentric assumption that man is the most rational of beings, for whom a benevolent nature has purposefully designed abundant natural resources. He opens his discussion of bees in Book 11, for example, by claiming that "they alone" among the insects "have been created for the sake of man," as producers of honey and wax.[44] Within Pliny's text, one can find clear traces of the *scala naturae*, the great "chain of being" that is held to progress from mineral matter through plants and animals to *homo sapiens*.[45] Nevertheless, this hierarchy of being rubs cheek by jowl with alternative structures and even reversals of hierarchy that challenge and complicate humanity's place within the natural order. In his ensuing discussion of the complex society of the beehive in Book 11, for instance, Pliny asks: "What men can we rank in rationality (*ratio*) with these insects, which unquestionably excel mankind in this, that they recognize only the common interest?"[46] In acknowledging that animals are capable of surpassing mankind in their commitment to social principles, he indicates where human *ratio* fails.

Here, as elsewhere in the *Natural History*, Pliny explicitly moves from a classificatory model of natural science to a mode of ethical discourse that holds far broader implications. His introduction of insects as a group of related species in Book 11 programmatically alerts us to a key distinction between the Peripatetic project and his own. In a much-celebrated passage in the *Parts of Animals*, Aristotle observes:

> Even in the study of animals disagreeable to perception, the nature that crafted them likewise provides extraordinary pleasures to those able to know their causes and who are by nature philosophers. . . . We should not be childishly disgusted at the examination of the less valuable animals, for in all natural things there is something marvelous.[47]

Here, the notion that even animals unpleasant to the senses can be of intellectual interest to those who practice certain forms of empirical analysis ("philosophers") is firmly wedded to an appreciation of a nature (*physis*) that is marvelous in its capacity as "maker": the aesthetic appeal of certain species is clearly distinguished from their value for natural science. Likewise, in a clear nod to his intellectual forebear, Pliny observes at the beginning of Book 11:

> We marvel at elephants' shoulders carrying castles, . . . at the rapacity of tigers and the manes of lions, whereas really *natura* is to be found in her entirety nowhere more than in the tiniest of her creations. I consequently beg my readers not to let their contempt for many of these creatures lead them also to condemn to scorn what I relate about them, since in the contemplation of *natura* nothing can possibly be deemed redundant.[48]

That is, no living entity, no matter how small or ugly, should be deemed superfluous (*supervacuum*) to the wondrous workings of the natural order, because every component is metonymic of Pliny's broader project—the ingenious *ratio* of the whole. Yet consider how Aristotle continues:

> Surely, it would be unreasonable, even absurd, for us to enjoy studying likenesses (*eikones*) of animals—on the ground that we are at the same time studying the art (*technê*), such as painting and sculpture, that made

them—while not prizing even more the study of things constituted by nature, at least when we can behold their causes.[49]

On the one hand, we might read this as a defense of empirical observation and a celebration of the natural over the manmade: examining the bodies of animals themselves is of greater value than studying mere likenesses of them (such as fig. 4), which in their vaunting of artistic skill (*technê*) might distract us from the intrinsic interest of those things "constituted by nature." On the other hand, Aristotle's teleological drive, his focus on the observation of *causes*, reveals the anthropocentric logic at work within his taxonomic system. Here, he celebrates the process of knowledge acquisition by the scientist-philosopher rather than the more holistic model of "contemplation" (*contemplatio*) suggested by Pliny, which focuses less on classificatory hierarchies and divisions, and more on the interrelatedness of the system as a whole. This latter approach carries important ethical implications that radiate throughout the *Natural History*, generating an unspoken conflict between a drive toward scientific inquiry and a celebration of the coherence and inherent value of all living matter. *Naturalis historia*, in this sense, is not only the study of the natural world, but also a "natural mode of inquiry," the practice of a form of *historia* that, in its seemingly random organicism, open structure, and encyclopedic range, is in accordance with the material logic of the cosmos itself.[50]

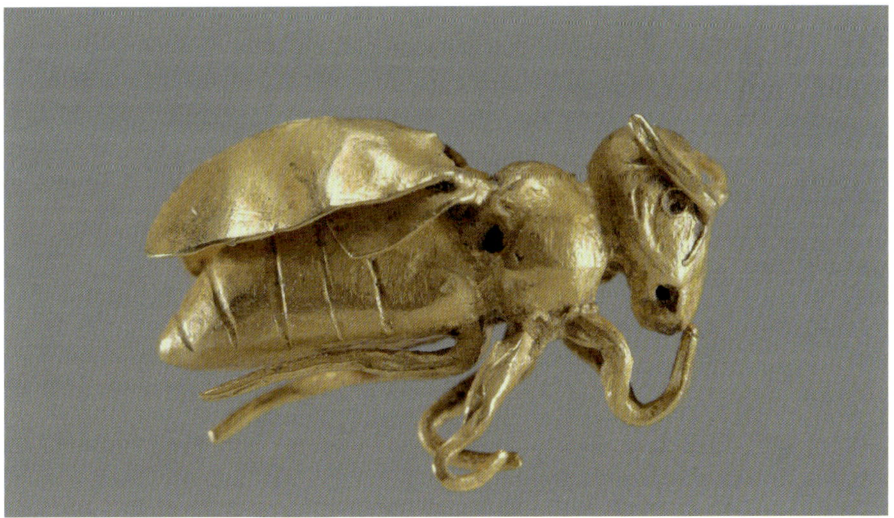

Fig. 4. Bee, 3rd–2nd century BCE. Gold, 9/16 in. (1.43 cm). Yale University Art Gallery, New Haven. Gift of Allison V. Armour, Class of 1884 (1935.17)

This is where Pliny's interest in the materials and techniques of the visual arts becomes so crucial to the ecological thinking of the whole. While both he and Aristotle subscribe to a model of *natura artifex* that looks back to Plato's *Timaeus*, the value assigned to living creatures as objects of representation (and to the artifacts that depict them) is very different in each case. In the *Parts of Animals*, Aristotle casts "painting and sculpture" as higher-order products, ontologically distinct from "things constituted by nature," and thus subscribes to a model of naturalism that is rooted in difference. For Pliny, finely wrought artifacts are co-constitutive of a *natura* that is itself infused with *ratio*—and which spontaneously produces images of its own.[51] Just as Pliny deems the tiniest of animals worthy of attention, so too are the tiniest of artifacts, such as precious stones, in which "the majesty of nature is concentrated" to such a degree that "for many people a single gem is enough to provide them with a supreme and perfect contemplation of the work of nature."[52] And just as nothing is *supervacuum* in the study of plants and animals, so for Pliny nothing is "superfluous" in the case of the visual arts—whether it be subsidiary decoration of cult statues, the "painting of lowly subjects" (*rhyparographia*) such as foodstuffs and cobblers' shops (known to us as still lifes; fig. 5),

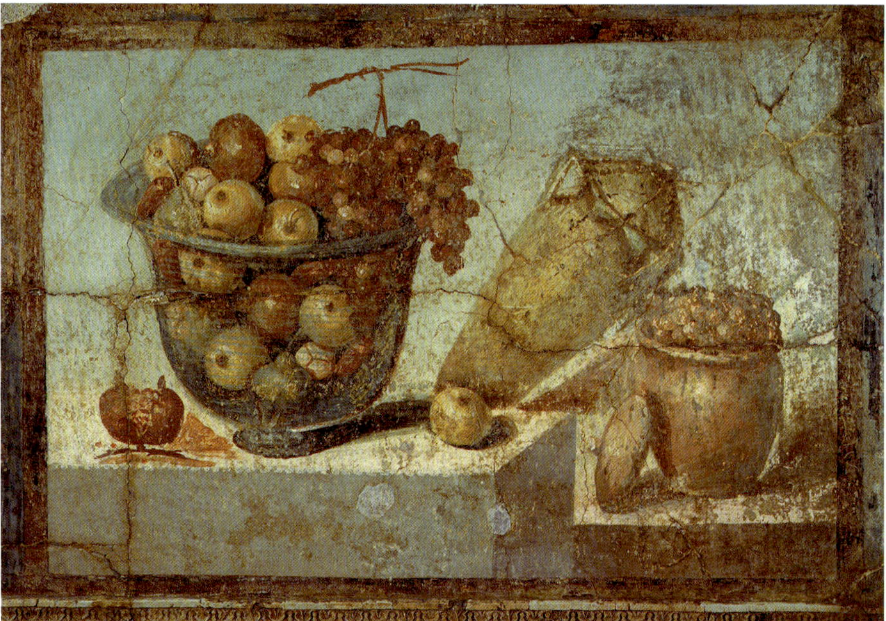

Fig. 5. Fresco depicting grapes, mid-1st century CE. From the Casa dei Cervi, Herculaneum (IV.21). Museo Archeologico Nazionale, Naples (8645A)

or portraits of philosophers' mothers.[53] Most importantly, in that they issue organically from Pliny's inquiries into metals, earth, and stones, the "art historical" components of the *Natural History* are ontologically aligned with the matter of *natura* itself, testifying to a *sympathia* between the organic and inorganic, the natural and the crafted.[54] As such, sculptures and paintings do not simply function as "likenesses" (*eikones*) of natural objects: they emerge from nature, partake of nature, and, through their application of *technê*, reflexively encourage contemplation of nature's own technical operations.

The Ethics of the "Natural" Image

What does all this imply for a more ecologically grounded art history? First, we must remind ourselves that Pliny is an observer, not an activist. As a member of the Roman elite devoted to public service, his preface is addressed to Titus, son of the emperor Vespasian and soon to be emperor himself. Pliny seeks to reassure him that he has not shirked his daytime responsibilities, for he has labored on the *Natural History* only at night: he has, in effect, painted both Phaestis *and* Alexander.[55] As admiral of the imperial fleet, Pliny arguably oversaw one of the major causes of deforestation within the Roman Empire; as a military commander in Germany and provincial governor in Gaul, Spain, and North Africa, he proudly furthered the cause of Roman imperialism, complicit in a massive colonization of peoples and depletion of natural resources that reached its peak during his own lifetime.[56] The vast knowledge on which he draws in the *Natural History* is dependent upon practices of colonization and subjugation that (quite literally) provide the text with its raw materials, while casting *natura* in terms that make it coterminous with the limitless expanse and ambition of the Roman Empire itself. While the *Natural History* promotes respect for a holistically conceived model of rational *natura*, then, it is not a work of proto-environmentalism. For all his observations on the exhaustion of natural resources in certain locations (of ivory, gold, pigments, and certain plants), Pliny chronicles the properties and qualities of these resources and the methods by which they are attained with relentless, often unreflective fervor.[57] That notwithstanding, the underlying ethics of the *Natural History* combine the Stoic principle of living "in accordance with nature" with a "vibrant" materialism, a boundless curiosity, and an old-fashioned Roman commitment to simple living, with all its distaste for luxury and avarice.[58]

In the work's final books, the visual arts provide the terrain on which the conflict between the imperial urge to map, conquer, and consume and a more ecological ethics of matter is fought out. Statues, paintings, precious vessels, and jewelry are made possible by the human urge to pillage the Earth of its resources, and yet they exhibit an integration of *res* (matter) and *animus* (spirit or intelligence) that is consistent with the skillful workings of *natura* itself. How are we to reconcile this contradiction? Significantly, Book 33 (which introduces metals, and thus the arts) begins with a meditation on the practice of mining:

> For in some places the earth is dug into for riches . . . and in other places for luxury, when gems and colours for tinting walls and beams are demanded. We trace out all the veins of the earth, and live above the hollows we have made in her, marvelling that occasionally she gapes open or begins to tremble—as if forsooth it were not possible that this may be an expression of the indignation of our holy parent! We penetrate her inner parts and seek for riches in the abode of the spirits of the departed, as though the part where we tread upon her were not sufficiently bounteous and fertile.[59]

This assault on Mother Earth cannot even be justified, Pliny claims, by a quest for healing remedies or nourishment, for these are predominantly supplied upon the surface:

> The things that she has concealed and hidden underground, those that do not quickly come to birth, are the things that destroy us and drive us to the depths below; so that suddenly the mind soars aloft into the void and ponders what finally will be the end of draining her dry in all the ages, what will be the point to which avarice will penetrate.[60]

The plundering of resources is here conceived as a violation of our *sacra parens* ("holy mother"), driven by a mindless thirst for luxury that fetishizes materials at the expense of their ecological integrity. Repeatedly, Pliny worries at the fault line between applications of human skill that distort, debase, or adulterate natural materials and those that apply a form of *ratio* that both respects and reveals their inner logic. Naturalistic art emerges from this ethics of matter not as Platonic imitation (a material distortion of abstract form), nor as mere illusionism; artists are not "inventors" of tricks or "rivals" of nature. Instead, marvels of naturalism

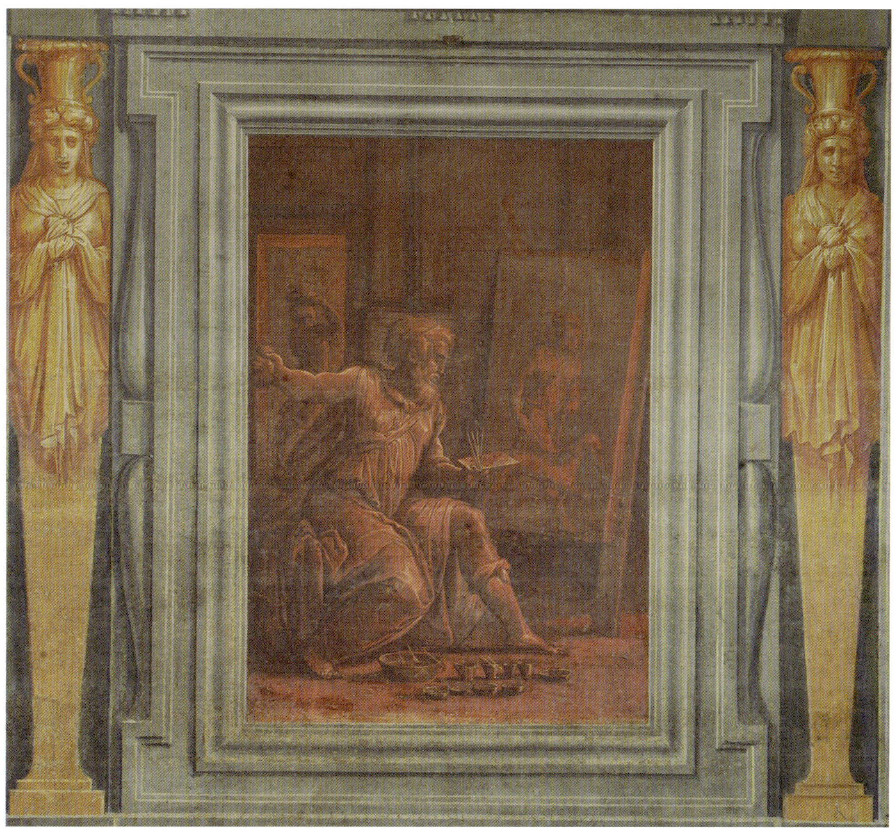

Fig. 6. Giorgio Vasari (Italian, 1511–1574), *Protogenes Throwing the Sponge*, 1518. Monochrome tempera, dimensions unknown. Sala del Trionfo della Virtù, Casa Vasari, Arezzo, Italy. Courtesy of the Ministry of Cultural Heritage and Tourism, Department of Archeology, Fine Arts, and Landscape for the provinces of Siena, Grosseto, and Arezzo. Photo by Alessandro Benci

are presented as *inventiones,* "discoveries" of the *ratio* of nature, which perform themselves as a form of "natural inquiry."[61]

Protogenes, the painter of "material causes," is best known not for his portrait of Aristotle's mother, but for his painting of the Rhodian hero Ialysus accompanied by a dog, which was displayed in the Temple of Peace at Rome as a prime example of imperial booty.[62] In a scene that would be memorably depicted by Vasari (fig. 6), Pliny relates that

> the artist's own opinion was that he did not fully show in it the foam of the panting dog . . . the foam appeared to be painted, not to be the natural product of the animal's mouth; vexed and tormented, as he wanted his picture to contain the truth and not merely a near-truth, he

> had several times rubbed off the paint and used another brush, quite
> unable to satisfy himself. Finally he fell into a rage with his art because it
> was perceptible, and dashed a sponge against the offending spot in the
> picture. And the sponge restored the colors he had removed, just as
> his diligence had desired, and chance produced nature in the picture![63]

Here, at the center of empire, we find an example of image making that does not simply imitate nature, but in which the painter works as nature's agent rather than a master of raw materials. Aristotle may have claimed in the *Parts of Animals* that "*Technê* is the *logos* of the work without the matter," associating skill with the abstraction and ontological superiority of dematerialized form.[64] The *Ialysus*, however, emphasizes the degree to which form and intelligence inhere within matter itself. It is not Protogenes's iconic imitation but rather the sponge's indexical impression that creates the most convincing image of foam in the painting, playing a causal role in the generation of a representation that is "true" rather than "truth-like" while revealing an underlying logic of form across diverse species and substances. The most precise imitator of the natural world, it turns out, is *natura* herself.

Protogenes may have objected to the fact that human *ars* "could be discerned" in his painting (*intellegeretur*), but as Pliny tells us in Book 9 (on marine animals), sponges are themselves "discerning" (*intellectum inesse*): as living beings that engage dynamically with their environment, they occupy an interstitial category between plant and animal.[65] Strikingly, this perceptual ability is demonstrated by the fact that "they regulate their movements by the sense of hearing, and at the slightest noise they contract themselves, and emit an abundant moisture."[66] The sponge's apprehension of Protogenes's rage, in other words, is what generates the release of pigment that enables its foam-like imprint. Impressed on the surface of the painting, the abstract textural effect created by the sponge's holes thus gives form to the most convincing mode of figuration, one that operates as an instantiation as well as a representation of its liquid matter. Protogenes's painting does not deceive an animal (as Zeuxis's grapes deceive the birds); rather, it is produced by a being that tests our most basic assumptions about the relationship between life and intelligence, matter and agency.

As both an investigation into and a demonstration of the operations of *natura*, Protogenes's painting stands itself as an example of *naturalis historia*. Pliny tells us that it was painted during the Siege of Rhodes, resulting in a suspension of military operations while the painter painstakingly worked on his panel, laboring in his garden cottage and subsisting on beans so as not to dull his wits.[67] Protogenes embodies a humble, mindful, and collaborative approach to materials, offering an ethical alternative to the discourse of power and consumption that drives the Roman imperial machine. At the same time, the interaction of human and nonhuman, accomplished artist and simple sponge, produces an object that not only challenges conventional distinctions between "art" and "nature," but that also seeks to draw closer together the concentric circles of care that constitute the practice of *oikeiôsis*: in its miraculous production of a "truthful" image, the *Ialysus* establishes a relational matrix that expands traditional notions of social allegiances beyond the kinship of the human *oikoumenê* to encompass a creature that sits at the very limits of sentient being.

Does Protogenes (as avatar of Pliny himself) merely offer the reader a form of false consciousness? He exists, after all, within a romanticized Classical past already far from the ethical and political conflicts of Pliny's Roman regime. Yet the unresolved internal conflicts of the *Natural History* remind us that from its very beginnings, Western art history has existed in dialogue with ecological crisis; that art making, and ways of thinking about art making, have sought to honor, illuminate, and engage with the materials and environments from which they emerge, even as they have shared in anthropogenic and anthropocentric practices that have distorted and exhausted those environments. The question of how to carve out an ethical space within a system with which we are hopelessly complicit continues to trouble our sleep. We might recall Pliny's comment of his nocturnal labors that "life consists in wakefulness" (*vita vigilia est*), a perpetual "being on the watch" that does not just describe the work of observation and inquiry, but also the practice of vigilance as a form of care for the stuff of life itself.

1. Pliny the Elder, *Natural History* 35.65 (*remoto linteo ostendi picturam*). Translations of Pliny are taken (with some modifications) from the Loeb Classical Library edition, trans. H. Rackham, 1952. For discussion, see (from a vast bibliography) Norman Bryson, *Looking at the Overlooked: Four Essays on Still Life Painting* (London: Reaktion Books, 1990), 30–32; Jaś Elsner, *Art and the Roman Viewer: The Transformation of Art from the Pagan World to Christianity* (Cambridge: Cambridge University

Press, 1995), 16–17, 89–90; Sorcha Carey, *Pliny's Catalogue of Culture: Art and Empire in the "Natural History"* (Oxford: Oxford University Press, 2003), 109–11; and Michael Squire, "Campanian Wall-Painting and the Frames of Mural Make-Believe," in *The Frame in Classical Art: A Cultural History*, ed. Verity Platt and Michael Squire (Cambridge: Cambridge University Press, 2017), 188–255, esp. 221–28.

2. I allude here to Stephen Bann's influential reading of Pliny's anecdote in *The True Vine: On Visual Representation and the Western Tradition* (Cambridge: Cambridge University Press, 1989), 27–40, and Norman Bryson's critique of representational dualism in *Vision and Painting: The Logic of the Gaze* (New Haven and London: Yale University Press, 1983). On animals as both naïve and ideal viewers of illusionistic artworks, see W. J. T. Mitchell, *Picture Theory: Essays on Verbal and Visual Representation* (Chicago: University of Chicago Press, 1994), 329–44.

3. On the rationalizing impulses of Greco-Roman art, and its focus on the body, see Jeremy Tanner, *The Invention of Art History in Ancient Greece: Religion, Society and Artistic Rationalisation* (Cambridge: Cambridge University Press, 2006). On mistreatment of the environment in antiquity, see J. Donald Hughes, *Environmental Problems of the Greeks and Romans: Ecology in the Ancient Mediterranean* (Baltimore: Johns Hopkins University Press, 2014).

4. See Johann Joachim Winckelmann, *History of the Art of Antiquity*, trans. Harry Francis Mallgrave (Los Angeles: Getty Publications, 2006).

5. On Winckelmann's "climate theory" and its intellectual history (which draws on the theories of Jean-Baptiste Dubos and Montesquieu and looks back to Greco-Roman models of environmental determinism), see Alex Potts, *Flesh and the Ideal: Winckelmann and the Origins of Art History* (New Haven and London: Yale University Press, 1994), 54–58, 158–61; Thomas DaCosta Kaufmann, *Toward a Geography of Art* (Chicago: University of Chicago Press, 2004), 15–38; and Katherine Harloe, *Winckelmann and the Invention of Antiquity: History and Aesthetics in the Age of Altertumswissenschaft* (Oxford: Oxford University Press, 2013), 114–28. On the "three ecologies" (fundamental to the thinking behind the conference that inspired this volume), see Félix Guattari, *The Three Ecologies* (London: Athlone Press, 2000).

6. For a critique of ancient pastoral from an environmental perspective, see Greg Garrard, *Ecocriticism*, 2nd ed. (Abingdon: Routledge, 2012), 37–65, with a nuanced response by Terry Gifford, "The Environmental Humanities and the Pastoral Tradition," in *Ecocriticism, Ecology, and the Cultures of Antiquity*, ed. Christopher Schliephake (Lanham, Md.: Lexington Books, 2017), 159–74. On Roman "sacro-idyllic" painting, which has a complex relationship to literary pastoral, see Bettina Bergmann, "Exploring the Grove: Pastoral Space on Roman Walls," in *The Pastoral Landscape*, Studies in the History of Art 36 (Washington, DC: National Gallery of Art, 1992), 21–46, and from a more eco-critical perspective, Diana Spencer, "Aesthetic, Sociological, and Exploitative Attitudes to Landscape in Greco-Roman Literature, Art, and Culture," *Oxford Handbooks Online*, 2017

(DOI: 10.1093/oxfordhb/9780199935390.013.121). For an overview of art historical eco-criticism, see Suzaan Boettger, "Within and Beyond the Art World: Environmentalist Criticism of Visual Art," in *Handbook of Ecocriticism and Cultural Ecology*, ed. Hubert Zapf (Berlin: De Gruyter, 2016), 664–82.

7. On the problematic role of Classical art within the discipline of art history more broadly, see Verity Platt, "The Matter of Classical Art History," in "What's New About the Old? Reassessing the Ancient World," special issue, *Daedalus* 145, no. 2 (Spring 2016): 69–78.

8. On the conceptualization of *Homo faber* as controlling, instrumentalizing, and destroying the environment through tools, see Hannah Arendt, *The Human Condition* (Chicago: University of Chicago Press, 2nd ed., 1998), esp. 136–74.

9. For an exploration of this dilemma in relation to Classical art, see "The Art of Art History in Graeco-Roman Antiquity," eds. Verity Platt and Michael Squire, special issue, *Arethusa* 43, no. 2 (Spring 2010).

10. For Pliny's influence on early modern art history, see Sarah Blake McHam, *Pliny and the Artistic Culture of the Italian Renaissance: The Legacy of the "Natural History"* (New Haven and London: Yale University Press, 2013).

11. Brooke Holmes, "Before Nature?," in *Ecocriticism, Ecology, and the Cultures of Antiquity*, ix–xiv (x), citing Bruno Latour, *The Politics of Nature: How to Bring the Sciences into Democracy*, trans. Catherine Porter (Cambridge: Harvard University Press, 2004); Timothy Morton, *Ecology without Nature: Rethinking Environmental Aesthetics* (Cambridge: Harvard University Press, 2007); and Philippe Descola, *Beyond Nature and Culture*, trans. Janet Lloyd (Chicago: University of Chicago Press, 2013).

12. On Stoic principles of *oikeiôsis* (discussed by Diogenes Laertius, *Lives of the Philosophers* 7.85 and Hierocles, *Elements of Ethics* and *On Appropriate Acts*), see Simon G. Pembroke, "Oikeiosis," in *Problems in Stoicism*, ed. Anthony A. Long (London: Athlone Press, 1971), 114–49, and Troels Engberg-Pedersen, *The Stoic Theory of Oikeiosis: Moral Development and Social Interaction in Early Stoic Philosophy* (Aarhus: Aarhus University Press, 1990). On *oikeiôsis* in its Roman context, see Gretchen Reydams-Schils, "Human Bonding and *oikeiôsis* in Roman Stoicism," *Oxford Studies in Ancient Philosophy* 22 (2002): 221–51. On its reception in later European philosophy, see Reinhardt Brandt, "Self-Consciousness and Self-Care: On the Tradition of Oikeiosis in the Modern Age," *Grotiana* 22, no. 1 (2001): 73–92.

13. Henry G. Liddell and Robert Scott, *A Greek-English Lexicon*, revised and augmented throughout by Sir Henry Stuart Jones (Oxford: Clarendon Press, 1940), s.v. οἰκείωσις. For the "concentric circles" theory of *oikeiôsis*, see Hierocles in Stobaeus's *Anthology*, 4.671.7–673.11, reprinted in Anthony A. Long and David N. Sedley, *The Hellenistic Philosophers* (Cambridge: Cambridge University Press, 1987), 57g, and Anthony A. Long, "Hierocles on oikeiôsis," in Anthony A. Long, *Stoic Studies* (Berkeley: University of California Press, 2001), 250–63.

14. Daniel Richter, *Cosmopolis: Imagining Community in Late Classical Athens and the Early Roman Empire* (Oxford: Oxford University Press, 2011), 75.

15. On the modern-day implications of *oikeiôsis* for environmentalism and animal rights, see Helen Karabatzaki, "Environmental Issues in Hellenistic Philosophy," in *Thinking about the Environment: Our Debt to the Classical and Medieval Past*, ed. Thomas M. Robinson and Laura Westra (Lanham, Md.: Lexington Books, 2002), 33–42; and Gary Steiner, *Animals and the Moral Community: Mental Life, Moral Status, and Kinship* (New York: Columbia University Press, 2008), 92–93, 134–40.

16. Astrid Schwarz and Kurt Jax, "Etymology and Original Sources of the Term 'Ecology'," in *Ecology Revisited. Reflecting on Concepts, Advancing Science*, ed. A. Schwarz and K. Jax (Springer: Dordrecht, 2011), 145–47.

17. On the role of Protogenes in the *Natural History*, see Carey, *Pliny's Catalogue of Culture*, 102–4, together with the commentary in Jean-Michel Croisille, *Pline l'Ancien, Histoire naturelle, Livre 35: La Peinture* (Paris: Les Belles Lettres, 1985), 212–17. For sources on Protogenes, see Sascha Kansteiner et al., eds., *Der Neue Overbeck. Die antiken Schriftquellen zu den bildenden Künsten der Griechen* (Berlin: De Gruyter, 2014), vol. 4, nos. 2993–3032. For more on Protogenes as the unlikely protagonist of Pliny's history of painting, see Verity Platt, *Beyond Ekphrasis: Making Objects Matter in Classical Antiquity* (forthcoming).

18. See *Natural History* 35.80, 101–6. On Pliny's celebrated workaholism (related by his nephew, Pliny the Younger, *Letters* 3.5.8), see John Henderson, "Knowing someone through their books: Pliny on Uncle Pliny ('Epistles' 3.5)," *Classical Philology* 93, no. 3 (2002): 256–84; and Roy K. Gibson, "Elder and Better: The *Naturalis Historia* and the *Letters* of the Younger Pliny," in *Pliny the Elder: Themes and Contexts*, ed. Roy K. Gibson and Ruth Morello (Leiden: Brill, 2011), 186–206. On his celebration of artists who sign their work in the "imperfect" tense (*Pref.* 26–27), see Verity Platt, "Orphaned Objects: The Phenomenology of the Incomplete in Pliny's *Natural History*," *Art History* 41, no. 3 (2018), with further bibliography.

19. On Protogenes's encounter with the Hellenistic leader Demetrius Poliorcetes (*Natural History* 35.105) and its influence on early modern reflections on the relationship between the artist and the prince, see Ernst Kris and Otto Kurz, *Legend, Myth, and Magic in the Image of the Artist. A Historical Experiment*, trans. Alastair Laing (New Haven: Yale University Press, 1979), 40–42, and McHam, *Pliny and the Italian Renaissance*, 281, 288.

20. *Natural History* 35.106.

21. On the Alexander Mosaic (now in the National Archaeological Museum, Naples) and its complex relationship to fourth-century BCE painting, see Ada Cohen, *The Alexander Mosaic. Stories of Victory and Defeat* (Cambridge: Cambridge University Press, 1997), and Paolo Moreno, *Apelles. The Alexander Mosaic* (Milan: Skira, 2001).

22. Diogenes Laertius (*Lives of the Eminent Philosophers* 5.1) tells us that Aristotle was "son of

Nicomachus and Phaestis." On Aristotle's parents (who both seem to have died when he was young), see Anton-Hermann Chroust, *Aristotle: New Light on His Life and On Some of His Lost Works* (London and New York: Routledge, 2nd ed., 2016), esp. 27–28, 55–56, 73–82, 148–49; and Carlo Natali, *Aristotle: His Life and School* (Princeton and Oxford: Princeton University Press, 2013), 9–17.

23. On the Vienna Aristotle (fig. 2), a first-century CE Roman copy of a Greek original dated c. 320 BCE, now in the Kunsthistorisches Museum, see Paul Zanker, *The Mask of Socrates: The Image of the Intellectual in Antiquity*, Sather Classical Lectures (Berkeley: University of California Press, 1995), 71, with Ralf von den Hoff, *Philosophenporträts des Früh- und Hochhellenismus* (Munich: Biering & Brinkmann, 1994), 27–33.

24. *Inscriptiones Graecae* II², 4261, dated to the Imperial period. See Sheila Dillon, *Ancient Greek Portrait Sculpture: Contexts, Subjects, and Styles* (Cambridge: Cambridge University Press, 2006), 106.

25. Diogenes Laertius, *Lives of the Eminent Philosophers* 5.15–16. For discussion, see Natali, *Aristotle: His Life and School*, 9–17.

26. See, e.g., *Physics* 194b23–35; *Generation of Animals* 732a2–10, 775a15: for discussion, see Nancy Tuana, "Aristotle and the Politics of Reproduction," in *Engendering Origins: Critical Feminist Readings in Plato and Aristotle*, ed. Bat-Ami Bar On (New York: State University of New York Press, 1994), 189–206; Cynthia A. Freeland, "Nourishing Speculation: A Feminist Reading of Aristotelian Science," in *Engendering Origins*, 145–88; Charlotte Witt, "Form, Normativity, and Gender in Aristotle: A Feminist Perspective," in *Feminist Interpretations of Aristotle*, ed. Cynthia A. Freeland (University Park: Pennsylvania State University Press, 1998), 118–37; and Sarah B. Sharkey, *An Aristotelian Feminism* (Switzerland: Springer, 2016), 81–111.

27. See especially Luce Irigaray, "How to Conceive (of) a Girl," in *Speculum of the Other Woman*, trans. Gillian C. Gill (Ithaca: Cornell University Press, 1985), 160–67; and "Place, Interval: A Reading of Aristotle, *Physics IV*," trans. Carolyn Burke and Gillian Gill, in Luce Irigaray, *An Ethics of Sexual Difference* (Ithaca: Cornell University Press, 1993); see also Luce Irigaray, *In the Beginning, She Was* (London: Bloomsbury, 2013); with Cynthia A. Freeland, "On Irigaray on Aristotle," in *Feminist Interpretations of Aristotle*, ed. Freeland, 59–92; and Rebecca Hill, *The Interval: Relation and Becoming in Irigaray, Aristotle, and Bergson* (New York: Fordham University Press, 2012).

28. Irigaray, "How to Conceive (of) a Girl," 162.

29. Irigaray, *In the Beginning*, 2: this source is explicitly identified by her as "nature, woman, Goddess" (2).

30. For more "emic" readings of the relationship between ontology, power, and sexual difference in Aristotle's philosophy, see Witt, "Form, Normativity, and Gender," and Marguerite Deslauriers, "Sex and Essence in Aristotle's *Metaphysics* and Biology," in *Feminist Interpretations of Aristotle*, ed. Freeland, 138–67. For a positive take on Aristotelianism's potential for feminism itself, see Martha C. Nussbaum, "Aristotle, Feminism, and Needs for Functioning," in the same volume, 248–59.

31. See James I. Porter, *The Origins of Aesthetic Thought in Ancient Greece: Matter, Sensation, and Experience* (Cambridge: Cambridge University Press, 2010).

32. See Tanner, *The Invention of Art History*, 212–19.

33. On the methodological challenges of reading "through" Pliny to his Hellenistic sources, see Verity Platt, "The Artist as Anecdote: Creating Creators in Ancient Texts and Modern Art History," in *Creative Lives in Classical Antiquity: Poets, Artists and Biography*, ed. Johanna Hanink and Richard Fletcher (Cambridge: Cambridge University Press, 2016), 274–304.

34. For an influential example of this excerpted tradition, see Eugénie Sellers and Katharine Jex-Blake, *The Elder Pliny's Chapters on the History of Greek Art* (London: Macmillan, 1896). On the role of Pliny's "art history" within the larger context of the *Natural History*, see Carey, *Pliny's Catalogue of Culture*, and Tanner, *The Invention of Art History*, 240–46.

35. On the structure of Pliny's text, see Thomas R. Laehn, *Pliny's Defense of Empire* (New York and London: Routledge, 2013), 6–31, for a summary of interpretations.

36. *Natural History* 7.191–215. On this passage, see Mary Beagon, *The Elder Pliny on the Human Animal. Natural History Book 7* (Oxford: Clarendon Press, 2005), 56–57.

37. For an accessible account of Aristotle's biological methods, see James Lennox, "Aristotle's Biology," *The Stanford Encyclopedia of Philosophy* (Spring 2017 ed.), ed. Edward N. Zalta, https://plato.stanford.edu/archives/spr2017/entries/aristotle-biology (accessed November 28, 2017).

38. As recounted by his nephew Pliny the Younger, *Letters* 6.16.

39. On the difference between Aristotle and Pliny, see Gustav A. Seeck, "Plinius und Aristoteles als Naturwissenschaftler," *Gymnasium* 92 (1985): 419–34; Jacob Isager, *Pliny on Art and Society: The Elder Pliny's Chapters on the History of Art* (Odense: Odense University Press, 1991), 43–47; and Beagon, *The Elder Pliny on the Human Animal*, 20–21. On Pliny's approach to natural history, see also Mary Beagon, *Roman Nature: The Thought of Pliny the Elder* (Oxford: Clarendon Press, 1992).

40. For a classic critique along these lines, see Gian Biagio Conte, *Genres and Readers*, trans. Glenn W. Most (Baltimore: Johns Hopkins University Press, 1994), 67–104.

41. Mary Beagon, "The Curious Eye of the Elder Pliny," in *Pliny the Elder: Themes and Contexts*, ed. Gibson and Morello, 71–88.

42. For a critique of the dematerializing impulses of both Aristotle and Plato, see Porter, *The Origins of Aesthetic Thought*, 14–17, 70–138. On the Stoic underpinnings of Pliny's cosmology (within the context of a broader "layman's" eclecticism), see Beagon, *Roman Nature*, 26–50; Tanner, *The Invention of Art History*, 236–37; and Verity Platt, "Of Sponges and Stones: Matter and Ornament in Roman Painting," in *Ornament and Figure: Rethinking Visual Ontologies in Graeco-Roman Antiquity and Beyond*, ed. Nikolaus Dietrich and Michael Squire (Berlin: De Gruyter, 2018), 241–278.

43. *Natural History* 2.2.

44. *Natural History* 11.11. On the significance of bees and their products in the *Natural History*, see Neville Morley, "Civil War and Succession Crisis in Roman Beekeeping," *Historia: Zeitschrift für Alte Geschlichte* 56, no. 4 (2007): 462–70; and Verity Platt, "Beeswax: The Natural History of an Archetypal Medium," in *The Nature of Art: Pliny the Elder on Materials*, ed. Anna Anguissola and Andreas Grüner (Berlin: Brepols, forthcoming).

45. See Conte, *Genres and Readers*, 102–3.

46. *Natural History* 11.12.

47. Aristotle, *Parts of Animals* 1.5 (645a). On this passage and its context, see James Lennox, "The Unity and Purpose of *On the Parts of Animals* I," in *Being, Nature, and Life in Aristotle*, ed. James G. Lennox and Robert Bolton (Cambridge: Cambridge University Press, 2010), 56–77.

48. *Natural History* 11.2–4.

49. Aristotle, *Parts of Animals* 1.5 (645a).

50. On the *Natural History* as an "open" text, see Platt, "Orphaned Objects"; for its conception as "a text as generous as nature itself" (248), see Brooke Holmes, "The Generous Text. Animal Intuition, Human Knowledge and Written Transmission in Pliny's Books on Medicine," in *Knowledge, Text and Practice in Ancient Technical Writing*, ed. Marco Formisano and Philip van der Eijk (Cambridge: Cambridge University Press, 2017), 231–51.

51. On the "spontaneous generation" of images within the natural formations of stone, see *Natural History* 36.14 and 37.5, with Platt, "Of Sponges and Stones."

52. *Natural History* 37.1.

53. See *Natural History* 36.18–19, 35.112, with discussion by Michael Squire, "Campanian Wall-Painting," 208–10, and Platt, "Of Sponges and Stones."

54. On the role of a Stoic-derived cosmic "sympathy" within the *Natural History* (as well as an internal system of Aristotelian sympathies and antipathies), see Holmes, "The Generous Text."

55. *Natural History, pref.* 18–19. On the complex politics of the preface, see Patrick Sinclair, "Rhetoric of Writing and Reading in the Preface to Pliny's *Naturalis historia*," in *Flavian Rome: Culture, Image Text*, ed. Anthony J. Boyle and William J. Dominik (Leiden: Brill, 2003), 277–99.

56. On Pliny's career, see Ronald Syme, "Pliny the Procurator," *Harvard Studies in Classical Philology* 73 (1969): 201–36. On Roman deforestation (and related anthropogenic crises), see Hughes, *Environmental Problems of the Greeks and Romans*, 68–87.

57. See, e.g., *Natural History* 8.7 (ivory), 22.100, 33.3 (gold), 33.160 (Lydian ochre), with Ken Parejko, "Pliny the Elder's Silphium: First Recorded Species Extinction," *Conservation Biology* 17, no. 3 (June 2003): 925–27.

58. I allude here to Jane Bennett, *Vibrant Matter: A Political Ecology of Things* (Durham: Duke University Press, 2010). While Bennett does not discuss Stoicism in her influential inquiry into

the agency of matter, she does draw on the materialism of the ancient Epicureans. On the ethics of luxury in the *Natural History*, see Andrew Wallace-Hadrill, "Pliny the Elder and Man's Unnatural History," *Greece and Rome* 7 (1990): 80–96, and Carey, *Pliny's Catalogue of Culture*, 102–37.

59. *Natural History* 33.1.

60. *Natural History* 33.3.

61. On this point, see Tanner, *The Invention of Art History*, 235–46.

62. See Eva Falaschi, "More Than Words: Re-staging Protogenes' *Ialysus*. The Many Lives of an Artwork between Greece and Rome," in *Re-staging Greek Artworks in Roman Contexts: New Approaches and Perspectives*, ed. Gabriella Cirucci and Alessandro Poggio (Milan: LED, forthcoming).

63. *Natural History* 35.102. On Vasari's painted cycle of artist anecdotes from the *Natural History* in the Sala del Trionfo della Virtù in his home in Arezzo (dated to the 1540s), see Liana DeGirolami Cheney, "Vasari's Depiction of Pliny's Histories," *Explorations in Renaissance Culture* 15, no. 1 (1989): 97–120, and Patricia L. Rubin, *Giorgio Vasari: Art and History* (New Haven and London: Yale University Press, 1995), 35–38.

64. *Parts of Animals* 1.5 (640a).

65. *Natural History* 9.148. For more on sponges in the *Natural History*, see Platt, "Of Sponges and Stones."

66. *Natural History* 31.124.

67. *Natural History* 35.105. On Protogenes's humble lifestyle, see Carey, *Pliny's Catalogue of Culture*, 102–4.

Ark Thinking

Jeffrey Jerome Cohen and Julian Yates

> If all architecture is architecture of the Holocene, then perhaps the Anthropocene is the end of architecture as we know it. The *arche* in architecture means something like origin, source, beginning, command or conditions of possibility, yet in the Anthropocene one can no longer imagine a practice of building from the same conceptual foundations. Perhaps rather than *arche*, the conceptual root has to be something else, something without that confidence of striving upward.
> —McKenzie Wark, "From Architecture to Kainotecture"

> Architecture could only in fact find its place *after* the Flood—or rather in its stead.
> —Hubert Damisch, "Noah's Ark"

Perhaps all art and architecture, as we know them, do indeed belong to the Holocene (entirely recent time). Perhaps, too, the arrival of what is named Anthropocene voids their conditions of possibility and today we bear witness to the closing of a parenthesis. But, perhaps also, against the seeming odds, we may recognize in this announcement of the closure of one epoch—in truth, the end of one way of marking time that enables us to discern a multiplicity of other scales and chronologies—not the voiding of the conceptual foundations that have oriented our practice of building and making, so much as an invitation, once again, to inquire into the ends (*telos*) of architecture and art.[1] How do our models of *poiesis*, of making, of process, program our relations with the crowded assemblage of beings, human and otherwise, with whom we come into being? Perhaps the *arche* in architecture refers less to an origin than to an ongoing economy or ecology (a structure, a terrain) that our ways of building and making seek to maintain and to manage. And perhaps, remote as the possibility may seem, the whole business of building and making, of art and architecture, have all along held within themselves the potential for rethinking and rezoning what we name *arche* (origin) and *telos* (end), in ways that welcome the host of agencies other than human with which we come into being.

In this essay, we explore one occluded, speculative, or perhaps forgotten origin or supplement to the word "architecture" that foregrounds the way the practice and study of building, of constructing shelter and refuge, cohabits with figures of flood, catastrophe, and inundation. As our epigraph from Hubert Damisch's essay "Noah's Ark" indicates,[2] we are eager to give the game away immediately: this alternate origin resides in the story of Noah and his Ark as we receive it from the book or anthology of beginnings we call Genesis. We are interested in how the story of Noah and his Ark might offer a set of conceptual resources that speak to the difficulty all manner of activists, artists, and writers face in responding to the task of somehow adequately representing and so responding to the prospect of anthropogenic climate change and mass extinction.

Genesis

In his essay "Noah's Ark," originally published in 1987 in the *Revue Critique*, art historian and self-styled "displaced philosopher" Hubert Damisch asks why it may be that the entry for "Architecture," written by celebrated architect Jacques-François Blondel, in Denis Diderot and Jean Le Rond's 1751 *Encyclopédie, ou dictionnaire raisonné des sciences, des arts et des métiers*, is so very short.[3] "Dispatch[ed] . . . in just three compact and carefully phrased columns," is how he puts it.[4] Damisch rewrote and augmented the essay over a period of years that witnessed the fall of the Berlin Wall, the first Gulf War, 9/11, the second Gulf War, and a growing awareness that anthropogenic climate change is the cause of the global rise in temperatures and sea levels, the potentially catastrophic interruption of seasonal meteorological norms, and a sixth mass extinction. Given that as he revises the essay, Damisch alludes to these events, it seems curious that the apparent paucity of Blondel's entry on architecture should demand his attention. Surely, there are other, more pressing, matters at hand? What then is at stake in Blondel's brevity and the apparent omission on the part of Diderot and Le Rond's otherwise encyclopedic urge?

It should be said that Blondel's entry is not completely lacking. He does manage a synoptic if skeletal architectural history from the Greeks to his contemporaries. He defines architecture as an art of proportion and measure and so both art and science. He also distinguishes architecture from the "simple art of building—in other words, *construction*" by insisting that the purview of his entry, of "Architecture" itself, concerns the "'art of *composing* and *constructing* buildings for the convenience [commodité] . . . and different purposes of life, such as sacred buildings, royal palaces, and private houses, as well as bridges, public squares, the-aters, triumphal arches, etc.'"[5] The word "composition," as Damisch comments, "is what distinguishes architecture from the simple art of building" or construction as in the case of military or naval architecture. Here Blondel's entry would seem to side with historians of architecture who ally the endeavor to the history of rhetoric and the human shaping of the world, and to dwelling or soft phenomenology. But Blondel's entry still, to Damisch, seems lacking. Where, for example, in the *Encyclopédie*, should readers look for some treatment of construction or what seems to be most important to Damisch, "'the art of building in relation to matter?'"

The results, initially, prove frustrating. The entry on "Construction," which runs to more than twenty pages, takes as its subject grammar and "gram-matical construction" with some reference to geometry. Some information is also to be found in the entries on "Carpentry," "Masonry," and "Joinery," but oth-erwise, "the art of building in relation to matter" appears to go missing, or to be included only as a partially occluded supplement. Damisch acknowledges that the 1777 *Supplément* to the *Encyclopédie* includes two additional articles on "Archi-tect" and "Architecture," that seem to speak to this omission, but he finds them just as "flat" as Blondel's original entry. Perhaps, then, Blondel's brevity might be the result merely of "the constraints imposed on the contributors by alphabetical order."[6] But, the fact that the entries on "Art," and "Composition" were "not used to remedy the problem," Damisch offers, "seems to indicate that neither the author nor the editors felt the need to do so." That said, perhaps generations of readers have merely been looking in the wrong place for further wisdom on the business of construction or "the art of building in relation to matter" that Blondel, as Damisch renders him, seems to wish to distinguish from architecture as a sci-entific art of proportion, measure, and perspective.

Directly prior to Blondel's entry on "Architecture" appears an entry on, of all things, naval construction, written not by a shipbuilder or architect, it must be said, but by a theologian: Abbé Edmé-François Mallet. Very excitingly, from Damisch's point of view, Abbé Mallet manages to produce what looks very much like "an authentically functionalist approach" to architecture or construction, "one that even goes into details,"[7] such as how to construct a space whose use changes over time, a space that must accommodate all manner of beings, feed and water them; how to care for them; and how to manage their waste. Readers who look to the *Encyclopédie* and feel frustrated that they find within its contents little discus-sion of such pressing matters that occupy architects and urban planners today, such as risk management, logistics, accommodation, questions of access and security, or even the tensile strength of materials, or who conclude that they shall have to wait for the likes of a Le Corbusier to encounter a purely "functional sense of proportion," shall find themselves transported, embarked on a story that might displace their sense of architectural history and forever alter their conception of architecture in relation to both the materials of construction and the urgent matters of catastrophe, human-authored and otherwise. The title of this entry on functionalist architecture, "on the art of building in relation to matter," written so many centuries ago—so very many more centuries in fact than the date of the *Encyclopédie*, as Abbé Mallet would be the first to attest—is, of course, "Ark."

The story of Noah's Ark as reported in Genesis 6:9–9:17, with its divinely ordained blueprint for a floating building and imminent weathering of an announced catastrophe, is, Damisch ventures, the first architectural treatise—enabling him to recast architecture with its attendant or necessary questions of accommodation and environing not as the besting of flood, failure, and catastrophe, but quite precisely as finding its origin, its birth, from the waters of the flood. "The art of building in relation to materials," writes Damisch, "has never ceased to" cohabit "with the prospect of a generalized catastrophe," which, typically, either "looks to stave off . . . by rendering it useless" or "merely aspires to furnish humanity with the means to survive . . . without too much damage."[8] Calculate the risks. Construct the necessary shelter. Navigate and so weather the storm. But, more fundamentally, or occluded by this survivalist narrative, which appears to subtend the more decorous and proportioned "'art of *composing* and *constructing* buildings for the convenience [commodité] . . . and different purposes of life,'" Damisch invites us to consider that the story of Noah's Ark might reveal the way architecture itself stands not in opposition to catastrophe, but as the art of constructive failure—as architecture's status as the "privileged domain of application" for catastrophe theory seems to confirm. Architecture designates, inhabits, and makes its home out of and within the rupture or failure of materials that reach their own individual "catastrophe points,"[9] and whose several catastrophes it must orchestrate or arrange in what is called "building in relation to materials," or what we might now name a whole ark of other than human agents, forces, entities, materials, ecologies.

Although he does not quite say it, Damisch seems to suggest that we should surrender the depleting hope that one day the art of building as rhetoric or as an art and science of dwelling will vanquish risk, failure, catastrophe, and

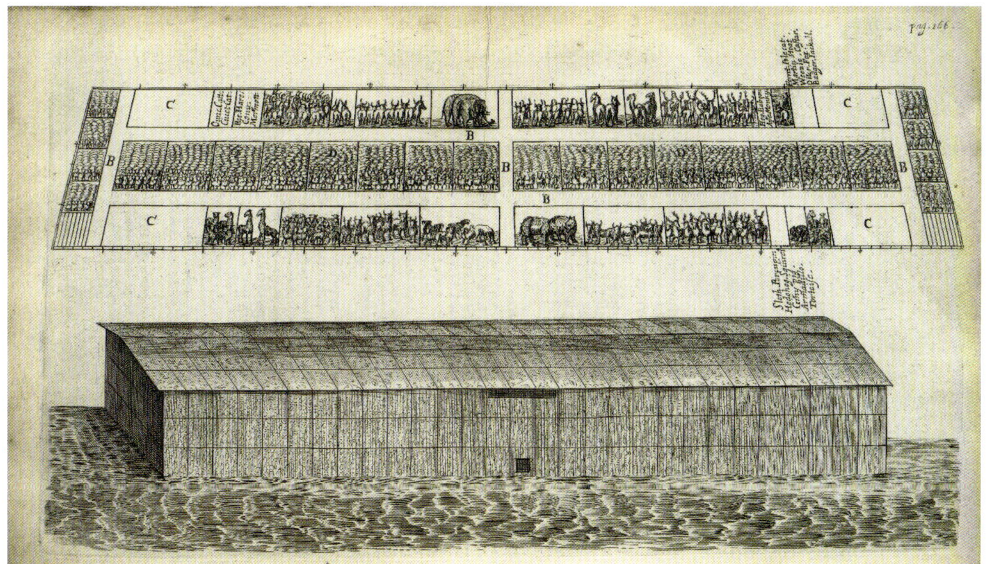

Fig. I. Floor plan and drawing of Noah's Ark in John Wilkins, *An Essay Towards the Real Character of Philosophical Language* (London, 1668), p. 166. Folger Shakespeare Library (shelfmark: W2196)

flood. The story of the Ark, as he seems to know, invites something else entirely, something implicit in the fact that the dimensions for the floating building that Noah and his family construct are not of his own design but are received directly from the divine. God, after all, is the architect; Noah, and family, God's builders. What then should we conclude from this co-announcement or double articulation of Flood and Ark, of inhuman catastrophe and design?

Here, Damsich and Abbé Mallet follow the seventeenth-century English theologian Bishop John Wilkins, who famously calculated the minimum dimensions of the Ark based on the space and resources he calculated necessary for Noah, his family, and their assembled animals in his *An Essay Towards the Real Character of Philosophical Language* (1668). For Wilkins, steeped as he was in the Patristics and in biblical commentary, the story of the Ark exists as an allegory whose shape reveals a fundamental, orienting episteme. The literalism of the story proves important (fig. 1). His essay is written ostensibly to counter detractors who seek to prove that the story of the Ark is impossible. But, beyond that, the true product of his essay lies less in proving the Ark's feasibility than in disclosing the higher order allegorical quotient to its feasibility. The efficacy of Noah's functionalist approach to architecture, as Damisch might put it, runs in tandem with a deeper sense of architecture as itself a structuring allegorical system whose lineaments are more than a shaping or remodeling of the world. Accordingly, the terms of Wilkins's calculus, his operationalizing or actualization of the Ark as a model, prove key and must be addressed point for point.

For example, Wilkins projects the way arrangements of space inside the Ark would alter as the carnivores ate their way through the flocks of sheep that served as their food. Over the course of the forty days and nights of the Ark's voyage, the sheep eat the fodder; their numbers diminish as they are eaten; and the amount of manure increases. Given that the Ark is sealed, the internal arrangements of space on board are understood to be dynamic, available to change as the functional requirements of the Ark alter.[10] His calculations, however faulty, are widely credited with anticipating the mathematics necessary for global trade from the seventeenth-century's sailing vessels of the East India Company, to the transatlantic slave trade or "middle passage," and, today, the integrated networks of container ships and transport links that, among other things, enable the global trade in industrialized flesh become meat, which the migrancy of displaced people and human trafficking networks parasitize.[11] At stake in his calculations, which mathematize animal lives as units, then, is what seems the pure neutrality of a system of structuring space as fungible units of habitation or accommodation, architecture become a sovereign science of space that processes different beings according to its own equivalences. Against this prospect, Wilkins offers the divine origin of the Ark's dimensions and materials as a tariff or moral ratio. He explains the divine origins of the design by offering that "the human mind tends to wildly exaggerate objects."[12] Left to his own devices, Wilkins feels that Noah and family would have "engendered a building infinitely greater than was necessary" and so which would have failed, listed, sunk, or whose accommodations would have been so errant as to result either in starvation or glut. Damisch reads Wilkins's reserve as evidence of "the propensity of modern societies to deal with difficulties they face by excess rather than by lack and to imagine solutions, to devise projects, to impose tasks on themselves, and to fuel dreams of an exaggerated scope . . . that are ultimately totalitarian."[13] Accepting, on the contrary (as the story of Noah's Ark offers), that the dimensions of survival emerge with and from catastrophe, and that therefore the arc of catastrophe radicalizes questions of accommodation, refuge, and survival, signals the way in which—for all its drawing down of boundaries, for all the closing of the door of the Ark or the limits of a building—the very structure of the Ark and of architecture necessitates and produces an open inquiry into structure and structuration. The Ark stands as both origin and expression, both allegory and rhetoric, a zoo-biopolitical crux or blueprint whose actualization decides everything.

Putting the "ark" back into architecture enables us to recognize that "catastrophe takes its place at the beginning of the tale."[14] "Architecture," as Diderot and Le Rond's alphabetic arrangement of entries apparently registers, "could only find its place *after* the flood—or rather in its stead."[15] Architecture, ark-building, sets in motion an awareness of system and interconnection *per se*, which is to say, of the way a building or structure exists as a set of environmental or environing functions that may prove hospitable, progressive, welcoming, or lethal. The Ark's calculus, the *arche* in architecture, remains neutral, a point of crossing between origin and expression that decides the limits of a world. If all architecture thus far, in human history, has, as McKenzie Wark suggests,[16] been architecture of the Holocene, which is to say an art of building that could anticipate a predictable set of ecological constraints and conditions; and if, today, in the epoch of anthropogenic climate change, architecture must somehow come to anticipate an entirely unpredictable set of circumstances and non-generalizable local conditions, then with Damisch, Abbé Mallet, Bishop Wilkins, and the Genesis story, we wish to offer the story of Noah's Ark as an open text on the conjoined questions of structure and accommodation, and as evidence that architecture has always cohabited with the disaster that it inhabits and prorogues.[17]

Welcome, then, to what we call "ark thinking"—a consideration of the way the story of Noah's Ark embeds an ongoing set of questions about construction, accommodation, air conditioning, environment, and catastrophe. We are interested in the way contemporary initiatives to combat the effects of global warming and the emerging genre of Cli(mate) Fi(ction) recycle and engage with the story of Noah's Ark, and so with figures of mobile or static refuge and storage amid a flood or inundation of catastrophic dimensions. Our contention is that the rich afterlife of the Genesis narrative, from the Middle Ages and Renaissance on, offers forgotten strands of thought, forgotten elaborations of the story, written from the perspective of Noah's wife and family, the animals on the ark, and crucially those excluded and so left behind to die, which speak more eloquently and compellingly to the ethical and political burdens of living through the Anthropocene than otherwise routine invocations of the Flood story in contemporary culture and science evince. Here we find ourselves in profound sympathy with Wark's desire to transform the study and practice of architecture into what he calls "a kainotecture," deriving from the word "*kainos* (which is also the root of *-cene* in

Holocene and Anthropocene), meaning a twist in the quality of time."[18] We take pride in sharing with him the hope that what may emerge from such an endeavor is an imaginative register of building that would constitute something like "a xenotecture, from [the word] *xenos*, the stranger, who could be friend or enemy," and who, nevertheless, requires some order of welcome and accommodation. We remain cautious, however, as regards the periodizing plot Wark conserves and that funds what becomes, for him, an archival sifting of the past for evidence of what he names "symbebekotecture, from *symbebekos*, the accident," architecture's accidents or accidental buildings that might prepare us for architecture's future as precisely as concerted building for the accident. We pause because we wonder to what extent architecture has ever been free of catastrophe, free, that is, of some management of imminent risk and immanent inhuman forces from which it derives the inadequate shelters and inadequate hospitality it offers.

What, then, does it entail to follow Damisch, Abbé Mallet, and Bishop Wilkins, and to inhabit the figure of Noah's Ark as an always-contested site at which the question of habitation, of refuge, and of hospitality opens and closes, only to open once again?

Ark Thinking

Everyone thinks they know what an ark is: the ark is a ship in which you place your animals to save them from catastrophe, or a strongbox in which you secure records, stories, sacred objects, and seeds of origin. But few realize the complicated histories from which our modern arks arrive, their strange detours and unexpected remakings. A term conveying refuge and conservation, "ark" has traversed troubled waters and long centuries on its journey into the narratives we tell. A space of sanctuary and preservation, an ark is built to convey some fragment of a turbulent present into a better future. We stow in virtual arks sequences of DNA (the Frozen Ark network) and upload images into databases meant to preserve animal diversity from oblivion (the Photo Ark). Sometimes we safeguard living creatures within physical structures christened with that name, carefully managing their reproductive habits to delay their extinction (the Amphibian Ark). Plants and seeds have their own special versions of arks—as do, in a way, the wealthy (gated communities and other havens to exclude the tumults of the world). In narratives of climate change, we turn to the ark as a microcosm secured against disaster, a chance to survive the world's end. In our speculative fictions, what was for Noah and his family a boat becomes a spaceship.

The book of Genesis has gifted us with our most powerful trope for envisioning how life endures beyond cataclysmic climate change. Noah builds a box-like vessel to sail the rising waters with his cargo of humans and animals, bequeathing to the Earth a chance to start over, to be populated anew. The odd-looking modern English word *ark* denotes primarily this boat that Noah constructed against deluge: Old English *ærc* anglicizes the posh Latin *arca*, a noun that for writers like Juvenal, Horace, Pliny, and Cicero named a chest for keeping precious things, especially money, safe from the perturbations of the world. *Arca* therefore makes a certain good sense for designating the vessel—but we will also recognize *ark* as signifying "chest," since the Ten Commandments were stored in a container which in English translations of the Bible is described as the Ark of the Covenant. After its deployment in the Latin Vulgate translation of the Hebrew Bible, the world filled with arks (*arches, Archen, arcas*). Versions of the Latin term have found their way into numerous contemporary languages, even non-Romance tongues. *Arca* in turn stretches back in time to Greek *arkhe*, designating beginnings, origins, and the source for civic authority (documents preserved in a strongbox), but also *archon* or witness. The word *ark* is itself quite literally an odd little archive that has been sailing the linguistic sea for millennia. As a chest full of hopes, we continue to connect the term to Noah's device for protecting family, food, and animals. Yet the Hebrew noun that names his cataclysm-enduring craft is *tava* (תֵּבָה, pronounced tayva). Used only one other time in Torah, to designate the basket of reeds preserving the infant Moses, *tava* may have little to do with the ark-chests that Latin translation spawned. The word *arcus* also gives us the word "rainbow"—the weapon suspended in the heavens like some inverse or archived sword of Damocles. Arks—whatever they are, however they gather their manifold stories—sail divergent currents. When viewed across the centuries, they constitute a divergent flotilla. Various religious groups and organizations are still building arks today (fig. 2). In its own way, this essay that we are writing constitutes its own en*ark*ment.[19]

One of the things that intrigues us about the story of Noah's Ark is the way the minimal scaffolding to the Genesis narrative seems to auto-produce or proliferate a series of differing perspectives: life and death inside the Ark; life and death upon landfall; life and death for those not on the ark—or *Not Wanted on the Voyage*, as the title to Timothy Findley's 1984 novel reads.[20] Positions shift; perspectives are imagined, inhabited, imaged, and scripted as the story is read, crucially remediated, and so reanimated by its readers and viewers. In the Chester Corpus Christi

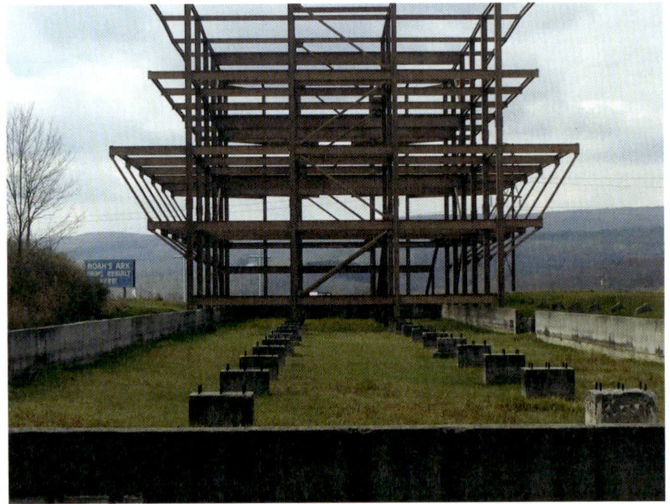

Fig. 2. God's Ark of Safety, Frostburg, Maryland

Cycle, for example, Mrs. Noah is summoned into being in order to voice resistance to the demand that she enter the Ark, leaving her gossips and friends behind to die. "I will not out of this town," she proclaims steadfastly, insisting further that unless "I have my gossips everychone, one foot further I will not gone" and that "they shall not drown."[21] Her resistance becomes a verbal and visual trope in representations that supplement the story of survival and covenant with an overarching sense of loss, or that retell the story as a boisterous, contested affair. Mrs. Noah, with a devil clinging to her back, figures as a patron saint of persistent, passive resistance. In the Chester Cycle, she has to be manhandled aboard (fig. 3). This urge to dwell with and imagine the Flood, to open the Ark to what it leaves behind, to the animals and persons it remainders, proves a compelling and recurring haunt within the visual imagination of medieval and early modern Europe (figs. 4–6). The afterlife of the Genesis story traces a non-consolatory or non-salvific story that testifies to the Ark narrative as very precisely something to inhabit and to think with and through.

Every ark is an invitation, an opportunity to reopen the question of structure and origin, of past, present, and future, even as that gesture of reopening comes premised on the drawing down of limits, the closing of a door, and the making of landfall. Materializing spaces of circumscription and confinement, sorting the various and the volatile into fixity, an ark may function as a museum, chancery, seed vault, biosphere, star craft, zoo, library, factory farm, slave ship, database, repository. Every ark preserves at a cost. To engineer such a structure is to perform a gesture of despair and desire at once: despondency for an Earth not to be saved, confidence that after disaster abates, a better home is to come. Yet that "better" conveys a narrowness, begging the question of *better for whom*? An ark is not launched in the expectation of a more survivable or commodious world

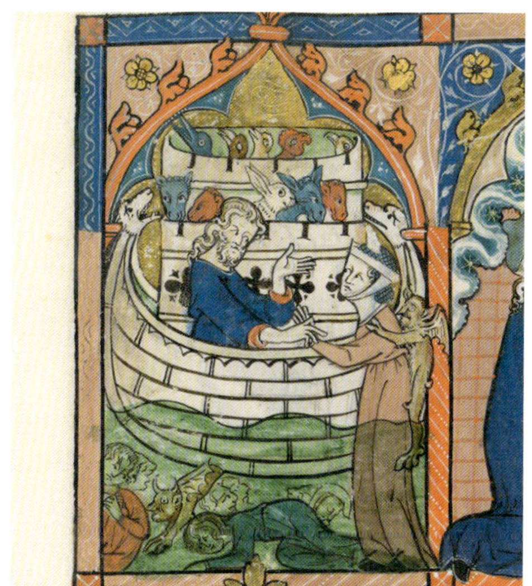

Fig. 3. *Noah's Wife Outside the Ark*, leaf from the Ramsey Psalter, East Anglia or London, England, c. 1300–1310. Painting on vellum, 10 1/2 × 6 1/2 in. (26.8 × 16.5 cm). Medieval Manuscript Folio Records, 256108, The Morgan Library & Museum, New York

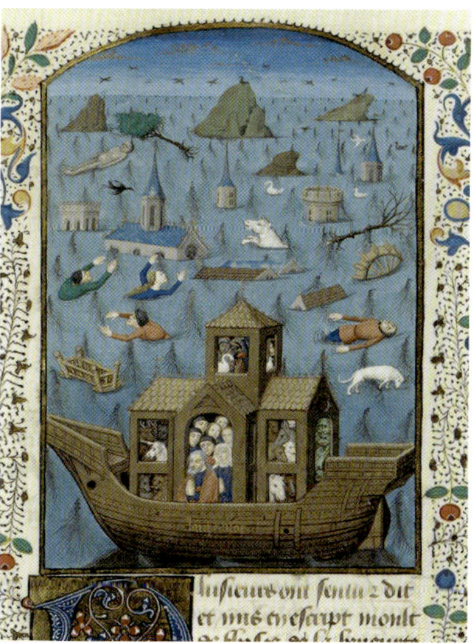

Fig. 4. Master of the Échevinage of Rouen, *The Flood*, from *La Cité de Dieu* (*City of God*), by Saint Augustine, c. 1470–75. Translation by Raoul de Presles. Painted manuscript on vellum, with miniatures and ornamented letters, 18 1/2 × 13 5/8 in. (47 × 34.5 cm). Manuscrits français 28, fol. 66v, Bibliothèque nationale de France, Paris

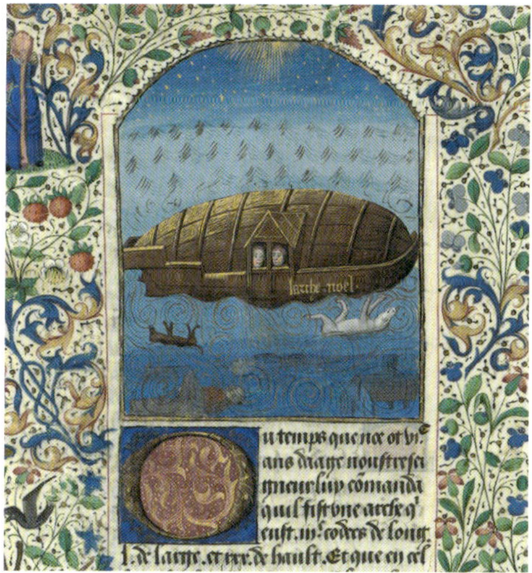

Fig. 5. *Le Livre des hystoires du Mirouer du monde, depuis la création, jusqu'après la dictature de Quintus Cincinnatus*, 1401–1500. Painted manuscript on vellum, with miniatures and ornamented letters. Manuscrits français 328, fol. 4v. Bibliothèque nationale de France, Paris

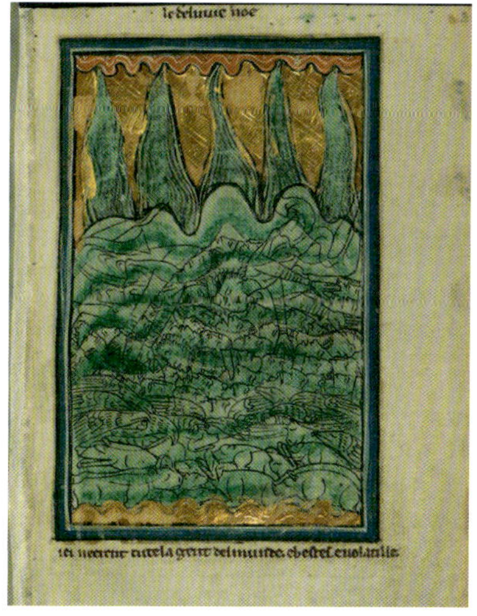

Fig. 6. William de Brailes (British, active c. 1230), *The Flood of Noah*, c. 1250. Ink and pigment on parchment, 5 3/16 × 3 3/4 in. (13.2 × 9.5 cm). The Walters Art Museum, Baltimore. Acquired by Henry Walters, Baltimore, June 6, 1903, by purchase; Walters Art Museum, 1931, by bequest (W.106.3R)

for all who dwelled upon its lands before and within catastrophe. Selective and small, its spaces are closed against a cosmic diversity of humans and nonhumans, conserving meager community against general ruin. Arks easily become prisons. Yet entangled within the closing of alternatives every ark attempts, the trajectories it sails will veer unexpectedly, will offer the unbolting of unforeseen possibilities. The same ark that reduces boisterous lives to sortable, storable units and attempts to regulate the plots of the stories it conveys will inevitably open up the imagination. An ark, so it seems, attempts to assert human agency within, upon, and against a world of noncompliant nonhuman actors, refusing containment. But as Damisch, Abbé Mallet, and Bishop Wilkins agree, creatures, elements, storms, oceans, climate, toxins, atoms, time, and every other force and object placed at the exterior of the ark environs, pushes back. There is an architecture that solicits these inhuman actors, that seeks to process the word "catastrophe" as several, a continual overturning that might alter our very sense of structure. Such is the effect, as we saw, of finding architecture's origin in the story of the Ark—in the unstable, non-foundations of the sea. To drown beneath a surge is not always to lose story, voice, and agency.

Of course, not all arks are mobile (fig. 7). The ark is always more of a floating building than a ship. In *The Age of Stupid* (2009), a documentary made in anticipation of the United Nations Climate Change Conference in Copenhagen

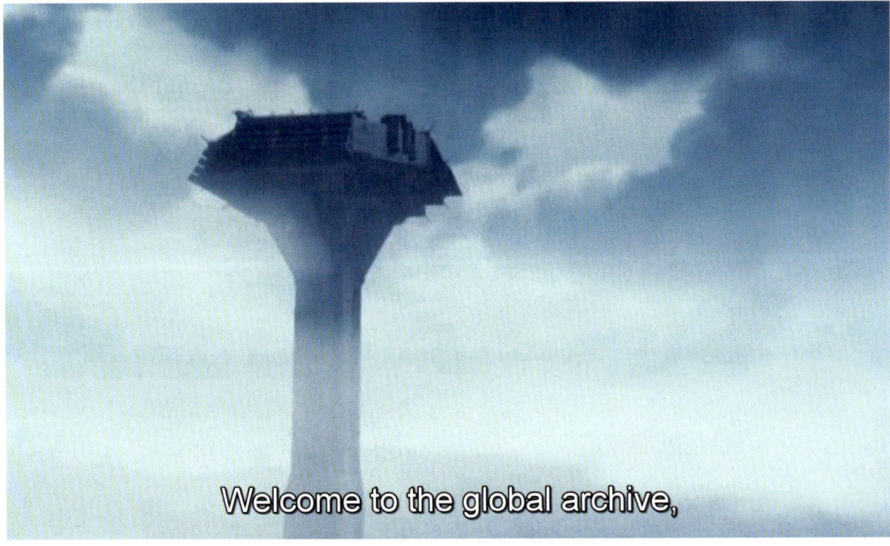

Fig. 7. Screenshot from *The Age of Stupid*, directed by Franny Armstrong (London: Spanner Films, 2009), DVD

in 2009, we meet a family-less Noah in the year 2055, playing the role of "the archivist." He welcomes us to the "global archive," a repository of pickled specimens of animals along with all the treasures of the art world, and records of human achievement, gathered together 800 kilometers north of Norway. You could be forgiven for thinking that this wind-powered building or tower, reaching up to the sky, epitomizes something closer to an ill-timed, after-the-fact Tower of Babel than to an ark. After all, it houses a sort of species-wide retrospective of human making (the pickled animals are also the products of human making) whose purpose now seems unclear, as no visitors queue to enter the museum turned mausoleum. But then the story of the Tower of Babel, that story of a human-authored, technological superlative that aspires to join all nations, peoples, and languages, runs in tandem with the differently timed and patterned story of the Flood. Indeed, the figure of this "global archive" might be said to hybridize the two stories, offering itself as both a repository/archive and a communication device that might commute the sins of climate change.

The film unfolds as the archivist attempts to understand how it may be that the human race managed to know that climate change was happening and failed to address it. How could the current circumstance have come to pass? The very texture of the film wrestles with the difficulty posed in recognizing climate change, in taking cognizance (again, and again, and again) and so owning, inhabiting, living in and up to the reality, of making, environing, and building within the altered circumstances of anthropogenic climate change—of understanding the ark in architecture. The film's structure juxtaposes many stories: Piers, a clean energy entrepreneur and wind farmer from the United Kingdom who, along with Lisa, his wife, and their kids, likes to go skiing in the French Alps; Fernand, their eighty-six-year-old guide, who lives on the glacier, protests the increase in traffic through the Alps, and offers firsthand testimony to how much the glacier has retreated since he was a boy; Jey, heir to a communications fortune in India, who launches India's third budget airline; Alvin, a chemist for oil companies off the coast of Florida, who experienced Hurricane Katrina firsthand, becoming something of a local hero after ferrying his friends, neighbors, acquaintances, and strangers, along with their pets and potted plants, to higher ground in a time of flood; Layefa, who works to become a doctor as she and her family scrape by in Nigeria in an economy decimated by big oil and a community terrorized by violence; Adnan and Jamila, children in an Iraqi refugee family now in Jordan, whose father was killed by United States soldiers.

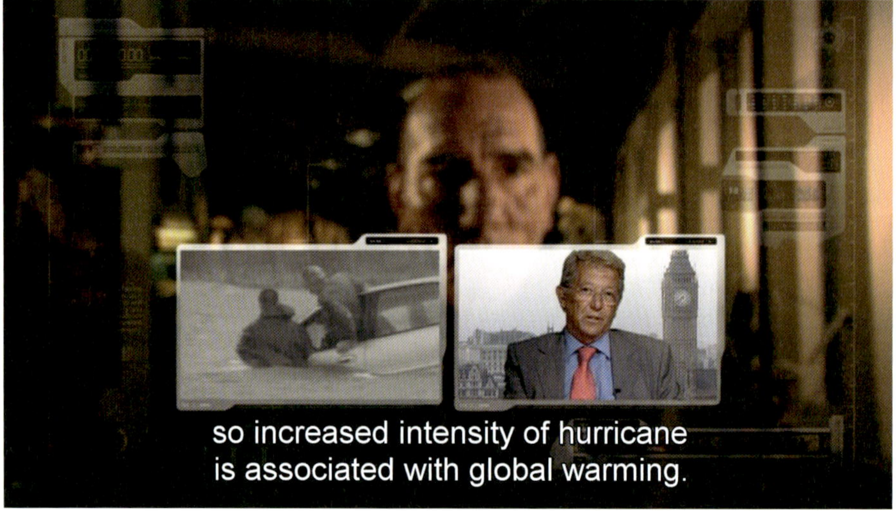

Fig. 8. Screenshot from *The Age of Stupid*, directed by Franny Armstrong (London: Spanner Films, 2009), DVD

The archivist summons up these stories as he searches the global archive for references to climate change in 2009, the year that might have counted. A succession of screens in the ark/tower become media ecology enables us to perceive the interpenetration and so relatedness of stories, localities, and sites via the juxtaposition of images and video (fig. 8). This retrospective solo media ecology enables the synoptic "god trick" that makes recognition possible. Although already in 2009, and especially now, given that we have passed the projected "tipping point" of 2011, this ecology proves solipsistic. The film periodically returns to images of Fernand's little roped party of glacier walkers that includes Piers and family as an image of the social, or sociality as the linkages between persons, animals, plants, and conditions that appear unrelated or at a distance. The roped party is, of course, the privileged icon of our condition in Michel Serres's *The Natural Contract* (1990).[22] But even as the film aspires, by the interlacing of images, stories, and places, to produce the praxis of the roped party, recruiting its viewers to reduce their emissions and lobby on behalf of carbon taxes or credits come Copenhagen, the retrospective cast to its 2055 inquiry proves at best salutary.

"So why did I build this archive?" asks the archivist as the film nears its apocalypse. "It's a cautionary tale," he offers from his eerie, last man scenario and extinction narrative. It is now that the archivist reveals the true purpose of this ark or tower (fig. 9). A few touches to the screen that frames his face sends the

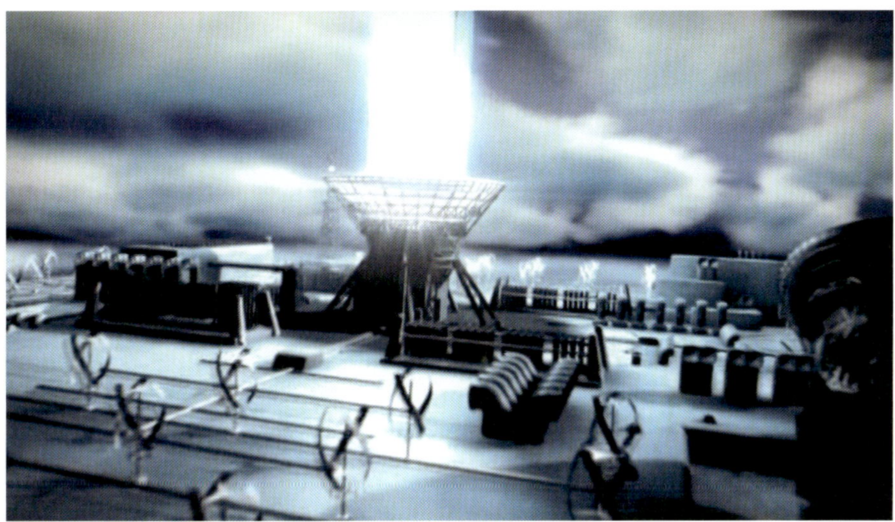

Fig. 9. Screenshot from *The Age of Stupid*, directed by Franny Armstrong (London: Spanner Films, 2009), DVD

message on its way and the ark/tower broadcasts the records of his search—or perhaps the entirety of the archive of human making—skyward, addressing whatever unknown beings might one day receive it. This radio wave is pictured as a flash of white light, a blinding techno-magical broadcast to the beyond that renders sublime the banal inability of the movie's mixed media imaging to render recognition of anthropogenic climate change as something we own, take cognizance of, and act upon. How could we not act? We were living, so it turns out, not in the Anthropocene or any of the other newly available names for our epoch, but, as Alvin the oil worker remarks, in *The Age of Stupid*.

Like the makers of this documentary, we subscribe to the necessity of mixed media, to a promiscuity of story, time, and place in the hopes of some future efficacy grounded in the actions of our present. It's the last man narrative that gives us pause. It's the loading of the ark with pickled animals and buried treasures we resist. Ark thinking demands more, we think, we know. Indeed, ark thinking already arrives crowded with differently timed historical persons and places who by their encounter with the story of the Flood have offered themselves as the wetware of ecological thought. Everyone who builds and boards an ark, whether they identify themselves as a Noah or not, is merely the latest and newest inhabitant.

These other voices and stories subsist within the skeletal arc and archive of the Genesis narrative and return in particular historical moments. In fact, we can feel one welling up inside us now. A flood of arks is coming that contributes to our ark thinking, our attempt, like Damisch, not to make concepts, as Gilles Deleuze and Félix Guattari write is the function of philosophy, but to displace them—to own and inhabit, and motivate all that the ark appears to decide.[23]

Flood

Not all arks reach landfall. Or, sometimes, come landfall, the ark disgorges another flood. The transport the story provides, from one world to another, from one covenant to another, fails to convince or to console. The rainbow pales. The story isolates and overwhelms. The ark's landfall provokes. It provides not relief and gratitude that we stand now on dry land, survivors of a watery violence that drowned not simply flora and fauna, but whole forms of life, whole environments. The Flood comes to register instead as an attack not on the so-called unrighteous but on the very "human-ambient thing without which people cannot remain people," a primordial act of environmental terror that "uses violence against the very air that groups breathe," the "air, the atmosphere—the primary media for life."[24] The creator, who breathed life into us all, engulfs the walking, talking clay he had sculpted and animated, with a medium that stills that being, transforms the autonomic facticity of breathing into a reflex for dying. Sometimes, against the arc of the ark, by its landing, by and through its attempt to communicate the good news that we who breathe today draw that breath from the lungs of Noah and his family, inheritors of the divine gift of air conditioning that was the Ark, the story provokes not joy or gratitude but horror. News of the Flood, narrating the Flood, produces a compensatory outpouring of affect, of feeling, a reciprocal movement of energy that seeks to recognize, remark, buoy, or even to revive all that has been lost. We sit open mouthed. We breathe. Then comes the noise, the anguish and anger, the air in our lungs—a medium that animates this loss, this terror, this outrage.

Artist Ellen O'Grady captures a vivid moment of such storytelling gone wrong, of an object lesson gone awry, in her book of pictures and handwritten words, *Outside the Ark: An Artist's Journey in Occupied Palestine* (2005). "When I was a little kid," she explains, "my favorite fantasy book was a Hallmark version of the Noah's Ark story." Her dream was to dwell comfortably within a family ark, a houseboat that was also a floating zoo. No matter how cold the rain outside, "inside the ark, all of us were warm and safe."[25] At Sunday school, however, everything changes. Her teacher Mrs. Graff reads the Noah's Ark story aloud to

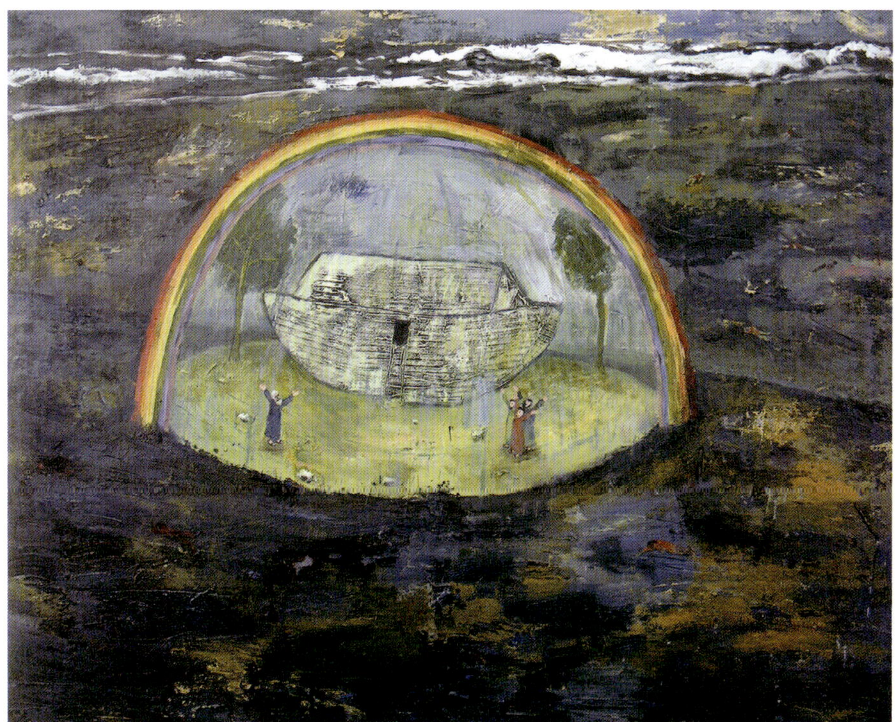

Fig. 10. Ellen O'Grady (American, b. 20th century), *Snowglobe Ark*, 2002. Mixed media on canvas, 36 × 48 in. (91.4 × 121.9 cm). Illustration in *Outside the Ark: An Artist's Journey in Occupied Palestine* (Durham: 55 Books, 2005)

her class. "When she came to the part about the floodwaters drying up," O'Grady writes, "she held the book open to the picture of the sturdy, gleaming ark surrounded after the flood by the lush green trees and colorful plants, all under the beautiful rainbow in the sky" (fig. 10). The author goes on to add that "the entire class was entranced except for Joel, the boy sitting beside me. Joel stared at the picture . . . and yelled suddenly."

"'WHERE ARE ALL THE BODIES?!?'"

"Our teacher looked puzzled and annoyed. She put her book down."

"'WHAT BODIES, JOEL?'"

"'THE BODIES!' he cried. 'WHERE ARE ALL THE BODIES OF THE PEOPLE AND THE ANIMALS THAT DIED IN THE FLOOD?!'"

Mrs. Graff "narrowed her eyes" and in a "gravelly, disapproving voice she told Joel he was 'a VERY RUDE BOY.'"[26] Joel resisted. Landfall and the rainbow fail to "entrance." Joel, whose world is not to be contained within a finalizing rainbow—a boy whose name literally, ironically, affirms that God is God (יוֹאֵל [Yo'el] signifies "YAHWEH is God")—refused to be transported. Or, more correctly, there is something to the telling of this story, something to Mrs. Graff's well-intentioned reading aloud, that transports only too well, that works upon the imaginative faculties of the little boy such that when she turns the book around, holds it "open to the picture of the sturdy, gleaming ark surrounded after the flood by the lush green trees and colorful plants, all under the beautiful rainbow in the sky," the transfer from the time-bound linearity of words in their telling to the synoptic image of landfall appalls. The reduction of the telling, which provokes a succession of nightmare images in Joel's imagination, to the good news of landfall provokes his grief, his outrage, his lament, and his question: "WHERE ARE ALL THE BODIES?" Joel, who indeed affirms, attends, objects. For him, the ark he conjures in his imagination resists the reduction that occurs come the moment of disembarkation. Joel refuses the disappearance that the switch from words to an image that would replace his own succession of images, would allow. Indeed, the oscillation of story, image, and imagined pictures, renders the story of the Ark mobile.

"As Joel's disquiet over the shiny, rainbow version of Noah's rescue narrative suggests, stories—tightly framed for time and space, and point of view—are convenient places for concealing bodies," observes Rob Nixon.[27] But Joel does not merely denounce this absence. He identifies the way the final image of landfall, with its "lush green trees and colorful plants," with its parade of cleansed animal bodies, exists quite precisely also as the going missing of the drowned. The explosion of Joel's words stands in strict relation to the vividness of this image that erases. But, so too, his question, his demand—which "puzzles and annoys"—signals the way the skeletal outline of the Genesis story produces, quasi-automatically, affectively charged counter-images in other media to the arc that this Ark appears to complete. The rainbow is a shimmering weapon. The Ark is a mixed media archive whose opening, come landfall, figures also as disintegration, its wake littered with affective flotsam and jetsam.

Joel's question makes an impression more lasting than the intended ending in rainbow.

"When our teacher continued with her story," writes O'Grady, "holding up for us that glorious rainbow in the book, I saw the bodies."

"Lifeless bodies lying across the weather-beaten landscape. Some bodies lived in the safe and protected ark, while some bodies drowned in the holy flood."

"It was the first time I was aware that there can be a story behind a story. A story we try to hide" (fig. 11).[28]

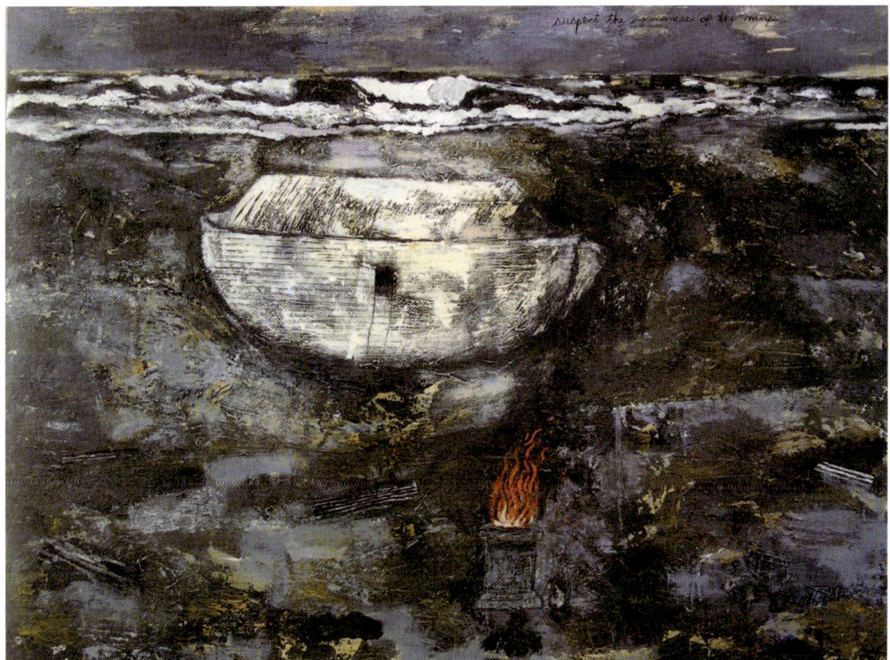

Fig. 11. Ellen O'Grady, *Suspect the Soundness of Maps*, 2002. Mixed media on canvas, 36 × 48 in. (91.4 × 121.9 cm). Collection of Michael Davey. Illustration in *Outside the Ark: An Artist's Journey in Occupied Palestine* (Durham: 55 Books, 2005)

Because Mrs. Graff reads the story aloud; because, for Joel, the images in the book do not accord with the images in his mind; because Joel asks his question; because Mrs. Graff handles things badly; a girl recognizes something of the way in which stories hide other stories, hold them in abeyance. The artist this girl becomes draws them—supplementing both the story of Noah and his Ark and producing a series of images that seeks to visualize the bodies and lives that go missing in the representation of occupied Palestine. Joel's interrogative leads O'Grady to wonder about what Noah actually beheld when he disembarked his little space of safety and so what Noah might have omitted from the narrative sent forward into history: "Did he speak only about a rainbow high in the sky and remain silent about the things he saw in the water and on the ground?"[29]

Landfall names the *topos* or moment at which a terrestrializing, localizing perspective grounds the mobility of the Ark story, here and now. And like Joel, like Noah's wife, we are flooded with the desire to keep writing and introduce you to so many more refugees, stowaways, or also-rans from the Ark story who ask us to imagine and so to fill in what goes missing when catastrophe is narrated. Indeed, we end this essay by refusing landfall and welcoming aboard the ark a whole school of questioning Joels: rude boys and girls; dubious, just, and affirmative narrators; attentive readers who find possibility in present and omitted detail. The flood of feeling that momentarily engulfs these creatures is also the story of ark thinking, of a story, which, for all its landing, knows that any covenant, any act that secures, that agrees to new air conditions, hides within its seeming completion "the stories behind the stories" (as O'Grady glosses Joel's searching query), the bodies of the dead.

Manifest

What we have called ark thinking proceeds by refusing to allow a story or the act of building to close, and the structure to be finished, its limits decided.[30] This act of thinking or concept troubling is not an act of un-building so much as a misuse or repurposing of times and spaces. It displaces concepts in the sense that Damisch and the setting of a building in motion (a building that must float) demand. As a reading practice, then, ark thinking refuses landfall. It aims to move between and among the disjunctive perspectives the story of the Ark generates, intermingling them, inhabiting them, and so exploring the contours and costs of an act of building. Not anti-historicist, this mode of reading is at least more than historicist, in that it includes the excess that historicism seeks to reduce. It refuses to assume only the point of view of the characters within the driving or main plot of the narrative, the authority figures who keep their intended storylines and pasts and futures locked in watertight archives. It refuses the pre-given narrative arc of the Ark—or prefers to notice and to note the way in which while Noah stories are so often about origins, nothing is all that original about them. In general, it prefers the company of those excluded from the ark: the wives and children who do not get to speak as they are ushered aboard; the ravens and the doves and the peacocks and the lions and maybe even the gopher wood of the naval timber that populate this ark. As a mode of textual and cultural analysis, it follows the most imaginative vectors of the story, sometimes even going overboard to dwell with the sea creatures who make their homes in the drowned cities now open to wandering. As an interpretive ethics, ark thinking stands with the drowned, or follows the wayward trajectories of the hungry raven away from the security of the ark and home.

Against what Donna Haraway has called "the god trick" (which pretends that the truth is to be discerned from above, from an abstract and disembodied perspective that privileges distance and detachment), ark thinking strives for saturated and embodied ways of knowing.[31] Always mobile, it grounds itself in the positions of actors or actants in the ark and the stories it proliferates. Ark thinking shifts positions—sometimes strategically, sometimes tactically—knowing that perspectives are always embodied, time-bound operations.[32] It is unafraid of affect and finds itself inundated, engulfed, submerged, in turbulent activations. Because it moves through air and water (and stone and fire)—because it is not willingly immured or immobilized—ark thinking means recognizing and embracing errant trajectories as we attempt to hold open the architecture of our arks, to widen the temporary refuge they offer, and we surrender to the multiple catastrophes in whose stead the ark in architecture emerges.

1. For a sense of the stakes about what to name our present moment, see, among others, Donna Haraway, *Staying with the Trouble: Making Kin in Chthulucene* (Durham: Duke University Press, 2016), 99–103; and *The Anthropocene and the Global Environmental Crisis: Rethinking Modernity in a New Epoch*, ed. Clive Hamilton, Christophe Bonneuil, and François Gemenne (London: Routledge, 2015).

2. Hubert Damisch, *Noah's Ark: Essay on Architecture*, ed. Anthony Vidler, trans. Julie Rose (Cambridge: MIT Press, 2016), 23. The essay originally appeared as "L'Arche de Noé," in *Revue Critique* 43 (January–February 1987).

3. For Damisch's self-description, see Hubert Damisch and Stephen Bann, "Hubert Damisch and Stephen Bann: A Conversation," *Oxford Art Journal* 28, no. 2 (2005): 159; quoted also in Damisch, *Noah's Ark*, xi.

4. Damisch, *Noah's Ark*, 1.

5. Ibid., 7. Throughout, Damisch quotes from the *Encyclopédie, ou dictionnaire raisonné des sciences, des arts et des métiers*, vol. 1, ed. Denis Diderot and Jean Le Rond d'Alembert (Paris, 1751).

6. Damisch, *Noah's Ark*, 9.

7. Ibid., 15.

8. Ibid., 18.

9. Ibid., 21–22.

10. John Wilkins, *An Essay Towards the Real Character of Philosophical Language* (London, 1668), 162–68.

11. On the dis-animating arithmetic of "livestock" as its origins find themselves routed from Noah's Ark, through early modern imaginary arithmetic, to the horrors of the "middle passage" and on to the interchangeable infrastructures of container ships, see Laurie Shannon, *The Accommodated*

Animal, Cosmopolity in Shakespearean Locales (Chicago: University of Chicago Press, 2013), 270–83.

12. Damisch quoting Mallet, "Arche," in *Encyclopédie*, vol. 1, 607. Mallet draws on Wilkins, *An Essay*, 168.

13. Damisch, *Noah's Ark*, 17.

14. Ibid., 23.

15. Ibid.

16. McKenzie Wark, "From Architecture to Kainotecture," in *Accumulation, e-flux* (April 2017), paragraph 1, http://www.e-flux.com/architecture/accumulation/122201/from-architecture-to-kainotecture/ (accessed November 20, 2017). See the epigraph for this essay.

17. Damisch's trouble with Blondel's entry in the *Encyclopédie* by way of Noah's Ark resonates with an earlier instance in which water seeps into the foundations of the history of architecture: Leon Battista Alberti's lost treatise on naval construction and building *De Navis*, which Leonardo da Vinci knew and refers to in *On Painting*. Indeed, the history of naval construction as a theoretical concern might be said to designate a watery supplement to the history of architecture. The prospect of building without a secure foundation, of building at sea, exposes architecture to invasion by what it seeks to manage or exclude. For a consideration of the evidence for what *De Navis* might have contained in the context of a larger interest in shipbuilding among Renaissance humanists, see Ennio Concina, "Humanism on the Sea," *Mediterranean Historical Review* 3, no. 1 (1988): 159–65. We are grateful to Christopher P. Heuer for alerting us to this confluence.

18. Wark, "From Architecture to Kainotecture," paragraph 4.

19. The etymology of the word "ark" is itself something of a bewitched spot in the annals of "arkana." Damisch offers one redaction in "Noah's Ark," 18–19. Two especially fine synopses of etymologies past are to be found in Daniel Anlezark's *Water and Fire: The Myth of the Flood in Anglo-Saxon England* (Manchester: Manchester University Press, 2006); and Sarah Elliott Novacich, *Shaping the Archive in Medieval England: History, Poetry, and Performance* (Cambridge: Cambridge University Press, 2017).

20. Timothy Findley, *Not Wanted on the Voyage* (Toronto: Penguin Canada, 2006 [1984]).

21. *The Chester Mystery Cycle*, ed. David Mills (East Lansing: Colleagues Press, 1991), lines 200–204.

22. Michel Serres, *The Natural Contract*, trans. Elizabeth MacArthur and William Paulson (Ann Arbor: University of Michigan Press, 1995), 103–4.

23. Gilles Deleuze and Félix Guattari, *What is Philosophy?* trans. Hugh Tomlinson and Graham Burchell (New York: Columbia University Press, 1994).

24. Peter Sloterdijk, *Terror from the Air*, trans. Amy Patton and Steve Corcoran (Los Angeles: Semiotext[e], 2007), 25–26.

25. Ellen O'Grady, *Outside the Ark: An Artist's Journey in Occupied Palestine* (Durham: 55 Books, 2005), 2.

26. Ibid., 4–6.

27. Rob Nixon, *Slow Violence and the Environmentalism of the Poor* (Cambridge: Harvard University Press, 2011), 200.

28. O'Grady, *Outside the Ark*, 8.

29. Ibid., 44.

30. On the violence of decision as cutting or the creation of an edge, in different registers, and as an act to be troubled and resisted, see, in different contexts, Serres, *The Natural Contract*, 55, and Jacques Derrida, *The Gift of Death*, trans. David Wills (Chicago: University of Chicago Press, 1995), 53–82.

31. Donna Haraway, "Situated Knowledges: The Science Question in Feminism and the Privilege of Partial Perspective," in *Simians, Cyborgs, and Women: The Reinvention of Nature* (New York: Routledge, 1991), 188–89.

32. On this formulation of tactics as momentary occupations or transformation of space and therefore as time-bound, see Michel de Certeau, *The Practice of Everyday Life*, trans. Steven Rendall (Berkeley: University of California Press, 1984), 29–42.

The Entropic History of Ice

Maggie M. Cao

In a recent work called *The Distance Between What We Have and What We Want* (*Arctic Ice Project*), the New York–based Bahamian artist Tavares Strachan harvested a 4.5-ton block of ice in Alaska and sent it by FedEx to his native Nassau, where it was kept frozen through a hot summer in a solar-powered freezer (fig. 1).[1] For Strachan, ice is a powerful medium, with certain sculptural qualities. Thus encased, it recalls a minimalist cube behind gallery glass. Yet ice is not so much a material as a *state*—one defined by tenuous chemical bonds, which means that Strachan's rigid block is constantly at entropic risk of melting, losing its ideal form or altogether vanishing.

In Strachan's piece, the potential ruination of the encased ice block speaks to both dark futures and troubling pasts. In its aesthetic, sculptural qualities, the artwork gestures toward environmental crisis—a topic often communicated today

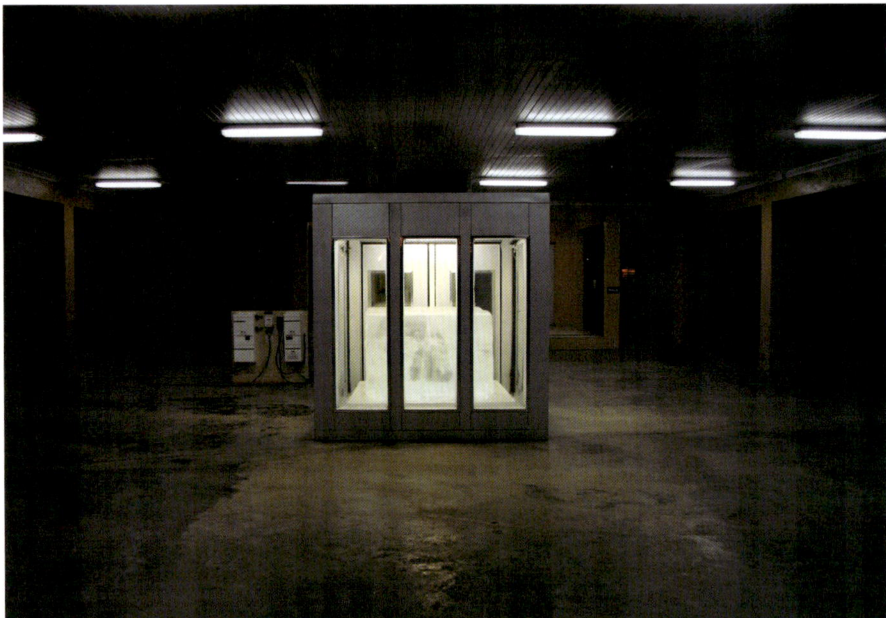

Fig. 1. Tavares Strachan (Bahamian, b. 1979), *Chamber with Ice: Elevator for the Reversal of Up and Down*, 2006, in *The Distance Between What We Have and What We Want*. Ice, refrigeration unit, solar panels, fans, flags, battery system, 96 × 120 × 96 in. (243.8 × 304.8 × 243.8 cm)

though images of majestic glaciers and stunning icebergs. Indeed, the ecological catastrophes on our horizon have led to a growing global consciousness about the material conditions of ice—we think of it as melting now more than ever. Yet the *geographies* of Strachan's piece ask us to look not forward, but back to our colonial pasts. The ice block's southbound route inverts the trajectory usually taken by perishable commodities—ones that travel in cooled containers not unlike the artist's. Moreover, the delicate technological equilibrium achieved in Nassau maps the ironic intimacy between the frigid North and torrid South that has long governed our global economy.

Although treating ice as *medium* is a more recent development in the history of art, a recognition of the unique aesthetic power of ice as *matter* is not. What follows is an attempt to locate the origins of the technological and commercial conditions thematized in *Arctic Ice Project*. I want to suggest that the historical encounters to which Strachan's artwork gestures, particularly in its spatial traversals, originate in an earlier moment when ice similarly loomed large: mid-nineteenth-century America, the heyday of Arctic exploration and global shipping.

Nineteenth-century artists and writers attempting to visualize the northern reaches of the hemisphere in paintings, prints, photographs, and prose imagined ice as an artistic material full of contradictions. In its seeming solidity yet ever-present liquidity, ice accumulated aesthetic, economic, and political meanings for Americans. In suggesting that Strachan's work gestures toward this history, I want to do more than offer an interpretation of his artwork by way of historical digression. Rather, I want to suggest that nineteenth-century encounters with frozen matter share with contemporary interventions by Strachan and other artists an awareness of ice as a material embedded in technological and economic concerns as well as natural and ecological ones.

As such, the history of ice presented here reveals the intersection of environmental and political imperialisms that have long fueled our dreams and fears of entropy. The melting Arctic is entropic in the simple sense. A nineteenth-century term from the laws of thermodynamics, "entropy" describes the tendency for matter in a closed system to reach a stable equilibrium: ice melts as the temperature of Earth's ecosystem increases. But the history recounted here is entropic in an expanded sense as well, for entropy also implies matter's tendency toward decay and formlessness. As such, the "entropic" supplies this history of ice with a fitting set of oppositions—of stability and chaos, passivity and agency, cold and hot—that expose the undercurrents of colonialism and racial politics in the aestheticizing of frozen worlds both then and now.

Picturing the Arctic

In the summer of 1859, the renowned American landscape painter Frederic Edwin Church and the art writer Louis Legrand Noble set out on a voyage "after icebergs." Their destination was the icy bays of Labrador and Newfoundland, where, as Noble later explained in his travel chronicle, icebergs and facilities for "studying and sketching them" abound.[2] Upon their return, Church undertook to paint his mammoth 1861 canvas *The Icebergs*, a panoramic rendering of a watery cove framed by towering cliffs, tunnels, and shelves, all of shimmering ice (fig. 2). The corresponding textual narrative, *After Icebergs with a Painter*, published by Noble that same year, was no less dramatic with its over three hundred pages of sublime and picturesque prose.

Church and Noble were among the many nineteenth-century Americans who ventured north to examine the continent's icebound regions. Mass culture enthusiasm for the Arctic had reached a fever pitch by the 1850s in the wake of several well-publicized commercial and scientific expeditions.[3] When the scientist Elisha Kane published his *Arctic Explorations*, an immensely popular account of the second Grinnell Expedition in 1855, it was said to have joined the Bible on "every parlor table in America."[4] And when Kane died two years later, his funeral

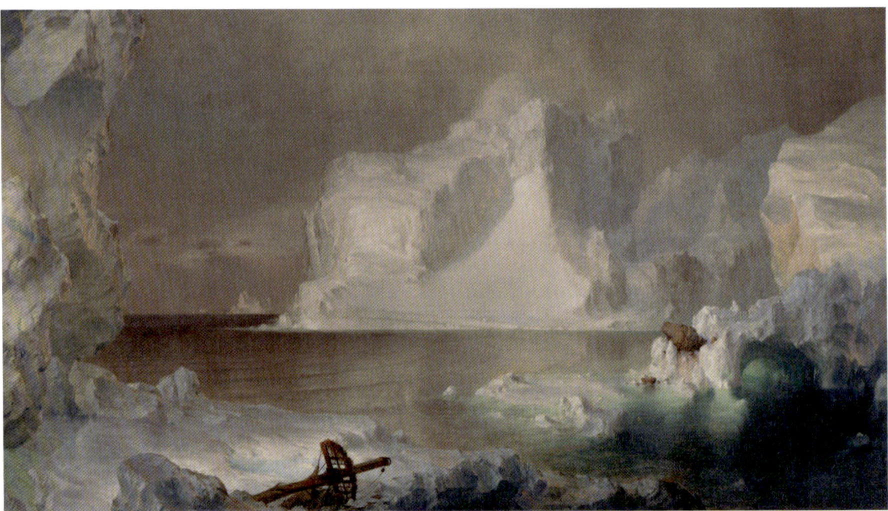

Fig. 2. Frederic Edwin Church (American, 1826–1900), *The Icebergs*, 1861. Oil on canvas, 64 1/2 × 112 1/2 in. (163.8 × 285.7 cm). Dallas Museum of Art. Gift of Norma and Lamar Hunt (1979.28)

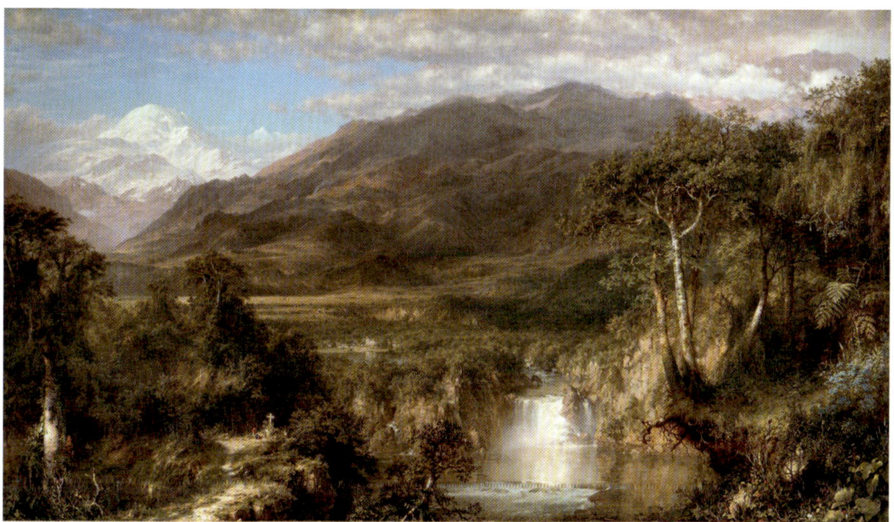

Fig. 3. Frederic Edwin Church, *The Heart of the Andes*, 1859. Oil on canvas, 66 ⅛ × 119 ¼ in. (168 × 302.9 cm). The Metropolitan Museum of Art, New York. Bequest of Margaret E. Dows, 1909 (09.95)

train was met at nearly every platform from New Orleans to Philadelphia by a memorial delegation that is said to rival only Lincoln's in the nineteenth century.[5]

Ever an enterprising artist, Frederic Church no doubt had aims to create the next Arctic masterpiece. Church's northbound journey followed the completion of his colossal South American landscape *Heart of the Andes* (fig. 3), which debuted with roaring success in New York and was poised to go on national tour (it would quickly become the most popular display of a single artwork in the Civil War era).[6] For his Arctic showpiece, Church incorporated signature elements of his landscape practice—dramatic topography and richly delineated detail. Yet these visual strategies, for which he had been praised in the reception of *Heart of the Andes*, only confounded viewers when transplanted from the fecund tropics to the frozen world. While beholders of *The Icebergs* today may be particularly attuned to its excess—the blindingly turquoise glowing caves and endless glimmering bluffs and spires arrayed across the nine-foot-wide canvas—period critics were troubled by the picture's blankness and formlessness.[7]

"One hardly knows what to say about it," began a critic for the *Boston Transcript*, who found it "difficult to realize that it [the painting] is a representation of nature." Another reviewer noted that "it will require some time to get even on speaking terms of the 'Icebergs.'" The scene resembled that "day of creation when the Earth was without form and void," mused another. For these viewers, the lack of human narrative in such an otherworldly landscape was troubling. "No trace of human associations whatsoever," reads one review, leads to "a complete abnegation of extrinsic interest."[8] (The broken mast in the foreground—suggesting a human footprint—was only added later, in 1863, perhaps in response to such criticism). With so much to look at, nineteenth-century viewers apparently found nothing to see.

The anxieties displayed by Church's critics betray the fact that Americans consumed Arctic expeditions in the nineteenth century in the form of narratives. It was narrative—the publication of memoirs, the circulation of images, and the delivery of touring lectures—that turned countless failed expeditions into heroic feats. On another level, the lack of eventfulness in Church's painting recalled genuine fears associated with Arctic encounters, which were liable to end in bodily disappearance—men lost, or worse, devoured in desperate acts of cannibalism. Most famously, the British explorer Sir John Franklin and his crew had disappeared without a trace in 1845, prompting dozens of rescue missions in subsequent decades that retrieved little but frozen relics of their tragic fate.[9]

The Arctic proved a unique challenge to nineteenth-century painters trained in the conventions of landscape, a genre whose narratives of masculine heroism were bound up with the culture of exploration. Following Church, the American artist most associated with the Arctic was William Bradford, who in 1869 organized a similar artistic expedition to the coast of Greenland. Trained as a marine painter, Bradford would go on to build a successful career painting Arctic scenes, which unlike Church's were populated with incident and story line.[10] The problem of unnatural formlessness, while avoided in the paintings themselves, nevertheless defined Bradford's experience in the Arctic itself. Particularly revealing is the artist's travel narrative, published in the form of a lavish, limited-edition album entitled *The Arctic Regions*. In it, Bradford discusses endless optical failures, particularly as they relate to ice and states of matter in general. In one instance, the artist describes seeing "far away on the eastern horizon . . . a low-lying cloud, which some thought another fog bank," though it would later prove to be land. Elsewhere he notes that it is "difficult to distinguish an iceberg from the dark grey rocks in the background." The Arctic, he resolved, was the "complete reversal of the whole order of nature." Ice, in Bradford's account, was particularly troubling and more akin to optical illusion than natural specimen. In their "multiform varieties of mass and outline," Bradford wrote, they resembled "the quick-changing views of a kaleidoscope."[11] Echoing the paradoxical view taken by Church's critics—that a monumental canvas filled with rich details could add up to void and nothingness—Bradford would conclude that Arctic ice was "bewildering" in the "infinite variety of their sameness."[12]

No doubt encounters with the frozen world have long destabilized aesthetic and geographic certainties. For centuries, explorers of the Far North returned to recount landscapes rampant with optical ambiguities and illusions impossible to picture.[13] In nineteenth-century America, artists had to contend not only with these visual challenges but also with their economic implications. For what is unique about this historical moment is that the perceptual paradoxes associated with ice were newly politicized in geographic terms. The American fervor for all things Arctic coincided with an economic globalization that demarcated temperate North and torrid South and, along with it, cold and hot matter.

Ice Breaking

When William Bradford painted scenes like his 1871 *An Arctic Summer: Boring Through the Pack in Melville Bay* (fig. 4), he underscored the fact that icescapes were a subject with global reach. With the inclusion of a tall ship "boring through"

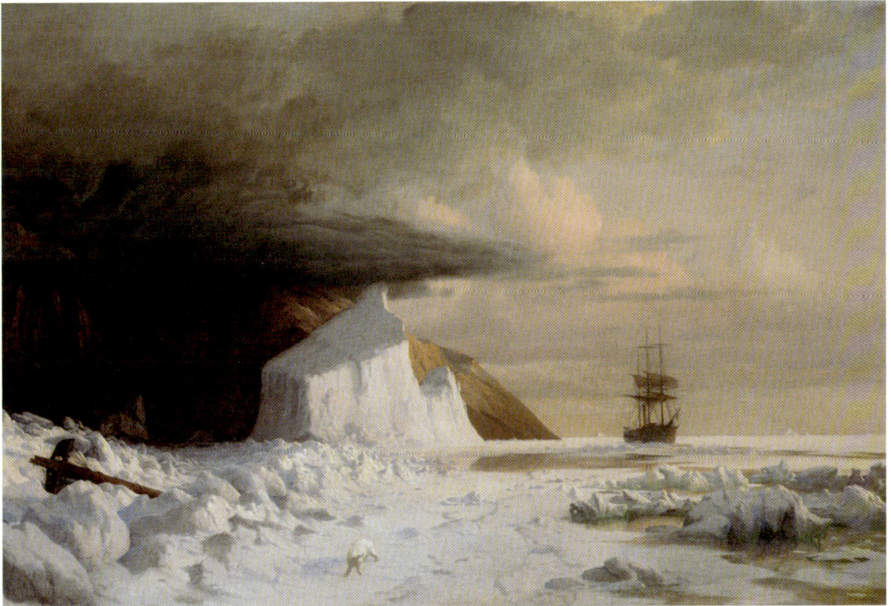

Fig. 4. William Bradford (American, 1823–1892), *An Arctic Summer: Boring Through the Pack in Melville Bay*, 1871. Oil on canvas, 51 3/4 × 78 in. (131.4 × 198.1 cm). The Metropolitan Museum of Art, New York. Gift of Erving and Joyce Wolf, in memory of Diane R. Wolf, 1982 (1982.443.1)

pack ice, as the title tells us, Bradford capitalized on an international, scientific obsession of the day: the hunt for the fabled Northwest Passage, the shortest route between Euro-American ports and trade destinations in East and South Asia. Thus, breaking through Arctic ice, which Bradford's ship is poised to do, meant clearing a route to the tropics. Looking north meant thinking south.

Accounts of a Northwest Passage have circulated since the sixteenth century, but it was pursued with greatest fervor in the nineteenth.[14] A new sea route over North America would drastically reduce costs and time in transpacific shipping, which then required sailors to round Cape Horn at the tip of South America. The British were the most ambitious explorers in the first half of the nineteenth century, followed by the Americans in the century's latter half. Between 1850 and 1910, more than two dozen US-based expeditions entered the Arctic Circle. Though traveling under the guise of humanitarianism (to recover Franklin's lost expedition), each was in hot pursuit of the very same seafaring route that Franklin had so tragically failed to locate.[15] Summing up the Anglo-American tradition of Arctic exploration in 1871, Matthew Maury, the author of *Physical Geography of the Sea*, the standard oceanography text of the period, observed: "Whatever may have been the immediate object of these various expeditions, whether to enlarge the fields of commerce, to carry the Bible, to spread civilization, to push conquest, or to bring back contributions of science, it has never lost sight of the promise made by Columbus of a western route to India."[16]

The possibility of a Northwest Passage structured nineteenth-century understandings of the Arctic's relationship to the rest of the globe. Dreams of global connectedness *sans* ice emerged in all aspects of culture. In 1826, John Cleves Symmes, a war hero turned trader living in the then-frontier settlement of St. Louis, publicized his theory that a hollow inner Earth connected the two poles: if you went far enough northward, he theorized, you would be transported through a hollow shaft to the other side of the world.[17] While the Earth's hollowness had some mathematical precedent, Symmes was the first to propose an expedition to explore what he thought was a habitable inner sphere via the North Pole. As an early American engaged in commerce across distances (he operated an Indian trading post at the frontier), Symmes, perhaps not surprisingly, turned to the rhetoric of globalization to promote his plan. In the treatise he produced with his collaborator James McBride, Symmes argued that such an expedition would be of "immense advantage to our commerce and national prosperity."[18] Though outlandish, the Hollow Earth theory generated considerable popular press attention and was cited as a primary motivation for a government-funded expedition to the South Pole.[19]

Less eccentric theories of a habitable Far North also circulated. Geographers hypothesized that a warm, open sea flowed over the Earth's poles just beyond the subarctic regions. Such balmy polar seas were richly imagined in literary accounts such as Edgar Allan Poe's *The Narrative of Arthur Gordon Pym of Nantucket*. In this 1838 novel, a Nantucket sailor encounters steamy, milky currents and white, ashen rain as he drifts in the Pacific toward the Southern Pole.[20] In the topsy-turvy world of Poe's fiction, the visual blankness associated with the icebound Arctic is populated with the exotic tropes of tropical exploration: the dark-skinned native and his mysticism. By the 1850s, numerous scientific studies were marshalled to prove the existence of more hospitable climes beyond the ice-jammed seas, which had time and again forced explorers to retreat. Observations about the circulation of deep-water currents, high-atmosphere airflows, and animal migrations between the poles and the equatorial regions provided further assurance that the Northwest Passage was more than maritime mythology.[21] Indeed, a best-case scenario would reveal a veritable tropics at the cardinal ends of the Earth. Thus, in claiming that warm, equatorial flows made the frozen North navigable, scientists neatly tied the Arctic (an imaginary tropics) to the true, equatorial tropics in a scientific defense of economic ambitions.

Ice Making

It is no coincidence that the global shipping of perishable commodities dates back to these most self-assured decades of Arctic exploration. As Church and Bradford painted the Arctic, the American ice industry was booming.[22] Large-scale harvesters hacked blocks of ice out of frozen rivers and lakes throughout the Northeast to literally supply the tropics with cold. As the historian of science Rebecca Woods has argued, cold, when harnessed as a technology and commodity, cheats both time and distance, connecting the food chains of North with South, temperate zones with tropical latitudes, metropoles with rural and colonial outposts.[23] It was with the commodification of ice that the tropics became the lifeline of our modern way of life.

In the early to mid-nineteenth-century United States, cold technologies revolved around the management of the material conditions of ice. Ice may have been a renewable resource acquired at no cost, but early entrepreneurs were well aware of its entropic properties. A pioneer in the ice trade, Frederic Tudor (a.k.a. the "Ice King") blamed his initial failures on the absence of environmental controls in his system. Only after investing in cargo-hold insulation and storage depots—the infrastructure and technology for keeping ice frozen—did he meet financial success.[24]

By the 1820s, ice had become an international commodity shipped as far as China and India. American ice companies imagined the global reach of their product from the outset when they identified the Caribbean as their key market. Tudor's first business venture involved sending a cargo of ice to Martinique; he then shifted his focus to establishing a monopoly in Havana. In a draft business plan, he offered investors assurance of the company's "advance in extending . . . [service] to all the tropical places."[25]

Arctic ice and commodity ice carried shared ambitions in the nineteenth century. Both their geographies were bidirectional—linking frozen North and tropical South. In the metropolitan Northeast, cities like New York and Boston, where Church and Bradford were exhibiting their Arctic landscapes, viewers likely connected the otherworldly scenery pictured on their canvases with the commodity harvested from their local rivers and ponds. In Noble's account of Church's expedition, sea ice in Labrador is described as akin to "our summer cakes, handed in by the ice-man."[26] Meanwhile, accounts of industrial ice trading evoked the landscapes of the Arctic. In an article about ice-harvesting technologies, the *Journal of the Franklin Institute* described one innovator in the trade as "the great transporter of icebergs to the torrid regions."[27] (And one did literally serve as the other in that mariners regularly harvested polar ice for storage in ship holds as a source of drinking water when on route to warmer seas.)

The irony in these nineteenth-century encounters is that the commodification of winter ice enabled the very transnational connectedness that polar ice geographically hindered. Both quests for more efficient, global commodity circulation were attempts in environmental and material control—the one icing, the other de-icing, we might say. And neither of these ambitions proved easy to realize. Explorers and mercantilists underestimated the material assertiveness of ice itself—that in melting, it speeds decay, and that in freezing, it entraps and kills. It took many trials before the so-called Ice King mastered the transporting of perishable goods in cargo holds. He eventually patented a method for packing ice with "non-conducting materials" that prevented "wasting, melting, and decaying."[28] On the *anti-freeze* front, we might say that nineteenth-century American expeditions found neither a warm polar sea nor Sir John Franklin's ships safe and sound.

They returned instead only with rumors of the lost crew's resort to cannibalism, the most dreaded end conceivable in maritime culture. (In fact, Franklin's ships were discovered only in recent years, in part because of melting sea ice in northern Canada.[29]) By the opening of the next century, Arctic exploration had shifted from searching for open routes to conquering the magnetic pole, and ice harvesting had largely been replaced by chemical-based compressed air refrigeration. And with that, the era of managing the material conditions of ice would end.

Ungrounding

It was precisely the nineteenth century's preoccupation with managing ice that shaped the way Arctic landscapes were perceived. Unlike Bradford's paintings of de-icing in action, Church's *Icebergs* was deemed unmanageable because it presented matter in a state of variability and volatility without signs of material control. In declaring itself a landscape painting, this absence was further compounded, for landscape was the American genre most associated with constructing narratives of industrial advancement tied to nature.[30]

The American discourse on landscape imagined a viewer in possession of land through his visual control from a privileged point, often in the picture's middle ground. In 1849, a critic in the *Bulletin of the American Art-Union* advised painters to include in their compositions "an open space on which the vision may rest—a patch of lawn or broad surface of rock . . . the place where we must be . . . an open place, where at least we may stand . . . this rule is of the first consequence."[31] In other words, the ideological machinery of nineteenth-century landscape relied on the illusion of solid earth because such fixed positions enabled viewers to imaginatively participate in narratives of national progress. Nowhere is this trope more visible than in Asher B. Durand's aptly entitled *Progress: The Advance of Civilization* (1853; fig. 5), a painting in which figures moving along the winding waterside path from foreground to background, in wagons, boats, and then trains, naturalized a narrative of westward expansion tethered to technological evolution.

Both Church and Bradford sought to connect ice to the physically sound matter of more familiar, terrestrial landscapes. Although his painting was lacking in narrative, Church still imagined *Icebergs* in earthbound terms borrowed from his earlier landscapes. In a broadside accompanying the painting's exhibition, the author, likely Church himself, locates the viewer at a privileged viewpoint commanding the surrounding space. "The spectator is supposed to be standing on

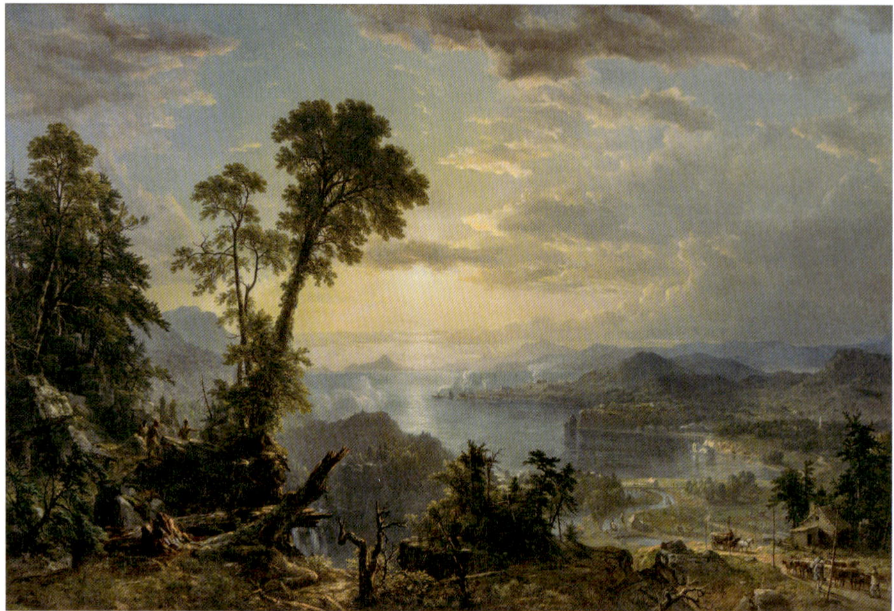

Fig. 5. Asher B. Durand (American, 1796–1886), *Progress: The Advance of Civilization*, 1853. Oil on canvas, 48 × 72 in. (121.9 × 182.9 cm). Location unknown

the ice," the narrative begins; "imagine an amphitheater, upon the lower steps of which you stand, and see the icy foreground at your feet, and gaze upon the surrounding masses, all united in one beneath the surface of the sea."[32] The text provides assurance of the spectator's all-encompassing vista and describes ice as a conquerable surface within a navigable landscape, solid despite appearances.

Church's textual description attempts to provide the same grounded security offered by the compositional details of Bradford's paintings. Omnipresent in Bradford's compositions are the icebreaking and sealing vessels that penetrate the otherwise frozen landscape—details that reinforce narratives of maritime conquest. Painting on a much smaller scale than Church, Bradford also relied on color to construct ice in more familiar, terrestrial terms. The golden and red hues of his ice fields at sunset and sunrise deflect the problem of blankness and vacuity viewers associated with Arctic conditions and found troubling in the cool, unearthly chromatic effects of Church's *Icebergs.*

Both artists, no doubt, were also contending with the very un-landed nature of the Arctic itself. Like the wetland, the other ontologically unstable environment of the American nineteenth century, the Arctic was neither fully land nor water. This troubling in-betweenness was what made swamps and marshes

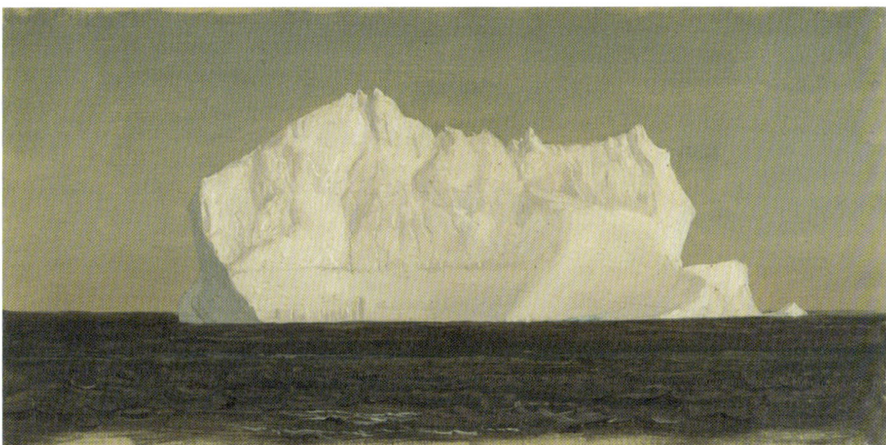

Fig. 6. Frederic Edwin Church, *Floating Iceberg*, 1859. Brush and oil paint, graphite on paperboard, 7 3/8 × 14 3/4 in. (18.7 × 37.5 cm). Cooper-Hewitt National Design Museum, New York. Gift of Louis P. Church (1917-4-296-a)

simultaneously wasteland and resource (if, that is, they were drained or dried out for building and agriculture).[33] Similarly, the Arctic was both a vast emptiness and potentially exploitable, though that exploitation involved turning solid to liquid rather than the other way around. This ambivalence of the Arctic landscape surfaces in the preparatory studies that both Bradford and Church produced during their respective expeditions. In Church's *plein air* sketches painted in Labrador, icebergs are isolated against blank backgrounds of sea and sky (fig. 6). While rich in textural and geometric detail, they float free like frigid islands, dramatically untethered to anything resembling firm ground. Back in the studio, Church would stitch together the textures and colors of these carefully observed specimens into a recognizable topographical setting for *Icebergs*: an inlet framed by towering cliffs, not unlike the grounded ones he and his fellow landscapists were famous for.

Bradford's work follows a similar pattern. His album *Arctic Regions* focuses, like Church's sketches, on monumental floating icebergs photographed by hired professionals (fig. 7), while his later paintings render ice as a surface on which to stand. Both Church's oil sketches and Bradford's photographs are mute renderings that confirmed the anxieties of period viewers. As one astute critic of Church's *Icebergs* noted: "In painting a scene, *where only water, in . . . its various forms . . .* is represented, many of the ordinary rules of painting are reversed."[34] Turning away from painting altogether for his travel album, Bradford explained that ice, in its "wild, rugged shapes, indescribable and ever-changing, baffle all

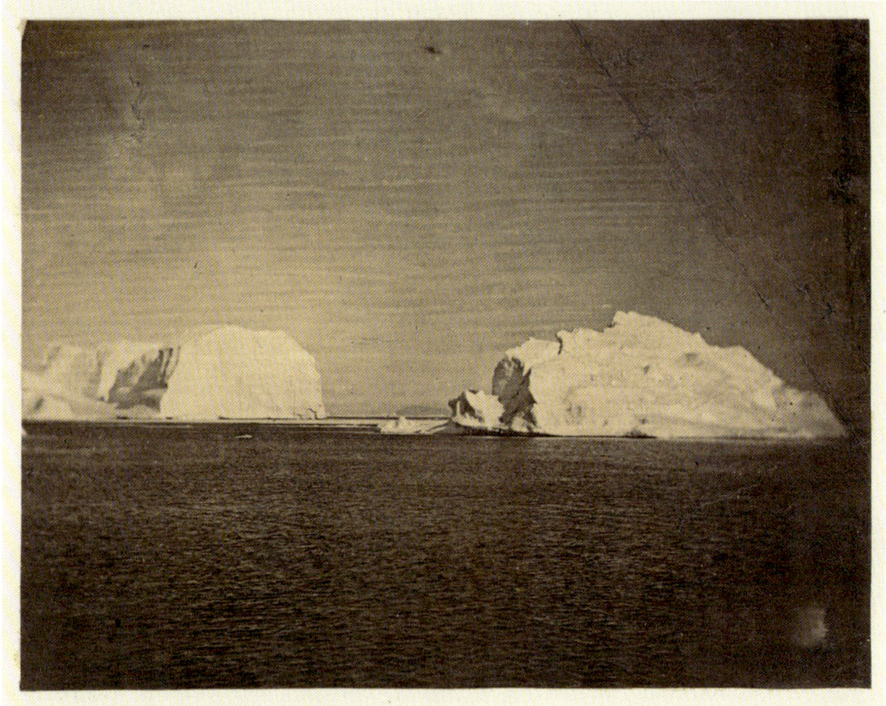

Fig. 7. William Bradford, plate from *Arctic Regions*, 1873. Albumen print. Rare Folio ND237 B6965a. Clark Art Institute Library, Williamstown, Massachusetts

description and nothing can do them justice but the sun-given powers of the camera."[35] While Church's and Bradford's paintings of the Arctic may have mimicked terrestrial landscapes in composition or visual effects, the genre's conventions ultimately proved incompatible with the material qualities of ice. Despite their best efforts to turn the Arctic into a proper landscape, ice offered neither the stable vistas nor that solidity underfoot on which imagined possession and conquest narratives relied. After all, it was not ice but its absence (a de-icing) that would constitute progress when it came to conquest of the Far North.

"Seeing-in"

To make sense of ice—to transform a troubling material into a manageable one—nineteenth-century artists and writers drew upon its resemblance to the solid materials of sculpture and architecture. Whereas Church's painting may have been mute to viewers, the text penned by his travel companion Noble offered viewers an endless stream of metaphors that gave ice legibility. For Noble, ice is everything but ice, so much so that toward the end of his narrative, he appears exacerbated by the premise:

> It is a combination of Alp, castle, mosque, Parthenon and cathedral. It has peaks and slopes; cliffs, crags, chasms and caverns; lakes, streams and waterfalls. It has towers, battlements and portals. It has minarets, domes and steeples; roofs and gables; balustrades and balconies; fronts, sides and interiors; doors, windows and porches; steps and entrances; columns, pilasters, capitals and entablatures; frieze, architrave and cornice; arches, cloisters, niches, statuary and countless decorations; flutings, corrugation, carvings, panels of glassy polish and in the rough; Greek, Roman, Gothic, Sarcenic, Pagan, Savage. It is crested with blades and needles; heaped here and there with ruins, blocks and bowlders [sic], splintered and crumbling masses.[36]

Noble's glutted text may be excessively verbose, but it uses rhetoric common to many nineteenth-century accounts of the Arctic. Bradford turned to similar metaphors in his narrative. Ice, he wrote, gave "scope for the imagination to picture forth all things wonderful and strange, whether it be gigantic form of man or beast, crenellated castle wall or donjon deep."[37]

Such descriptions focus on chance resemblances, specifically "seeing-in"—an imaginative or associational mode of perception dating back to antiquity and most often applied to immaterial substances such as clouds and smoke.[38] Leon Battista Alberti had proposed that such accidental visual resemblances were associated with the birth of art itself—that sculpture began when humans found objects whose appearance needed only "slight alteration" to become a striking imitation of something else.[39] In the nineteenth century, this mode of perception was aligned not with landscape painting—a genre associated with empirical vision and concrete details—but with the then-popular art form of ideal sculpture, Neoclassical marbles depicting literary, historical, and mythical figures. In their metaphor-heavy rhetoric, Arctic narratives regularly evoked connections between ice and sculpture, highlighting the chromatic and textural affinities between marble and frozen water. Bradford, for instance, described icebergs rising from the sea as "perfectly smooth, and white as the purest marble, well-proportioned and as finely rounded by the action of the water as if fashioned by the chisel of a sculptor."[40]

Moreover, the discourse of chance perception, so pervasive in nineteenth-

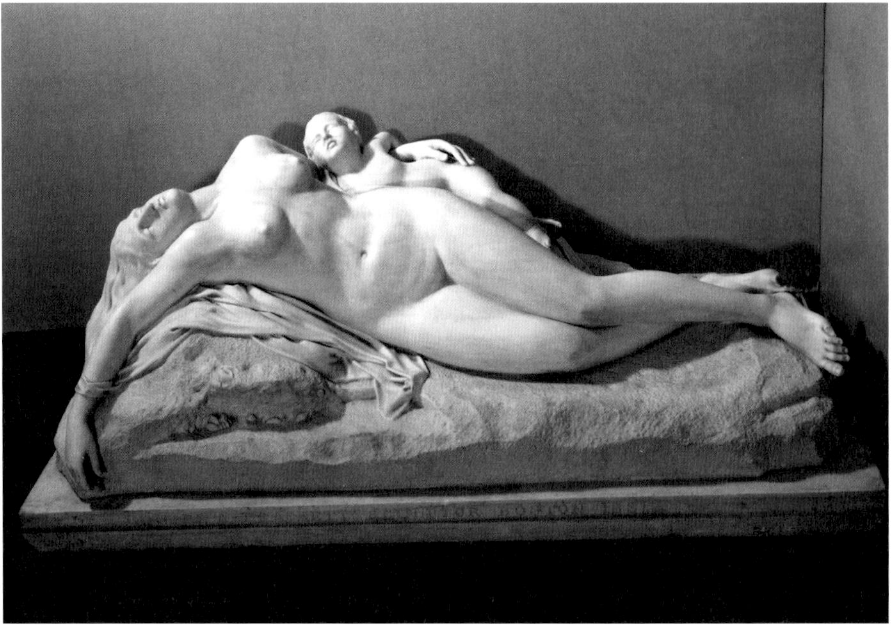

Fig. 8. Edward Brackett (American, 1818–1908), *Shipwrecked Mother and Child*, 1848–51. Marble, 72 × 33 ⅛ × 23 ½ in. (182.9 × 84.1 × 59.7 cm). Worcester Art Museum, Worcester, Massachusetts. Gift of Edward Augustus Brackett (1904.64)

century Arctic narratives, modeled a mode of looking specifically associated with marble sculpture.[41] Exhibition pamphlets and etiquette manuals codified sculptural sight as an associational practice, a kind of "seeing-in" that, as Joy Kasson has argued, facilitated a viewer's access to an artwork's allegorical meaning.[42] Instructing viewers on proper behavior before Edward Brackett's *Shipwrecked Mother and Child*, a work about maritime disaster (1848–51; fig. 8), the sculptor Horatio Greenough suggests the following: "Sit quietly on the several sides of the room, and even there survey it with half-closed eyes. The work is of marble: it is vain that you will seek aught else by crowding upon it. By remaining at a proper distance, you will find that it is no longer marble, but poetry."[43] In other words, to see beyond the meaningless, stony surface, a spectator had to purposefully reduce his or her visual acuity.

While surveying artworks from afar, viewers of ideal sculpture used precisely the opposite skill set that they would have needed for looking at landscape painting. Spectators of landscape were instructed not to look from afar but to approach the canvas (Church even encouraged visitors to bring their opera glasses to his exhibitions to facilitate this up-close scrutiny).[44] Nineteenth-century accounts of the Arctic, which so indulged seeing-in, evoked not the meticulous inspection of the landscape enthusiast but the distant, passive gaze of the student of sculpture.

To see ice as sculpted stone rather than frozen water entangled the Arctic in marble's racial ideologies. Nineteenth-century American sculptors invested heavily in marble's natural whiteness because it facilitated the sublimation of sensual flesh that risked curtailing a work's allegorical meaning. Artists disparaged their artistic predecessors for using pigments to tint their surfaces, and critics deemed the practice "a ghastly thing" and a "falsification . . . without any adequate motive."[45] As Charmaine Nelson has shown, this rejection of color by Neoclassical sculptors follows a colonial logic, pitting the pure, restrained, noble White body against the sensuous, unruly Black body, which was rarely a subject of ideal sculpture, even after emancipation.[46] Seeing with half-closed eyes also favored marble's intangible whiteness—a smooth, flawlessness that pushed sculpture toward poetic abstraction rather than coarse materiality. Indeed, when the most famous marble sculpture of the nineteenth century, Hiram Powers's *Greek Slave* (fig. 9), toured the antebellum South, it was almost universally praised for its portrayal of ideal femininity rather than read as a critique of the institution of slavery (as it had been by Northern abolitionists).[47]

The racial ideologies of marble became ever more acute during the Civil War. When Union soldiers defaced a Hiram Powers

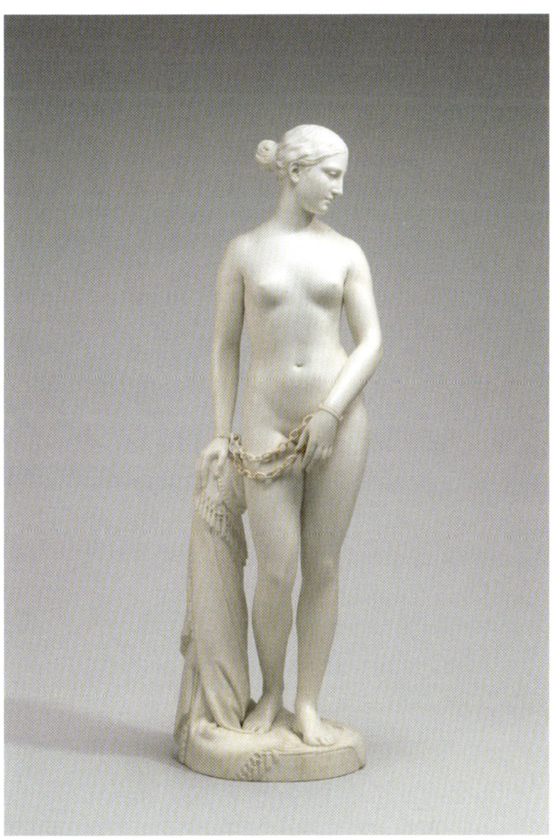

Fig. 9. Hiram Powers (American, 1805–1873), *The Greek Slave*, modeled 1841–43, carved 1846. Marble, 65 $^{15}/_{16}$ × 20 $^{1}/_{4}$ × 18 $^{1}/_{2}$ in. (167.4 × 51.4 × 47 cm). National Gallery of Art, Washington, DC. Gift of William Wilson Corcoran (2014.79.37)

bust of secessionist John C. Calhoun in North Carolina's senate chamber during occupation, they chose to cover it with black ink. An army doctor recorded in his memoir that he came across the vandalized bust with an inkwell crowning his head. Black fluid had "descended in copious streams over the face" and "besmutted the features," he wrote. Racially motivated iconoclasm had put the "Father of Secession" in blackface.[48]

Images of ice cannot be divorced from these contested geographies. To passively admire icebergs from afar as marble palaces was also to sublimate the racial implications of ice into the aesthetics of smooth, shimmering surfaces. Questions of race, as Martin Berger has suggested, animate even those nineteenth-century cultural products without obvious racial imagery, even Arctic landscapes.[49] When Church debuted his *Icebergs* at a New York gallery less than two weeks after the outbreak of the Civil War, he chose a politicized title, *The North: Church's Picture of Icebergs* (only later did he rebrand it with the simple descriptive title we know today.) Church, a staunch Unionist, no doubt wanted viewers to contemplate questions of racial and geographical politics in so naming his painting.[50] He reinforced an alignment of Arctic North with the Union and tropical South with the Confederacy, which emerged out of Arctic exploration itself. The scientist Isaac B. Hayes, who returned from an Arctic voyage in 1861, for instance, described his mission as one of carrying "the flag of our Republic, with not a single star erased from its glorious Union, to the extreme Northern limits of the earth."[51] The Confederate South, meanwhile, was coded as tropical, filled with swamps that bred epidemics and harbored runaways. Politically, the slave economy linked the Confederacy to the veritable tropics, particularly the Caribbean, and not just during the Triangle Trade. Just prior to the Civil War, Southerners had tried but failed to realize their dream of a tropical slave empire in Cuba, Mexico, and Central America.[52]

In the Civil War era, ice may have been righteously tethered to Union politics by Church and others, but it can hardly be pardoned from problematic racial constructs. As a commodity, it was a colonizing material, quite literally. Based in the Northern states, the American ice industry's largest international markets were colonial outposts with significant Euro-American populations: the Caribbean and India. There, ice was a luxury good intended only for the White populations of these tropical locales. To set up a successful ice business, one Boston entrepreneur spent time visiting with local governments of a dozen Caribbean islands seeking exclusive rights to sell only to "resident foreigners."[53] Ice was seen

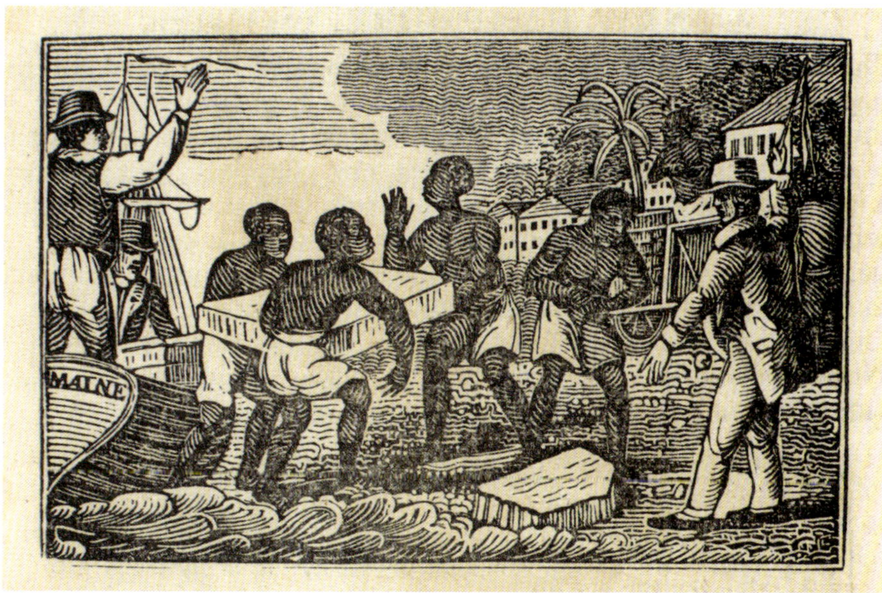

Fig. 10. Detail of "Ship to Shore in the Tropics, 1828," published in *A System of School Geography Chiefly Derived from Malte-Brun*, by Samuel G. Goodrich (1836). The Henry E. Huntington Library and Art Gallery, San Marino, California (RB 117650)

as incompatible or unfit for those native to tropical climes. In a nineteenth-century print depicting ice being unloaded in Cuba from the holds of a ship marked "Maine," Black, enslaved laborers are shown unable to tolerate the extreme temperature of the imported blocks (fig. 10). The food historian Hi'ilei Hobart, who studies the introduction of ice to nineteenth-century Hawaii, has argued that Indigenous accounts of ice as "burning" and "so hot" rather than freezing or too cold was interpreted by colonists as a marker of biological racial difference.[54] The importation of cold—which ushered in modern patterns of what one might call "imperial" eating—was indelibly tied to the exploitation and consumption of nonwhite bodies.[55] In the nineteenth-century Americas, ice, art, and race were inextricably bound together by practices of perception as well as technologies of globalization.

Ice / Sculpture

Yet, it was only in the 1960s and later that artists have tackled this critical nexus in their practice. In particular, a number of artists associated with the Caribbean and Latin America have productively utilized the material conditions of ice and its connection to sculpture to expose the racial ideologies of globalization. Among the

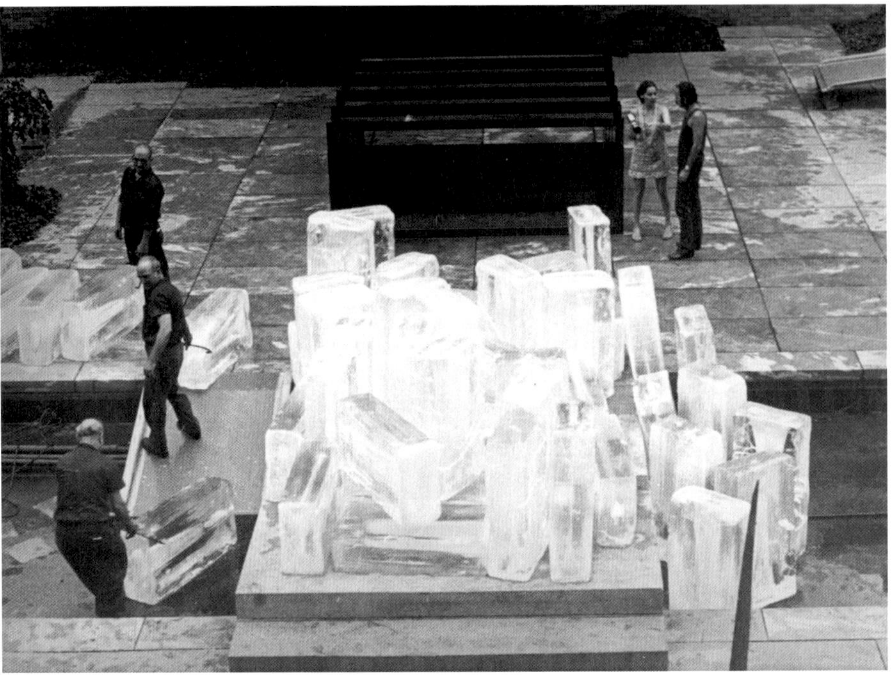

Fig. 11. Rafael Ferrer (Puerto Rican, b. 1933), *50 Cakes of Ice*, 1970. Collection of the artist. Art © Rafael Ferrer/Licensed by VAGA, New York, NY

first practitioners to work in such terms was the Puerto Rican-born Rafael Ferrer, whose melting "environments" constructed of large ice blocks (first at the Whitney and later at MoMA) ironically reenacted the White-male heroism of minimalism (fig. 11).[56] Recalling his Puerto Rican upbringing, Ferrer explains that he chose to work with ice because "a man from the tropics views ice as a magical substance," perhaps referencing Gabriel Garcia Marquez's novel *One Hundred Years of Solitude*, in which a character mistakes ice for "the biggest diamond in the world."[57] It is precisely the incommensurability of ice and "a man from the tropics"—a notion at the forefront of the racist ideology animating nineteenth-century global encounters—that Ferrer and other contemporary artists have put at the center of their work.

Unlike many recent, straightforwardly eco-critical artworks using ice—for instance, Olafur Elliason's *Ice Watch* (a clock-shaped installation of Greenland icebergs melting away in downtown Paris, in 2015) or Roni Horn's *Library of Water* (a minimalist gallery in Iceland filled with clear columns of melted local glaciers, which is ongoing)—the particular subset of artworks I want to introduce here

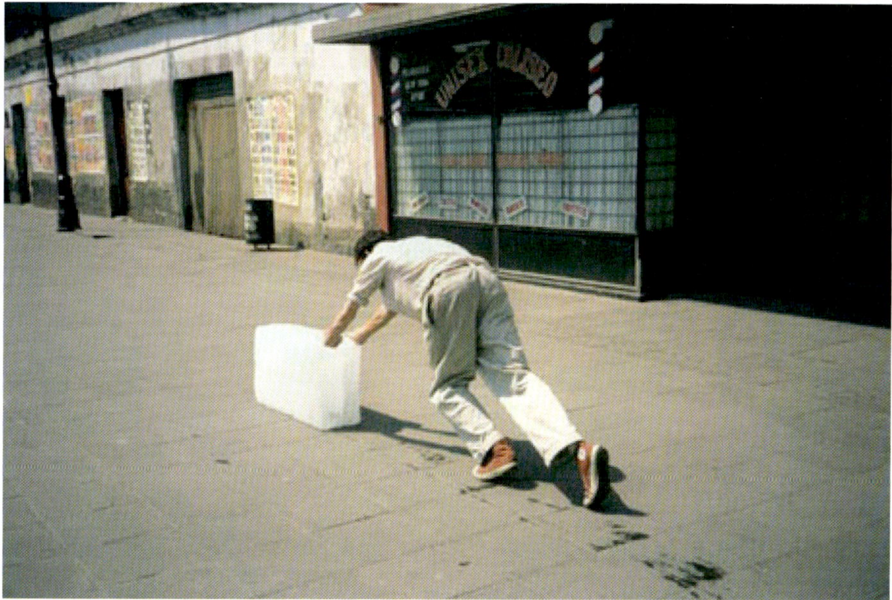

Fig. 12. Francis Alÿs (Belgian, b. 1959), *Paradox of Praxis I (Sometimes Doing Something Leads to Nothing)*, 1997. Video documentation of an action, Mexico City. Photo: Enrique Huerta

turn away from the visual mode of the sublime. They instead underscore the fact that the aesthetics of ice go hand in hand with commerce and politics. The artists working with ice on such terms are, not surprisingly, associated with the tropics, spaces where hot and cold matter have long been politicized.

Ice, for many of these artists, is not a precious, nonhuman substance whose melting is meant to be poignantly lamented, but human-centered—a sign for the disenfranchised body of the colonial other. In artworks such as Francis Alÿs's *Paradox of Praxis* (1997), this human context is physically enacted. In this performance piece, the Belgian-born, Mexico-based Alÿs pushed a torso-sized block of ice through the streets of Mexico City until it had completely melted into the hot asphalt (fig. 12). The artist's arduous but pointless task—akin to the grueling work of Mexican street vendors (which Alÿs also documented in other media in the same years)—transforms melting ice into a sign of nonwhite labor in the global South.[58] More recently, the Brazilian artist Néle Azevedo has literally used ice to sculpt the bodies of the oppressed. Her *Minimalist Monument*, first installed in Brazil in 2005, consists of an army of miniature human figures cast in ice and designed to quickly melt away in urban public spaces (fig. 13). Conceived as an "anti-monument," Azevedo uses the drama of melting to critique the dis-

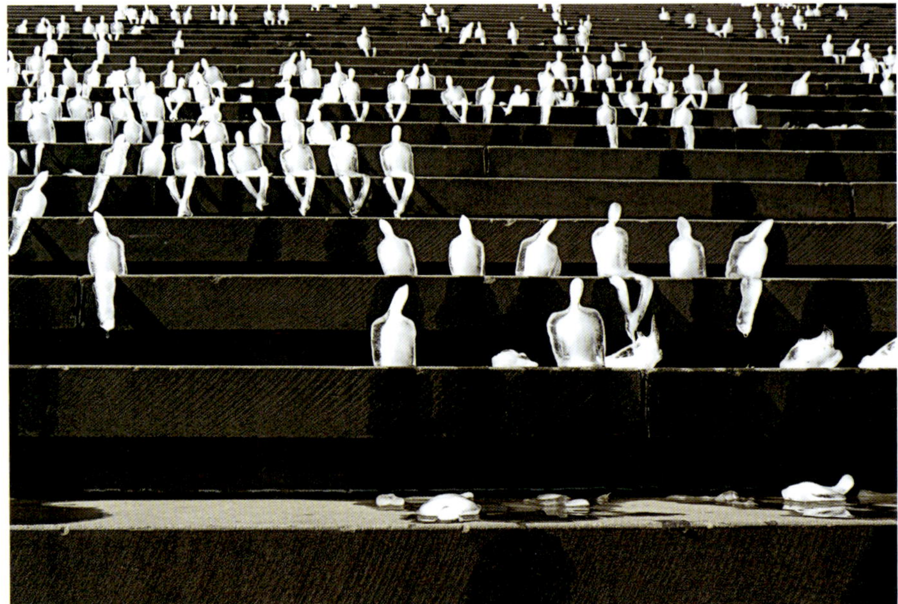

Fig. 13. Néle Azevedo (Brazilian, b. 1950), *Minimum Monument*, 2014. Installation. ©Néle Azevedo, Minimum Monument, Berlin 2009. © 2017 Artists Rights Society (ARS), New York / AUTVIS, Sao Paulo

connection between monumental sculpture and local history. Ferrer, Alÿs, and Azevedo each constructed a narrative of ice melting that is human rather than Anthropocene, political rather than natural, racialized rather than universal.

Sculpting ice, for those contemporary artists who are looking to or from the tropics, is ultimately about using ice as a kind of anti-sculpture. Each notably turned to ice that was mechanically made rather than naturally occurring, referencing the industrial history of their material and its geopolitics. The minimalist cube and the civic monument of today (much like the marble goddesses of the nineteenth century) are constructed from hard, durable matter that speaks to perpetuity—to the maintenance of essentializing narratives. To re-create them in ice, itself a product of the economic colonization of the tropics, is to marshal entropy as a weapon against the legacies of imperialism.

Today, in the midst of climate change and growing awareness of the fragility of Arctic ecosystems, melting ice has become far too easy to exploit artistically. When Azevedo's *Minimalist Monument* was installed in Berlin in 2009 under the auspices of the World Wildlife Fund, the artist's melting bodies were recast as an emblem of global warming even though the artist has never explicitly defined the work in environmental terms. Like the misreading of Powers's *Greek*

Slave that took place in the antebellum South, this rebranding of frozen water as stand-in for glacier and iceberg unfortunately erases an important history—that in the nineteenth century and today, the properties of ice connect ecological fragility to racial politics. Now, as melting ice is slowly turning the once-mythical open polar sea into a troubling reality, we need to look south as much as north. As the tropics get closer than ever in nautical miles, they also become the region of the world most vulnerable to rising sea levels and warming temperatures. Not only will this result in a loss of land and livelihood for much of the developing world, but it will no doubt lead to the deterioration of global supply chains on which the North has long relied. The consequences of climate change are not just aesthetic, as the melting away of icebergs artistically installed may suggest, but deeply economic and disconcertingly political.

Entropy, then, can be dangerously universalizing. We live in a moment when ice as artistic medium has largely lost its history. An installation of icebergs, melting away, offers viewers a critique of environmental destruction that is cleansed of political implications, prompting a kind of passive gaze not unlike that of nineteenth-century Americans before their sculpted marble allegories. I began this essay with Tavares Strachan's *Arctic Ice Project* because it maintains an eco-critical currency while gesturing to that now-lost history. The key to its effectiveness, I would suggest, is its ability to combine a narrative of the vanishing Arctic sublime with the mundane mechanics of freezing. Though Strachan's final installation of a frozen cube recalls the work of Ferrer and Alÿs, the ice in question is not mechanically made but harvested from the remote North. In Strachan's turn away from the romantic, the iceberg imitates the ice cube. Staging a reversal of our usual encounter with ice, Strachan's project also asks us to return to narratives of encounter and expedition more generally. The piece might be read as a rescue mission wherein the nonwhite explorer from the tropics masters the Arctic.[59] He excavates its most precious matter and preserves it by using cooling technology powered by heat itself. The work thus centers not on melting but on freezing— not the chaos implied by entropy but on material equilibrium. We might say that *Arctic Ice Project* conveniently realizes the very material control that drove once-failed nineteenth-century pursuits concerning frozen matter. But with its revised agents and sites, we can begin to situate today's ecological concerns of melting in a politicized history of freezing.

1. Robert Hobbs, "Tavares Strachan's Infinite Games," in Tavares Strachan, *The Distance between What We Have and What We Want* (New York: Pierogi and Ronald Feldman Fine Arts, 2006).

2. Louis Legrand Noble, *After Icebergs with a Painter: A Summer Voyage to Labrador and Around Newfoundland* (New York: D. Appleton and Co., 1861), vi.

3. On the cultural impact of Arctic exploration, see Michael Robinson, *The Coldest Crucible: Arctic Exploration and American Culture* (Chicago: University of Chicago Press, 2006).

4. Quoted in Barry Alan Joyce, "Elisha Kent Kane and the Eskimo of Etah," in *Surveying the Record: North American Scientific Exploration to 1930,* ed. Edward C. Carter II (Philadelphia: American Philosophical Society, 1999), 104.

5. Robinson, *The Coldest Crucible*, 45.

6. Kevin J. Avery, *Church's Great Picture, "The Heart of the Andes"* (New York: Metropolitan Museum of Art, 1993).

7. Jennifer Raab discusses this characteristic of *The Icebergs'* reception in *Frederic Church: The Art and Science of Detail* (New Haven: Yale University Press, 2015), 87–122, arguing that Church purposely evaded narrative in order to explore formal qualities of painting.

8. For a compilation of period reviews of *Icebergs*, from which these quotations are drawn, see Gerald L. Carr, "Early Documentation of *The Icebergs*," in Eleanor Jones Harvey and Gerald L. Carr, *The Voyage of the Icebergs: Frederic Church's Masterpiece* (Dallas: Dallas Museum of Art, 2013), 91–94.

9. On the function of narrative in relation to failure in Arctic expeditions, see Adriana Craciun, *Writing Arctic Disaster: Authorship and Exploration* (Cambridge: Cambridge University Press, 2016) and Lisa Bloom, "Science and Writing: Two National Narratives of Failure," in *Inscribing Science: Scientific Texts and the Materiality of Communication*, ed. Timothy Lenoir (Stanford: Stanford University Press, 1998), 328–50.

10. On Bradford's career, see Richard C. Kugler, *William Bradford: Sailing Ships & Arctic Seas* (Seattle: University of Washington Press and New Bedford Whaling Museum, 2003).

11. William Bradford, *The Arctic Regions: Illustrated with Photographs Taken on an Art Expedition to Greenland* (London, 1873), 7, 46, 78, 47.

12. William Bradford, "Life and Scenery in the Far North," *Journal of the American Geographical Society of New York*, Jan. 1, 1885, [n.p.].

13. On artists encountering ice in the early modern period, see Christopher P. Heuer, "Arctic Matters in Early America," in *Scale*, ed. Jennifer L. Roberts (Chicago: University of Chicago Press, 2016), 180–214.

14. On historical attempts to discover the Northwest Passage, see Glyn Williams, *Voyages of Delusion: The Quest for the Northwest Passage* (New Haven: Yale University Press, 2003).

15. On the history of American expeditions to the Arctic, see Robinson, *Coldest Crucible*; Pierre Berton, *The Arctic Grail: The Quest for the North West Passage and the North Pole, 1818–1909* (New

York: Viking, 1988); and Lisa Bloom, *Gender on Ice: American Ideologies of Polar Expeditions* (Minneapolis: University of Minnesota Press, 1993).

16. Matthew Maury, *The Physical Geography of the Sea and Its Meteorology* (New York: Harper & Brothers, Publishers, 1871), 204.

17. The Hollow Earth theory first appeared in John Cleves Symmes, "No. 1. Circular," *Niles' Weekly Register*, June 20, 1818, 294. Interest in the theory outlasted Symmes's own lifetime. His writings on the topic were published as an anthology in 1878 by his son: Americus Symmes, ed., *Symmes's Theory of Concentric Spheres: Demonstrating That the Earth is Hollow, Habitable Within, and Widely Open About the Poles, Compiled by Americus Symmes, from the Writings of his Father, Capt. John Cleves Symmes* (Louisville, Ky.: Printed by Bradley & Gilbert, 1878).

18. *Symmes Theory of Concentric Spheres, Demonstrating That the Earth is Hollow, Habitable Within and Widely Open About the Poles—by a Citizen of the United States* (Cincinnati: Morgan, Lodge, and Fisher, 1826), 144.

19. An early convert to Symmes's theory, Jeremiah Reynolds undertook an expedition to the South Pole in 1829. On this and other failed attempts to fund expeditions to test the Hollow Earth theory, see John Weld Peck, "Symmes' Theory," *Ohio Archeological and Historical Publications* 18 (1909): 29–43.

20. Edgar Allan Poe, *The Narrative of Arthur Gordon Pym of Nantucket* (New York: Harper & Bros., 1838).

21. See, for instance, William W. Wheildon, *Atmospheric Theory of the Open Polar Sea: With Remarks on the Present State of the Question* (Boston: Elmwood Typographia, 1872); and Isaac Israel Hayes, *The Open Polar Sea: A Narrative of a Voyage of Discovery Towards the North Pole in the Schooner "United States"* (New York: Hurd and Houghton, 1869).

22. On the history of the ice-harvesting industry in the northeastern United States, see Richard O. Cummings, *The American Ice Harvests: A Historical Study of Technology, 1800–1918* (Berkeley: University of California Press, 1949); and Joseph C. Jones Jr., *America's Icemen: An Illustrative History of the United States Natural Ice Industry, 1665–1925* (Humble, Tex.: Jobeco Books, 1984).

23. On the impact of cold storage on global shipping in the nineteenth century, see Rebecca J. H. Woods, "Nature and the Refrigerating Machine: The Politics and Production of Cold in the Nineteenth Century," in *Cryopolitics: Frozen Life in a Melting World*, ed. Joanna Radin and Emma Kowal (Cambridge: MIT Press, 2017): 89–116.

24. Jones, *America's Icemen*, 93.

25. Cummings, *The American Ice Harvests*, 142.

26. Noble, *After Icebergs with a Painter*, 175.

27. "Specifications of American Patents," *Journal of the Franklin Institute* 27 (April 1839): 245.

28. Jones, *America's Icemen*, 13.

29. "Ship Found in Arctic 168 Years After Doomed Northwest Passage Attempt," *The Guardian*, September 12, 2016.

30. On the conventions of landscape and its ideological underpinnings, see Angela Miller, *Empire of the Eye: Landscape Presentation and Cultural Politics, 1825–1875* (Ithaca: Cornell University Press, 1996).

31. "Some Remarks on Landscape Painting," *Bulletin of the American Art-Union* 2 (November 1849): 23.

32. Frederick Church's broadside entitled "The North" was published on the occasion of the exhibition of the painting in 1861 at the Boston Athenaeum. The quote comes from a reprint published in Harvey and Carr, *The Voyage of the Icebergs.*

33. On the cultural history of wetlands, see David C. Miller, *Dark Eden: The Swamp in Nineteenth-Century American Culture* (Cambridge: Cambridge University Press, 1989).

34. "Art," *New York Evening Express*, February 26, 1861, 1.

35. Bradford, *Arctic Regions*, 12.

36. Noble, *After Icebergs with a Painter*, 247.

37. Bradford, *Arctic Regions*, 14.

38. On chance methods and early modern painting, see Dario Gamboni, *Potential Images: Ambiguity and Indeterminacy in Modern Art* (London: Reaktion Books, 2002). On the theory of seeing-in, see Richard Wollheim, *Painting as an Art* (Princeton: Princeton University Press, 1987), 45–48.

39. Leon Battista Alberti, *On Painting; and On Sculpture*, trans. Cecil Grayson (London: Phaidon, 1972), 121.

40. Bradford, *Arctic Regions*, 46.

41. This idea has a longer history: Michelangelo, for instance, was reputed to see figures emerge from his marble blocks.

42. Joy Kasson, *Marble Queens and Captives: Women in Nineteenth-Century American Sculpture* (New Haven: Yale University Press, 1990).

43. Horatio Greenough, *Edward Brackett's Marble Group of the Shipwrecked Mother and Child* (New York, n.d.), quoted in Kasson, *Marble Queens and Captives*, 36.

44. On Church's relationship to detail, see Raab, *Frederic Church.*

45. Anne Brewster, "American Artists in Rome" (1868) and James Jackson Jarves, *Art Hints, Architecture, Sculpture and Painting* (1855), quoted in Charmaine A. Nelson, *The Color of Stone: Sculpting the Black Female Subject in Nineteenth-Century America* (Minneapolis: University of Minnesota Press, 2007), 60, 62.

46. Nelson, *The Color of Stone*. See also Kirk Savage, *Standing Soldiers, Kneeling Slaves: Race, War, and Monument in Nineteenth-Century America* (Princeton: Princeton University Press, 1997), 52–88.

47. Nelson, *The Color of Stone*, 75–112.

48. On the provenance of this bust and its history of vandalism, see John W. Coffey, "Arms for Art, and Other Shenanigans: The Curious Case of a Marble Bust of John C. Calhoun," *Southern Cultures* 19 (Winter 2013): 5–21. I am grateful to the author for bringing the history of this piece to my attention.

49. Martin A. Berger, *Sight Unseen: Whiteness and American Culture* (Berkeley: University of California Press, 2005).

50. Carr, "Early Documentation of *The Icebergs*," 59–66.

51. See ibid., 65.

52. Robert E. May, *The Southern Dream of a Caribbean Empire, 1854–1861* (Gainesville: University Press of Florida, 2002).

53. Cummings, *The American Ice Harvests*, 137.

54. Hi'ilei Julia Hobart, "Tropical Necessities: Ice, Territory, and Taste in Settler Colonial Hawai'i" (PhD diss., New York University, 2016).

55. As Kyla Tompkins has shown, eating in the nineteenth century is central to what she calls "the performative production" of racialized bodies. See Kyla Wazana Tompkins, *Racial Indigestion: Eating Bodies in the 19th Century* (New York: New York University Press, 2012).

56. On Ferrer's work, see Deborah Cullen, *Rafael Ferrer* (Los Angeles: UCLA Chicano Studies Research Center Press, 2012); and Deborah Cullen et. al., *Retro/Active: The Works of Rafael Ferrer* (New York: Museo de Barrio, 2010).

57. Edward J. Sullivan, "Rafael Ferrer in the Tropical Sublime," in Cullen et. al., *Retro/Active*, 55.

58. On Alÿs, see Mark Godfrey, ed., *Francis Alÿs: A Story of Deception* (New York: Museum of Modern Art, 2010).

59. Though it remains unstated, Strachan's visual documentation of his expedition to harvest his ice block seems to ask viewers to recall the often-forgotten presence and contributions of nonwhites in the history of Arctic expeditions. In a general way, published narratives of Arctic expeditions regularly ignored the significant role that Indigenous guides played in the routing and survival of explorers. More specifically, Strachan may be referencing the achievements of Matthew Hensen, the African American member of Robert Peary's 1909 expedition that first reached the North Pole, a self-described "general assistant, skilled craftsperson, interpreter [of the Inuit language], and laborer" whose accomplishments were celebrated only posthumously.

A Post-Critical Arctic?

Christopher P. Heuer

As a hackneyed symbol of climate change (and its touching denials), the Arctic is everywhere today.[1] Yet as spectacle, cartographic abstraction, symbol, or lode, the Far North remains something of a non-site, a constellation of images and geographies rapturously optical and grimly unseen: the place where city-sized glaciers slide spectacularly into the sea on IMAX, and also where resource extraction and military surveillance operate in legal and optical darkness. Such unsettledness imparts to certain art practices engaging the Far North a dynamism that critiques— and often redoubles—neoliberal binaries of nature versus culture.

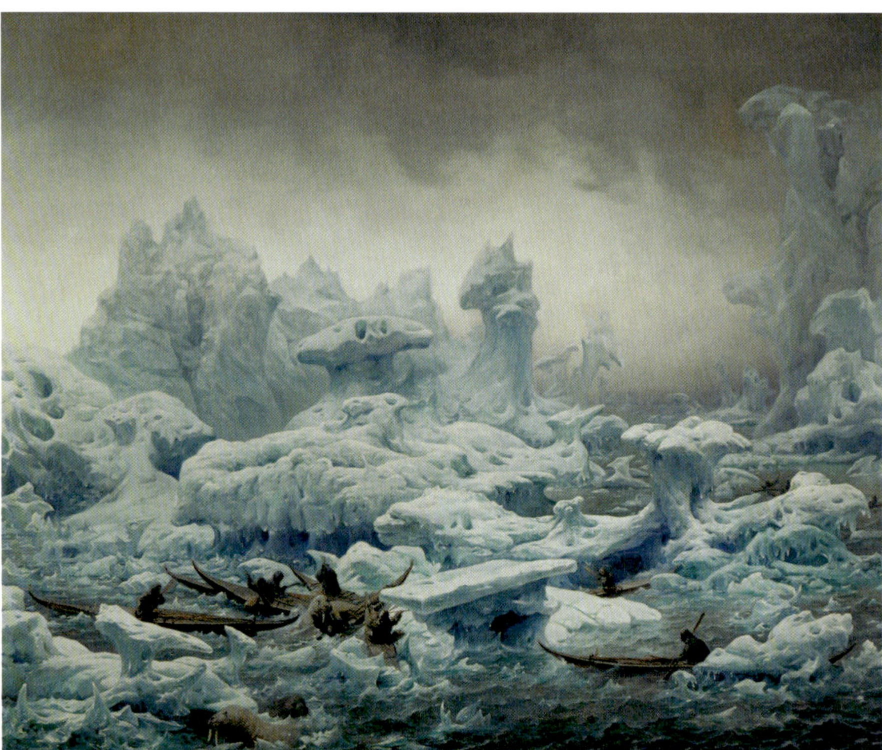

Fig. I. François-Auguste Biard (French, 1799–1882), *View of the Polar Sea, Greenlanders Hunting Walrus*, 1841. Musée du Chateau, Dieppe, France

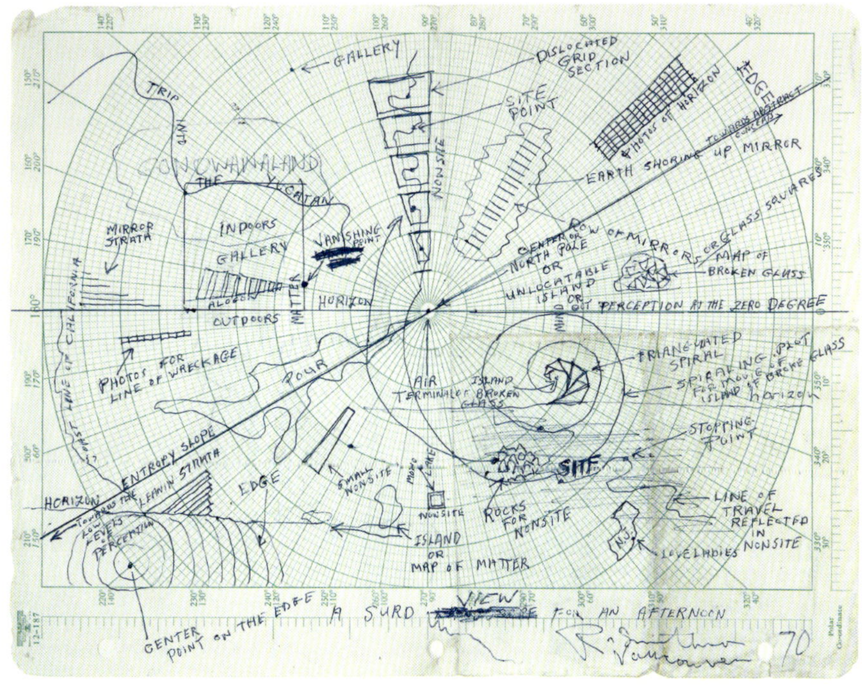

Fig. 2. Robert Smithson (American, 1938–1973), *A Surd View for An Afternoon*, 1970. Ink on paper, 8 ½ × 11 in. (21.6 × 27.9 cm). Collection of the Vancouver Art Gallery, Vancouver Art Gallery Acquisition Fund, VAG 98.71.1. Art © Holt-Smithson Foundation / Licensed by VAGA, New York, NY. Photo: Vancouver Art Gallery

The notion of an "Arctic sublime" was once identified by Victorianist Chauncey C. Loomis as an aesthetic of monsters, shipwreck, heroism, and death (fig. 1), an aesthetic in which one is "privileged or doomed briefly to experience power, mystery, and terror."[2] It is a situation endlessly critiqued in postwar art (fig. 2). Yet the sublime has remained the Arctic's main mode of engagement for contemporary visual culture, even in (or because of) an era of warming seas. For some artists, however, the Arctic's physical status as a broken land, a literal archipelago, mimes its unsettled role as archive, documentee, or performative condition, its unsecure status as an actual "place."[3] In the Far North, cleavages between ideas of environment as an either/or proposition of knowledge or experience simply are not sustainable;[4] and conventional ideas of what counts as "activist" art often dissolved.

Sameness

On September 25, 1969, a group of North American art figures flew to the Canadian village of Inuvik, just inside the Arctic Circle. The travelers were all loosely associated with Conceptualist practice in New York and Canada: critic Lucy Lippard, artists Iain and Ingrid Baxter, Harry Savage, Lawrence Weiner, and curators Bill Kirby and Virgil Hammock. The group spent thirty-eight hours in the town creating ephemeral artworks and photographs, all intended for a show entitled *Place and Process* at the Edmonton Art Gallery.[5] Most of the pieces involved the movement of earth, stones, or waterways, or ironic photographic interventions in the marshy land around town. Gestures were both placid and violent: Weiner arranged rocks and sticks around a stream (fig. 3), while Harry Savage shot flares into the night sky.

Lippard later published a diaristic account of the trip.[6] Her commentary, offering selective descriptions of artworks, established a relationship between a barren Arctic landscape and the divided hamlet of Inuvik as a kind of newly globalized colony. At first, Lippard mapped the artworks onto an ideal of an eerie wasteland. "Northern spaces are grand, bleak, infinite, and reject autonomous man-made objects almost by definition."[7] This is an anti-property aesthetic, Lippard argued, akin to "the Eskimo language [which] contains no words for measurement of space or time."[8] Certain *process* artworks, however, turned away from such grandiosity to confront the local, chiefly in cartographic terms. In *Circular Walk inside the Arctic Circle Around Inuvik, NWT*, and *Sixteen Compass Points inside the Arctic Circle*, for example, Iain and Ingrid Baxter, operating as "N. E. Thing Co.," made C-print photographs at stages along a 3.5-mile

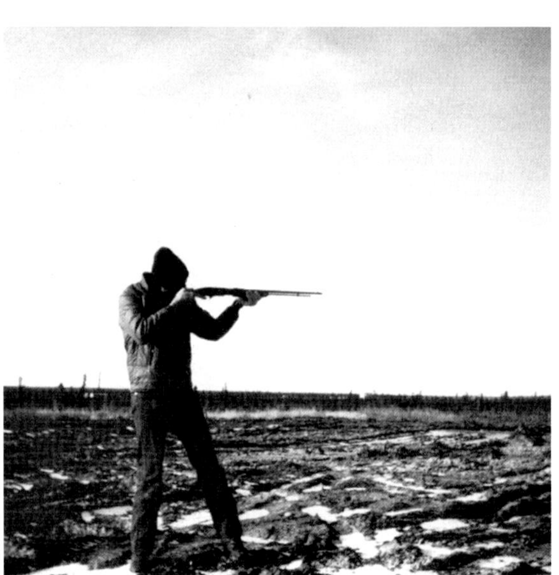

Fig. 3. Lawrence Weiner (American, b. 1942), *The Arctic Circle Shattered*, in Lucy R. Lippard, "Art Within the Arctic Circle," *Hudson Review* 22, no. 4 (Winter 1969–70), plate 2. In the collection of Lucy R. Lippard. © 2017 Lawrence Weiner/Artists Rights Society (ARS), New York

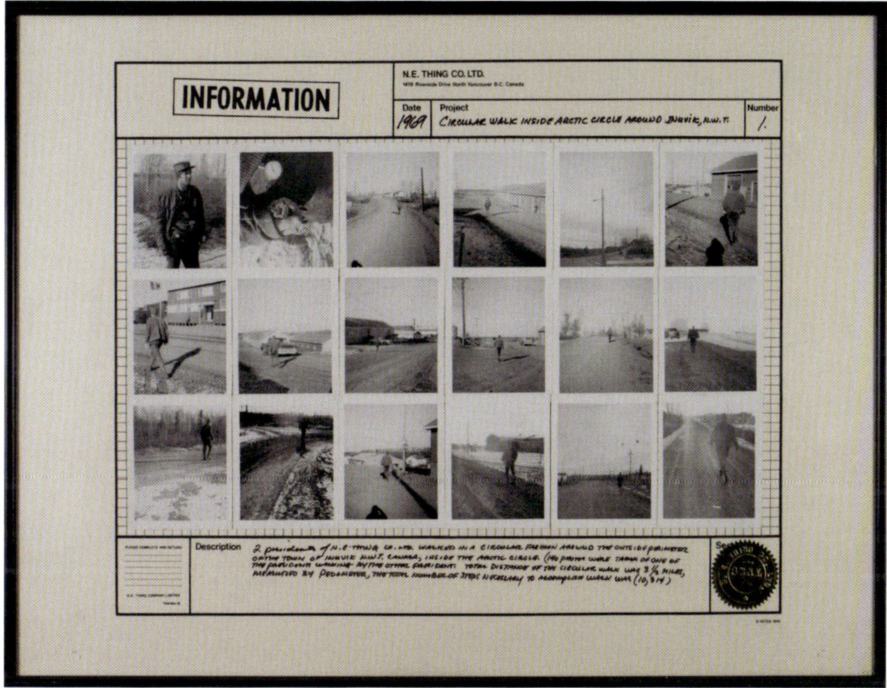

Fig. 4. N. E. Thing Co., *Circular Walk Inside Arctic Circle Around Inuvik, N.W.T.*, 1969. Collage, 17 7/8 × 24 in. (45.5 × 60.9 cm). Collection of the Morris and Helen Belkin Art Gallery, The University of British Columbia, gift of Iain Baxter and Ingrid Baxter, 1995 (BG1394). Photo: Howard Ursuliak

hike, a total of 10,314 steps (fig. 4). For the Edmonton show, these NETCO images were mounted on gridded paper alongside maps or framed as snapshots from a mobile viewpoint. In them, the landscape was gritty and unscenic; haphazardly framed garbage bins, marshy roadways, muddy tundra, telephone poles—all sutured into a cold informational matrix. In another piece, known only through Lippard's account, Baxter spray-painted a white East–West paint line directly in the brushy taiga. And in still another NETCO work, "Territorial Claim" photos were made of a small patch of ice that had been urinated on by Baxter. Invoking the bureaucratic processes of mapping and measuring, but also the animal gesture of territory-marking, the pieces parodied the southern mythology of the Arctic as a space of grandeur and majesty resistant to human presence. Instead, repeated Kodachrome images show mud-spattered trucks in fields, bulldozer tracks on puddled ground. "The [Arctic] landscape is not so exotic as I expected," Lippard wrote. "What makes it so uninteresting to describe . . . is the infinite sameness of the terrain."9

While these entries within the *Place as Process* show were not the first engagements of 1960s practice with an extreme landscape, they were among the first dealing with the Far North. In their bifurcating of advocacy and aspersion toward the Arctic environment (and its construction by exterior forces), the sortie marks an obscure return, and simultaneous travestying, of old notions of the Far North as unmappable, the ultimate quest; the kind of muted spectacle we find in August-François Biard (fig. 1), or, as Loomis once saw it, Samuel Coleridge's *Mariner.* Yet in her essay, Lippard went on to adapt this sublime to a by-then familiar Conceptualist poetics of resistance—to the gallery, to the object, to the highly wrought and picturesque. Much later, Lippard even suggested that her own photo-documentation of certain Inuvik work—haphazardly framed, unsystematically printed—was similarly de-skilled, if only by accident: "I didn't even own a camera," she modestly admitted, "someone somewhere chose me. Bad choice in terms of photography!"[10] The Baxters' Arctic work, for one, was framed as a midwestern reaction to the culture of super-cool New York minimalism and an inchoate land art movement (Virginia Dwan's legendary *Earthworks* show had been mounted the year before; critics had responded specifically to its recalibration of the idea of wastelands.[11]) Like these, documents of the Arctic installations often relied upon a sense of moving as the piece itself; and artists' experience of the terrain as stuff, rather than cartography or history.

The *Place as Process* artists, with their banal defilement of the Inuvik landscape (rifle shots, spray paint, and urination, interventions by transient artists), amplified as well as critiqued the Arctic landscape's debasement and possession by visiting forces, both material and academic. Vancouver critic Charity Mewburn argued how this staged a symbolic combat against a Greenbergian, flatness-based high-art discourse; the Arctic works were simultaneously *participating* in the project of aesthetic takeover themselves. As Mewburn puts it, the Inuvik works represented "a parodic exercise against the colonizing pretentions of high art formalism" while also a "highly ironic symbol *itself* of neo-colonialism."[12] In 1961, Greenberg had written a piece for the journal *Canadian Art* asserting "Northern" aesthetics as the logical locus, and landscape mode, for advanced painting now that its New York profile was dead. And in 1962, Greenberg had actually hosted a writers' workshop at Emma Lake, on the Saskatchewan tundra.[13]

Conspicuously absent in all the Inuvik works' engagement with the tundra is the silence about or lack of interest in Indigenous presence, and an outright polluting of an environment later understood as fragile and symbolic. While Lippard stopped short of presenting any of the 1969 Inuvik pieces as "activist" in any overt sense, she proved sensitive to the nominally ecological slant (her words) of NETCO's pieces, specifically, *vis à vis* the Arctic surroundings. The "intricate balances of organisms and their environments"[14] are particularly well queried in such settings, Lippard wrote. But environmental observation was paired with the ruined social and physical state of Inuvik's own fabric, a sensitivity that she, writing in 1968, in the midst of the American civil rights movement, saw as an upshot of economic inequality. The town of Inuvik, in fact, was an opportunistic "instant" site built by the Canadian government in the 1950s to anchor mineral extraction, the town manned by a transient white executive class and an increasingly disenfranchised Inuit population living in neglect and in appalling housing conditions. A disgusted Lippard described "one of Canada's newest slums . . . a miserable conglomeration of lean-tos, tents, and shacks."[15]

The "Arctic," here, designated a zone of relative indifference. Lippard cast the Arctic as a terrain of the *social*, a dire and riven one, to be sure. It was one acquitting new visibility just as it became *less different* than the rest of the industrialized world. As much as the *Place as Process* works were interested in the tension between lived landscape and mobile *traces* of such a landscape, Lippard's *Hudson Review* piece found itself unexpectedly distracted by the real-world exigencies of Arctic sites *outside* the gallery. Arctic "dematerialization," after such an experience, was a process within art *and* life.

The Administrative Sublime

Today, work ostensibly about the poles, as about other environmental precarities, often rehearses certain speculative realist tendencies, or object-oriented ontologies, as a kind of profligate existentialism. There seem to be two main issues at stake: on the one hand, art is manifesting alternatives to (and retrenchments of) mainstream environmentalist activism; on the other, in the face of climate emergency, practices are querying the real-life place of ecological concerns in neoliberialism. And yet, they do this in vastly different ways.

In 2007, Guido van der Werve premiered a large-scale single-channel video installation, *Nummer Acht, Everything is going to be alright*. The piece, originally filmed on a single strip of 16 mm film, was shot in the Bothnian Sea in northern Finland.[16] In the work, van der Werve blithely walks toward a tracking,

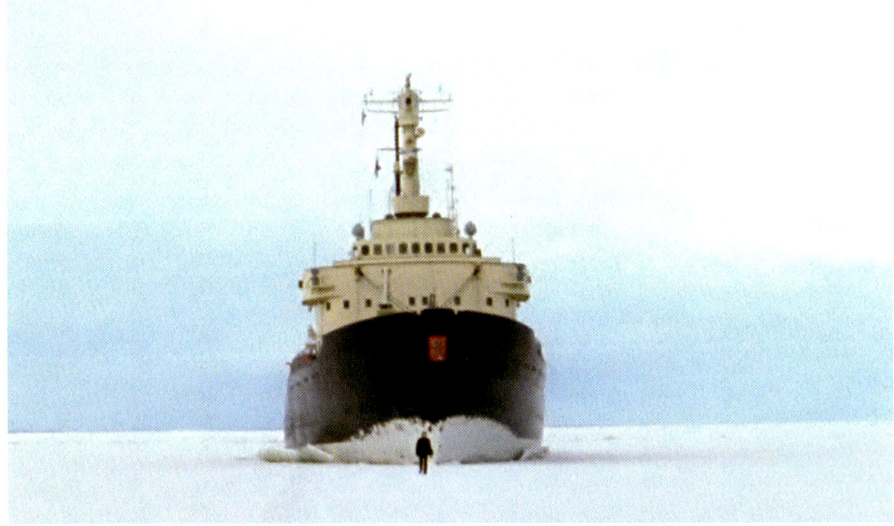

Fig. 5. Guido van der Werve (Dutch, b. 1977), still from *Nummer acht, everything is going to be alright*, 2007. 16 mm film transferred to video (color, sound). The Museum of Modern Art, New York, Fund for the Twenty-First Century (70.2009)

retreating camera in front of a colossal icebreaker, never arriving, never progressing—no destination for ship or man (fig. 5).[17] It is as if he is quietly, mightily chased, not oblivious to the hulking ship behind him, but moving toward some larger end point of contact. Ten minutes and ten seconds of film unfold, then loop, with the thudding bass of the ship's engines the only sound; the work turns the sublime aesthetic—think Caspar David Friedrich's *Wanderer* or Walter Benjamin's retreating angel of history—into a pictorial statement about futility, not in the *face* of some cowing Arctic landscape, but through apparent disregard for it.

Van der Werve's work would almost seem another allegory for environmental catastrophe: the solitary Westerner, expensively clad against the cold, plodding passively onward, all while the colossal, heaving forces of capital slowly and surely make ice disappear. But the piece makes no overt comment about climate change (there is no text in the film and van der Werve's other "numbered" artworks are sited elsewhere). Yet the disparities of (say) scale here actually look to other engagements within the polar regions, the sublime that Lippard sought to counter.

The artist-in-the-Arctic reappears in Marja Helander's *Modern Nomads* series from 2001. The piece consists of large photographs of northern landscapes in which a modern-looking flight attendant walks through a landscape wearing a

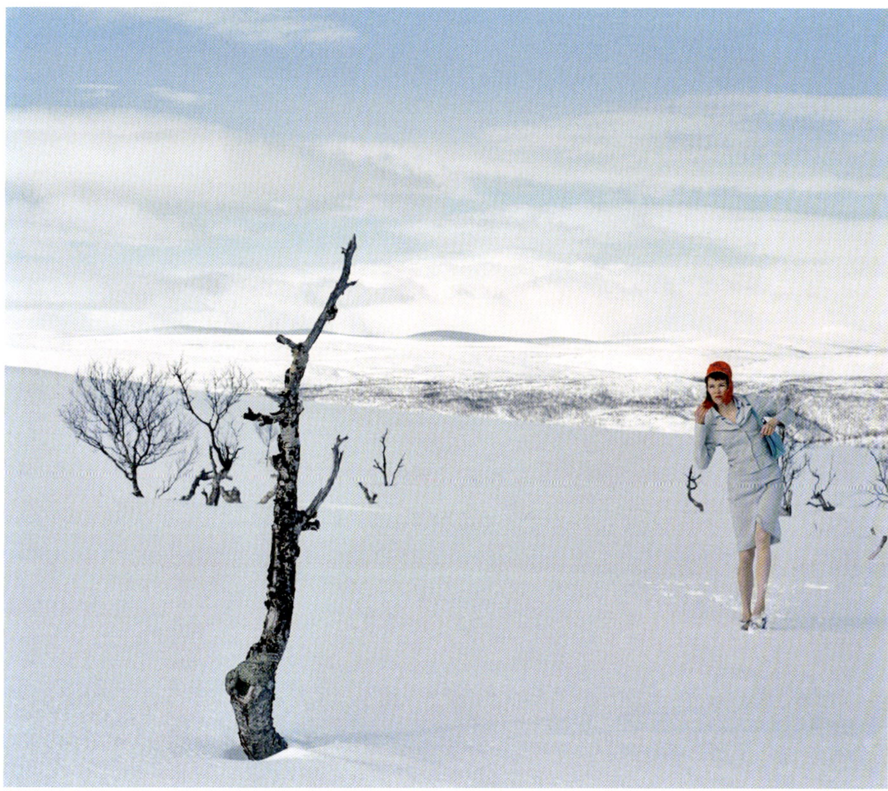

Fig. 6. Marja Helander (Finnish, b. 1965), *Mount Palopää, Utsjoki*, 2001. C-print on aluminum, 28 × 33 ¹/₂ in. (71 × 85 cm)

sarvilakki, a traditional Sámi headdress (fig. 6). As Helander writes: "The photos in the Modern Nomads tell about a modern person, who is totally lost in her traditional Sámi environment. She doesn´t understand her position. She walks on the mountains following the footsteps of her ancestors, reindeer-herdsmen. The movement continues, but the frame of reference is different."[18] The use of staged photography is quite different from van der Werve's use of crafted video, although both seem in dialogue with art history; the film gives a lived sense of duration in the now-repetitive actions, again in the north of Finland. Yet for Helander, this whiteness has specificity, a Sámi specificity, about the politics of dislocation.

But what happens when dislocation takes place for declaredly Arctic *matter*? Olafur Eliasson's much-adored *Ice Watch* was installed in Paris in November 2015, in collaboration with the Danish geologist Minik Rosing.[19] The piece consisted of twelve large blocks of ice harvested from the sea off eastern Greenland. The shards were towed through the North Sea, loaded on freezer trucks, driven

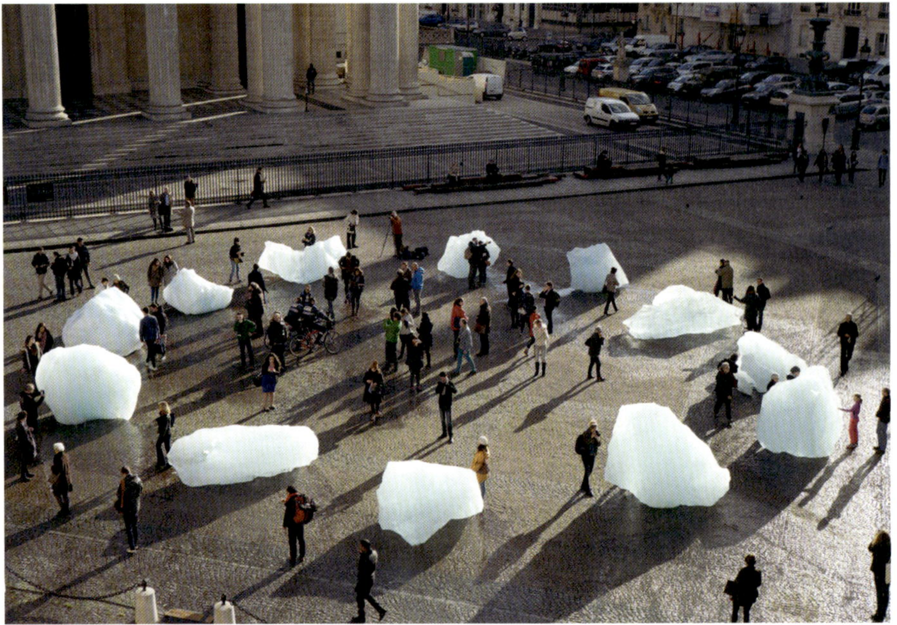

Fig. 7. Olafur Eliasson (Danish, b. 1967), *Ice Watch*, 2014–2015. Twelve ice blocks. Place du Panthéon, Paris

to Paris, and then arranged on the Place du Panthéon to coincide with the United Nations Climate summit of 2015 (fig. 7). The shards—giant, cumbersome, militantly sculptural—were meant to be left at an indeterminate span to melt away: pops and cracks of ancient water now discernable, a localization of far-off climate change, a wholly sensory snapshot of its effects.

Eliasson's piece, in fact, entered something of a canon of melting-ice-as-artwork, together with works by Francis Alÿs, Rafael Ferrer, and others, discussed elsewhere in this volume by Maggie M. Cao.[20] To this list we should add Jane McMahan's *Arapaho Glacier*, first installed in the *Weather Report* show at Boulder in 2007, curated by Lucy Lippard (fig. 8). McMahan constructed a small metal box apparatus with a solar panel. She then appropriated a one-foot-square block of ice from not far away, but from a nearby glacier in Colorado. She installed it and kept it cold with machines powered by the sun. The scale was intimate, the visual mundane, and the apparatus constantly struggled to keep pace with natural entropy. McMahan likened the work to an altarpiece, mourning, like Eliasson, for a seemingly doomed present, nevertheless arguing not for castigation and wonder but for active human solutions—utopian and inconclusive as they might seem—all while admitting technology's uneven capacity for salvation.[21]

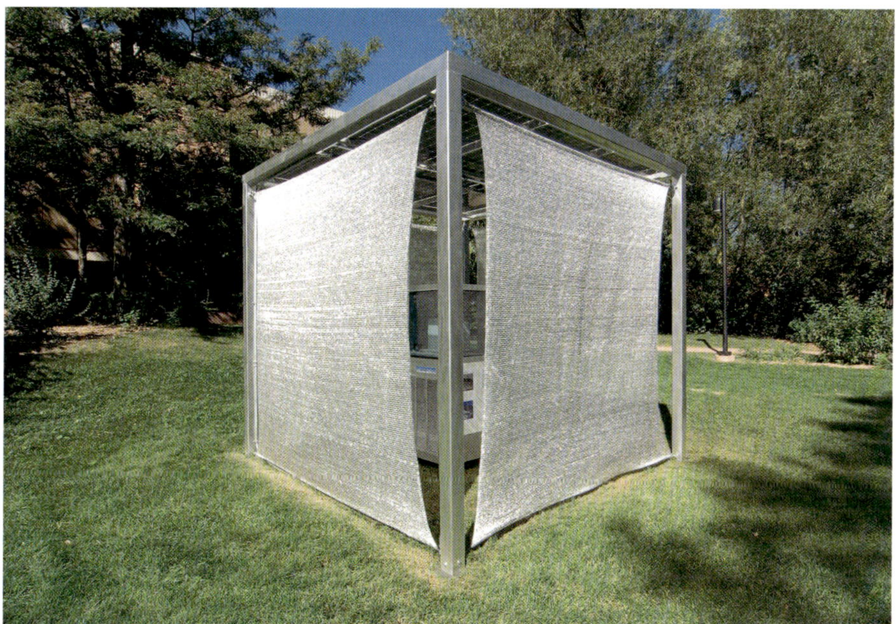

Fig. 8. Jane McMahan (American, b. 20th century), *Arapahoe Glacier*, 2007. Ice, glass, steel, refrigeration equipment, solar panels, batteries, and aluminum screen, 120 × 120 × 120 in. (304.8 × 304.8 × 304.8 cm)

McMahan made ice a relic, both sustained and eroded by its environment. The idea of *Arapaho Glacier* "meaning" something specific about climate change was pushed to the side, making it actually a far more trenchant engine for thought.

Eliasson's *Ice Watch* installation, of course, was different. Its appearance came to coincide with the Paris terrorist attacks of November 13–14, 2015. In the Place du Panthéon, now redoubled as a pilgrimage site, the ice accrued (for some) a poignancy of loss and tears, and more morbidly, the fragility of bodies, of spilled blood—the social centrality of such phenomena, all while cleaving to its stated intent of making climate change sensible. Eliasson spoke of the work: "Let's appreciate this unique opportunity—we, the world, can and must act now. Let's transform climate-knowledge into climate action. . . . I hope it will inspire shared commitment to taking climate action."[22] And indeed, for a paralyzed Paris, Eliasson's literalism was romantic and hopeful, the intimacy of a desperate local and global situation made viscerally clear. Over the course of five weeks, the imported sculptures disappeared, a foil to the preservational gesture of the Pantheon nearby. Michael Bloomberg's foundation (which sponsored Eliasson's project in part) lauded the piece as "a great example of how public art can spur people to action."[23] Eco-literary theorist Timothy Morton championed *Ice Watch*'s potential to "start a conversation" about the Earth.[24]

But a conversation among whom? What would the actually existing action that people might be "spurred to" look like? One critic pointed out that "the carbon footprint resulting from *Ice Watch Paris* is 30 metric tons (about 33 US tons) of carbon dioxide . . . largely based on the transportation of the 12 blocks of ice, weighing a total of 80 metric tons (~88 US tons), from the Nuup Kangerlua fjord outside Nuuk to Paris."[25] Maybe the piece somewhat inaccurately universalizes the idea of the "human" who is actually behind Anthropocene warming, ignoring who is forced to work to render such melancholic spectacle possible. Climate change affects all spheres of human activity differently, a factor that often drops out of much traditional environmentalism's tone of self-righteousness, as its mostly First-World proclamations are about "us." Jason Moore diagnoses this with his concept of the Capitalocene, a paradigm for thinking about the politics of environmentalism that refuses to universalize climate change's agents.[26] And this might be how any "activist" angle for *Ice Watch* needs rethinking: at the level of spectatorship and production, the piece tended to emphasize the self.

Maybe we could be crassly schematic and say that a work like *Ice Watch* marks a neo*materialist* turn in Arctic art practice. The human's ontological continuity with things or matter is framed; not much is specifically asked of us; "being," a kind of theology, replaces epistemology.[27] We intuit what these pieces want us to think. These are dynamics that have been institutionalized across art-critical discourse, but that, arguably, retain special relevance to "environmental" practice, concerned as it is so concretely with the symbolic qualities of matter *qua* matter—not necessarily as "place" in various models of thought. There might be an unexpected historicity here, but there is also a paradox: material like Eliasson's in Paris helps mobilize a public in its icy actuality and metacommentary about it, but it is a public that, in its institutional framing, tends to be limited as to its socioeconomic makeup. Bits of Greenland expensively dragged to Paris reveal an inconvenient truth, but also *franchise* that critique and then largely walk away.[28] Dialectically, the state of Eliasson's piece summarizes a binary that faces most works dealing with climate change: art's capacity either to "raise awareness" about global crisis—often by seeing a bunch of stuff that is supposed to change our minds (struggling polar bears, speeding Greenpeace zodiac boats)—or to interrogate its actually existing (and unevenly distributed) effects upon social spheres.

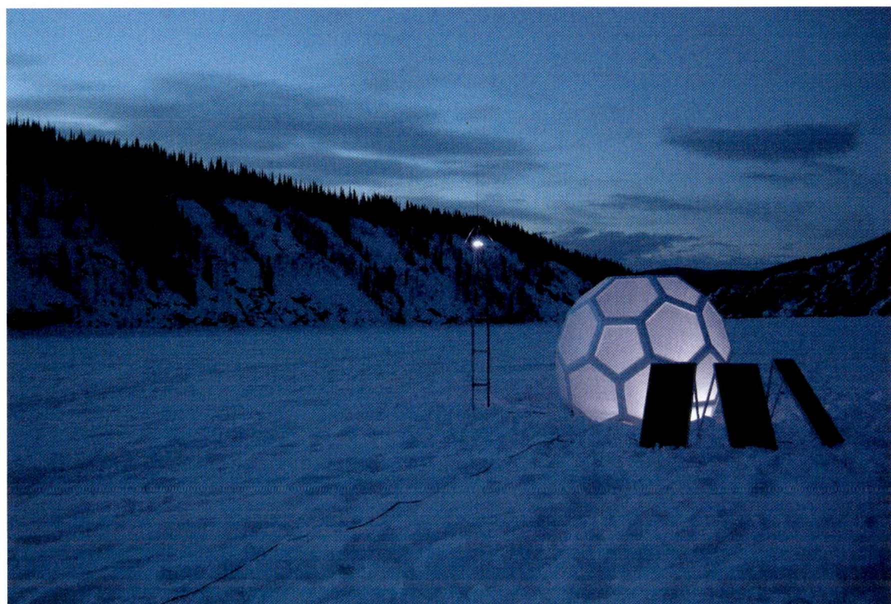

Fig. 9. Charles Stankievech (Canadian, b. 1978), *The DEW Project* (installation view), Confluence of Klondike + Yukon Rivers, Yukon Territory, Canada. 64°03′ N, 139°27′ W

On the latter, there is the work of Charles Stankievech, a founding member of the Yukon School of Visual Arts, the northernmost art school on the North American continent. His work moves between video, installation, performance, film, interviews, and research to embrace the Far North's science-fictional imagination. In Stankievech's 2010 *DEW Project*, for example, electromagnetic waves were recorded around disused American radar stations in the Far North of Canada (fig. 9). In interviews, the artist noted how the construction of the DEW lines in the 1960s was contemporaneous with minimalist sculpture, the white space of the Arctic recalling the white cube of the gallery.[29] Like Stankievech's other "fieldworks" (his term), the *DEW Project* was difficultly visual; it contained other components like writings "possibly" authored by the artist in various venues, and stories about geodesic domes. Not an eschewing of sincerity, the combined practices raised the possibility that "Arctic" art might be capable of framing a discursive mode that is not entirely recognizable to a para-Arctic public, one that often yearns for exoticism at all costs. Of his work, the artist has written: "The only taboo would be in making an absolute distinction between theory and fiction or art and writing."[30]

The sprawling practice of the Center for Land Use Interpretation (CLUI), based in Culver City, California (represented elsewhere in this volume),[31] has been an important influence for Stankievech's research aesthetic. In 2006, CLUI staged *Ultima Thule*, a fixed-video installation set in extreme northern Greenland, detailing the famous Arctic underground city and radar surveillance base (fig. 10). In an arrangement of photographs and video at the National Museum in Nuuk, CLUI displayed details of military listening equipment from the base *in situ* on the barren tundra. Less about the Arctic than its militarization, the document-heavy installation was viewed by only a few hundred people. Like Stankievech's piece, it agnostically framed the Cold War as a conflict of the unseen—of radar, submarines, radio transmissions, front lines across the North Pole. Yet the project militantly de-centered expressive presentations of data and explanation. The implication was subtle: with climate change, a site-specific, static Cold War Arctic of missiles and lines has given way to a fluid Warm War Artic of tankers, space, and land claims.

Defining itself as a "research organization involved in exploring, examining, and understanding land and landscape issues," CLUI has quietly pursued this—the interpretation not of the Earth but of human intervention with the Earth across various landscapes, militarized or not—in heterogeneous activities since the 1990s. As with Greenland's Arctic tundra, CLUI looks at places that are not conventionally beautiful, but places where people actually live and work, places subject to climate change as much as anywhere. Although this seems parodic, CLUI intends dead-serious social practices for a world in which, as one critic puts it, "the ability to change people's minds through argument [is] seen as [an] exhausted mode."[32] As with the *Thule* piece, most CLUI work is not blatantly critical either of the human alteration of the Earth or of its preservation; as Matthew Coolidge has written: "Humans are a part of nature and nature shouldn't be something considered exclusive of humans."[33] Discarded with the practice are ecologies simply of mankind *versus* "environment"; these are exchanged for ecologies of politics, information, capital, and history. "There is something performative in how CLUI refuses to allow their activities to be categorized exclusively as art, geology, land reclamation, or political activism," states historian Cornelia Butler, "preferring instead an amalgam of these."[34] A work like CLUI's *Ultima Thule* might be compelling because it doesn't *brandish* itself *as art*—at least not in the conventional way. It suggests that the critical work of (say) "Arctic" art is not making stuff (even tragic stuff) visible and *meaningful* in easily recognizable ways,

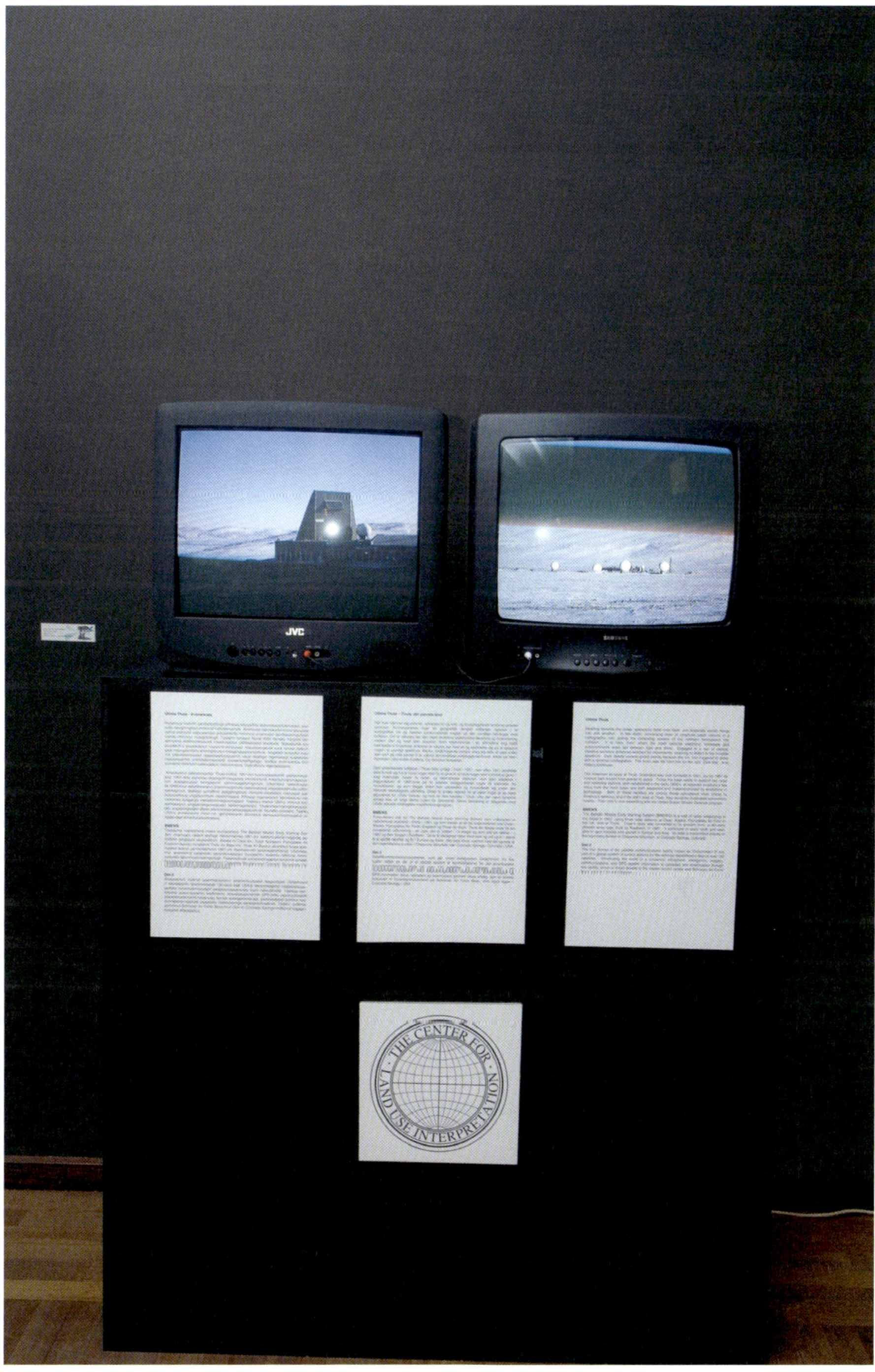

Fig. 10. Center for Land Use Interpretation, *Ultima Thule* (installation view, detail), 2006. Two videos on podium, each two-minute loops

but in interrogating the *limits* of Arctic visibility, of Arctic meaning, via practices which the art world (as complicit in polar melt as any capital-based force today) cannot easily frame.

Perhaps we could put it this way: in comparison to the Greenland of Eliasson's *Ice Watch*, the Greenland of the Center for Land Use Interpretation was collaborative, softly anonymous, de-centered, hard to get to, unironically bureaucratic, oriented toward the permanent. It was kind of boring. CLUI installations often swap out romantic sentiment for an "administrative sublime."[35] But they are not cynical, and not hectoring. Of course, such studied ambiguity runs the risk of sounding a lot like miasmic neoliberal shrugging at intellectual commitment of any kind. And yet, across its practice CLUI rigorously complicates any fetishization of "place" as a site of Heideggerian intimacy with the local; it often reads places as half-connected networks, ones that can fail, decay, disconnect. In its vast archive of photographs, for example, CLUI charts the unexceptional: sites like shopping malls, sewer pipes, and water towers. Through CLUI we think about land—such as Arctic—less as experience than as land as inventory. A preservation operation, yes, but one far more engaged with the notion of nature as something everyday rather than as an excursionary respite.

But across the realm of other art in and *of* the extreme North, we are otherwise threatened by a post-critical turn.[36] Certain contemporary art practices engaging the polar regions, although well meaning, tend to ape globalization's uncritical adoration of connectivity, with works dawdling into either technologized scolding or a limp aesthetic of "edgy," mashed-up tourism.[37] Fair enough. But castigating human behavior on the Earth does not translate into actually saving the Earth. Maybe we can say that any Arctic practice which is stentorian about what it is *about* might be the most problematic. Lippard, after her own polar junket, touted the power of questions raised "out of sight."[38]

If the Far North's original place within early modern culture was as terrain of flight and madness, then surely we are seeing both a return and a *détournement* of the tradition today, for better or for worse. At least for now, the art world's own ecosystem has yet to ruin completely what it might just mean for an art *of* climate change—an art of urgency—to intervene critically in the vitally *unscenic* world of public democracy, itself human, itself public, itself precarious.

1. On this phenomenon see, most recently, Julie Decker and Kirsten J. Anderson, eds., *Up Here: The North at the Center of the World* (Seattle: University of Washington Press, 2016).

2. Chauncey C. Loomis, "After the Arctic Sublime," in *Nature and the Victorian Imagination*, ed. Ulrich C. Knoepflmacher and G. B. Tennyson (Berkeley: University of California Press, 1977), 99.

3. The survey literature on such practices is already extensive: for a sample, see Nicola Triscott, "Critical Art and Intervention in Technologies of the Arctic," in *Arctic Geopolitics and Autonomy*, ed. Michael Bravo and Nicola Triscott (Berlin: Hatje Cantz, 2010), 19–36.

4. Benjamin Morgan, "After the Arctic Sublime," *New Literary History* 47, no. 1 (Winter 2016): 2. On the "archipelagic" episteme of the early modern North, see Adriana Craciun, *Writing Arctic Disaster* (Cambridge: Cambridge University Press, 2016).

5. Iain and Ingrid Baxter organized the Edmonton show. See Nancy Shaw, "Siting the Banal: The Extended Landscapes of the N.E. Thing Company," in *Beyond Wilderness: The Group of Seven, Canadian Identity, and Contemporary Art*, ed. John O'Brian and Peter White (Montreal and Kingston: McGill-Queen's University Press, 2007), 63–68; and Grant Arnold and Karen Henry, *Traffic: Conceptual Art in Canada, 1965–1980*, exh. cat. (Vancouver: Vancouver Art Gallery, 2012), 73–74.

6. Lucy R. Lippard, "Art Within the Arctic Circle," *Hudson Review* 22, no. 4 (Winter 1969–70): 665–74.

7. Ibid., 672.

8. Ibid., 673.

9. Ibid., 666.

10. Lucy Lippard, personal communication with the author, April 14, 2015, and further: "I have no idea where the other prints or negatives [from the Inuvik trip] are. I certainly took more than what was in the article." See also the work of Caroline Kelly, which engages with the Lippard photographs explicitly, at http://carolinekelley.com/section/207755-Arctic-Circle-Project-I-II.html (accessed November 20, 2017).

11. Cf. Sidney Tillim, "Earthworks and the New Picturesque," *Artforum* 7, no. 4 (December 1968): 42–45.

12. Charity Mewburn, *Sixteen Hundred Miles North of Denver* (Vancouver: Belkin Art Gallery, University of British Columbia, 1999), 26–28.

13. Ross Fox, "The Greenberg Factor," in *The Canadian Painters Eleven (1953–1960) from the Robert Mclaughlin Gallery* (Amherst, Mass.: Mead Art Gallery, 1994), 26–37.

14. Lippard, "Arctic Circle," 669.

15. Ibid., 666.

16. See Tineke Reijnders, "De atleet die het landschap voorbij doet rollen: Over kunstenaar Guido van der Werve," *Ons Erfdeel* 2 (2013): 80–89.

17. Christine Ross, *The Past is the Present, It's the Future Too: The Temporal Turn in Contemporary Art* (New York: Bloomsbury, 2012).

18. https://www.grossestreffen.org/marja-helander (accessed November 20, 2017).

19. http://icewatchparis.com (accessed November 20, 2017).

20. See Maggie M. Cao, "The Entropic History of Ice," in this volume.

21. Lucy Lippard, Stephanie Smith, and Andrew Revkin, eds., *Weather Report: Art and Climate Change* (Boulder, Col.: Museum of Contemporary Art, 2007); on the history of such an approach, see SueEllen Campbell, *The Face of the Earth: Natural Landscapes, Science, and Culture* (Berkeley: University of California Press, 2011), 118.

22. Eliasson's comments appeared on the various versions of icewatch.com; on the problematics of the idea of "action" herein summoned with regard to the environment, see T. J. Demos, *Against the Anthropocene* (Berlin: Sternberg Press, 2017.)

23. http://www.artists4climate.com/en/artists/olafur-eliasson (accessed November 20, 2017).

24. Quoted in Cynthia Zarin, "The Artist Who Is Bringing Icebergs to Paris," *The New Yorker*, December 5, 2015.

25. http://hyperallergic.com/260217/olafur-eliassons-sundial-of- melting-icebergs-clocks-in-at-half-past-wasteful (accessed November 20, 2017). See David Balzer, "The Carbon Footprint of Art," *Canadian Art*, February 20, 2017.

26. Jason W. Moore, "The Capitalocene, Part I: On the Nature and Origins of our Ecological Crisis," *Journal of Peasant Studies* 44 (2017): 594–630.

27. Emily Apter et al., "A Questionnaire on Materialisms," *October* 155 (Winter 2016): 3.

28. Website notwithstanding: see *icewatch.org*.

29. See Joshua Bolchover and Jonathan D. Solomon, *Sustain and Develop* (New York: Princeton Architectural Press, 2010), 298–300.

30. Anna-Sophie Springer, "Traversals," in Charles Stankievech, *Loveland* (Berlin: K. Verlag, 2011), 203.

31. See the final essay in this volume, "Photo Essay: Peripheral and Central Places in the USA."

32. Astra Taylor points out that "activist" began as a slur in the 1930s leveled against leftist protesters by reactionary forces of management. "Organizer," by contrast, is a word self-applied in trade union and labor circles during the same decade. See Astra Taylor, "Against Activism," *The Baffler* 30 (2016): 123–31, esp. 127.

33. In Kate L. Haug, "The Human/Land Dialectic: Anthropic Landscapes of the Center for Land Use Interpretation," *Afterimage* 25, no. 2 (September–October 1997): 3–5.

34. Cornelia Butler, cited in Eugenie Tsai, Cornelia Butler, Thomas Crow, and Alexander Alberro, *Robert Smithson*, exh. cat., Museum of Contemporary Art, Los Angeles (Los Angeles, 2004), 237.

35. Michael Ned Holte, "The Administrative Sublime or the Center for Land Use Interpretation at the Circumference," *Afterall* 13 (Spring–Summer 2006): 25.

36. Hal Foster, "Post-Critical," *October* 139 (Winter 2012): 3–8.

37. See, for example, Paul D. Miller's *Terra Nova: Sinfonia Antarctica* project (2009) or its related book, *The Book of Ice* (New York: Mark Batty Publisher, 2011).

38. Lippard, "Arctic Circle," 674.

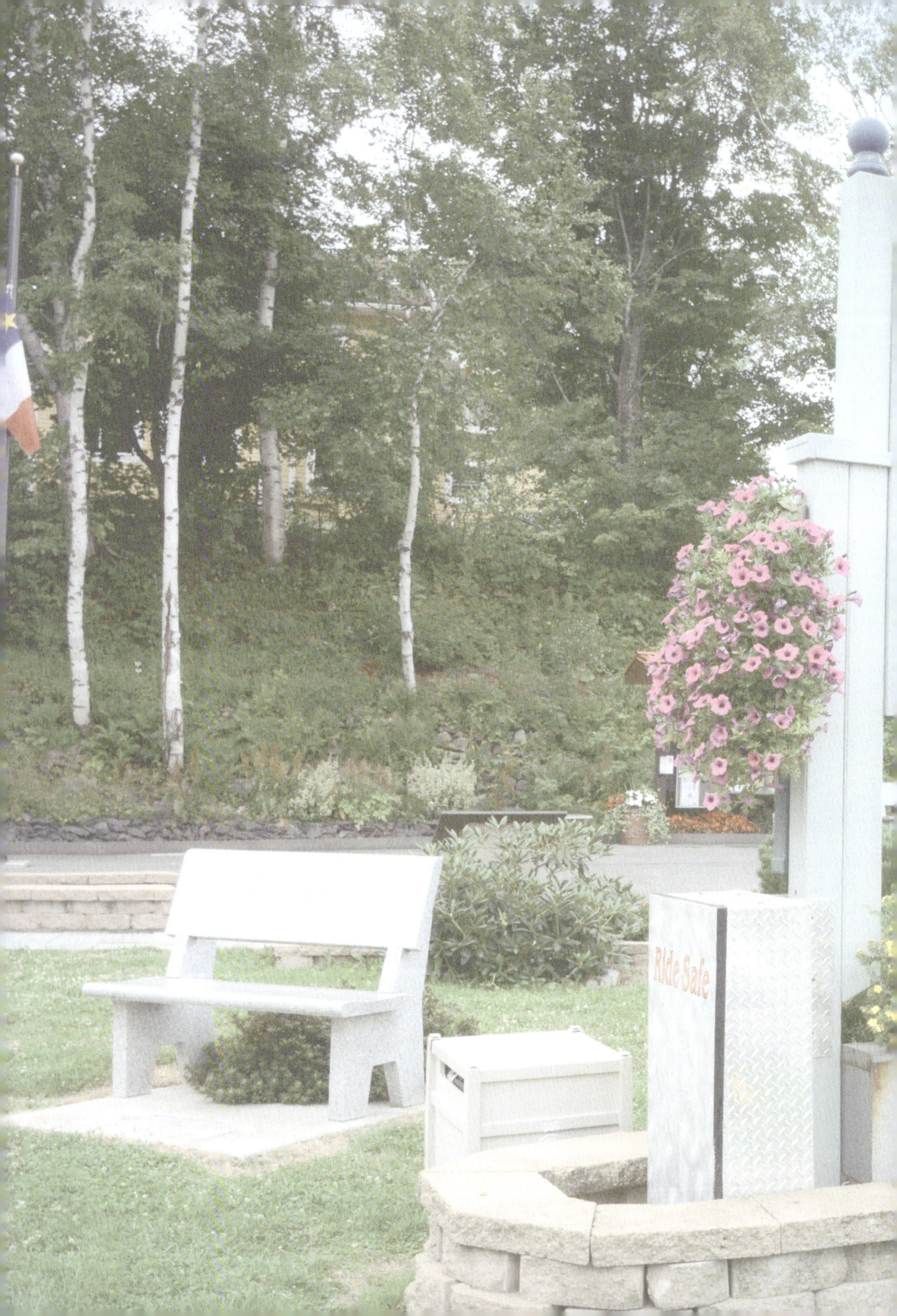
Ride Safe

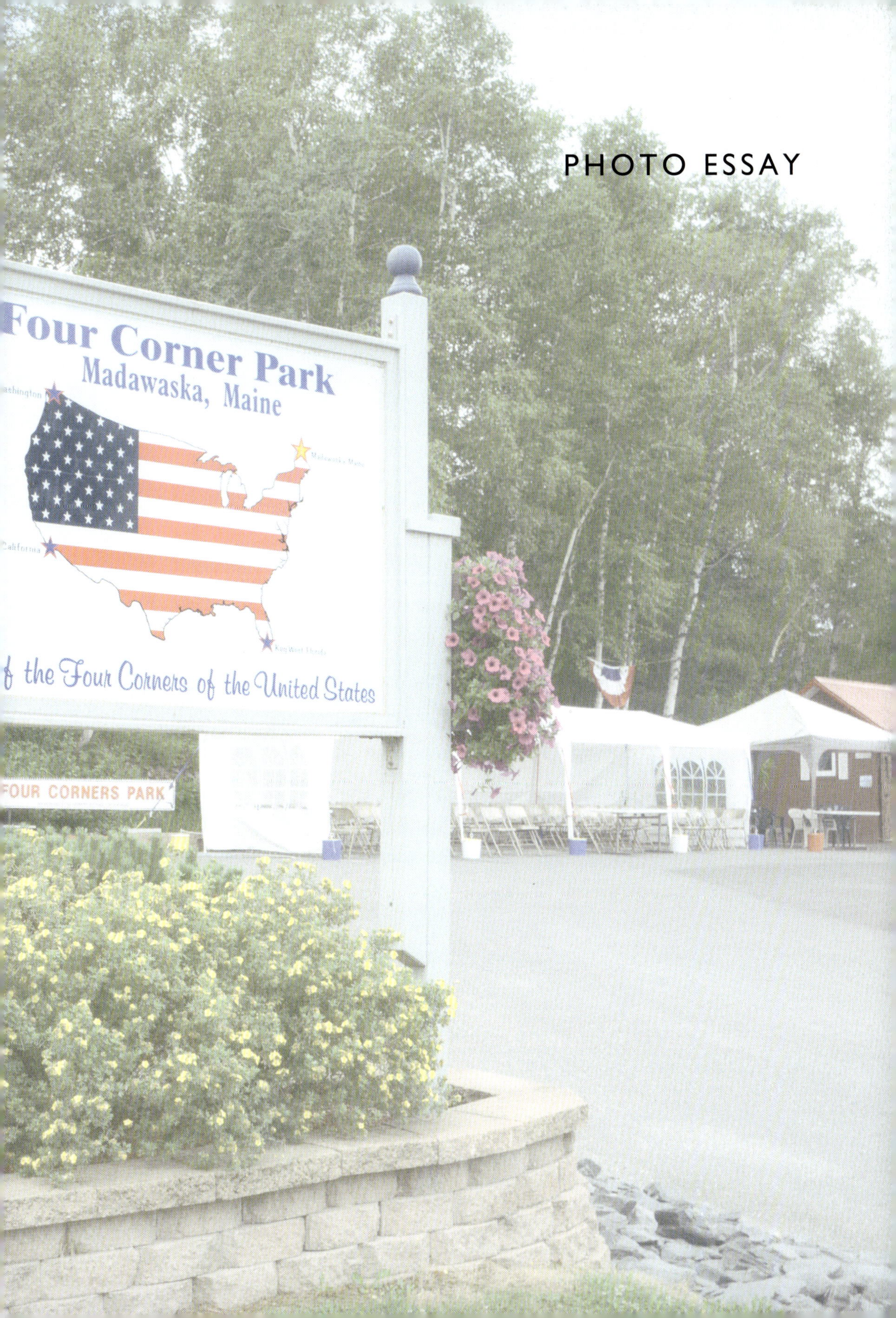
Four Corner Park
Madawaska, Maine
Washington
Madawaska, Maine
California
Key West, Florida
f the Four Corners of the United States
FOUR CORNERS PARK

Peripheral and Central Places in the USA

Center for Land Use Interpretation

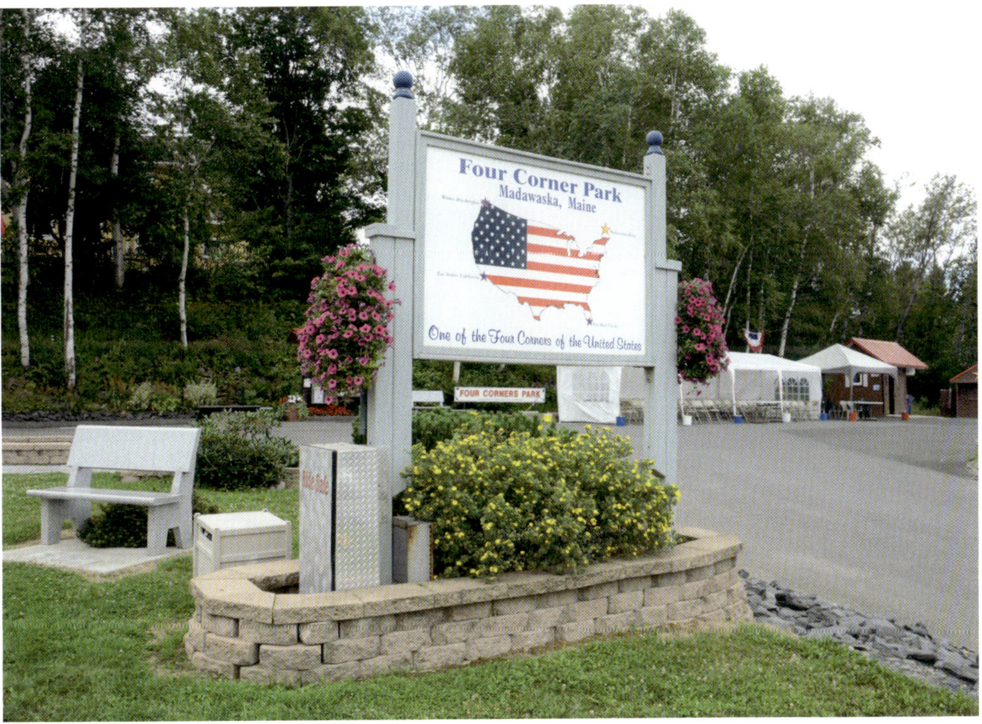

Fig. 1 (and detail, pp. 310–311). Center for Land Use Interpretation, Four Corners Park, Madawaska, Maine, 2014. CLUI photo

Madawaska, Maine, considers itself the most northeasterly town in the nation, and therefore one of the four corners of the United States. This fact is promoted especially at Four Corners Park. The park was opened in 2007, primarily to celebrate motorcyclists who do a four corners trip, visiting each corner of the United States in as few as twenty-one days.

The northernmost point in the continental United States (outside Alaska) is part of the area known as the Northwest Angle, on the shores of the Lake of the Woods, Minnesota. This point sticks up north of the 49th parallel, a straight line that serves as the border for more than 1,200 miles westward, to the Pacific Ocean. East of this point the border meanders across 1,300 miles of waterways, until it

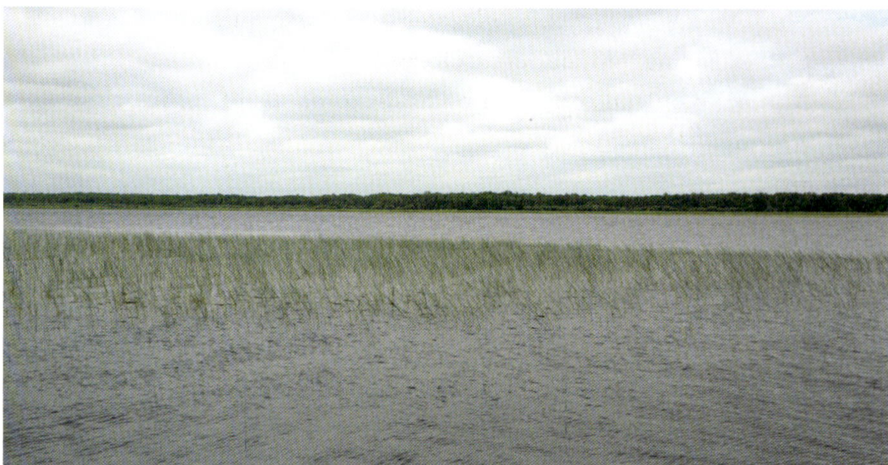

Fig. 2. Center for Land Use Interpretation, Angle Inlet, Minnesota, 2014. CLUI photo

picks up the 45th parallel at St. Regis, New York. Treaties establishing the border in the eighteenth century named the most northwestern point of the Lake of the Woods as the limit of the water boundary. Later surveys found this point actually lies 27 miles north of the 49th parallel, so the border was drawn due south from here to the 49th, resulting in this northernmost bulge in the boundary. The actual point is in the water, and is unmarked.

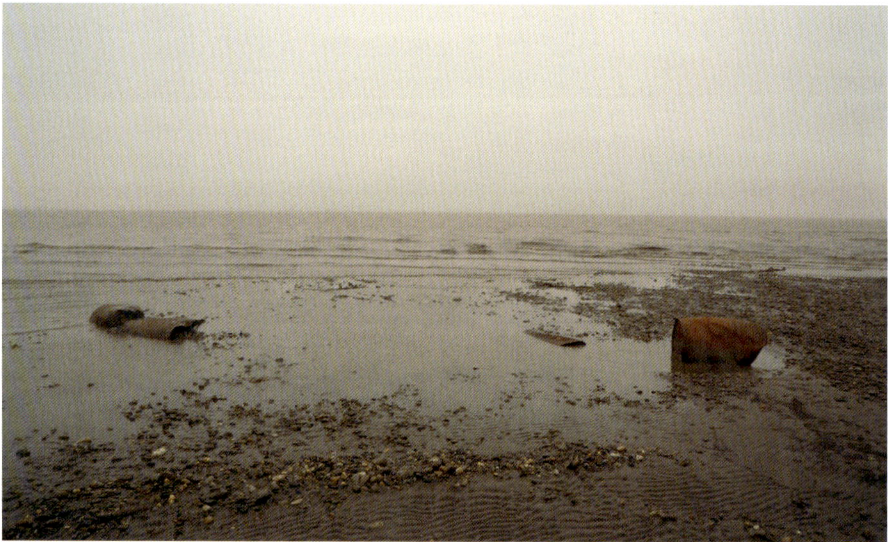

Fig. 3. Center for Land Use Interpretation, East Dock, Prudhoe Bay, Alaska, 2008. CLUI photo

East Dock is a loading and storage area on a constructed promontory extending into the Arctic Ocean at Prudhoe Bay, Alaska. It is the northernmost point of land connected by roads to the rest of the continent and accessible by the general public. Tour buses take visitors the last few miles from the town of Deadhorse to this point, as road access to the Arctic Ocean is restricted, on land controlled by oil companies. Point Barrow, 200 miles away, is the northernmost point in Alaska, but it is not connected by roads.

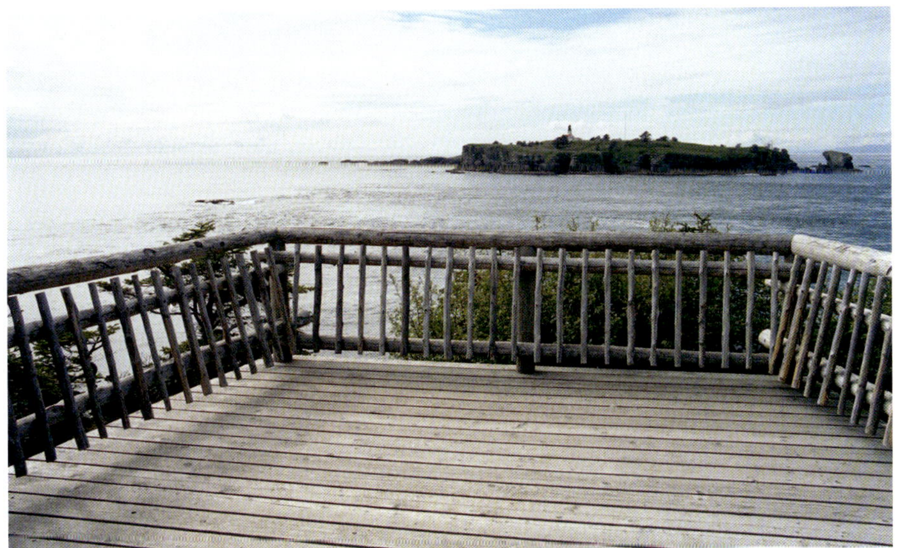

Fig. 4. Center for Land Use Interpretation, Cape Flattery, Washington, 2000. CLUI photo

This point of land and the bush that grows upon it is generally considered the most north and west point on the contiguous landmass of the continental United States (the "lower 48")—a sort of Northwest's northwest. It is located on Cape Flattery, between the Strait of Juan de Fuca and the Pacific Ocean, on the Makah Indian Reservation. A half-mile-long path through the woods from a parking lot at the end of a dirt road leads to a rustic platform on top of a cliff. Ten miles south of Cape Flattery is Cape Avala, an even more remote and unheralded lump on the Olympic Peninsula, which is actually 350 feet farther west.

On the southern coast of Oregon is Cape Blanco, the second-most-western point on the West Coast, after Cape Flattery/Cape Avala in Washington. This stretch of coast is a favored landing point for undersea cables, connecting America to the rest of the Pacific world.

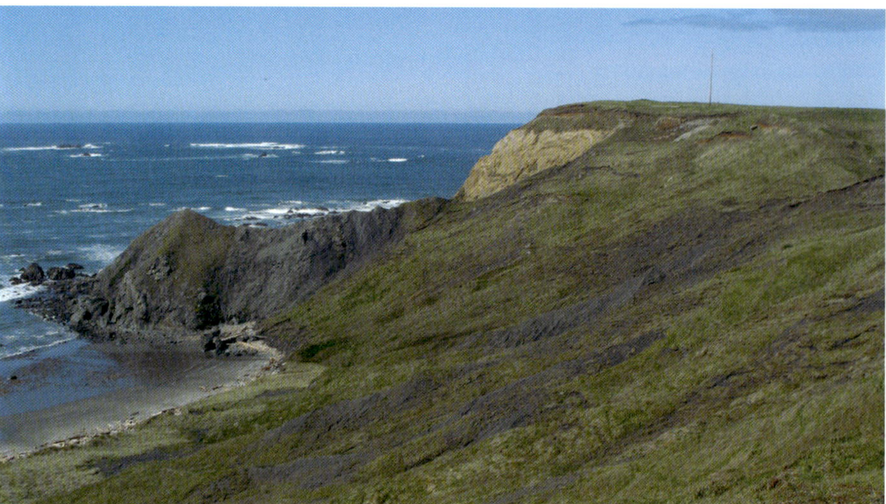

Fig. 5. Center for Land Use Interpretation, Cape Blanco, Oregon, 2003. CLUI photo

The border with Mexico physically manifests as a metal fence emerging from the Pacific Ocean and crossing the beach here at Border Field State Park, the southwestern corner of the United States. From here, the fence goes east as a series of straight lines over the land for 600 miles, to El Paso, where the border enters the meandering channel of the Rio Grande.

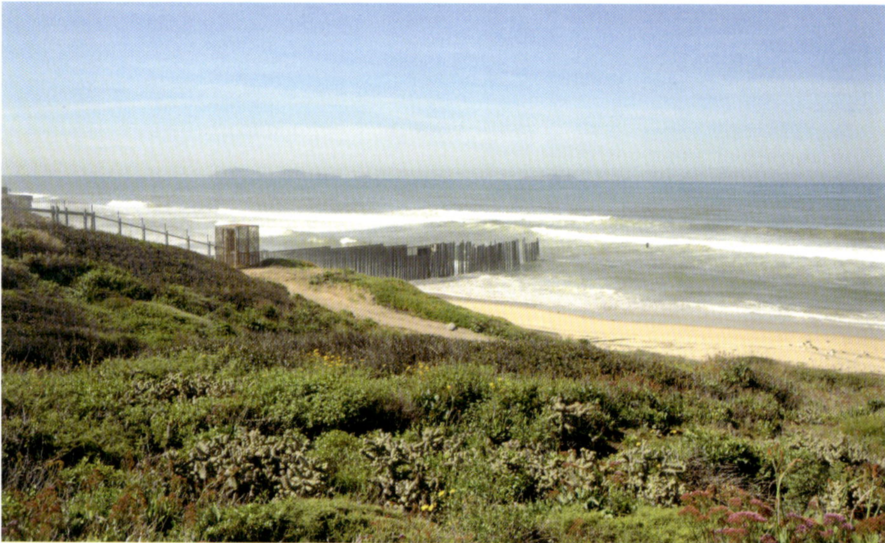

Fig. 6. Center for Land Use Interpretation, Border Field State Park, San Diego, California, 2010. CLUI photo

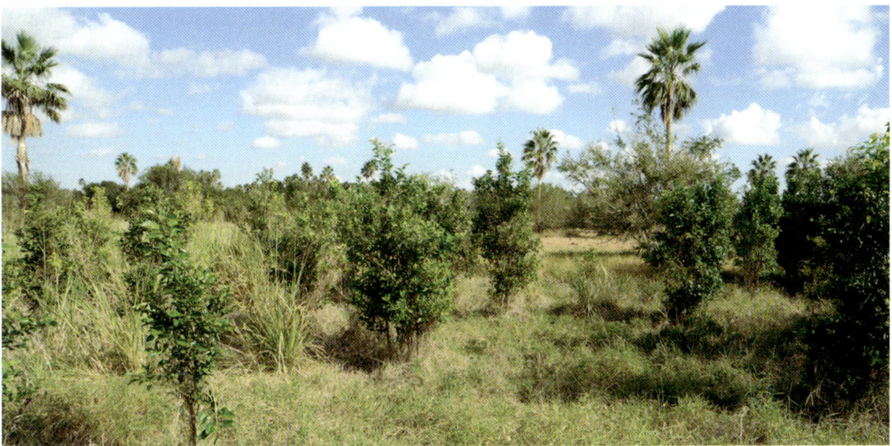

Fig. 7. Center for Land Use Interpretation, Southmost Ranch, Cameron County, Texas, 2008. CLUI photo

The Rio Grande meanders dramatically as it approaches its terminus at the Atlantic Ocean near Brownsville, Texas. A bend in the river on the Southmost Ranch, across from Ejido Longereño, Mexico, is the southernmost point of land in the United States, besides Hawaii and Florida. Levees protect the agricultural land on the American side of the river.

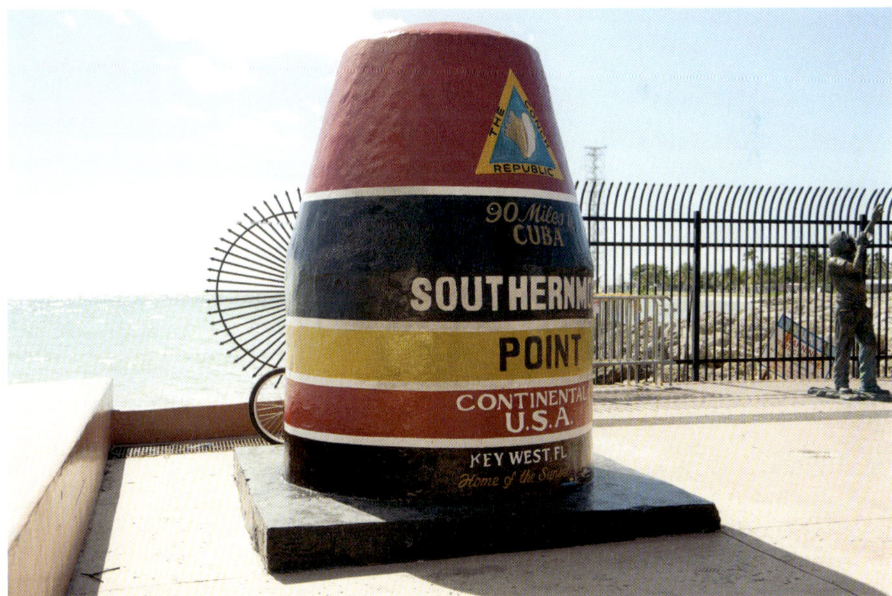

Fig. 8. Center for Land Use Interpretation, Southernmost Point Monument, Key West, Florida, 2016. CLUI photo

A popular monument at the southern end of the Florida Keys marks the southernmost point on the continental United States. Though the Keys were originally islands, they are now connected to the shore by highway and railway causeways, extending the continental national perimeter in a 100-mile-long arc to the last island on the chain, Key West. The Southernmost Point Monument, however, is not the southernmost point, but rather the southernmost point to which the public has access. Next to the monument is the fence of the Key West Naval Air Station, where a point of land named Whitehead Spit projects farther south, into the sea.

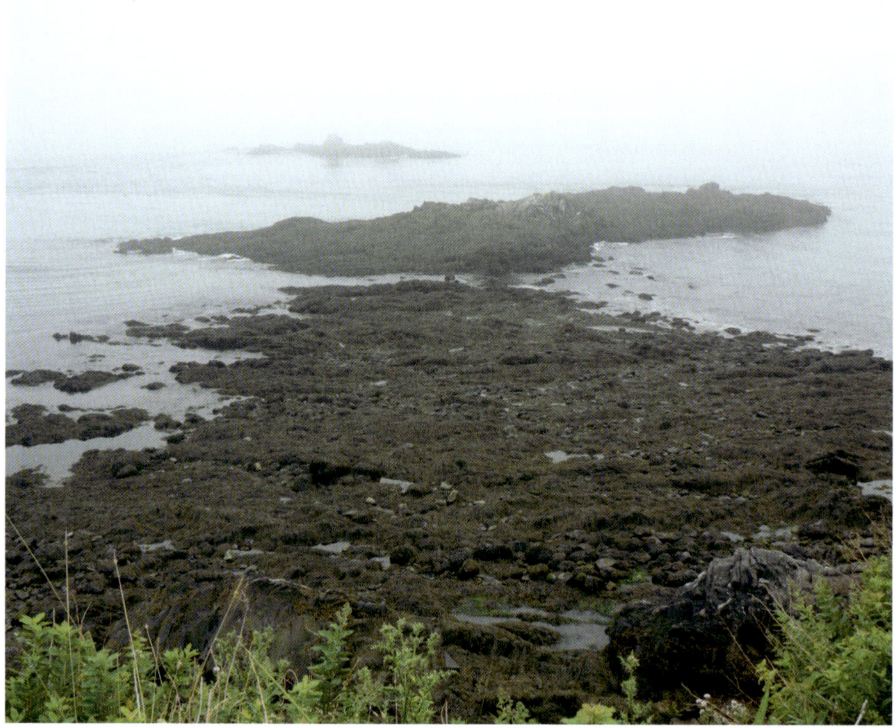

Fig. 9. Center for Land Use Interpretation, West Quoddy Head, Maine, 2014. CLUI photo

The rocky peninsula at the bottom of the bluff at West Quoddy Head is the easternmost point in the United States. The international boundary emerges from the sea off the Head and runs inland, past the West Quoddy Head lighthouse. The area is often socked in by fog, and a fog horn periodically sounds off next to the lighthouse.

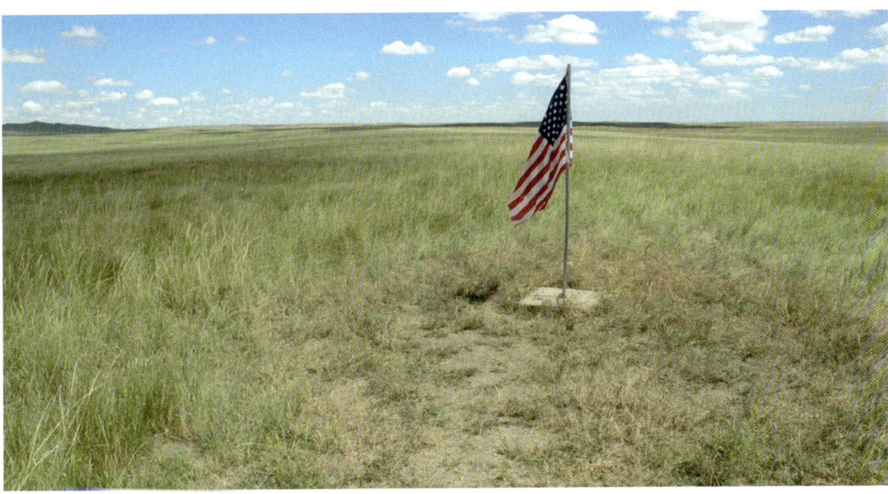

Fig.10. Center for Land Use Interpretation, Geographic Center of the Fifty United States of America Site, South Dakota, 2010. CLUI photo

The geographic center of the United States is generally accepted to be at this point, in a field, 20.8 miles north of Belle Fourche, South Dakota. This was determined as the point at which an arc connecting the geographic center of the forty-nine states and the geographic center of Hawaii would balance. This point was established on the admittance of Hawaii into the Union, in 1959, and a small ceremony was held here to celebrate.

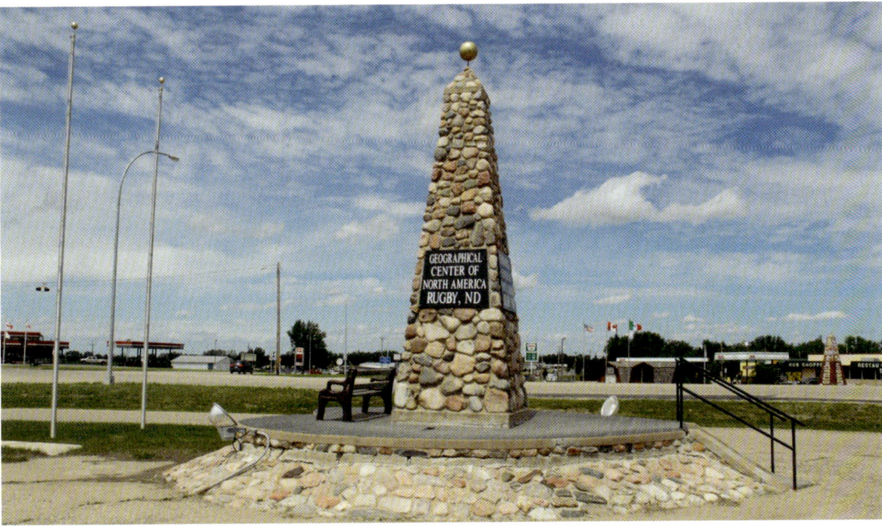

Fig.11. Center for Land Use Interpretation, Geographic Center of North America Monument, Rugby, North Dakota, 2007. CLUI photo

The geographic center of North America is marked with a pyramidal monument in the town of Rugby, North Dakota, despite the fact that the mathematically determined location fell in a lake sixteen miles away.

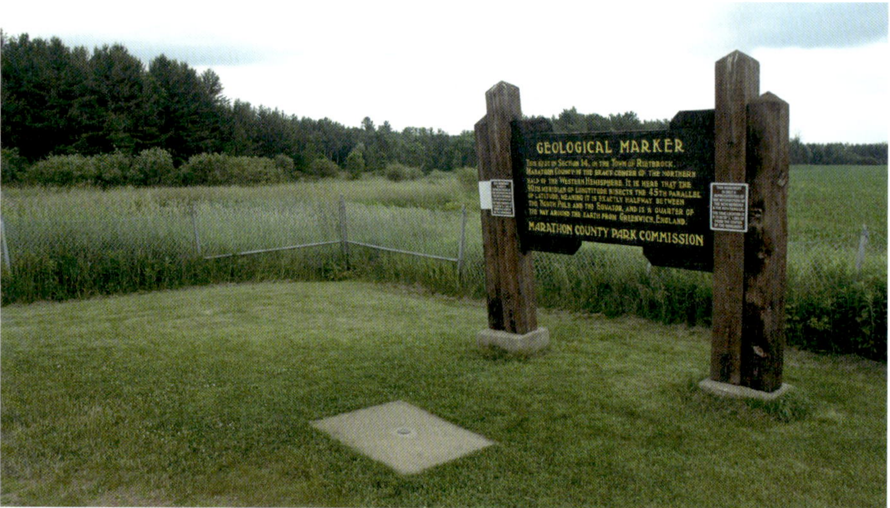

Fig. 12. Center for Land Use Interpretation, The Center of the Northern Hemisphere Monument, Rietbrock, Wisconsin, 2011. CLUI photo

The center of the northern hemisphere is marked with a monument outside Rietbrock, Wisconsin, where the line of 45° latitude north, the point halfway between the North Pole and the equator, meets the line of 90° longitude west, one quarter of the way around the world from the prime meridian in Greenwich.

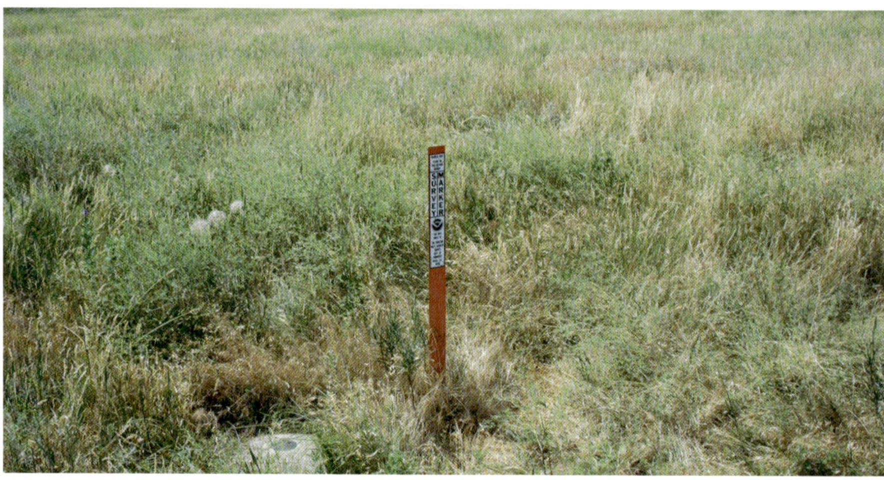

Fig. 13. Center for Land Use Interpretation, Geodetic Center of the Nation, Kansas, 2010. CLUI photo

The geodetic center of the nation is marked with a small bronze disc in a field north of Lucas, Kansas. Known as Meades Ranch, this is one of the most significant survey points in the world. In surveyor's parlance, this was the "primary station" for all Mexican, American, and Canadian surveys, known as the North American Datum of 1927 (NAD 27), from which nearly a sixth of the world's surface was geodetically referenced, until 1983, when a new, more accurate global surveying system was adopted, which moved the datum point from Meades Ranch to the Earth's center of mass.

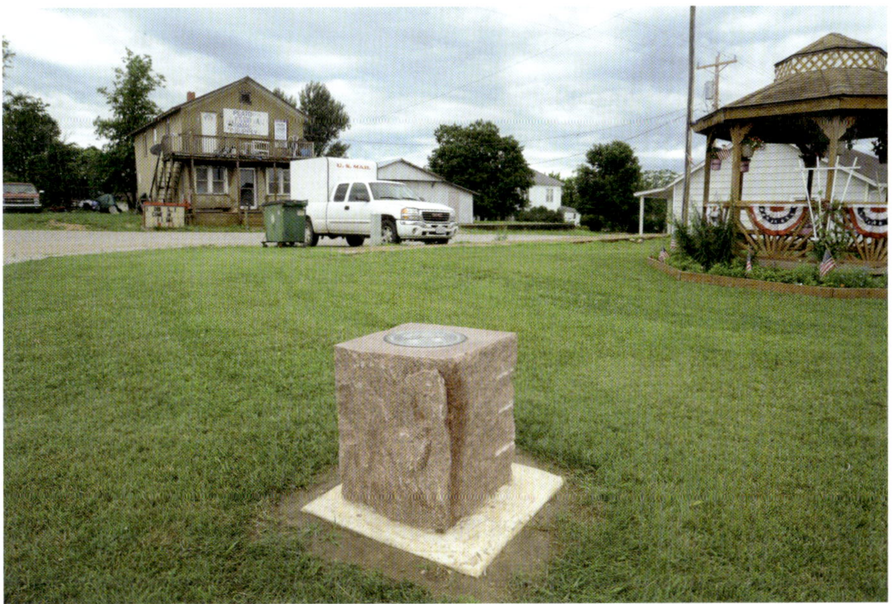

Fig. 14. Center for Land Use Interpretation, Current Official Population Center of the Nation Monument, Plato, Missouri, 2011. CLUI photo

The official population center of the United States, as determined by the 2010 national census, was declared to be at Plato, Missouri. The calculation has been made every decade since 1790, when it was in Maryland, and the population center has been moving west/southwest since then. Based on 2010 census data, the mathematical point was actually 2.7 miles east of Plato, in the woods on private property. The chief geodetic surveyor from the National Geodetic Survey negotiated with local officials to put the monument in a public place near the middle of town so that it would be more accessible.

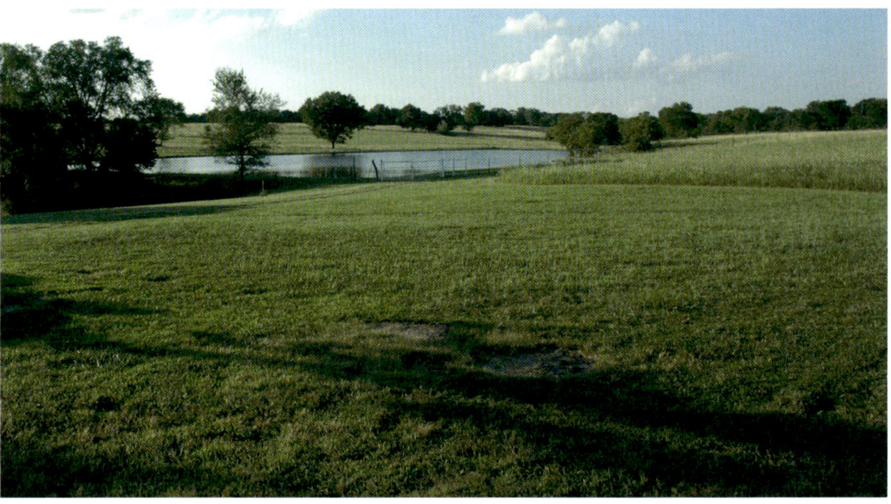

Fig. 15. Center for Land Use Interpretation, Google Center of the United States on a Mac, Dearing, Kansas, 2010. CLUI photo

Searching for the United States of America in Google Maps or Google Earth on a computer running Mac-based software renders a map of the United States that is centered on a point at the southern edge of a small pond on a farm north of Dearing, Kansas. This is apparently because Dan Webb, the Google engineer who worked on the coding, grew up on this farm and selected it as the default site.

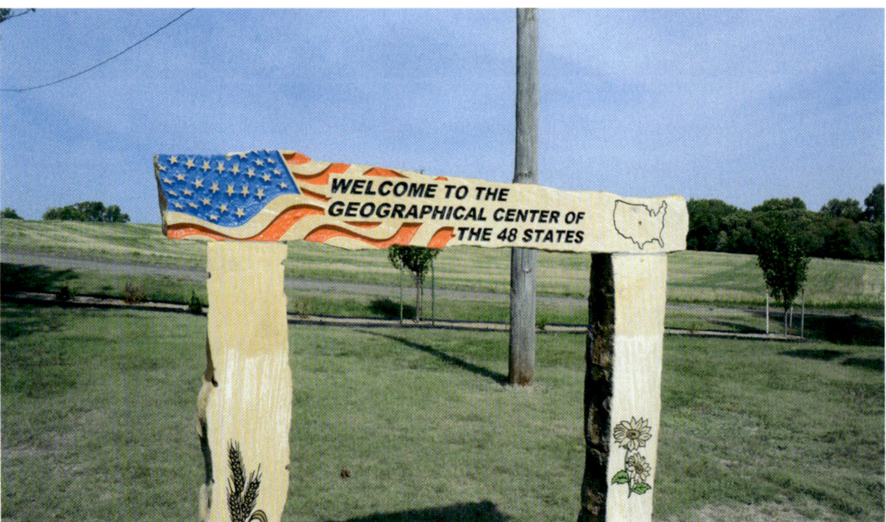

Fig. 16. Center for Land Use Interpretation, Geographical Center of the Contiguous Continental United States, Lebanon, Kansas, 2012. CLUI photo

As early as the 1920s, the Geographical Center of the United States was considered by most officials to be located at 39°50' north latitude by 98°35' west longitude, determined as the point where a flat map of the forty-eight states would balance if it were of uniform thickness. This point was determined mathematically, and by mounting a large map of the nation on cardboard, trimming the edges off, and balancing it on a string, hanging from above. On the ground, this location, which had been approximate to begin with, and rounded off to degrees and minutes, landed in an active hog farm north of the town of Lebanon, Kansas. A nearby area was cleaned up into a park, complete with a new highway and a motel, to celebrate the site.

Contributors

Maggie M. Cao is the David G. Frey Assistant Professor of Art History at the University of North Carolina at Chapel Hill. She received her PhD from Harvard University in 2014 and completed postdoctoral work at the Columbia University Society of Fellows. Her new book, *The End of Landscape in Nineteenth-Century America* (2018), examines the dissolution of landscape painting as a major cultural project in the late nineteenth-century United States. She is currently at work on a project titled "New Media in the Age of Sail," which examines art forms that emerged from contexts of global commerce in the long eighteenth century. She is also involved in collaborative projects centered on the environmental humanities and new approaches to art and economics.

The Center for Land Use Interpretation (Matthew Coolidge and Aurora Tang) is a research and education organization interested in understanding the nature and extent of human interaction with the surface of the earth, and in finding new meanings in the intentional and incidental forms that people individually and collectively create. The organization was founded in 1994, and since that time it has produced dozens of exhibits on land use themes and regions for public institutions all over the United States, as well as overseas. The Center publishes books, conducts public tours, and offers information and research resources through its library, archive, and website. The Center exists to stimulate discussion, thought, and general interest in the contemporary landscape. Neither an environmental group nor an industry-affiliated organization, the work of the Center integrates the many approaches to land use into a single vision that illustrates the common ground in "land use" debates. At the very least, the Center attempts to emphasize the multiplicity of points of view regarding the utilization of terrestrial and geographic resources.

Jeffrey Jerome Cohen is dean of humanities at Arizona State University. His research examines strange and beautiful things that challenge the imagination, phenomena that seem alien and intimate at once. He is especially interested in what monsters, misfits, inhuman forces, objects, and matter that won't stay put reveal about the cultures that dream, fear, and desire them. Cohen is widely published in the fields of medieval studies, monster theory, posthumanism, and eco-criticism. His book *Stone: An Ecology of the Inhuman* received the 2017 René Wellek Prize for best book in comparative literature from the American Comparative Literature Association. With Julian Yates he is co-writing *Noah's Arkive: Towards an Ecology of Refuge*. He currently serves, with Stacy Alaimo, as co-president of the Association for the Study of Literature and the Environment (ASLE).

Vittoria Di Palma is associate professor of architectural history and theory at the University of Southern California. Before joining USC, she taught at Columbia University, Rice University, and the Architectural Association School of Architecture. She has held visiting positions at the University of Calgary and the Oslo School of Architecture and Design, and has received fellowships from the Canadian Centre for Architecture, Dumbarton Oaks, the Paul Mellon Centre for Studies in British Art, the William Andrews Clark Memorial Library, and the Huntington Library. She is a co-editor of *Intimate Metropolis: Urban Subjects in the Modern City* (2009), and the author of *Wasteland, A History* (2014), which received the 2016 Herbert Baxter Adams Prize, the 2016 Elisabeth Blair MacDougall Award, the 2015 Louis Gottschalk Prize, and a 2015 J. B. Jackson Book Prize.

Robert Felfe is professor of seventeenth- and eighteenth-century art history at the Universität Hamburg and a member of the Naturbilder/Images of Nature research group. He received his PhD in art history in 2000 with a thesis on the natural sciences and book illustration around the turn of the eighteenth century. Subsequently he was a postdoctoral scholar at the Freie Universität Berlin where he completed his habilitation on art and nature in the context of early modern collecting. In 2012–13 he was fellow at the Kunsthistorisches Institut Florenz and held a visiting professorship at the Universität der Künste Berlin (art academy). Between 2010 and 2016 he was a member of the editorial board of *kritische berichte - Zeitschrift für Kunst- und Kulturwissenschaften*.

Chelsea Mikael Frazier is a PhD candidate in the department of African American studies and a fellow in the Science in Human Culture Program at Northwestern University. In her scholarship and pedagogy, she brings eco-critical approaches to the study of contemporary Black women artists, writers, and activists. Grounded in Black feminist theory, eco-criticism, decolonial studies, political ecology, and new materialism, Frazier probes the ways in which dominant theoretical and disciplinary frameworks in environmental studies obscure the legibility of a Black feminist ecoethic as it manifests in Black women's writings, visual art, and activism across the African diaspora. Frazier's research has been generously supported by the Social Science Research Council, the Mellon Mays Fellowship program, and the Alumni Association of Barnard College. Her published work appears in the *Journal of Critical Ethnic Studies.*

Ghana ThinkTank (John Ewing, Maria del Carmen Montoya, and Christopher Robbins) is an artist collective known for its unconventional approach to negotiating social conflicts. Using a blend of public art and community organizing, they have been "developing the First World" since 2006. They collect problems in the "developed" world, and send them to think tanks they establish in Cuba, Ghana, Palestine, Iran, and a facility for incarcerated teenage girls in the United States. They then work with the communities where the problems originated to implement those solutions—whether they seem impractical or brilliant. In 2017, Ghana ThinkTank worked with the Williams College Museum of Art on a year-long initiative focusing on climate change. They began by working with an Action Team of students and faculty to ask residents in Williamstown environs "How does climate change affect YOU?" These problems were sent to think tanks in Indonesia and Morocco—countries already grappling with the impacts of climate change—that provided solutions to these problems and then journeyed to the United States to help implement these ideas.

Christopher P. Heuer is associate professor of art history at the University of Rochester. He is the author of *The City Rehearsed: Object, Architecture and Print in the Worlds of Hans Vredeman de Vries* (2009) and coauthor of *Vision and Communism* (2011). The recipient of Fulbright, Getty, Mellon, Kress, Humboldt, and CASVA fellowships, he formerly taught at both Columbia and Princeton Universities. He remains a founding member of the media collective Our Literal Speed, based in Selma, Alabama. A new book on the Renaissance arctic, *Into the White*, is forthcoming from Zone Books/MIT Press.

Jessica L. Horton is an assistant professor of modern, contemporary, and Native American art history at the University of Delaware. She is the author of the book, *Art for an Undivided Earth: The American Indian Movement Generation* (Duke University Press, 2017), which was awarded a Wyeth Foundation for American Art Publication Grant and included in the Andrew W. Mellon Foundation Art History Publication Initiative. Her essays about globalization, space, materiality, ecology, and Indigenous politics have appeared in publications such as *Art Journal, Art History, American Art, Third Text,* and *The Journal of Transnational American Studies.* Her research has been supported by the Getty Research Institute, the Smithsonian Institution, the Center for Advanced Study in the Visual Arts, the Social Science Research Council, and the Terra Foundation for American Art, among others. She is helping to design and build an earth-sheltered, solar-powered house in rural northern California.

Sarah Kanouse is an interdisciplinary artist and writer examining the politics of space, memory, and the built environment. Her research-based creative projects trace the production of landscape through political processes, ecological agents, and the practices of everyday life. Her feature-length film, *Around Crab Orchard*, addresses the imbrication of military, carceral, and conservation spaces in an American wildlife refuge. The image-text book *Re-Collecting Black Hawk* (with Nicholas Brown) explores vernacular landscapes of settler commemoration in the American Midwest. Kanouse has screened or exhibited at Documenta 13, the Smart Museum, the Cooper Union, the Museum of Contemporary Art Detroit, and in other international venues. She has written on site-based and critical art practices in such publications as *Art Journal, Acme,* and *Leonardo,* and in numerous edited volumes. She is currently associate professor in the department of art and design at Northeastern University, where she directs the MFA program in interdisciplinary art.

Sonya S. Lee is associate professor of Chinese art and visual culture at the University of Southern California. She has published widely on the material culture of Chinese Buddhism, including *Surviving Nirvana: Death of the Buddha in Chinese Visual Culture* (2010). Currently, Dr. Lee is completing a book manuscript titled *Cave Temples of Sichuan and Chongqing in Eco–Art History*, in which she explores the interrelationship between art and the environment by focusing on Buddhist cave temples in southwest China.

Dylan Miner is a Wiisaakodewinini (Métis) artist, activist, and scholar. He is director of American Indian and Indigenous studies and associate professor at Michigan State University. He is on the Michigan Indian Education Council and is a founding member of the Justseeds artist collective. Miner holds a PhD from the University of New Mexico. In 2010, he was awarded an Artist Leadership Fellowship through the National Museum of the American Indian, Smithsonian Institution. He has been featured in more than twenty solo exhibitions. His book *Creating Aztlán: Chicano Art, Indigenous Sovereignty, and Lowriding Across Turtle Island* was published by the University of Arizona Press. In 2017, Miner published an artist's book titled *Aanikoobijigan // Waawaashkeshi* with Issue Press. He is currently completing a book on Indigenous aesthetics and writing his first book of poetry.

James Nisbet is associate professor in the department of art history and director of the PhD program in visual studies at the University of California, Irvine. He works on modern and contemporary art, with special interests in environmental history and the history of photo-based media. Nisbet's book *Ecologies, Environments, and Energy Systems in Art of the 1960s and 1970s* was published by MIT Press in 2014.

Verity Platt is professor of classics and history of art at Cornell University, where she also curates the Cornell Cast Collection. She is the author of *Facing the Gods: Epiphany and Representation in Graeco-Roman Art, Literature and Religion* (2011) and editor, with Michael Squire, of *The Art of Art History in Graeco-Roman Antiquity* (2010) and *The Frame in Classical Art: A Cultural History* (2017). She currently holds a fellowship at Cornell's Atkinson Center for Sustainability and the Environment, where she is working on an eco-critical reading of Pliny the Elder's *Natural History*.

Julian Yates is professor of English and material culture studies at University of Delaware. He is the author of some forty essays on medieval and Renaissance literature and culture, questions of ecology, the posthuman, and literary theory; and author or editor of four books: *Error, Misuse, Failure: Object Lessons from the English Renaissance* (2003), which was a finalist for the Modern Language Association's Best First Book Prize; *What's the Worst Thing You Can Do To Shakespeare?* (2013), co-authored with Richard Burt; *Object-Oriented Environs in Early Modern England* (2016), co-edited with Jeffrey Jerome Cohen; and, most recently, *Of Sheep, Oranges, and Yeast: A Multispecies Impression* (2017), which won the Michelle Kendrick Memorial Best Book Prize from the Society for Literature, Science, and the Arts.

Rebecca Zorach is the Mary Jane Crowe Professor of Art History at Northwestern University. She teaches and writes on early modern European art (fifteenth–seventeenth century), contemporary activist art, and art of the 1960s and 1970s. Particular interests include print media, feminist and queer theory, theory of representation, and the multiple intersections of art and politics. Before joining the faculty at Northwestern she taught at the University of Chicago and was a visiting faculty member at Yale University, the École des hautes études en sciences sociales, and Williams College, where she was Robert Sterling Clark Visiting Professor in 2013–14. Her books include *The Passionate Triangle* (2011) and *Blood, Milk, Ink, Gold: Abundance and Excess in the French Renaissance* (2005). She is currently completing a book on community art and Chicago's Black Arts Movement.

Photography Credits

Permission to reproduce images is provided courtesy of the owners listed in the captions. Additional photography credits are as follows:

Heuer and Zorach, Introduction: National Archives Catalog. Record Group 412: Records of the Environmental Protection Agency, 1944–2006 (fig. 1); Museum of Contemporary Photography, Columbia College Chicago (fig. 2)

Nisbet, The Ecological Site: courtesy of Richard Serra Studio (fig. 2); excerpts from PASSAGES IN MODERN SCULPTURE by Rosalind E. Krauss, copyright © 1977 by Rosalind E. Krauss. Used by permission of Viking Books, an imprint of Penguin Publishing Group, a division of Penguin Random House LLC. All rights reserved. Any third party use of this material, outside of this publication, is prohibited. Interested parties must apply directly to Penguin Random House LLC for permission (figs. 3 and 4); © Queen's Printer for Ontario, 2008–2017. Reproduced with permission (fig. 5)

Lee, An Eco-Art History of Weathered Stone Sculptures from Southwest China: photos by author (figs. 1–13); left-hand photo by Angela Howard and right-hand photo by author (fig. 14)

Di Palma, Character and the Climatic Imaginary: photo by Mike Agee (fig. 1); © RMN-Grand Palais/Art Resource, NY, and photo by Franck Raux (fig. 2); © RMN-Grand Palais/Art Resource, NY, and photo by Michèle Bellot (fig. 5); © RMN-Grand Palais/Art Resource, NY, and photo by Gérard Blot (fig. 6)

Horton, "All Our Relations" as an Eco-Art Historical Challenge: photo by Sebastian Kriete (fig. 1); courtesy of Alan Michelson (fig. 2); courtesy of Postcommodity (fig. 3); to locate, see https://jewschool.com/2016/11/77979/heres-why-i-took-action-as-a-jew-in-solidarity-with-standing-rock/ (fig. 4); photo by F. Peter Weil (fig. 5); photo by Daniella Zalcman (fig. 6); © President and Fellows of Harvard College, Peabody Museum of Archaeology and Ethnology, Harvard University (fig. 9); image still from drone footage by Rory Wakemup (fig. 11)

Ghana ThinkTank, Coggins, and Washington, Talking About the Man in the Moon: all photos courtesy of Ghana ThinkTank

Felfe, Premodern Geosphere: photo courtesy of Nick Crowe and Ian Rawlinson (fig. 1); © RMN-Grand Palais / Art Resource, NY, and photo by Stephane Marechalle (fig. 4); © Victoria and Albert Museum, London (fig. 5)

Miner, *Gichi-mookomaanan miinawaa Gichi-maazhigaa-aabkook* // From Big Knives to Big Pipelines: digital image © 2017 Museum Associates / LACMA. Licensed by Art Resource, NY (fig. 2); © The Trustees of the British Museum. All rights reserved (fig. 3)

Zorach, "Welcome to My Volcano": videography by Alyssa Bistonath (figs. 5, 8); Courtesy of Chicago Film Archives (figs. 6, 7)

Frazier, Thinking Red, Wounds, and Fungi in Wangechi Mutu's Eco-Art: digital image © The Museum of Modern Art / Licensed by SCALA / Art Resource, NY (figs. 1 and 3); courtesy of the artist (fig. 2); National Trust Photo Library / Art Resource, NY (fig. 4); York Museums Trust (York Art Gallery), UK / Bridgeman Images (fig. 5); by kind permission of the Earls of Mansfield. Copyright the Earls of Mansfield, Scone Palace, Perth (fig. 8); Scala / Art Resource, NY (fig. 9)

Kanouse, My Electric Genealogy: all photos courtesy of the author

Platt, Ecology, Ethics, and Aesthetics in Pliny the Elder's Natural History: Erich Lessing / Art Resource, NY (fig. 1); KHM-Museumsverband (fig. 2); photo by Yale University Art Gallery (fig. 4); Scala / Art Resource, NY, and photo by Fotografica Foglia (fig. 5)

Cohen and Yates, Ark Thinking: by permission of the Folger Shakespeare Library (fig. 1); © RMN-Grand Palais / Art Resource, NY (fig. 4)

Cao, The Entropic History of Ice: courtesy of the artist (fig. 1); Bridgeman Images (fig. 2); © Smithsonian Institution, Cooper Hewitt, Smithsonian Design Museum / Art Resource, NY, and photo by Matt Flynn (fig. 6); photo by Mike Agee (fig. 7); Image © Worcester Art Museum (fig. 8); courtesy National Gallery of Art, Washington (fig. 9); photo by Don Roger Gill (fig. 11); courtesy of the artist (fig. 12)

Heuer, A Post-Critical Arctic? Erich Lessing / Art Resource, NY (fig. 1); © 2017 Guido van der Werve. Image courtesy of the artist and Galerie Juliette Jongma, Amsterdam (fig. 5); © Olafur Eliasson and photo by Martin Argyroglo (fig. 7); courtesy of the artists (figs. 6 and 8); photo by C. Stankievech (fig. 9); photo © Knud Josefsen. Courtesy of Center for Land Use Interpretation (fig. 10)

CLUI, Peripheral and Central Places in the USA: all photos courtesy of the Center for Land Use Interpretation Photo Archive

Clark Studies in the Visual Arts

The Two Art Histories: The Museum and the University (2002)
Edited by Charles W. Haxthausen
With essays by Dawn Ades, Andreas Beyer, Richard R. Brettell, Stephen Deuchar, Sybille Ebert-Schifferer, Ivan Gaskell, Eckhard Gillen, Richard Kendall, John House, Patricia Mainardi, Griselda Pollock, Mark Rosenthal, Barbara Maria Stafford, Gary Tinterow, William H. Truettner, and Michael F. Zimmermann, and an afterword by Richard Brilliant

Art History, Aesthetics, Visual Studies (2002)
Edited by Michael Ann Holly and Keith Moxey
With essays by David Carrier, Philip Fisher, Hal Foster, Ivan Gaskell, Jonathan Gilmore, Thomas DaCosta Kaufmann, Michael Kelly, Karen Lang, Stephen Melville, Kobena Mercer, Nicholas Mirzoeff, W. J. T. Mitchell, Griselda Pollock, Irene J. Winter, and Janet Wolff

The Art Historian: National Traditions and Institutional Practices (2003)
Edited by Michael F. Zimmermann
With essays by Mieke Bal, Stephen Bann, Horst Bredekamp, H. Perry Chapman, Georges Didi-Huberman, Eric Fernie, Françoise Forster-Hahn, Carlo Ginzburg, Charles W. Haxthausen, Karen Michels, Willibald Sauerländer, Alain Schnapp, and Michael F. Zimmermann

Anthropologies of Art (2005)
Edited by Mariët Westermann
With essays by Hans Belting, Janet Catherine Berlo, Suzanne Preston Blier, Steve Bourget, Sarah Brett-Smith, Shelly Errington, David Freedberg, Anna Grimshaw, Jonathan Hay, Howard Morphy, Ikem Stanley Okoye, Francesco Pellizzi, and Ruth B. Phillips

The Lure of the Object (2006)
Edited by Stephen Melville
With essays by Emily Apter, George Baker, Malcolm Baker, John Brewer, Martha Buskirk, Margaret Iversen, Ewa Lajer-Burcharth, Karen Lang, Mark A. Meadow, Helen Molesworth, Marcia Pointon, Christian Scheidemann, Edward J. Sullivan, and Martha Ward

Compression vs. Expression: Containing and Explaining the World's Art (2006)
Edited by John Onians
With essays by Cao Yiqiang, Wilfried van Damme, Rita Eder, James Elkins, Arlene K. Fleming, Derek Gillman, Jyotindra Jain, Cecilia F. Klein, Yves Le Fur, Dominic Marner, Anitra Nettleton, John Onians, Edmund P. Pillsbury, Michael Rinehart, David Summers, and Georges S. Zouain

Asian Art History in the Twenty-First Century (2007)

Edited by Vishakha N. Desai

With essays by Frederick M. Asher, Melissa Chiu, John Clark, Gao Shiming, Yukio Lippit, Saloni Mathur and Kavita Singh, Kaja M. McGowan, Rana Mitter, Alexandra Munroe, Jerome Silbergeld, Nancy S. Steinhardt, Akira Takagishi, and Gennifer Weisenfeld

Architecture between Spectacle and Use (2008)

Edited by Anthony Vidler

With essays by Mario Carpo, Beatriz Colomina, Mark Dorrian, Kurt W. Forster, Hal Foster, Sarah Williams Goldhagen, Michael Hays, Mark Jarzombek, Felicity D. Scott, Terry Smith, Anthony Vidler, and Mark Wigley

The Meaning of Photography (2008)

Edited by Robin Kelsey and Black Stimson

With essays by Geoffrey Batchen, François Brunet, Mary Ann Doane, José Luis Falconi, Robin Kelsey, Douglas R. Nickel, Blake Stimson, John Tagg, and additional contributions by Lars Kiel Bertelsen, Anne McCauley, Jorge Ribalta, John Roberts, Eric Rosenberg, Eric C. Shiner, and Bernd Stiegler

Photo essays by Sharon Harper, Lilla LoCurto and Bill Outcault, Fiona Tan, and Akram Zaatari

The Migrant's Time: Rethinking Art History and Diaspora (2011)

Edited by Saloni Mathur

With essays by Stanley Abe, Esra Akcan, Iftikhar Dadi, Jennifer González, Ranajit Guha, May Joseph, Miwon Kwon, Kobena Mercer, W. J. T. Mitchell, Aamir R. Mufti, Nikos Papastergiadis, Richard J. Powell, Edward W. Said, and Nora A. Taylor

Fictions of Art History (2013)

Edited by Mark Ledbury

With essays by Paul Barolsky, Thomas Crow, Gloria Kury, Mark Ledbury, Ralph Lieberman, Maria H. Loh, Alexander Nemerov, Joanna Scott, Cole Swensen, Marianna Torgovnick, Caroline Vout, and Marina Warner

Art History in the Wake of the Global Turn (2014)

Edited by Jill H. Casid and Aruna D'Souza

With essays by Esra Akcan, Jill H. Casid, Parul Dave-Mukherji, Aruna D'Souza, Talinn Grigor, Ranjana Khanna, Kobena Mercer, Nicholas Mirzoeff, Steven Nelson, Todd Porterfield, Raqs Media Collective, Kishwar Rizvi, David J. Roxburgh, and Alessandra Russo

Art History and Emergency (2016)

Edited by David Breslin and Darby English

With essays by Thomas Crow, Kajri Jain, Molly Nesbit, Caroline Arscott, Anatoli Mikhailov, Mary Miller, Howard Singerman, Patrick D. Flores, Manuel J. Borja-Villel, Our Literal Speed, and Theaster Gates